Buon Appetito; Niagara's early Italian-American culinary traditions

The Italian Research Group
Lewiston Public Library

DEDICATION

This book is dedicated to those who came before us.

Contents

ACKNOWLEDGMENTS

Thank you to all of the people who helped with this book. It was truly a labor of love. Thank you to the Macri family for galvanizing this project. Thank you to Barbara Coppock for editing and for supporting this project from the beginning. Thank you to the director of the Lewiston Public Library, Jill Palermo, for making this happen. Thank you to all of our writers: Beverly Barthel, Beverly Bidak, Robert Borgatti, Marcia Buzzelli, Patricia DiNieri, Peggy Taylor-Hulligan, Eleanor Novara and Dan Sicoli. Thank you to all of you who have shared your wonderful stories, recipes and family sayings.

Most of all, thank you to my beautiful grandmother, Jean Ann (Fortuna) Borgatti, for helping me put this book together and for being my inspiration.

Introduction

Although I represent the third generation of my (mother's) family to have been born in America, I was the last generation to have had the privilege of knowing the relatives who had come from the Old Country. Unfortunately my children were born many years following their deaths and they will never know them firsthand. I was on the fringe—embracing that last link to another world. I was young and they were old. We were very different—yet I knew they were *mine*. I fondly recall holding onto my Grandmother Fortuna's hands and tracing the smooth lines, the roads that led me back in time. There were stories of Italy and stories of early times in America—where they carved out a place of their own. Still living in the city in which they had chosen to replant themselves—I have stumbled among their ghosts. With each birthday that passes, I long to reach back. I have researched my family tree—attempting to make myself more complete. We are a giant puzzle of those who came before us. I love to share what I find with the children—because they are the most interested. Their eyes light up as if our stories are but a fairy tale. And they are... in a way. They are magical stories from lost worlds—but they are so much better because the characters have *our faces, our mannerisms*. They laugh how *we laugh*—they are moved by the things that *move us*.

The idea for a book such as this came about after a special benefit Macri's Italian Grille restaurant held for the Lewiston Public Library in 2013. In gratitude, we decided to use the funds generated and share some of our Italian history in a book. With many of us having ties to these early Italian-Americans we found it quite impossible to tell their stories without telling about their beautiful food. The more we researched, the more we realized how integral these traditions were and still are today. Italians attempted to bring the warmth of their homeland into their new city through their dinner tables. They grew *little Italies* in their gardens, baked them into their biscotti, ground them into their meats, pressed them into their vino, sold them in their shops. This is the story of the businesses that grew around these culinary traditions. The stories of restaurants, dairies, taverns, beverage dealers, bakeries, grocery stores and delicatessens, meat markets and confectionaries. We have also thrown in some special stories about holiday memories, local traditions, gardening, the Italian tradition of foraging for cicoria and cardoons, and, of course, a few recipes and some colorful family sayings! Most of all this little book is a celebration of the people, the Italians, and what they contributed to American cuisine and to the traditions and history of the city of Niagara Falls.

We hope that by putting these stories and these traditions into print they will find new life in our children and grandchildren.

Michelle Ann Kratts, Lewiston Public Library

THE D'AVOLIO AND MACRI FAMILIES
MACRI'S ITALIAN GRILLE
BY BEVERLY BIDAK

Macri's Italian Grille is located at 810 Center Street in historic Lewiston New York. The restaurant business is not new to owner Gary Macri, who is a third generation restaurateur. The restaurant features many traditional and specialty Italian dishes from some family recipes that date back more than 50 years.

Gary's maternal grandfather, Vincent D'Avolio, was born in May 1908 in Cumberland, Maryland. Vincent's parents, Antonio and Pasqua (nee Aquila) D'Avolio, came to the United States to find the American dream. When Antonio D'Avolio was killed in a construction accident in 1908, his wife had no choice but to take her two infant children, Vincent and Marietta, back home to Collarmele, L'Aquila, Italy.

Vincent worked as a laborer for the D'Alessandro family in Italy. He married Erma D'Alessandro about 1928. Erma was the eldest of six children. Her mother died when she was 12 years old and she raised her younger siblings. In March 1931, Vincent set sail for the United States. His final destination was Niagara Falls, NY, where he had relatives. He left behind his wife, daughter, Antonina (Anne), and unborn son, Concezio (Ezio). Erma and the children arrived in New York in May of 1935 and the family was reunited. Another daughter, Theresa, was later born into the family.

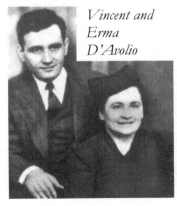

Vincent and Erma D'Avolio

In the early 1950s, Vincent D'Avolio opened a tavern at 1018 Grove Avenue called Vincent's Grill. Erma did most of the cooking and the children worked there too. The grill became known as the Soup Bowl Restaurant. In the 1960s, they sold the business and bought DelFredos Restaurant on Main Street. Mrs. D'Avolio continued as the cook in the new restaurant and her husband helped out in the kitchen. He wanted to write down her recipes but Erma always measured ingredients by the handful. Vincent, having had much bigger hands, would take his wife's handful and put it in a container to get the proper measurements. The couple's children also worked alongside their parents at DelFredo**s**. Vincent ran the restaurant until his death in 1968.

In the meantime, Anne D'Avolio met and married Jimmy Macri on October 7, 1950. James Vincent Macri was the son of Dominic and Carmella (Bel Castro) Macri of Niagara Falls, NY. Dominic Macri was born July 30, 1872 in Cavlonia, Calabria, Italy. He immigrated to Niagara Falls, NY, in April of 1903. His wife, Carmella, was born in about 1889 in Italy, as were their first two children. Jimmy was born in Niagara Falls and was the second youngest of eight children.

In 1954, Jimmy Macri opened The Clock Restaurant with his nephew, Joe DeGennaro, located at 1727 Pine Avenue. After several years, they closed the restaurant and Mr. Macri went to work at DelFredos, the family restaurant.

Main Street in Niagara Falls was deteriorating and a new location was required. DelFredos Restaurant was closed.

MR. AND MRS. JAMES MACRI

James Macri opened Macri's Palace in the City Market in 1973. The new enterprise was owned and operated by the Macri family, Jimmy, Anne and their son, Gary. Erma D'Avolio remained involved in the restaurant. Macri's has been well known for its Italian and American meals, its great banquet facilities and for 32 years was a family favorite for most of Niagara Falls.

Courtesy Niagara Falls Public Library

In the mid 2000's, the restaurant downsized a bit and moved to the Summit Park Mall and operated under the name, Macri's Italian Grille. The food remained of the highest quality, but several events took place. On November 11, 2005, Erma D'Avolio passed away. She was a strong and positive person and left a legacy of a great work ethic to her children. She was known to say "Don't trip over every little stone or you'll wear out your shoes." Another tragedy occurred on November 5, 2008, when James Vincent Macri died. He left behind a wife, four children and several grandchildren. His motto was "you need to cook with love". Shortly thereafter, the restaurant was forced to leave the Summit Park location when the mall owners decided to close the shopping and business center.

"Mama D'Avolio"

Gary D. Macri contemplated retirement, but his mother, Anne, said "What am I going to do?" In August 2009, he returned to the business his family started more than 60 years ago and opened Macri's Italian Grille in the Clarkson House in Lewiston, New York. His mother works with him at the new location.

The menu consists of many traditional and specialty Italian items, homemade pastas, homemade sausage, many wonderful grilled items, seafood and much, much more.

When I interviewed Mrs. Macri and Gary, I was inspired by their love for and commitment in continuing to own and operate a business that has been in their family for three generations.

THE FORTUNA FAMILY
FORTUNA'S RESTAURANT
BY MICHELLE ANN KRATTS

Special thanks to my uncle, Robert Borgatti, for capturing so much of this information many years ago in a family history of the Borgatti and Fortuna families.

What I remember most of my great grandfather, Francesco Fortuna,

 was the rhythm and the melody of his beautiful Italian voice. Although he lived in this country for over sixty years, he never lost the thick accent rendered to him at the place of his birth. He loved to express himself; to talk and to lecture. There was never a quiet moment at our family table and no subject was off-limits. My sister and I would spend weekends with him and our great grandmother and he would use most of the time teaching us the Italian words for ordinary things. He was adamant that we would know our heritage. He would also tell us remarkable stories from his youth— tales of heroism during the First World War, of the time he wrestled a bear, anecdotes relating to his immigration to America. At large family gatherings at the restaurant it was inevitable that he would stand up and speak to all of us. This was always in Italian. I had no idea what he was saying but he was so passionate and powerful as he commanded the room. He would pound his cane or his fists--his voice rising and falling with the mood of his words. Somehow I knew he was mentioning things like *respect*

and *family* and, of course, *food.* There was no doubt that he was the patriarch and the *king of our family.*

My great grandfather was no ordinary man. The eldest child of Giuseppe Fortuna and Maria Bonanni, Francesco was born on the first of June, 1895, in Sommati-- a little town located in the commune of Amatrice and the province of Rieti, in what is now the region of Lazio. He always loved to cook. Perhaps it was inevitable as Amatrice is considered one of the culinary capitals of Italy.

An early picture of my great grandfather

Amatrice is the birthplace of *Sugo all'amatriciano*—one of the most well-known pasta dishes in Italy and especially in Rome. Legend also reveals that the popes often chose chefs from Amatrice for their personal cooking needs at the Vatican.

As idyllic and romantic as a childhood in Italy can strike an American granddaughter's imagination, things were not always as I envisioned— and my great grandfather would not hesitate to let me know the details of a difficult existence. First of all--work began at a very young age. My great grandfather assisted his father on the family farm through part of the year and during the remainder accompanied him to Sardinia to help with the manufacture of goats' milk cheese in a firm called Paulo Luparini Landucci. But the spirit of adventure caught up with him and— just a young boy—he ran away from home. He stayed with his uncle, Pietro Valentino—who operated a butcher shop in Rome. Afterwards he left that uncle to apprentice under another uncle, Baldo Bonanni. Baldo was a chef at *"Il Ristorante Vigliani"* –also in Rome, and he represented the seventh generation of chefs in Francesco's mother's family. My great grandfather dreamed that he would represent the eighth generation and Baldo taught him all of his family cooking secrets—Italian family culinary traditions that Francesco brought to America.

During the First World War my great grandfather served as an information dispatcher in the Italian Army. On November 1, 1915, near the city of Parmenova (on the Italian-Austrian front) he found himself trapped behind enemy lines. Holding off the German fire with only a machine gun in a small bunker he was soon overcome. He remembered nothing more—only awakening in the safety of an Italian hospital. He had been shot seven times and left for dead until Italian forces finally found him.

Great grandma, grandma, great grandpa and "Jackie"

He spent the rest of the war recovering from his devastating wounds. Hoping to start a better life for himself my great grandfather arrived at the port of New York on March 12, 1921. He took a train to Niagara Falls where he met up with his cousin, Lorenzo Bonanni. In fact, the day he arrived in the city he cooked for his cousin's wedding reception.

Great grandma

Francesco worked various jobs in Niagara Falls. He first worked for the Niagara Junction Railroad—which proved portentous as he fell in love with a fellow railroad worker's daughter and soon after married Clementina Ventresca (my great grandmother) on December 12, 1923, at St. Joseph's Church. They had two children: my grandmother, Gina, and my uncle and godfather, Joseph.

My great grandfather obtained a barber's license from the city of Niagara Falls and operated various barber shops until settling at 827 19th Street—the

The barber shop

future site of his restaurant. In the 1930's he had saved up enough money to purchase the building. He moved his barber shop to an upstairs room and leased out the downstairs to Sylvester Sozio, another Italian immigrant who managed a tavern and restaurant called *Sylvester's Grill*.

On Sundays when the barber shop was closed my great grandfather would cater parties in private homes for weddings and other family celebrations. In 1945 his dream of owning his own restaurant came to fruition when Sozio moved out and the *Deluxe Grill* was born. Sometime before 1960, the name changed to *Fortuna's Deluxe Restaurant* and finally years later to *Fortuna's*.

Originally, the *Deluxe Grill* was a partnership between my great grandfather and my uncle, Victor Ventresca. Uncle Victor, a recently returned veteran of World War Two, was able to procure the liquor

license and help with funds to get the restaurant off the ground. My grandmother, Gina, a full time student at Niagara Falls High School, also helped with funding the restaurant by handing over most of her wages from her work at Bell Aircraft during the war.

Not unlike the other Italian businesses in Niagara Falls, my great grandfather's business was family operated. Most of the family was somehow associated with the restaurant. My great grandmother, Clementina, worked alongside my great grandfather—putting in just as many hours. Early kitchen staff included: Rachel Sicoli, my Aunt Antoinette Valenti, Evelia Volpe, Fanny (her last name could not be recalled) and Ann Pasquantino. My cousin, Sandra Tecchio, worked in the kitchen doing various jobs. My Aunt Phil (Felicetta Ventresca Tecchio) and my grandmother were waitresses. Other well-known waitresses through the years included: Polly, Sherry and Pat. Uncle Victor tended the bar. Our cousin, Peter Valenti, also worked for many years as the bartender at Fortuna's and his two sisters, Nellie and Carm Valenti, were waitresses. Eventually, my Uncle Victor opened his own restaurant, the very popular, "Mr. Steak," in the Town of Niagara. My Uncle Joe worked for the business and took over when my great grandfather retired. His wife, my Aunt Carmela (Ferlito), was the vivacious hostess at Fortuna's for many years, as well as a spectacular baker. My cousin Joseph, Jr. and my uncle Bob Borgatti, worked as busboys. My cousin David, the oldest son of my uncle, learned to cook here as well. There was even a time when my great grandfather's brother, Fernando, and his wife, Italia, came from Italy to live in Niagara Falls with their children: Mana and Francesco. During those years Fernando and Italia worked in the kitchen.

Joseph, Jr. now owns and operates the family business along with his wife, Michele (Milkie). David Fortuna brought the family culinary traditions to California where he owns and operates Wholey Ravioli, an Italian restaurant (offering "Traditional Italian Goodness") in Galt.

Great grandpa in the kitchen at Fortuna's

My grandmother related to me that the entire family even participated in the cleaning and maintenance of the restaurant. Several mornings a week my grandfather, Henry Borgatti, would stop at Fortuna's before working at DuPont and clean the toilets, vacuum the rugs, wash the kitchen floor, empty the garbage. My uncle, Sam Tecchio, also helped with the cleaning and maintenance on a regular basis. As for the major spring cleaning...again, this was a family affair. The restaurant would close for two weeks in order to completely clean the building, shampoo the carpets, paint and fix anything that needed fixing.

Fortuna's has had its fans through the years. Someone recently confessed to me how (back in the old days) the neighborhood boys used to take the bread that they had stolen from area bakeries and run by the kitchen window at Fortuna's—where my great grandfather would set the sauce to cool—and dip their bread into it for a nice treat. I wonder if my great grandfather ever knew about this! There were also large groups of men who frequented the restaurant on a regular basis. They would come to watch the Yankees games, for a drink and a bite to eat. The group of men grew and grew. As the Korean War began, and as Niagara area men were called to serve, there were going-away parties for the men who left for the war. My great grandfather made a special snack for the men during this time. He was constantly trying out new recipes and sharing with others. For these men he would make his own sausage mix, flatten it into a large oval shape that would fit onto a chunk of Italian bread, fry the meat and then serve to them—often piled high with fried onions and peppers. It was a sort of early submarine sandwich. In those days the Italian bread never came pre-sliced and it was usually the waitress's job to slice the bread. My grandmother is not sure if this sandwich was even listed on the menu. But it was certainly a favorite and perhaps one of the last meals some of these men had in Niagara Falls before leaving for Korea… and eventually for Vietnam.

Some of the servicemen and Fortuna's "regulars" in the 1950's. Victor Ventresca is standing, left front. To the center towards the back in an apron is my great grandfather. Beside him in an apron is my great grandmother. Next to her is my grandmother, in a dark shirt. Third from the front right in dark vest and tie is my Uncle Joe Fortuna, future owner of the restaurant.

DELUXE GRILL
827 - 19th Street
ITALIAN RESTAURANT
SATURDAY NIGHT SPECIAL
RAVIOLIS... with MEATBALLS or CHICKEN
SPAGHETTI EVERY DAY
BLUE PIKE FISH DINNER EVERY FRIDAY

ON THE JOB — Now going on 82, Frank Fortuna can still be seen in the wee hours of the morning preparing food for the day at Fortuna's Restaurant on 19th St. He believes if you like what you're doing, you should keep on doing it. Gazette photo.

My great grandfather never tired of working at his restaurant. Eventually building a home a few blocks away on Woodlawn Avenue, Francesco walked to the restaurant every morning. Sometimes his beloved German shepherd, Champ, would accompany him. Around 3:00 or 4:00 am he would begin the daily routine of preparing the lard and olive oil for frying--as well as the sauce. When the restaurant first opened the hours were grueling. Closing time was at one in the morning on weekdays and two on weekends.

My great grandfather always believed in using only fresh ingredients. He never believed in steam tables. He was particular about every food-thing that was used in the kitchen. I recall the delight of being at their house when the freshly baked bread was delivered from Canada. The aroma was over-powering. My great grandfather also insisted that everything would be made to order. As for Francesco's specialties...they included his raviolis, his signature sauce and his salad dressing. Other favorites were his eggplant parmesan, his greens and beans soup (which was not "wet" or "soupy," but of a thicker consistency) and his veal cacciatore. He also served excellent American style food such as fried chicken and steaks. Sometimes my great grandfather would have deer brought in that had been cleaned. Usually it was from his good friend, Enio Baldassarre, who was a great hunter. In fact, my great grandfather used to save all his meat scraps for Enio's hunting dogs. With this deer meat he would make various dishes and serve them to Enio's friends and other good friends who frequented the restaurant. I suppose this is where the deer head came from that graced the breezeway at their house on Woodlawn Avenue. I knew he wasn't a hunter....but now it all makes sense.

My great grandfather was puzzled over many American food customs. He did not care for soft white bread—preferring the chewy Italian bread. He also claimed that Italians—who sometimes ate pasta three meals throughout the day—maintained a healthy weight because they used less sauce and cheese than Americans. I also remember how in his old age he would sweeten his coffee with grapes and various fruit as he was forbidden sugars due to his diabetes. He worked hard his entire life—refusing any idle moments. When he wasn't cooking or experimenting with recipes he enjoyed working in his garden. He told me a little secret one day after I stopped in for a visit on my way home from school. He had such a love affair with some roses in Italy that he had hidden their seeds in his hatband on the trip to America. So, in a way, he had brought a part of Italy to Niagara Falls. And here they were growing beautifully in his little garden on Woodlawn Avenue. That day he picked a rose and handed it to me. He said (in his Italian accent, of course): *a rose for a princess.*

Uncle Joe, my grandma, my great grandma and my great grandpa

My great grandfather died on August 18, 1990. He was ninety-five years old. He is buried in the mausoleum at Riverdale Cemetery in Lewiston, New York, with my great grandmother, Clementina, who happened to die one month before he did. But in a way, he never died, for his dream still lives on the corner of 19th and Forest Avenue in Niagara Falls, New York.

Fortuna's Restaurant today

My cousins making meatballs at Fortuna's

Uncle Joe (Fortuna), my dad (Bob Barthel), Joey and Maria Fortuna, Grandpa Borgatti and Uncle Bob Borgatti

THE ANTONACCI FAMILY
THE COMO RESTAURANT
BY ELEANOR MIGLIAZZO NOVARA

I well remember my first time eating out in a restaurant other than an ice cream parlor or one of the pizza hangouts when I was in Junior High School. It was June 1956 while in the 9th grade at South Jr. High School, I was singing in the chorus in our year-end production show. After the performance several of my classmates and I were walking out of the school and before I knew it we were sitting in a storefront that was known as the "Como Restaurant" located at 2220 Pine Avenue, Niagara Falls, NY.

FEATURE PHOTO

Francesco Antonacci and Don Florio stand outside of Antonacci's Bakery on 20th Street in 1919. Later Francesco opened the Como Restaurant.

Courtesy the Niagara Falls Gazette Calendar

It was a very busy, small restaurant with a few wooden tables and chairs crowded into a storefront with two large windows on each side of the windowed doorway. The kitchen was in the back of the room and I remember the hustle and bustle of many dishes being brought out from table to table. It was like being in a fish bowl because you could see people walking along the sidewalk as they looked in the windows. Being in this Pine Avenue area was like being in another city because at that age there weren't many times when I ventured out of my neighborhood. It was a new experience for me as I grew up in an Italian family and we never went out to eat in a restaurant. And, it was a good thing it was an Italian restaurant because I ate only Italian food. Needless to say, my selection from the menu was a dish of spaghetti. Thankfully I had enough money with me as I think the spaghetti cost something like a quarter back then.

The restaurant was founded by Francesco Antonacci who was born in Abruzzo, Italy on August 8, 1889. He immigrated to the United States in 1903, settling in Windber, Pennsylvania, following in the same path that many immigrants from Italy did when first arriving in America; working in the coal mines. It was hard work, but through the years he was able to save enough money to enable him to move to Niagara Falls.

FEATURE PHOTO

The original Como Restaurant. 1927

Inset Picture

Francisco Antonacci & Dominec Florio in from the Antonacci Bakery Truck (located on 20th St.) in 1911

1997 Niagara Gazette Calender

Courtesy the Niagara Falls Gazette Calendar

As a young man growing up in Italy, Francesco learned the skill of baking bread and soon after arriving in Niagara Falls, he began his first business endeavor, the Antonacci Bakery Shop, located at 440 – 20th Street.

Courtesy the Niagara Falls Gazette Calendar

Shortly thereafter, he met and married his wife, Maria Giuseppa (Cubello) Antonacci, on September 19, 1919. By 1927, he saved enough money to purchase a house with a store front on Pine Avenue. He opened the Como restaurant in the storefront and lived upstairs with his wife, where they raised their three children; Adeline, born, July 29, 1923, Nick, January 29, 1925, and Mario, August 1, 1927. He named his restaurant the "Como" after the famous Lake Como resort in northern Italy. [When you enter the second set of doors on the right side you will see a photo of Lake Como hanging on the wall].

Over the years the restaurant became increasingly popular with the locals and tourists from all over the country. Many celebrities representing the entertainment and professional sports world, along with many political figures were welcomed into the restaurant by the ComoFamily; to name a few: Joe Lewis, Joe Conway, Joe Torres, Frank Sinatra, Frankie Lane, Liberace, Sammy Davis, Jr. and many more. Adeline recalls how one night Sammy Davis, Jr., after performing at Melody Fair in North Tonawanda, came to the Como and ended up dancing on the tables.

Eventually two houses adjacent to the restaurant were purchased and demolished, allowing for further expansion.

The Como 1980

Eventually two houses adjacent to the original restaurant were
purchased and demolished allowing for further expansion,
as shown above.

Living upstairs from the restaurant Francesco's children learned the
business from an early age especially Adeline who at age twelve worked
part-time as a waitress. Eventually she became the hostess. She married
Dominic Colucci on April 20, 1940, at St. Joseph's Church, in Niagara
Falls, and they also lived upstairs from the restaurant where they raised
their two sons; Dominic and Frank. Dom began bartending part-time
while working a day job. Soon the business was thriving and Dom quit
his day job and became a full time bartender.

Each of Francesco's sons had his own talents and interests which
complemented each other to the hilt: Nick became the chief chef in the
kitchen while Mario utilized his talents in tending the bar and
welcoming the numerous customers. He was known for greeting his
many close friends with his famous expression, *"gotta pay the mortgage
fellas."*

Second Generation: Dominic Colucci, Mario and Nick Antonacci

Sampling the **"COMO"** Restaurant's Delicious Sauce
Prepared by, Chief Chef, Nick

Adeline's son Dominic was first to make his mark at the Como setting the pattern for his younger brother Frank to follow. Both learned the "hard work" ethic growing up in the business by washing dishes at an early age.

Dominic manages the Como restaurant, on Pine Avenue, and Frank manages the Como Airport restaurant, on NF Boulevard. Nick's son-in-law, Steve Hall, is now the head chef, a skill he learned from Nick. Steve worked during his college years washing dishes. Nick took a liking to him and started training him to cook. Little did Nick know that one day he would walk his daughter down the aisle to marry him! There are several cousins who have chosen to follow in the footsteps of Adeline's boys, namely; Lou, Frank and Mario Antonacci. You can see Frank in the dining room and Mario tending bar. Lou manages the Deli next door.

Many of the recipes prepared by Francesco were brought over with him from Italy and are still used in the restaurant today. Francesco was not only well known for his excellent food preparation skills, he was also admired for his generosity.

Francesco Antonacci died in 1963. His son Nick died in 1987 and Mario in 2005. His son-in-law Dominic died in 2001. Since 2007, Adeline, age ninety-one, is still working three nights a week at the Como Airport restaurant located across from the Niagara Falls International Airport.

Prior to that, she was hostess at the Goose's Roost restaurant (located near the NF Bus Terminal in downtown Niagara Falls) from 1974, until the restaurant property was purchased by the Niagara Falls, NY Seneca-Niagara Casino in 1984.

Over the years, through economic times good and bad, the Como family has more than survived – it has thrived! They built two banquet halls; the bar was enlarged in 1958 and again in 1959. In 1978 the Deli was expanded along with the kitchen and the Francesco Banquet Hall was added adjacent to the Deli.

There aren't many restaurants these days where you are served an array of home-made Italian bread, rolls and one of their favorites - pizza bread. And, of course we can't forget their home-made bowties. In all these years in the restaurant business, their menu hasn't changed much. Those special pastas, gnocchi and fettuccini, and soups are still made in their kitchen. Francesco's baking and cooking skills (made with Francesco's recipes brought with him from Italy) helped keep those favorites a primary item on the Como's menu.

Since 1927 the Como restaurant has become the largest and most famous Italian-American Restaurant in Niagara Falls. For all those customers from Western New York and Southern Ontario have been blessed to have memories of the Como in our lives as many weddings, anniversaries, showers, baptisms, graduations, special dinner and luncheon events, and more have been held there.

The present generation (Dominic II, his sons Dominic, III and Christopher) are continuing the family tradition of operating Como restaurant and Como at the Airport restaurant, 10158 NF Boulevard, Niagara Falls, NY.

Much of the generosity and consideration to the employees of the Como have seeped into the generations and employees (or shall I say the Como family) working there today which is a testament to Francesco. This has been a remarkably close family who continue to fill Francesco's vision brought to America so many years ago as a young man.

GOOD HEALTH
COMES WITH
GOOD EATING
All That and More at
THE COMO
THE FINEST IN ITALIAN FOODS
We Specialize in
PARTIES — BANQUETS — WEDDINGS

COMO RESTAURANT
2220 PINE AVENUE   PHONE 2-9618

Auguri per altri 100 anni! (Best Wishes for another 100 Years!)

Third and fourth Generation, Dominic Colucci, Jr. with his son Dom, III.

Adeline Colucci and son Frank Colucci Como at the Airport Restaurant

THE CRUGNALE FAMILY
LA HACIENDA RESTAURANT
BY MICHELLE ANN KRATTS

Believe it or not, one of Niagara's most legendary Italian restaurants, La Hacienda, (the one with the mysteriously Spanish name) was founded by an Irishman, Frank Fitzgerald. A chauffeur before he opened a restaurant in 1936, located at 1672 Ontario Avenue, called The Modern Grill, Fitzgerald did not open La Hacienda until about a year later. Initially situated at 922 Pine Avenue, La Hacienda offered Spanish and Italian cuisine, while The Modern Grill served American and Chinese food. Apparently, this is why the "Spanish" theme was established at La Hacienda Restaurant and still carries through today. Perhaps one of the most popular dishes the original La Hacienda served was called "Chicken in the Rough." It included half a chicken, French fried potatoes, salad, hot biscuits and syrup and cost $1.25. By 1947, Joe Pellicci and Nick Mariello took over as owners. According to the directories, Joe first worked as a bartender at La Hacienda's cocktail lounge. They ran the restaurant until about 1957, when the Crugnales heard that the business was for sale.

—NOW OPEN—
NIAGARA'S MOST MODERN GRILL
AND RESTAURANT
La Hacienda—922 Pine Ave.
Our Mixed Drinks Never Fail to Satisfy
Delicious Foods, Liquor, Wines, Beer
SPANISH—
ITALIAN—   DISHES   —AMERICAN
—CHINESE
LaHacienda   Frank Fitzgerald, Prop.   Modern Grill
922 PINE AVE.   NIAGARA FALLS, N.Y.   1672 ONTARIO AVE.

JOSEPH PELLICCI

Patsy (Pasquale) and Clara (Di Censo) Crugnale, my friend, Mike's grandparents, and friends of my family, were working at the Nabisco Biscuit Company when Joe Mozzarello told them. Patsy had always wanted his own business and Clara was a wonderful cook...so why not? The Crugnales purchased La Hacienda in 1957 and the business is still in the family today. Generations of Niagarans savor the recipes that were passed on down from Clara Crugnale...recipes she had learned in San Pio, Italy. My children have admitted that it is one of their favorite places to eat. Their order is always the same: a thin crust New York style cheese pizza and a chef salad piled high with mozzarella cheese and sprinkled with ceci beans and that delicious house dressing that can be purchased by the gallon.

Recently I had the pleasure of spending an afternoon around the kitchen table with Patsy and Clara, their daughter and their grandson's wife. They welcomed me as if I were family...since, actually, Patsy and my great grandmother, Clementina, were paesan, or from the same town in Italy. They all had known each other back in the day. This was all new to me. In fact, as I learned about the history of the owners of La Hacienda, strangely, I learned things about my own family. I especially loved the sound of their accents for they reminded me of my grandparents.

Patsy (who laughingly claims the name, Patsy, was rendered to him by his wife, Clara, for she thinks he is "Irish" and not Italian for some reason) was born in Bugnara, Italy. His father came to America around 1910. First, Patsy worked at the City Market on market days. Then he took a job at the Nabisco Biscuit Company. His family actually lived across the street from my family, the Fortunas, on 19th Street. During the war, Patsy joined the Navy. But that was short-lived because as soon as the Japanese saw him "coming....they give up too." When the war ended there was one thing left to do...find himself a bride. He planned on going to Europe to find the perfect woman; to Italy. A friend of his took fate into her own hands, though, and told him about her beautiful niece who lived in Italy. She showed him a picture of this young niece and her name was Clara. He decided that, yes, she was the one. So the family, eager to ensure their daughter would have a good life in America following the devastation of the war in Italy, sent her to Niagara Falls. It was a terrible voyage for poor Clara. She had never left home before and here she was on the ocean! She was so seasick that she said if the windows hadn't been bolted shut, she would have thrown herself into the water to end her misery. The boats that Italy still had in the late 1940's were in terrible condition. She did make it to America, though. And she had a suitcase filled with cheese...for it was always the custom to bring food from the hometown to your family when you made that long trip.

Patsy met her at the train depot, holding her picture in his hands, and they were married soon after. As it was Lent they could only be married by the mayor, and not in the church. A church wedding at St. Joseph's soon followed. Their wedding feast, which was celebrated at the Como Restaurant, was beautiful. There were sandwiches, pizza, biscotti and a cake that weighed just about 65 pounds, according to Clara. Italian weddings were day-long affairs in those days. The marriage ceremony took place at 8:00 am, followed by breakfast, lunch, dinner and then they would spend the evening dancing.

The Crugnales had three daughters: Patricia, Mary and Lillian. Patricia actually met her husband in the restaurant. Of course, owning a restaurant sometimes involves grueling hours which don't leave much room for a social life. Today the restaurant is run by Aldo Evangelista, who is married to Lillian. They are grateful to Aldo, who makes his own sausage and bread. "He cooks real good," Clara told me. Of course, she taught him all of her recipes. "My son in law...God bless him...I show him everything..."

Patsy and Clara reminisced about the old days at La Hacienda. When they first took over a small cheese pizza cost ninety cents and a beef on weck cost seventy five cents. During these years, the city was thriving and the restaurant would be packed to capacity on a regular basis. As the midnight shift at the factories would let out there would be a rush of people wanting dinner. There were some nights that they would have to put up a rope to keep people back. One Friday, Clara made forty-five pounds of fish. Her kitchen was in the basement at first so everything had to be brought up by a dumb-waiter on ropes. She cooks by hand, with no set measurements. Her favorite dish to cook is ravioli. She would make it from scratch with a rolling pin. One day she was talking with a woman who mentioned how she had to rush home to fix gnocchi for her family by 5:00. Clara wondered however she could make gnocchi so quickly! The secret was that she used ricotta cheese instead of potato. After this, Clara also made gnocchi with ricotta.

Clara and her daughters did all of the shopping. They would go to the Acme Store by the Wedge to purchase the groceries and then push shopping carts back to the restaurant. It was a difficult life. They would finally go to sleep around 5 am, only to wake up at 10:30. They would take care of their children, go to mass and then go back to work.

There were some crazy antics they mentioned, too. Clara loved to dress up for Halloween. One year she dressed like a hobo and frightened the people in the pizza room!

Pizza was always one of the specialties of La Hacienda. Clara's brother, Lorenzo, ran the bar and made the pizzas. There was actually a special pizza room at La Hacienda. On some busy nights they made about 300-400 pizzas.

When the Spallino Towers were built, during the late 1960's/early 1970's, La Hacienda was forced to move. It was at this time that the restaurant relocated to its present day location at 3019 Pine Avenue. Another restaurant called Monaco's Grill, owned by Gene Monaco, was at one time in that spot. Monaco's Grill had quite a bit

of musical entertainment and Italian food, as well. It was a good central location and it definitely worked for La Hacienda and for the Crugnales.

Before I left the Crugnales I asked them if they had any secrets that they would like to share concerning how others can live such long and healthy lives as they have lived. Clara eagerly announced that it was the "EVOO"...the Extra Virgin Olive Oil. Good food, of course. Lots of greens and fruits. And a glass of wine every day. And not just any wine...homemade wine. She gave me a glass and it was the most beautiful glass of red wine I have ever had. I thought it was cute that

she had her grandson's wife bring us a little picture frame. Clara had enclosed a thank you card that Mike's wife had written. It mentioned how she enjoyed spending "quiet" time with Clara drinking wine. I laughed because I know how much my own grandmother loves thank you cards but I never knew her to frame one! Every little thing has meaning to Clara. She also took me to her curio cabinet and showed me some of her favorite things: a Madonna (from her son-in-law, Aldo), little knick-knacks, and most precious were the three little ceramic cows. She took them out and showed them to me. When she first saw these three little cows in a shop she was struck by them and had to have them no matter what the cost. She had taken care of the cows in Italy and they had reminded her of her own cows.

There was one more little precious tidbit Clara left for me, personally: a new picture of my great grandmother. Throughout the afternoon she had mentioned my great grandmother's friends, the places they had been together. She said that my great grandmother's ravioli were the best of all. And she also mentioned that when she had first come to America, a frightened and lonely young girl, my great grandmother (who was much older) offered to help her and to give her a position at her restaurant, the Deluxe Grill. And…she told me about my great great grandfather's wine. It was, perhaps, the best made in Niagara Falls. Everyone would go to his home on 19th Street for a bottle. I never knew any of this! How strange to learn about my own family one afternoon with the Crugnales!

Our afternoon together was truly a wonderful gathering of past and present and, of course, of the memory of food and its place in our lives.

THE BUZZELLI FAMILY
BUZZELLI'S DAIRY
BY MARCIA BUZZELLI

Remarkably the Buzzelli family is still actively involved in the dairy business. Five generations have been in the same line of work since Francesco (Frank) Buzzelli decided to operate a dairy in 1912 at 521 19th Street in Niagara Falls, NY. In the city directory of 1917, Frank is listed as a dairyman and his son Guy as a driver. Later Guy became the owner of the dairy with his son Frank.

Buzzelli dairy farm on 19ᵗʰ Street, Niagara Falls

According to the US census of 1915, Francesco arrived in the USA in 1888. His older brothers, Mauro and Antonio arrived in 1884 and settled in Niagara Falls where power was being developed. The power brought paper mills along the river and much work. In the next 6 years, they brought their other siblings and mother to Niagara Falls. The family came from Castel di Sangro, L'Aquila, Abruzzo, Italy. Castel di Sangro is a two hour drive southeast of Rome, in the Apennine Mountains. Today it is a town of about 5,000 people. In WWII, a great deal of the town was destroyed by bombing as it was in the path to Rome. It has been rebuilt today and continues to grow as it is close to Rome and a good place to ski.

After arriving in the United States, Francesco began to use the English translation of his name, Frank. He was born on April 23, 1871, the 6th child of Gaetano Buzzelli and Fiorangela Sconciafurno. After their father died in Italy, the family came to Niagara Falls, NY. They first settled on N. Stedman Street which by 1893 became 19th Street. This area of Niagara Falls was farm land and good for grazing. Having come from an area in Italy where there were cows they bought cows and soon neighbors were asking for milk. Nineteenth Street was a little Italy with most residents from Italy, including Frank's brother Mauro (Mike), my grandfather. Also, on the street was the Palumbo family. Their daughter, Margaret, would marry Frank's son, Guy. Guy and Margaret would have two children: a boy, Frank, and girl, Norma.

They started bottling the milk and delivering to homes, restaurants and grocery stores in the city of Niagara Falls. In the 1940's they sold milk, chocolate milk, butter milk, orange drink and ricotta cheese. Easter week was especially important for the ricotta cheese sales and they gave out a recipe for Ricotta Pie to customers. Their recipe for ricotta pie was used later at Cornell University.

Frank married Rosina Mandia on January 7, 1897.   They had 6 children: Guy, Arthur, Edward, Carmella, Bessie and Daisy.   The boys became part of the dairy business.   After Frank passed away in 1931, Guy took over along with his brother, Arthur.   The farm was moved off 19th street and on to property at Route  104 and 429, where it remained from 1939 to 1944.   On the property was a large stone home that was built around the Civil War, and continues to stand there.   Edward opened his own dairy, known as E.A. Buzzelli's Dairy about 1940.   The milk came in pint jars and quart bottles including the baby face bottle. All bottles were made of glass.   The milk came in a glass baby face bottle with the top being cream.   They supplied customers with a tool that would take the cream out so it could be whipped and left skim milk to drink.

At one time Niagara Falls had 32 Dairies.   Their Dairy's motto was "you can whip our cream but you cannot beat our milk".   On the truck was the phrase "always a head". It was not until the late 1940's that milk became homogenized   and the cream was no longer on the top.

About 1950, Guy's son, Frank, joined the family business after graduating from Cornell University and serving 2 years in the Navy. In 1952, they merged with Niagara Milk Cooperative and stopped bottling their own milk.   Frank next opened Creamland Dairy; where he made his own ice cream, custard and lemon ice located at the corner of Niagara Falls Blvd and Cayuga Drive.   Frank tells how he was trying to get the recipe for the lemon ice right and would give it to the neighbors to try. At the same time, he was working for Niagara Milk

Cooperative. Niagara Milk Cooperative bought Buzzelli's, Wendt's, and Diffine's Quality Dairies in 1967. In the Early 1970's, Creamland was sold to Thiele's Dairy from North Tonawanda and today it is known as Dee Dee's.

FRANK G. BUZZELLI

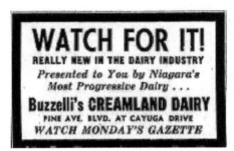

Today, his son Frank, Jr. is Assistant Plant Manager at Upstate Niagara Milk Cooperative. Frank, Jr.'s wife, Mercille, and son, Craig, also work there.

THE CASALE FAMILY
CASALE'S TAVERN AND MOTEL
BY BEVERLY M. BIDAK

Joseph F. Casale is the proud owner and operator of Casale's Tavern & Motel located at 6908 Buffalo Avenue in the LaSalle district of Niagara Falls, New York. The business has been in the Casale family since 1950 and at its current location since 1962. The motel has six fully furnished rooms, including refrigerators, microwave ovens and internet service. The tavern is friendly and cozy and offers light lunches, munchies, pizza as well as all your favorite beverages.

I interviewed Joe at his establishment to find out more about him, his family and his business. I know some of the family history, as he is my husband's second cousin. He was very enthusiastic to discuss the trials and tribulations that the family endured in maintaining the family enterprise.

Joseph F. Casale was the second child born to Francis Salvatore and Marie A. (Sawma) Casale in July 1939 in Niagara Falls, New York. He grew up in LaSalle, attended local schools and graduated from LaSalle Senior High School. He served in the military at the Corryfield Naval Auxiliary Air Station in Pensacola, Florida and Barcelona, Spain. Joe married Donna Leah Jensen the day after Christmas in 1964. Together they raised three children and have several grandchildren.

From 1981-1999, Joe worked at his job at HSBC, bartended at the tavern at night and played the piano at Kings Butler in Lockport and private parties on weekends. In 1999, he retired from the bank with 30 years of service and took over the business full time. He is also known as "The Piano Man." He played piano in a combo in the '80s and today voluntarily plays at Northgate Manor Nursing Home for the residents. Joe also plays piano at small family functions. He is really good and everyone joins in singing and having a grand time.

"The Piano Man," 1980's

The first member of this Casale family to settle in Niagara Falls, New York, was Joe's grandfather, Joseph M. Casale, later known as J.M. Mr. Casale was born Giuseppe MangiaCasale on June 23, 1877, in Gimigliano, Catanzaro, Calabria, Italy, to Salvatore and Maria Angela (Cubello) MangiaCasale.

When Joseph M. Casale was twenty years old, he built and operated a flourmill in Italy. Mr. Casale's thoughts were directed to the United States. He landed in the Port of New York in April 1899. He worked in a small store with his cousin in Copake, NY, for six months. He then went to New York City, where he found employment in a grocery store. In 1904 Mr. Casale came to Niagara Falls, where he went to work for the Crick Brothers Grocery for eighteen months as a clerk. He then ventured into business for himself, building a small store on Eleventh Street, where he sold groceries for a short time and then sold the business.

In 1906, J.M. boarded a ship and sailed back to Italy. He married Saveria Gaglianese in Gimigliano and together they returned to the United States and settled in Niagara Falls in 1907. He went back to work for Crick Brothers for another eighteen months then went back into business for himself. He built a building at 627 19th Street and opened a well-stocked grocery store. In 1912, Mr. Casale built the Star Theater at 625 19th Street. The theater was a comfortable, well- planned cinema house seating 300. He added to his business interests by adding a steamship agency, a foreign exchange and became a notary public.

J.M. and Sarah Casale had five children. Joseph M. Casale, prominent business entrepreneur in Niagara Falls, New York, met his untimely death in 1922. He was discovered electrocuted in the basement of his famed Star Theater. His widow, Sarah, with five children then married Antonio Girasole, who clerked in the Mr. Casale's grocery store. Mr. and Mrs. Girasole later sold all the businesses and the property, moved to LaSalle and had three additional children.

Antonio Girasole, clerk, JM Casale grocery store

Francis Salvatore Casale was born on July 16, 1915, in Niagara Falls, New York. He was the youngest child of Giuseppe and Saveria MangiaCasale. He grew up in LaSalle and his formal education ended after 6th grade. On October 14, 1933, Frank married Marie A. Sawma in Niagara Falls, NY.

Marie was the daughter of Massoud N. (Martin) Sawma and Halabee (Rose) Carma. Marie's parents immigrated to Niagara Falls at the turn of the 20th century from Lebanon (Syrian Arab Republic). They married in Niagara Falls and raised six children. Mr. Sawma owned and operated various businesses at 1106-1108 Eleventh Street, a grocery store, a dry goods store and a confectionary store. Martin Sawma died on July 10, 1948 and his wife, Rose, died on October 15, 1971.

Frank and Marie Casale both having parents, who owned their own businesses, started their first business endeavor in the early 1940's with a grocery store located at 186 56th Street. The building was two stories with a storefront and apartments above. The family lived in one of the apartments. Joseph F. Casale remembers that his parent's grocery store made deliveries to the local neighborhood.

When the Casales closed the store they opened a gas station on Buffalo Avenue. They then procured property across the street at 6515 Buffalo Avenue. The 56th Street store later became Mom's Pizzeria. The property on Buffalo Avenue consisted of a small restaurant, house, two cottages and enough riverfront to dock 25 boats. Frank moved his family into the house. He rented out the two cottages and rented out the boat docks. In 1950, Frank and Marie opened one of the first pizzerias in Niagara Falls, Casale's Pizzeria.

CASALE'S PIZZERIA
6515 BUFFALO AVENUE
PIZZA
EAT HERE OR AWAY
HOT DINNERS — SANDWICHES
BEER—WINE — PHONE 3-3072

In 1958, Mr. Casale learned that the State Power Authority was going to appropriate his land for Niagara Parkway developments. He was told not to make any improvements to the property that it would be taken in the near future. His long-term objective was to demolish the cottages and construct a small motel in their place. In 1960 he bought a house and a lot on 69th Street and Buffalo Avenue. The near future turned into four years later when the State Department of Public Works gave him notice to vacate immediately.

Because he had made no improvements to his current home and business property, its value had declined. The amount of compensation offered by the State would have bankrupted Mr. Casale and put his family and livelihood in peril. While negotiations continued, Frank Casale moved his family to the 69th Street home and began erecting a new building to house his business. The construction project took thirteen weeks of hard work with help from family and friends and for thirteen weeks a local union picketed daily claiming that scab workers were being used. In 1962 the new Casale's opened at 6908 Buffalo Avenue. Eventually a compromised settlement was reached between Mr. Casale and the State.

Two years later, Frank began building the motel behind the tavern. As with the building of the tavern, he did the construction work himself, with the help of family and friends. As before, a local union picketed daily claiming that scab workers were being used. The picket signs were put down in the afternoons when Frank informed the picketers that "Genesee was buying."

Marie Casale took care of her home and family and also did all the cooking and cleaning at the restaurant and motel. Time to make a decision…pizzeria or tavern. Tavern won out. Thus the current name, Casales' Tavern & Motel was born.

Marie and Frank Casale in the 1970's

Frank and Marie Casale operated a very prosperous and friendly establishment. The current owner, Joe, remembers his father as a "tough task master." All the family and customers knew Marie as Mom Casale. She is remembered as gracious, always greeting the customers and making everyone feel a part of her family. Joe says she was a "sweetheart", and a very hard worker. She was the nuts and bolts of the family and involved in the business until her death.

Joseph F. Casale took over full ownership and operation of Casales' Tavern & Motel in 1999. He still maintains a fun social split club started by his parents in 1958 called the "Dumschitt Club." This group of customers and friends now total about 200 members. They pay $30 annually, $4 is for a membership card. The remainder is for 25 weeks of split club and on the 26th week a picnic and split club is held. A new president is elected annually. Proceeds from the split club and raffles held during the year are donated to charities such as Hospice, Heart & Soul, the Salvation Army and Community Missions.

Casale's Tavern & Motel is very community and family orientated. Their customer base is made up of local people and tourists. There are many repeat customers and some being fourth generation families. Joes' grandson, Dom, is employed there now and is bringing in a younger clientele. Joe's son, Joe, is planning on becoming part of the business when he retires from the Niagara Falls Police Force.

Joseph F. Casale

THE LOTEMPIO FAMILY
RAINBOW GRILL
BY MICHELLE ANN KRATTS

It isn't often that Niagara's Italian culinary history merges with Hollywood and the entertainment world…but, just once, it did in the story of the Donia, Cardone and LoTempio families.

As a little girl, I always enjoyed a lazy Sunday afternoon at my grandparents' home. After my stomach was full from a wonderful dinner and after the lively conversation had subsided…it was inevitable that I would find myself in my grandparents' bedroom going through their old photo albums and scrapbooks. My grandparents always kept things perfectly organized and labeled all of their photographs so neatly. They took great care in preserving our family history. I particularly recall the clippings of the beautiful singer, April Stevens, and her musically talented brother, Nino Tempo. Of course, those were their stage names, and of course, there was a family story.

The LoTempios lived on Pine Avenue, near 15th Street, and before the war (during which my grandmother worked at Bell Aircraft making airplanes) she babysat little Antonino and Carol LoTempio. They lived near St. Joseph's Church and Levy Brothers Furniture Store. Across the street was the Amendola Theater. My grandmother enjoyed their antics and would never forget the kindness of their grandmother, Mrs. Donia, (Sarah Cardone, who had come from Parma, Italy) for she always invited her to eat her delicious Italian soups, or whatever she was cooking. Bart Donia (also born in Italy) had a tavern on the corner of Pine and 15th Street. Later, he ran the Rainbow Restaurant/Grill. Samuel LoTempio, the singers' father, owned the L & L Food Store which was located at 1618 Pine Avenue. Mrs. LoTempio (Anna Donia) would also serve my grandmother lunch at times. It was the first time she had ever had jello and white American bread sandwiches with mayonnaise and tomatoes.

WINS HONORS—Fifteen-year-old Carol Lo Tempio, daughter of Mr. and Mrs. Samuel Lo Tempio, of Garden avenue, will make her singing debut Saturday evening at Kleinhan's Music Hall, Buffalo, at the Curtiss Aircraft club "Fiesta Ball." Carol sings under the name of Carol Tempo.

ANNA DONIA
Who recently became the bride of Samuel LoTempio

During the early 1960's, Carol and Nino signed a contract with Atco Records. It was soon after that fame and fortune followed. They continued to have a string of billboard hits and even earned a Grammy for "best rock and roll record of the year" for the single, "Deep Purple."

Carol and Nino (who became April Stevens and Nino Tempo) performed locally for many years preceding their national success. In fact, the duo had entertained servicemen during the war alongside Benny Goodman and Glenn Miller. April became well-known as a torch singer and Nino was a musical prodigy. An old news article reveals that little Nino had become Glenn Miller's "handy-boy" and ran scores of errands for the musicians when the band played in Buffalo. In return, Nino was taught the songs that had made Miller famous. Miller appreciated Nino's exceptional talent and often took him along to sing whenever he played benefits in the Buffalo area. It was said that Miller had even offered Nino a job and promised it would come to fruition when he returned from Europe. Unfortunately, Miller was killed in a plane crash while entertaining troops overseas.

These "jukebox favorites" departed with their parents to Los Angeles, California, and the rest is history. Nino was also an actor in several films, including *The Glenn Miller Story*. Ironically, he played a thinly veiled alias for Benny Goodman. In 1975 he played saxophone on John Lennon's album, *Rock 'n' Roll*.

A few years ago, my grandmother and I were talking about April Stevens and her brother, Nino Tempo. She kept hearing the song that made them famous, "Deep Purple," on the Canadian radio station, AM740 from Toronto, and thought it would be so nice to hear from those famous kids she had, at one time, babysat. I found their official website and emailed them asking them if they remembered my grandmother. They responded immediately and said that they would always remember her fondly. They had some kind words and even sent her a CD with their latest music. I was excited to finally "meet" them, as well. For, after so many years of looking at scrapbook clippings, I felt that we were family.

THE RICCIUTO, VIOLA AND TARDIBUONO FAMILIES
VIOLA'S SUBMARINE HOUSE
BY MICHELLE ANN KRATTS

One of Niagara's most iconic stops is Viola's Submarine House. Established in 1958 by Luigi Ricciuto, Otto Viola and Joseph (Rita Viola) Tardibuono, it was initially located at 1717 Elmwood Avenue in Niagara Falls. In 1960, a second location was added at 1539 Military Road, in the Town of Niagara. Viola's is most well-known for its famous "steak and cheese" submarine.

Greetings

Only the best
to our patrons
Viola's Submarine
House

1539 Military Road
297-3550
1717 Elmwood Avenue
282-7094

It's not uncommon for people who leave Niagara Falls to long for Viola's subs. So many friends of ours have been known to wrap them up for loved ones in suitcases. What a great treat it is to present our displaced Niagarans with this piece of "home!"

Back in the late 1990's, my husband, Mike, served with the United States Air Force, Security Police Squadron, at Dyess AFB, in Abilene, Texas. We were a long way from home. For a time he manned the front gate which had a rotating sign that signified the name and hometown of the airman on duty. One morning, a retired colonel came through the main entrance while Mike was on duty. Before the colonel drove on, he lowered the window and said something to my husband.

"I bet you're thinking of a Viola's steak and cheese sub right now."

My husband paused for a moment in disbelief. He could hardly believe what he had heard. Obviously, the colonel was also from Niagara Falls...for he knew about the Viola's subs. One thousand six hundred and fifty miles is quite the distance, but the thought of a Viola's steak and cheese sub certainly brought my husband back home to Niagara Falls...like magic.

THE MAGADDINO FAMILY
POWER CITY DISTRIBUTING COMPANY
BY PEGGY TAYLOR-HULLIGAN

Stefano Magaddino was born on October 10, 1891, in Castellammare del Golfo, Sicily, to Giovanni Magaddino and (mother unknown). His family immigrated to the United States around 1902 and settled first in Brooklyn, New York. The 1930 census of Niagara Falls reveals the family at Whitney Avenue. It also lists that Mr. Magaddino was, at the time, operating a grocery/saloon.

In 1938, Mr. Magaddino, the owner of the Power City Distributing Company of New York, introduced his latest "brew," Niagara Bud Beer.

Niagara Bud Beer had a short lifetime. But the Power City Distributing Company continued to operate for many more years. It featured such beers as Empire, Beer, Black Horse Ale, Carlings Red Cap, Schlitz, Budweiser Beers and other famous beverages.

Mr. Magaddino served as the President of the Power City Distributing Company of New York from the Roaring 20's through the Prohibition Era, until approximately 1958. Great history was made locally during this vibrant and exciting era.

RELIABLE MEN
Three Wanted
AS TRUCK DRIVERS
CHAUFFEUR'S LICENSE NECESSARY
APPLY
POWER CITY
DISTRIBUTING CO.
1113 LA SALLE AVENUE
Men Working in Defense Plants
Do Not Apply

Mr. Magaddino died on July 19, 1974, and is buried at St. Joseph's Cemetery in Niagara Falls.

A recent drive by the old location of this site was found to be a vacant lot, which could probably tell many a story if we listen hard enough.

THE DI CAMILLO FAMILY
DI CAMILLO BAKING CO., INC.
BY MARCIA M. BUZZELLI

The Di Camillo Baking Company was founded in 1920 by Tommaso and his wife, Addolorata Di Camillo, at 565 14th Street in Niagara Falls, NY. Today the company is run by second, third and fourth generation members of the Di Camillo family. Three of Tommaso and Addolorata's twelve children have survived to this day: Joseph, Teresa Hargrave and Angelica Di Camillo. Teresa and Angelica continue to go to the office on Linwood Avenue, where the main bakery is currently located. Tommaso's grandsons David, Thomas, Francis (Skip), and Michael compose the executive officers. Cousins and grandsons are working together and doing everything from baking to sales.

Tommaso Di Camillo, the son of Francesco Di Camillo and Euphemia Ferrara, left his home in Villamagna, Chieti, Abruzzo, in Italy, in 1897. He went to Quebec and after one year immigrated to Niagara Falls, NY. His wife, the former Addolorata Iannotti, born in Ari, Chieti, Abruzzo, and raised in Villamagna in Italy, came to the United States and to Niagara Falls in 1903. Tommaso and Addolorata were married at St. Mary's Church on September 20, 1903.

Joe, Babe - Bread Wagon - Circa 1929

Tommaso and Addolorata Di Camillo

They became the proud parents of 12 children; five boys and seven girls. Sadly, the first burial at St. Joseph's Cemetery was the 18-month old son of Tommaso and Addolorata, Anthony Di Camillo. The three oldest girls and their mother opened a grocery store on 14th Street, where the father and his sons baked bread in the basement. The baked breads were delivered to their neighbors and about 200 little Italian delis all over town using horse-drawn wagons. Interestingly there were no sweets made until after the war. The famous Di Camillo's bread—which takes five hours from scratch to slice to produce-- was developed at this time with a special recipe that did not include sugar or shortening. It has since become the trademark for the bakery.

Home Delivery - Circa 1929

BULLETIN!!!

So that our employes may enjoy the Christmas Holiday Weekend with their families

ALL DI CAMILLO STORES WILL BE CLOSED
SAT., DEC. 25th & SUN., DEC. 26th

Di Camillos Bakery
• 531 Third St., • 467 20th St., • Pine Plaza

• Shop early *tomorrow* for the largest assortment of

Christmas Goodies

• Xmas Cut-Out Cookies
• Filled Cookies
• Fruit Cakes
• Tea Cookies

HAPPY HOLIDAY FROM EVERYONE AT DI CAMILLOS

Remember: All Di Camillo Stores
Closed Saturday & Sunday

Di Camillo
LIKE HOME BAKING

BAKERY SPECIALS

PLACE YOUR ORDER TODAY FOR
DI-CAMILLO'S
DONUTS *for*
HALLOWEEN

Full 7 inch
Layer
CAKES ea. **59¢**

These Delicious
Coffee
CAKES ea. **39¢**

Generous Size Squares
PIZZA ....ea. **10¢**

DOUGHNUTS
Fryer Fresh
Over 30 Varieties

HALLOWE'EN
Decorations on Cakes and Pastries

Eventually, all of the boys found themselves working in the bakery. Three of the daughters became nuns, three married and one remained single.   One daughter, Asunta, married and ran a gift shop in the town of Pittsford outside Rochester for several years.   She returned to Niagara Falls in 1979.   Son, Thomas, married and started working as a driver.   Later he became a retail store manager.   He and his wife had two daughters.   One continues to work at the bakery, Betty King. Frank was the first CEO of the company.   He had four sons, who run the company now.   At the present time, David is CEO.   Brothers Tom, Skip, and Michael are Vice Presidents.   A daughter, Ann, married and had four sons. Nicholas married and had twins: a boy and girl. He started as a driver and then was a master baker from 1920 to 2001. His son, Jim, has followed in his footsteps and after having a career in the Niagara County Probation Department retired to work at the bakery.   Joseph was a driver, master baker and sales manager from 1930 to 1971.   He married and had two sons. Angelica, a daughter who recently celebrated her 90th birthday, continues to work in the office of the company, having started in the grocery store that had been operated by her mother.   She works in the retail store as office

manager.   Teresa also continues to work in the office.   Teresa married Frank Hargrave and they have two children.   She started to work in the bakery at age 13, and in 1938 became the office manager.

ORIGINAL OVEN 19th Street

Tommaso died in 1941 and his children and grandchildren and great-grandchildren continued to run the company.

From 14th Street the business was moved to 467   20th Street.   From 1942 to 1976, bread, pizza and donuts were baked at this location until 1976 when the bakery was moved to 811 Linwood Ave.   With the advent of cars they had trucks delivering the bread.

A pastry store and bakery was opened at 531 Third Street in Niagara Falls from 1953 to 1976 years.   Son, Nicholas, a master baker, did the pastry baking here.

Today, the company has grown with retail stores on Linwood Avenue, Niagara Falls Boulevard, Pine Avenue, Lewiston and Williamsville, NY. In 1979, grandson, Michael Di Camillo, opened a Gourmet Department, which continues to this day. Di Camillo's products can be found in many cities around the United States. As printed in the Niagara Gazette December 1, 2013, popular Di Camillo gifts are in tins or ceramic jars of biscotti or cookies---several of which are featured in the famous Neiman Marcus mail order catalog.

TU SCENDI DALLE STELLE
(YOU COME DOWN FROM THE STARS)
BY MICHELLE ANN KRATTS

When I think of my great grandmother, Clementina Fortuna, during the holidays, my memories are always framed in wonderful food and song. Of course, food…but there was also music. Tears would come to her eyes when one particular song would play and forever I will see her when I hear it. And in Niagara Falls, one does hear this song at Christmastime. It's called "Tu scendi dalle stelle," and it's one of the most beautiful Christmas songs ever composed. I never really thought of the significance of the words until now. It is clear why the Italians loved this song. This song celebrates the story of a king born of the stars into dire poverty. Of a child who gives his life as a result of his great love for the world.

Perhaps for the Italians of Niagara Falls this song held some other significance, as well. For in the spring of 1920, one poor Italian child opened the gates of heaven. Literally.

The story probably began over the holidays in 1919/1920. Tommaso and Addolorata Di Camillo's infant son, Antonio, would not live. Suffering from pneumonia, he barely made it through La Festa dell'Epifania - the Feast of the Epiphany. He breathed his last on January 14, 1920. There must have been much heartache from the little house at 565 14th Street. The Di Camillo family, an immigrant family that eventually would found a baking empire in the Niagara region, did not have much during these early years. A funeral was held from the home on January 15 and the child was moved to the vault at Oakwood Cemetery for a charge of $2.50. It was winter and the ground was probably frozen over so a burial was not likely at this time.

It was customary to keep bodies in the vault until the ground was ready for burial in a plot. However, a plot in Oakwood was never chosen for little Antonio. Instead, there was another plan that would make history.

I had never heard about this other "plan" until a Di Camillo descendant approached me one afternoon in Oakwood Cemetery. He asked me if I knew anything about the baby who had founded a cemetery. I was ashamed to tell him that I knew nothing about this— but I would definitely look into it. After looking into his "story" it quickly became apparent that Mr. Di Camillo was correct. A child from his family had been the first burial at St. Joseph's Cemetery in Niagara Falls.

In fact it might be said that St. Joseph's Cemetery was born in Oakwood Cemetery one starlit evening in April when Father Augustine Billerio took the child's body from the vault and secretly buried it in the land that had been purchased by the Church—the eleven acres that is now St. Joseph's Cemetery.

It's hard to imagine today that the world was such a different place back in 1920. During this period there was a great amount of prejudice leveled at the Italian immigrants who had taken Niagara Falls by storm. Their dress and customs were strange and wild, they were full of passion and independence, they sang and they danced in the streets. They were outspoken and their superstitions and religious customs were seen as unusual. They were impoverished. By 1920, one of the most prominent of the Italian leaders, Father Billerio, purchased land for the purpose of consecrating a special ground for Roman Catholic burials. The Niagara Falls City Council responded by saying: "ABSOLUTELY NOT A CHANCE," and washed their hands of the situation. But Father Billerio was not about to accept defeat. For him, the establishment of a Roman Catholic Cemetery within the city of Niagara Falls was an integral part of his service to his people. So he took matters into his own hands.

It was recorded that on April 22, 1920 (some accounts say April 21) the body of little Antonio Di Camillo was removed from the vault at Oakwood Cemetery and secretly buried that evening in the "new Italeon cemetery." Father Billerio believed that in burying little Antonio on the property the nearby property owners who were against the establishment of an Italian cemetery, and the city fathers, would be left without an argument as it would be impossible to disinter the child's body.   When called upon by the City Council, Mr. Angelo Scalzo, Father Billerio and others revealed the history of the land they had recently purchased—including the story of the burial of Antonio Di Camillo-- and again, insisted upon being granted the right to turn it into a Roman Catholic burial ground. The City Manager reported that the sanitary code had been violated with Di Camillo's illegal burial and a permit would be necessary from the health officer—which would not be allowed. It was continually stated that the land was ill suited for a cemetery because of drainage issues, that the illegal burial would be a health risk to the community and that it should immediately be removed and reinterred at another location.

Finally, miraculously, on May 3, 1920, after much debate, the health officer, the corporation counsel and the city manager had a sudden change of heart. They had inspected the location, and after being informed of the manner in which the sanitary code would be met, finally agreed to allow for the establishment of a Roman Catholic burial ground within the city of Niagara Falls. St. Joseph's Cemetery was officially established.

On Memorial Day in 1920, the opening of the cemetery was formally observed and the ground consecrated. All of the Italian societies marched from St. Joseph's church on Pine Avenue to the new cemetery and were led by Scalzo's band. The men from Niagara Falls (of Italian heritage) who had given their lives in the First World War were memorialized. By May 29, there were twenty five bodies buried at St. Joseph's cemetery.

I have read that there is a stone in St. Joseph's that commemorates the life and death of Antonio Di Camillo. My daughter and I tried to find him one autumn afternoon but no one seemed to know the location. One of the grounds workers told me where the oldest part of the cemetery is and that I might find him there. Luckily, it was near the area where my own great great grandparents are buried. We walked along the fence and marveled at the beautiful angels that paved our way. There are many graves from the 1920's and 1930's in this section. Graves with beautiful Italian engravings and ceramic photographs offering the passerby a glimpse into the soul of the dead.

We never did find little Antonio. I snapped a few pictures of tombstones that caught my eye. Some belonging to beautiful Italian children that left the earth too early. They probably keep company with our little Antonio and honor him for opening the gates and letting everyone else in.

My daughter, Jillian, at her great great great grandparents' graves. Possibly nearby little Antonio's burial site.

THE TRUSELLO FAMILY
TRUSELLO'S BAKERY
BY MICHELLE ANN KRATTS AND DAN SICOLI

Trusello's Bakery was founded in 1917 on 20th Street in Niagara Falls by Antonino Trusello—an Italian immigrant. After moving to their iconic location on 19th Street, Trusello's Bakery quickly become one of the most well-known traditional Italian eateries in the city of Niagara Falls. The simple pizza, which was made from bread flour dough, tomato sauce and oregano was legendary. Some have boasted that "every first communion, baptism, birthday party, or family event in the Italian households of Niagara Falls had Trusello's sheet pizza." Antonino died in April of 1985 and Trusello's Bakery closed in 1996. For a short time the restaurant re-opened in Lewiston at 742 Center Street. Great grandson, Anthony Trusello, manned the ovens and used the recipes that were handed down from his grandfather. This location is also now closed.

Today, another pizzeria, DG Bread and Pizza, is located in the old green building where Trusello's pizza was born. Many locals flock to the pizzeria to enjoy what some consider a "close" version of Trusello's original Old Fashioned style pizza.

"What did you say about Trusello bread?"

By Dan Sicoli

The "regulars" as well as casual customers of the now closed Trusello's Bakery near the corner of 19th Street and Elmwood Avenue in Niagara Falls, NY, will no doubt recall the painted cartoon sign that hung for years on the building in the lot of the Sicilian bakery. Adapted from on old print ad for guns, it depicted one man holding another man by the collar and yelling, "What did you say about Trusello bread?"

This slogan, although rudimentary, perfectly captured the sentiment many loyal customers felt about the handmade loaves baked in a stone oven. Since its closing back in the 1996 many have tried, though none have been able to re-capture the original flavor of the saucy pizza or those crusty and tasty Italian loaves. Former customers still reminisce about their beloved Trusello's to this day.

Having been employed there during my high school and college years, I have many fond memories of the family-owned bakery. There was nothing like a hot loaf fresh from the oven, then splitting it in half, drizzling in some olive oil, sprinkling it over with salt and pepper, and then slowly sinking your teeth into the deliciousness of it all. It tasted better than the best steak in town.

Ironically, I was diagnosed with celiac sprue in my 30s and was forced to change my diet or risk serious consequences. Avoiding gluten, the only treatment, meant eliminating Trusello bread from my supper table as gluten is prevalent in wheat flour--the main ingredient in bread. But at least I was fortunate enough to enjoy Trusello's bread and pizza for those 30-odd years and retain the pleasure of those wafting memories which I can "smell" even now.

HOT PIZZA
Trusello Bakery
Every Nite 'Til 10:30
Phone 2-1506   840 - 19th

Two poems about Trusello Bakery
Courtesy Slipstream Magazine

what did you say about trusello bread?
By Dan Sicoli
i

wwI immigrant finds
sicilian sweat & flour make bread
courageous slave
finds america where
"there's gold in the streets"

ii

handmade
stone-cooked
over 40 years
10 billion loaves
the dago way

"can no be beat"

the old man died last week
but i swear i
heard him at the shop bench
this morning
smelled his coffee royal
just before the sun showed

"hey danny you weak
no squeeze right...how many times you do?
godda damma i tol' you roll...
roll an' squeeze...roll an' squeeze
squeeze SQUEEZA! li'e dis...
my hands all crook'd
i still shape-a bedder bread..."

but looking up from my hangover

i only saw a shadow
move by the screen window
heard a dog barking in the distance
a near-perfect loaf
in my hand

what i liked about
working
in the old stone sicilian bakery
during those teenage years
was the quiet quarter mile neighborhood walk
in the still dark morning
with the distant din of the falls
purging my half hung-over dreams

and how the trust of a season was a
molting bird of a cloud
in a northeast winter

making the lung of that brick oven more inviting

and how the taut spring of the wooden screen door
snapped it shut behind me
proclaiming my entrance
to the early morning preppers of industrial mixers

and how i'd catch their guarded smiles
knowing my young muscles would relieve them from lifting
the 100-lb sacks of high-gluten grain
as i waged through
the perpetual cloud of flour dust
gathering my apron and hat from the back room

and how subtle the changes
in this neighborhood
in this shop
in the minds of us men
so slovenly occurred

FOR SERVICE, AN AWARD—Anthony Trusello, connected with the baking business here for decades, was honored Tuesday at the installation dinner of the 18th-19th Sts. Business and Professional Men's Assn. A plaque presented Mr. Trusello called atten- tion to his years of service in his profession. Here, from left, are Salvatore Marasco, vice president of the association and dinner chairman; Mr. Trusello; Felix Palermo, president, and Frank Raymond, retiring president. — Gazette Photo.

THE SPACONE AND PROIETTI FAMILIES
PEE WEE'S PIZZERIA
BY MARCIA BUZZELLI

I went to visit my cousin and he told me the story of the first pizzeria in Niagara Falls.   When he returned from World War II, a friend of his suggested they open a pizzeria.   My cousin, Nunzio Spacone who was born in Prezza, L'Aquila, Abruzzo Italy, and his friend Albert Proietti, who was born in Niagara Falls, started Pee Wee's Pizzeria. It was around 1946; Albert who was stationed in the area of Naples could not get over how all the American soldiers would line up to eat pizza.   Nunzio and Albert started the business about the middle of Nineteenth Street, between Pine and Elmwood Avenue.   Business was such a success that they moved to a larger location closer to Pine Avenue. Saturday and Sunday evenings after the movies ended, they had long lines of people waiting to buy pizza.   They only served pizza using various toppings.   When they started, they went to Buffalo to buy a used oven.   Nunzio took a trip to Pittsburgh to see how they ran pizzerias, as there was a large Italian population in Pittsburgh.

Now Open for Business:
In New Location at 2005 Pine Ave.

Pee Wee's Pizzeria

2005 PINE AVE.   PHONE 4-1675

Pizza To Eat Here or Take Out

After a couple of years, Nunzio gave his share to Pee Wee and the business was moved to 20th and Pine Avenue.   I believe many of us would stop there on our way home from N.F. High School.   It closed about 1960.

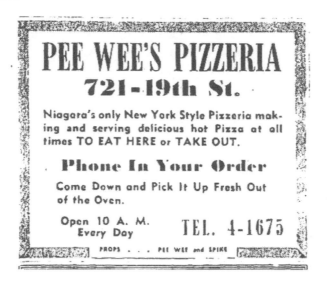

Recipe:

The pizza was sold in 9 inch plates with crushed tomatoes, mushrooms, pepperoni, anchovies, and a lot of oregano and grated Romano cheese.

4 cups of flour

1 1/3 cups of water

1 pkg of dry yeast

4 tbsp oil

½ tsp salt

Mix, knead and let rise in bowl. Form into pizza and add topping.

Bake at 375 for 40 minutes.

THE MERANTO, MIGLIAZZO AND GRANTO FAMILIES
THE M & M MARKET
BY ELEANOR MIGLIAZZO NOVARA

When I began researching my Migliazzo family history, I grew up knowing only one family, who were my father's first cousins, living in Niagara Falls, as the rest of the Migliazzo relatives lived in Italy. To my surprise, I came across a few cards from a family in Arizona who occasionally wrote to my parents expressing that they missed us and always wished our family well during the holidays. I learned that this family was my father Rocco Migliazzo's first cousins, who were twins, Giovanni (John) Migliazzo and Antonio (Anthony) Migliazzo [along with Anthony's wife Josephine (Govannini) and young son Bruno]. My sister, Connie (Migliazzo) Paolone, remembers the twins, who were born on August 5, 1893, in Girifalco, Catanzaro, Calabria, Italy, and to her knowledge they later left Niagara Falls for Arizona due to health reasons.

The twins, as they were referred to, were partners in a well-known and prosperous business that opened in or around 1934 in Niagara Falls, namely: MIGLIAZZO and MERANTO CITY MARKET [also known as the M and M City Market]. Connie recalls that our father Rocco also helped his cousins with the business for a brief period of time. Not knowing much about the business or the Migliazzo twins, my research consisted of seeking out a few of the Meranto family members, and this is where my story begins.....

74

I interviewed Elaine Meranto, daughter of Nicholas and Mary Meranto. Nicholas was also associated with M and M City Market. Elaine did remember the twin brothers, but didn't know much about them and knew they were not her relatives. At various holidays, especially Easter, Elaine remembers the large display of flowers and baby chicks and recalls the big snowstorm in 1936. She did find photos of the market along with various family members and many employees of the market. I am grateful to Elaine for copies of these photos and taking the time to talk and tell me that her cousin, Ralph Meranto, would be the person with more knowledge about the market.

Off I went to the Main Street Library in Niagara Falls to meet with Ralph where I picked his brain for information and learned that there were actually two different market businesses that had eventually merged into one. Sure enough, Ralph was a great source of information.

Shown in the middle is Elaine Meranto and her sister on the right

Ralph and Elaine's grandfather, Salvatore "Sam" Meranto, born on December 24, 1882, in Catanzaro, Calabria, Italy, and his wife, Mary (Talarico) Meranto raised a family of three boys and two daughters on their farm in Lewiston, NY. As a farmer Salvatore sold produce to various wholesale businesses in Niagara and Erie Counties. In 1919 he became the founder of the "original" Meranto Meat Market located in the Niagara Falls City Market.

Ralph believes his father, Thomas Meranto, must have inherited his father's genes for the produce business. [Maybe because of all the children born to Salvatore and Mary he is the only child born in Italy while they were on vacation visiting their family]. In 1929 he formed a partnership with Giovanni (John) Migliazzo in the Migliazzo and Meranto City Market (aka M and M Market), where they sold fresh fruits, vegetables and meats, with Carmen Granto, Sr. as Manager. The market was located at 1800 Pine Avenue, Niagara Falls, NY. Others involved in the business were Nicholas Meranto and Anthony Migliazzo.

Later, Carmen Granto, Sr., Thomas Meranto and Nicholas Meranto (Nicholas' wife Mary F. (Critelli) Meranto was the bookkeeper) opened a grocery/meat market [also known as the G and M Giant Market] located at 740 – 19th Street, Niagara Falls, NY. Eventually both businesses worked together closely as one market.

When Ralph was around 10-years old, he remembers his father bringing him into the business and said it was "because he knew how to read." This is where he learned that there was always an orderly way for arranging each grouping of produce on the tables. The most commonly used method was to place the many fruits on the tables in the shape of a pyramid; vegetables were laid out overlapping each other in a long row horizontally or vertically and large squash, pumpkins, etc. also had their own sequence of design to help appeal to the customer. Employees would trim lettuce, celery, broccoli, etc. and throw the trimmings on the floor. It was Ralph's job to sweep everything up.

Another job Ralph was given was to fill large bags with potatoes. He would open the bag, insert a large funnel and then fill the bags to the top, then slip the funnel up and out the top of the bag. The bags were then placed on a table for display and left opened for customers to purchase.

One comical memory is the "watermelon" ritual. A chain gang of employees would unload the trucks by transferring each watermelon from one person to another. When the final watermelon was handed to the last person, it would purportedly fall to the floor, allowing the employees to scramble for a refreshing slice along with lots of laughter.

The Migliazzo and Meranto Market

Ralph told me he especially remembers enjoying working along with John Migliazzo and Carmen Granto, Sr. and how they "took him under his wing" teaching him the produce/meat business. One thing that came to his mind, John was always worried whether he had eaten by telling him "If you get hungry just take some fruit and eat – you don't have to ask just take something."

By the time Ralph was 14-years old the market had moved and more or less merged with the G and M Market which was next to the M and M Market in the City Market. The two businesses primarily sold produce and meat. Both of these businesses, known as "vendors", had to apply for a permit to do business by renting a "stall with a number." These stalls were located in the City Market of Niagara Falls and each year they were required to renew their permit.

The M and M Market and G and M Market ran various ads in the Niagara Falls Gazette, especially for fundraisers or a newly opened business. Some of their ads were as follows, "BEST WISHES FROM MIGLAZZO AND MERANTO, FRESH FRUITS, VEGETABLES AND MEATS, 1800 PINE AVENUE AT CITY MARKET" and "SUCCESS IS OUR WISH To the new HIPPODROME THEATRE G&M Giant Food Market, 740 19th STREET, On City Market Square."

According to Ralph, Thomas Meranto was named Temporary Chairman of the First Independent Food Dealers meeting of Niagara Falls in December 1946, in the Chamber of Commerce building to complete plans for organization of an Independent Food Dealers' Association. Invitations were sent to several food dealers in Niagara Falls to attend. Thomas said "the meeting is open to all independent grocery and meat dealers in the city, whether or not they receive an invitation." Thomas, thereafter, became the Chairman of this newly formed association. This association grew to be known as the now existing Pine Avenue Business Association.

Well I guess the "apple doesn't fall far from the tree" because Ralph worked in various markets prior to going into business with his father. In 1958, after Ralph graduated from the University of Buffalo, he and his father opened their own business. The business services were expanded to include wholesale foods of every phase of social and business activities. Their first endeavor was the frozen goods service that extended to sales of large quantities which must have been one of the first markets in Niagara Falls to sell this large a quantity of frozen foods. This business was located on Portage Road, and continued until the Meranto Meat Market moved in 1971 to 1608 – 18th Street, Niagara Falls, NY.

GRAND OPENING—City officials met with vendors at the City Market today to mark the grand opening of the new city market building. From left are, George Petos, owner of the building's coffee shop; City Manager Edward H. Pottheff Jr., Ellwood Kysor, market superintendent; Mayor Calvin L. Keller, Harry Stahl, a vendor; Russell Larke, the architect who drew the plans for the new building; Carmen Granto, owner of the building's grocery, and John Migliozzo.—Gazette Photo.

The growth of the Meranto Meat Market that prospered for over 55-years was attained through the families' devotion to serving the public with quality service.

Following my interviews with Elaine and Ralph, it was time to contact Cynthia (Granto) Bianco for more information on the Migliazzo, Granto and Meranto Giant Market, particularly since her father, Carmen Granto, Sr., born on January 26, 1906, in Calabria, Italy, was a partner. Another hard working Italian who emigrated to the United States and joined fellow Italians to form an even bigger city market complex.

1929

MERANTO'S MEAT SERVICE
1209 PORTAGE RD.
THOMAS MERANTO AND
RALPH MERANTO, PARTNERS

Mr. Meranto started in the meat business in 1929 as a partner under the name of Migliazzo-Meranto at the City Market. After his son graduated from U. B. in 1958, they opened their own business. The business services were expanded to include catering service of every phase of social and business affairs. The freezing goods service extended to sales of large quantities, 1 to 1000 lbs. and over.

Celia (Simone) Granto, Cynthia's mother, a delightfully 93-year young and beautiful woman, who is the last of the original owners of the business, joined us for the interview. She appears to have lived a long and healthy life. She happily reminisced that she worked for the G & M Giant Market as a cashier where she met and married Carmen on January 3, 1942. This little story brought a twinkle to her eyes. Carmen and Celia raised two children, their son Carmen Granto, Jr. and Cynthia.

Big winter storm in 1936

Cynthia was familiar with many of the same employees who continued on when the Granto and Meranto Giant Market was formed, so it was, she says that the many employees and others associated with the market, like John Migliazzo and Nicholas Meranto.

Her great enjoyment was working for her father and as she sits back in her chair begins to tell me that one of her favorite memories of special times spent with him was when "after school each day I would wait on the stoop of my home and look down the street to watch for my father... upon seeing him returning home from work, I would run down the street to meet him and he would catch me in his arms and swing me around and we would both walk home."

Another pleasant memory was when Carmen invited her to ride with him to Buffalo to purchase the produce. They would leave at 4:00 a.m. which seemed like forever to get there, as in those days there were no thruway systems in the area. It was an exciting outing as Buffalo was a bustling city. It had become a ritual that after the Buffalo trip on the way home they would stop for breakfast at a restaurant not far from the market. Already the early morning start was beginning to feel like they had been out all day, especially after their breakfast.

They would return around 6:00 a.m., the truck filled with a variety of produce. Just as Ralph had expressed earlier, Cynthia has vivid memories of how the hard work really began as all the produce had to be cleaned, trimmed, organized, and ready for the customers to arrive for the day's business. These were "very long hard working days." Mixed in were happy times as well. As a matter of fact, Cynthia remembers the comical "watermelon ritual" along with the arrangement that went into the "displaying of the fruits and vegetables," the same as Ralph described.

When she became older, Cynthia recalls helping her father with more advanced jobs. He taught her how to count the day's receipts efficiently so that all the bills were facing one way and stacked in proper order to bring to the bank.

Cynthia, like Elaine, enjoyed the vast variety of flowers that were for sale: hydrangeas, lilies, tulips, dahlias, etc. They were very romantic and made the market look like a huge flower garden.

Christmas was always special to Cynthia when the Niagara Falls city workers would arrive with a large Christmas tree for display in front of the market. Celia remembers that the market had a special area set aside for selling Christmas trees. Each year field trips were arranged for schools to bring the children to visit the market and the trees.

Cynthia and Celia remember all the hard work required to make the market a success. Carmen will always be remembered as a wonderfully kind man who, according to Cynthia would feed anyone in need and if they didn't have enough money to pay their bill, he would take what they had and they went off with their bag of groceries. In time the market began selling more merchandise other than produce and meat.

It appears that the Migliazzo, Meranto and Granto families were the precursors for what we now know as a "Supermarket."

I was so proud to learn that two of my immigrant ancestors along with other immigrant families came to America and together developed these market businesses in Niagara Falls.

Celia (Simone) Granto

Caterina (Mariano) Migliazzo Wedding Photo. This is my mother, Caterina (Mariano) Migliazzo's, wedding photo with her siblings and parents. Starting from the extreme left is Anthony S. Mariano, Angelina (Mariano) Nudo, Mother, Maria Saveria (Paonessa) Mariano, Father, Salvatore Agostino Mariano, Bride, Caterina (Mariano) Migliazzo behind her parents. To the left of the Bride is Luigi Tommaso Mariano. To the right of the Bride is Thomas J. Mariano, and Maria (Mariano) Lentine, Critelli. Not shown in the photo is another son – Joseph Mariano.

THE CURTIS, SCIOLINO AND MARAZZO FAMILIES
LATINA FOOD SERVICES, INC.
BY MICHELLE ANN KRATTS

In the beginning…before the Italians…there were the Greeks. For it was in November of 1928, that two brothers, Aleck and John Curtis (Kouroumalli), from Delphi, Greece, officially founded the Sicilian Olive Oil Company, Inc., located at 1621 Pine Avenue. By 1937, this olive oil import company became the Niagara Importing Company, and was located at 1805 Pine Avenue. It carried specialty Mediterranean imported products. In 1954, Anthony Sciolino founded the Columbia Market, located at No. 5. 1908 Pine Avenue, which sold imported Italian foods and sundries. This served the needs of the Italian neighborhoods surrounding the Pine Avenue area. Charles Marazzo, Sr., who had started out as a stock boy at Sciolino's Columbia Market, eventually partnered with Mr. Sciolino and helped to form a wholesale distributorship in addition to the grocery store called Latina Importing Company. In the 1970's Mr. Marazzo purchased the Niagara Importing Company from Nick Curtis, Aleck's son. The Latina Importing Company and the Niagara Importing Company merged and became Latina's Foods, Inc. Because of the great demand, and also as a result of the movement of many Niagara Italians to the Wheatfield and Amherst areas, Latina's has grown significantly over the past decade. Today the distribution area spans from as far north as Lake Ontario, south to the Pennsylvania border and east to Rochester, New York. At the present time, Latina Food Service is under the direction of Charles Marazzo, Sr., his son (Charles, Jr.) and his daughter, Ann. The Niagara Falls location is presently located at 1712 Pine Avenue, by the City Market.

I think we all have our own personal memories of Latina's. The smell of Italian cheeses usually hits you as you walk through the doors. I love to bring my children and let them choose a box of pasta each. For me, I love to pick up a can of caponata, as well as some cheese and meats from the deli…which I intend to take home and eat with a loaf of bread from the Portage Bakery. My friend, Jerri "Brusino Hopper" Schultz, recalls the bread as well. Her mother would send her out to Latina's to get a fresh loaf of bread *at the specific time it was delivered*. It made the best tomato sandwich, she recalled. But, of course, there are the cannoli. We can't ever leave without a few cannoli.

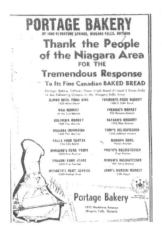

ANTHONY SCIOLINO   MRS. ADA GIARRIZZO

As for the name…Latina's…I found a sweet story in an old newspaper. La Tina is actually the name of a city in Lazio, Italy. It is the second largest city in Lazio, the first being Rome. In 1962, Mr. and Mrs. Elario of 16th Street in Niagara Falls, visited the shop and remarked about a poster that hung upon the wall. There was a section of the poster blown up which revealed a portion of the Appian Way…and the city of La Tina. When the Elario's looked closer they noticed that *they could clearly see the homes in which they were born* in the blown up section of the poster.

Latina's has always been a little picture window into the past; specifically into the origins of our Italian-Americans of Niagara Falls.

THE CASTELLANI FAMILY
TOPS MARKETS
BY ELEANOR MIGLIAZZO NOVARA

ARMAND J. CASTELLANI

A Self-made Businessman, Philanthropist, and Patron of the Arts

As a volunteer at the Castellani Art Museum and the gift shop since 2002, I have enjoyed learning about the many accomplishments of Armand J. Castellani. Working closely with his sister, Anna (Castellani) LaBarbera, I enjoyed many conversations about life with her beloved siblings and family, and especially how Armand's life was filled with new visions in the supermarket business and how he developed an interest in the arts.

Anna mentioned how Armand recruited her to become the Head Cashier in 1960, when the company was ready to open its first modern supermarket, located at Portage Road in Niagara Falls, NY. She wasn't very excited at first because she was raising two young daughters and wanted to be at home. He finally persuaded her and she continued to work for him in the market business until she retired. That is, she thought she would retire. Not so, said Anna! When Armand and Eleanor (Romano) Castellani, his wife, began their new venture purchasing works of art and subsequently building an art museum, he again sought out her help along with his daughter, Carla, in 1990 to open and manage a small gift shop along with organizing a plan to recruit and train volunteers for the Castellani Art Museum of Niagara University.

Now, I'm getting ahead of myself, because there were many years in the supermarket business prior to opening the museum that led to Armand's appreciation of the arts.

I've seen the loyalty and love the siblings and family have had for this great man. I never had the opportunity to meet Armand, but did get to meet his wife. Armand's life is one of the most fascinating and successful stories of an Italian immigrant who succeeded not only in Niagara Falls, Western New York and in New York State, but throughout the country. Much has been written about Armand, but I came to realize that a lesson in *"true grit,"* I guess you can say, and determination without a formal education can help pave the way to an extraordinary life.

Armand was born on June 6, 1917, in Giuliano di Roma, a village outside of Rome. He immigrated to the United States when he was three years old with his father, Ferrante, and mother, Elissa, along with his brother Alfred, and sisters Agatha and Riccarda. They lived in Utica, NY for several years prior to permanently settling in Niagara Falls around 1921. In 1922 Ferrante opened a small *"mom and pop"* grocery store named the *"Castellani Grocery Market"* at 1031 Fairfield Avenue in the north end of Niagara Falls. Armand's exposure to the retail grocery business at a very young age set the stage for becoming one of the owners of the largest market chains and an art museum in the years to come.

Armand was 16 years of age and in the 10th grade when his mother passed away. He quit high school at that time to help his father and brother, Alfred, manage the store on a full-time basis.

Prior to WW II, a second deli and self-serve butcher shop was opened and managed by Alfred. This was the first *"Great Bear Market"* on Pine Avenue, in Niagara Falls where customers came to purchase various cuts of meat from the freshly "hanging cow" stored in a refrigerated case. Prepared foods of tomato sauce and meatballs were also sold. Ferrante continued to cut his prosciutto by hand until he was ninety years old.

Armand and Eleanor, who was born on September 20, 1919, in Brantford, ON Canada, were married on December 27, 1941. They resided in Niagara Falls, NY and over the years were the proud parents of twelve children.

GREAT BEAR MARKET
ONLY LOCATION
636 19th ST. (Near Pine)

Armand was in the Army during World War II. While in the service he took the opportunity to obtain his GED and enroll in an extension course in business management where he could attend Officer Candidate School. It is this course that led him to learn the skills to run a successful business. He once said *"That course had a profound effect on my business future – it was the best $500 I ever spent."* After his discharge he credits his rank as captain to be one of his greatest accomplishments. As for his education received in the Army it appears to have been the jump start for his many undertakings. Among his duties Armand was the Manager of the Mess Hall, supply and transportation functions at an Army Air Base in Columbia, SC where he purchased food and supplies. He was later transferred to Fort Niagara in Youngstown, NY and continued with the same duties. At that time he and his wife had three children, Robert, Lawrence and Carla and their fourth child James Ferrante was born at the fort.

During his service at Fort Niagara he experienced working with German prisoners of war that were housed at the fort. He developed a plan for them to prepare a garden to grow vegetables in a small plot of land at the fort to be used in the Mess Hall.

Upon his return to Niagara Falls after his Army service, he joined his brother, Alfred who had opened and managed Ferrante's second store, the "Great Bear Market" in 1951, on 19th Street which was later relocated to Pine Avenue and 18th Street.

Armand's mother became ill and Ferrante was unable to keep his Castellani Grocery Market open as it was not economically feasible to have two stores in operation. Thomas A. Buscaglia, Sr., a grocery salesman, formed a friendship with the Castellani family from his sales visits to the store and they had an opportunity to discuss their situation with him. He also owned a business, T. A. Buscaglia Equipment Company. Thomas and Armand met with their attorneys it was decided to dissolve the the Castellani Grocery Market.

Shortly after they opened the Great Bear Market, Alfred died unexpectedly in 1951. Around 1954, Thomas and Armand became business partners. Thomas maintained the equipment part of the business and Armand continued on with the retail food business.

They negotiated with franchisees of the Bell's IGA to purchase their first Bell's store in 1954, located at the corner of North Avenue and Hyde Park Boulevard in Niagara Falls. With their first store came quality and value and after kicking around a name or two, it was a NFS associate, Albert DiMino, (and the franchisee of Tops in Lewiston) who came up with the name "Tops." This was their first small store to be named "Tops" formed under their partnership, followed by two more stores by 1960. It was around this time that Armand and Thomas decided to put the new Tops markets, the equipment company and some other operations under a corporate roof known as "Niagara Frontier Services, Inc. (NFS)." Thomas became CEO and Armand became President.

Before long Savino P. Nanula, a Great Bear Meat Department Manager rose in the ranks to become President and CEO. Nanula was followed by Armand's son Lawrence. Several of Armand's children were also active in the business as well as Lawrence. Robert rose to Tops' Vice-President for Marketing Development, Alfred went on to become Director of Operations, and James Ferrante was in charge of the Restaurant Division.

Armand and his partners converted their smaller markets into convenience stores, namely: Wilson Farms and B-Kwik. Their sales by this time were now in the millions and a combined employment of more than 7,000. They eventually went public, acquired several large businesses along with two Ferrante's Restaurants in Amherst, NY that were named after Armand's father.

Ferrante didn't use written recipes, he measured everything by hand. His daughter Agatha (Castellani) Valery known as "Aunt Aggie," had the job of measuring all of his recipes for the chefs to use in the restaurant. Her father showed her his technique of weighing and measuring the ingredients. For example, a piece of butcher paper was put on the table and each piece of meat, flour, sugar, etc. was placed on the paper and the weight was recorded for the recipe.

In 1960, their first modern supermarket (a 25,000 square foot store) on Portage Road in Niagara Falls was designed by NFS' architect Thomas Moscati, and was constructed, followed by two more. The corporation's first President, Armand, along with Nanula and Buscaglia, expanded the company into Buffalo in 1962 where their headquarters was moved to Dingens Street, located where Buscaglia maintained the T. A. Buscaglia Equipment Company another wholly owned division of NFS. At this time Anthony B. Buscaglia became Vice-President of Information Technology.

The negotiating team of NFS continued to branch out into many different business ventures leading up to purchasing three of Bell's IGA Franchises in Niagara Falls. Shortly after the NFS was founded they franchised Tops stores to several of their associates, namely: the Pernas, DiMinos, Dashes, Catalonos, Duesels, and others.

The Tops logo was taken from Bell's logo which was a "diamond" around each letter spelling Bells, and so it was decided to have the Tops logo become Tops with a diamond placed before the letter In 1962 Bells IGA on Pine Avenue was renamed Tops.

Future purchases of other businesses were made by NFS, the parent holding company of Tops, B-Kwik and Wilson Farms.

In 1967 Thomas A. Buscaglia died, and Armand took over as president and chief executive officer of Niagara Frontier Services: soon afterwards he was made chairman. As founder of Tops, Armand retired in 1989, and the company was bought out in 1991 by the Netherlands-based Koninklijke Ahold NV, a major international food retailer. When he retired he was Chairman of the Board and was named Chairman of the Board Emeritus. He was Chief Executive Officer from 1967 to 1985.

In the 1970's, Niagara Frontier Services was ranked in the highest percentile of the country's largest publicly held companies with profitability, growth and stock market performance by Forbes magazine.

Armand was pleased to retire from Tops Friendly Market as he was proud of the dedicated employees trained throughout the years with a good Tops philosophy. And so, Armand went on to other interests. Eleanor was very proud of her husband and was very supportive of him through their many endeavors. She felt she was blessed to be able to spend her golden years with her husband walking on the beach in Siesta Key, FL. It was here that they spent much time and where he was busy with a new hobby, working at his 24-acre flower and plant nursery.

ARMAND's MUSEUM CAREER.... A family trip in the 1960s, to Armand's birth place in Giuliano di Roma, a village outside of Rome, opened a whole new interest in the eyes, ears and heart of his life. He didn't know it then, but the "arts" would soon be his next endeavor.

A cousin of his, who was a professor at a university in Italy, took him to the Sistine Chapel and most especially wanted to show him a Giotto. He didn't quite understand what was so remarkable about it, but he told his father about it and he was very impressed. It was then that he decided he should learn more about it.

What he did learn about the Giotto is that it created a true feeling of depth in 14th century art. Thereafter, the more Armand read and saw it brought him to feel the arts and develop the skills to purchase a collection of art work.

For several years Armand developed skills in the arts by trial and error from his own personal observation of art, especially in relation to early art works purchased for his personal art collection in Italy He soon found that they were not of high quality to donate to art galleries or impress art dealers for purchase. Yes, his collection was admirable, but not yet sophisticated enough for the professional art world. Many family and friends who received gifts of his early art collection I'm sure are grateful to have them today simply because of his importance in the art world. Armand was on the Board of Directors of the Albright-Knox Art Gallery, located not far away in Buffalo, where he extended his knowledge through its staff and collection.

Armand J. Castellani
(6-6-1917 – 1-31-2002)

Eleanor (Romano) Castellani
(9-20-1919 – 12-8-2008)

Eleanor was a big influence on Armand's art ventures, travelling with him to various art galleries and auction houses in NYC where together, they were able to purchase many worldly pieces of art soon worthy of a professional collection. Eleanor is said to have "had an eye for art" and many times Armand would consult her before purchasing an art piece. If Eleanor didn't like it or didn't think it was a good enough piece for their collection, Armand would often dismiss the piece respecting Eleanor's skill. In most cases she was right. You know what they say "Behind every successful man is a woman."

From the 1960's to 1978, after extensively studying art, he slowly developed a "feel" for it. Armand was not shy about asking questions of the many art historians at various museums and galleries in NYC. This helped his second career of becoming an investor in the arts that led to the founding of the Buscaglia-Castellani Art Gallery in Niagara Falls, NY on November 26, 1978.

This is a very interesting and heartwarming story of sentiment and a great respect for friendship. Thomas A. Buscaglia, died suddenly in 1967. Armand began looking for a way to memorialize his good friend and business partner. As a member of the Board of Trustees of Niagara University, Armand expressed his wishes to the Niagara University administrators with an idea that a building be constructed on the NU campus to be named in honor of Buscaglia. Unfortunately, at that time the economy made it far too costly to construct. In 1976, NU had an opportunity to purchase the DeVeaux School (a private preparatory school for boys at 3100 Lewiston Road, Niagara Falls, NY). Armand agreed to support the purchase and suggested an art gallery be part of the new campus building they wished to build previously but couldn't afford at the time.

While at the NU DeVeaux campus, funding was met from contributions made by Armand and Eleanor, various Western New York benefactors and the Heritage Foundation for the Buscaglia-Castellani Art Gallery. Armand and Eleanor were honored at the dedication of the newly constructed $3.5 million *"Castellani Art Museum of Niagara University,"* on September 22, 1990, which was built in the center of the Niagara University campus in Lewiston, NY, with a formal public opening on September 23, 1990. The new 23,000-square foot museum would better accommodate the extensive collection of modern art which grew since 1976. The museum was designed by Thomas Moscati, architect who founded TRM Architect firm in 1977.

Armand's plan for the museum was *"to encourage study and love of art by sharing his personal collection with the students of Niagara University and with the entire Niagara Frontier community."* Since 1978, Armand and Eleanor increased their collection from 300 works of art tenfold through their patronage along with generous gifts from alumni, corporations, artists, and friends of the museum.

One of Armand and Eleanor's greatest of gifts to the Niagara Frontier community is the Castellani Art Museum of Niagara University.

The children of Armand and Eleanor continue to honor their parents through their continued involvement in the museum. Their son Robert, up until recently, was a Trustee on the NU Board of Trustees. Sons Christopher and James are very generous and give great support to the museum. Daughter, Carla, who is on the gala committee that organizes the museum's yearly fundraiser, is also a great supporter of the museum.

In October 2014, the Castellani Art Museum will celebrate its Twelfth Annual Gala, the proceeds of which support educational programming including Art Express family workshops, scholarships for our kids n' arts summer camp, and school tours that provide access to the visual arts for students throughout Western New York. Each year the theme for the gala is taken from an exhibition of works from the Castellani Art Museum of Niagara University's distinguished permanent collection.

Armand's son, Christopher summed up his devotion for his father this way…*"I am the proud son of a native Niagara Falls entrepreneur. Armand Castellani, founder of Tops Markets. What I learned from this remarkable man has helped me discover the secrets of success. Play by the rules, Offer a great product at a competitive price, Treat your employees fairly and honestly, Give generously to the community, Work hard, and always mind the store."*

(Photo courtesy of the Castellani Art Museum Facebook)

We in Western New York have long known that the Castellani Art Museum of Niagara University is a real *"gem"* on the Niagara University Campus. The museum is a mere ten minute drive from another *"gem"* – "Niagara Falls."

So we weren't surprised when Katherine Brooks of Huffington Post on March 24, 2014, placed the Castellani Art Museum of Niagara University in their top ten list of "13 of the Best New York Art Spots That Aren't In NYC."

Here are just a few of the many accolades awarded Armand:

1. **1964** – Niagara University honored Armand with an Honorary Doctor of Commercial Science Degree.

2. **1969** – He received the Niagara County Catholic Veterans' Award.

3. **1976** – He was the recipient of the Israel Prime Minister's Medal for "service in the cause of mankind."

4. **1987** – He received a secondary honorary doctoral degree from St. John's University and shortly thereafter, he received the State University of Trustees Distinguished Citizen Award.

5. **1988** – A candidate nominated by directors of the Greater Buffalo Chamber of Commerce, he was selected Western New Yorker of the Year by a panel of former award winners.

6. **1989** – He received the Outstanding Citizen Award from the Buffalo Council of World Affairs.

7. **1989** – He was awarded Chairman Emeritus at his retirement in 1989.

8. **1990** - On the dedication of the Castellani Art Museum, on September 22, 1990, both Armand and his wife received the

President's Medal from Niagara University for their "magnificent generosity as patrons of the arts and benefactors of the university."

In addition, Armand was a member of the Senior Advisory Committee of Marine Midland Bank; a member of the Board of Trustees for the Albright-Knox Art Gallery; a member of the Niagara University Board of Trustees and Chairman of the Buffalo and Erie Botanical Gardens Advisory Board.

THE FRATELLO FAMILY
FRATELLO'S GROCERY STORE
BY MARCIA BUZZELLI

Cosimo SanFratello left his home in Caltavuturo, Sicily in 1894. He arrived in Niagara Falls, NY, a 21 year old man, and needed to work. In about 1896, he opened his first grocery store with a partner, Mr. Pellicano. It was located at Main and Linwood.

In about 1900, he married Antonia D'Anna, a young girl from the same town in Sicily. She was living with her family in the city of Mt. Morris, NY. Together, they had twelve children and eventually his sons would be running the store. The oldest was Charles born in 1901, in Niagara Falls. The information and picture were given to me by his daughter Charlotte (Fratello) Tompkins. In 1903, Cosimo became a naturalized citizen. Sometime later he shortened his last name to Fratello.

Between 1896 and 1910, Cosimo had different stores with different partners. In 1910, he bought property at 128 Eleventh Street and had a building constructed. The first floor was a store and upstairs was an apartment for his family at the time: eight boys and four girls.

Picture courtesy Charlotte Tompkins

The picture on the preceding page was taken in the Eleventh Street store about 1930. Pictured are from left to right are Charles (behind the counter), Anthony (Fats), Salvatore (Tootie), and Cosimo. Cosimo died in 1936 and his sons, Charles and Salvatore, took over the running of the meat market. They were assisted part-time by their brothers, Joseph, Anthony, Dominic, and Thomas. They formed what was to become Fratello Bros. Grocery and Meat Market of Niagara Falls, specializing in tasty Italian sausage.

In 1946, the store had to move from Eleventh Street to 3010 Pine Avenue. They were forced to sell the Eleventh Street property to the city, so the building could be raised for what has now become the Niagara Frontier Transportation Garage. In 1946, the Pine Avenue store was run solely by Charlie and Salvatore. Eventually they took in a partner, Charlie's son-in-law, Tom Schiro. They had a successful business known throughout the city for their quality meats and sausage. You could also find friendly banter and cooking advice in the store. Their "Fratello Brothers" delivery truck could be seen daily driving through many parts of the city of Niagara Falls.

The men working in the store placed the wicker covers on their arms to cover the sleeves of their clothes. This can be seen in the picture.

Early in 1961, the store was sold to Salvatore, who ran it until January 1968, when due to health reasons he sold the store to Richard and Larry Scipione. He also sold them the sausage recipe which the next generation is using today. Scipione brothers ran the store specializing in prime quality meats. Richard's son, Dave is now operating it as Scipione Catering in the same Pine Avenue location.

Note:
Charlotte Fratello Tompkins reports the best part of the store was that she worked at the check-out counter after school. While working there and being friendly with the stock boys she met her husband, Ken Tompkins, whose family lived on 30th Street. They probably never would have met if the store was not on Pine at 30th Street.

FRATELLO BROS.
3010 PINE AVE.

WED. SPEC.

FRESH, ITALIAN
(Hot or Mild)
SAUSAGE
lb. 65¢

Jack Sprat Mild Cured
BACON
lb.
sliced 39¢

NABISCO, NEW
Lemon Chip, Choc. Chip
or
Oatmeal Cookies
Reg. 29¢
pkg. 23¢

CHASE & SANBORN
COFFEE
2 lb. tin 1²⁹
Regular or Drip Grind

ARMOUR'S STAR
Whole or Sliced
BOLOGNA
lb. 41¢

Fresh, Hot or Mild
ITALIAN SAUSAGE

THE PALERMO FAMILY
PALERMO'S CHICKEN SHOPPE
BY MICHELLE ANN KRATTS

I had heard of the Palermo chickens from my grandmother. Everyone bought Palermo chickens. They were usually still alive, in cages. The smell was horrendous!! You picked one. They butchered it right there and you took it home. Or, some people took the live chickens home; their heads popping out the top of a brown paper bag. They would be taken into the basement to be killed and their blood drained. The children often had the miserable task of plucking the feathers from the chickens. My grandmother said the chicken soup from a Palermo chicken was heavenly. The broth was golden. The frozen store-bought chickens we purchase today just cannot compare to a Palermo chicken. So I sought out the story of the Palermo chickens. Who were the Palermos? How did they start selling chickens? There was also a Palermo's Restaurant.

Many of Niagara's Italians first began their careers in the food industry as grocers. The Palermo family was no different. One of the earliest references to this family was in the Niagara Falls City Directory of 1910, listing Felix Palermo, 494 20th Street, grocer. Felix (also called Felice, Phil, or Philip) had several brothers who came to America from Italy. According to censuses, directories and obituaries, there were at least five brothers: Felix, Salvatore, Joseph, Charles and Nicholas Palermo. There were also at least three sisters (with married names): Maria Pugliese, Lucy Gallina, and Rose Mangione. Felix, Joseph and Nicholas may have been the only brothers to live in Niagara Falls. Early records show many variations on the surname such as Palmero and Palarino.

Felix, possibly the oldest sibling, was born in September of 1878, in Italy. He came to the United States in 1891 and lived in Niagara Falls for 59 years before his death on July 18, 1965. He and his wife, Maria Riggi, had two sons: Joseph and Charles Palermo. They also had two daughters: Jennie Amato and Josephine Viscuglia.

FOR LIVE
POULTRY
Freshly Dressed and Cleaned

CALL 2-3637

Free Delivery—LaSalle and DeVeaux
Thursday

Joseph Palermo & Son
452 - 19th STREET
Between Niagara & Ferry

Felix was an enterprising man. It might also be stated that he certainly had his share of *pluck*. For several years, he did, indeed, operate a grocery business from 494 20th Street. According to Niagara Falls City Directory records he did so from 1910 until 1913. In 1913 he opened a saloon at 2007 Ferry Avenue. This address would be associated with Felix for most of his life…and would be the site of some commotion from time to time. For once the 18th Amendment and Prohibition was enacted life would change for proprietors of taverns and saloons—especially for Felix Palermo. Almost immediately, the business operated out of 2007 Ferry Avenue transformed from a saloon to Palermo and Co. Bottling Works where soda and carbonated drinks were manufactured….along with other more risqué beverages. On July 6, 1927, it was reported that Federal Prohibition agents had raided a "wildcat brewery" at 2007 Ferry Avenue. Upon the premises, owned by Felix Palermo, agents seized various illicit equipment worth about $20,000. Apparently the building was constructed to resemble a ten-car garage. "Doors opened on the front, but a brick wall from floor to ceiling set off the interior of the building." Very crafty business! No one was arrested, however, "samples of the brew were taken" and city police were requested to guard the place. A raid by federal agents in 1930 brought more trouble to Felix. On April 1st, he was arrested and charged with violating prohibition law by being in possession of intoxicants. Four barrels of home brew beer were found on the premises. Others were also arrested during this raid. Interestingly enough, according to the Niagara Falls City Directory from 1928, there were almost 200 soft drinkeries in the city of Niagara Falls during this time period. It's only natural to wonder if many of these businesses were also secretly manufacturing alcoholic beverages.

During the latter part of the 1920's, the Palermos officially became involved with the poultry business with the creation of the Live Poultry Market, located at 431 19th Street and 1128 Falls Street, which was managed by Reginald Palermo. Although it is unknown if Felix was a part of this operation, he did hold the world championship as a chicken-plucker. According to accounts in the Niagara Falls Gazette he could strip a fowl of its feathers in less than four seconds. The New York Post even reported his strange skills in an article from January 22, 1935. Contests were held annually in the City Market. Felix's brother, Salvatore, had established a record in Buffalo, as well, only to be beaten by Felix. Salvatore operated a poultry store at 145 Busti Avenue in Buffalo.

By 1934, Palermo's Restaurant was officially established —although Felix's obituary states that he had been serving food since 1926. Felix and his wife, Maria, managed Palermo's until his retirement in 1945. Felix passed away on July 18, 1965 at the Restwell Nursing Home on Buffalo Avenue in Niagara Falls. He was buried at St. Joseph's Cemetery. Maria Riggi Palermo, Felix's wife, died several years before him, on November 20, 1963 at Memorial Hospital. Maria was also buried at St. Joseph's Cemetery.

WEIGHING THEM IN Maid of the Mist Family Picnic co-chairman Gene J. Virtuoso weighs chickens selected for the chicken barbeque to be held at Hyde Park picnic grounds from 4 to 9 p.m. on Thursday. Writing down the figures is Joseph Palermo, right. More than 1,000 live chickens have been received for the dinner. Teen-agers will dance to area rock 'n' roll bands on the Hyde Park tennis courts starting at 7:30 p.m. the same evening. There also will be a band concert.

Poultry Pluckers Compete for Championship

Photo by Frank O. Seed.

Feathers literally flew last night at the poultry market of Richard Morgan, in Eighteenth street, when five of the city's speediest poultry-pluckers stripped the feathers from five chickens in a contest to decide the 1937 poultry-plucking champion. The above picture shows the pluckers at the height of the contest, which occupied but a few seconds, with Joseph Dimlino, third from right, being declared the champion. Dimli-no was awarded a gold chicken foot, emblematic of the city championship, after he had plucked his bird in six seconds flat. Those in the picture are, reading from left to right: Phil Palermo, timekeeper, who holds the all-time plucking championship of 3½ seconds; Richard Morgan, judge, and Carl Gallini, Samuel Palermo, Joseph Dinono, Joseph Morganti and Joseph Vanni, contestants. The slowest of the contestants required only nine seconds to complete his job.

As for Palermo's chicken market, the directories and censuses of Niagara Falls shed some light on various locations and owners of the family-operated business. Along with Reginald (who is documented as the first manager), there were other Palermos connected to the business in 1927 and 1928: Salvatore and Joseph Palermo, residing at 453 19th Street; and Nicholas Palermo, another manager of Live Poultry Market, was listed as residing at 1128 Falls Street. By 1929 the directory notes that "Reginald moved to New York City." He is never mentioned again. By 1931, Felix and Clara and Joseph and Theresa are operating the Niagara Live Poultry Company out of 451 19th Street. Through the 1930's Niagara Live Poultry was located at both locations. By 1938 Niagara Live Poultry was at 1800 Pine Avenue at the City Market. However Joseph and Son were still operating out of the 451 19th Street shop. During the war years, Niagara Live Poultry was located at 625 18th Street and Joseph Palermo dealt poultry from 451 19th Street. By 1949 another location was added—708 19th Street. Felix and Clara ran this business.

To our knowledge there are no longer any members of the Palermo family operating poultry businesses in the Niagara area. In fact, many of the sites mentioned have been bulldozed long ago. But the memories of the Palermo chickens, and the recipes, live on in Niagara's history.

THE LOPRETE FAMILY
LOPRETE CONFECTIONARY
BY ELEANOR MIGLIAZZO NOVARA

I was very excited to be able to interview my second cousin Viola LoPrete (Fingerlow), who is the youngest daughter of Dominic LoPrete. Viola related a very interesting family story as follows:

Viola was very proud to have been able to work with her father to help establish a very successful business in the city of Niagara Falls, NY. She recollects at age twelve to almost eighteen she worked along-side him to help with his ice cream business and now was approached by me to tell about how an immigrant father and mother worked very hard to accomplish their dream in America.

Dominic LoPrete was a very well-known and prominent business man in the Niagara Falls area for many years starting in the late 1920's. Dominic was born on May 7, 1892, in Catanzaro, Calabria, Italy and emigrated to the United States. He departed Naples, IT on the SS Pesaro arriving in New York City, NY on October 26, 1920.

Dominic and Sarah LoPrete

He met and married her mother, Sarah (Paonessa) LoPrete, who was born on April 11, 1906, in Gimigliano, Catanzaro, Calabria, Italy. They were married on January 19, 1928, in Niagara Falls, NY.

Viola learned that one of Dominic's earliest endeavors in Niagara Falls was a restaurant he operated in 1927, on 513 Third Street. And sometime around 1934, he operated a confectionary store located at 24th Street next to a small movie theater known as the "Colonial" (long since torn down).

At a very young age Viola remembers two confectionary stores her father opened. One was located at 22nd Street and East Falls Street. Her parents resided in the rear of the store where her mother worked very hard in the home raising her three daughters, Mary LoPrete (Castiglione); Josephine "Joan" LoPrete (Ebbole) and Viola LoPrete (Fingerlow) as well as single-handedly operating the store.

The second store was operated solely by Dominic, located next to the old State Theater on East Falls Street near Portage Road. Viola's older sister Mary was a great help to her father while spending many hard-working hours at the store during her school years.

Viola tells me that she was told by many that her father made the best "lemon ice" in town which he sold at the two confectionary stores. Everyone just loved it. He had a special secret to it.....his own recipe!!! Even the Nuns and priests from Holy Rosary Church would come to the stores to purchase it. This lemon ice along with his ice cream sold in these stores must have stimulated his urge for his future love of the full-time ice-cream business.

Moviegoers on their way to see a movie at the State Theater would frequently stop in her father's store for candy, lemon ice, ice cream etc. He was a very generous man and there were times if the kids didn't have enough money he would treat them.

He never believed in putting all his eggs in one basket, so it was in 1947 that even as a little girl Viola remembers so well when he brought home that brand new 1947 Dodge truck with fancy bright yellow letters written on it…"Dominic LoPrete Wholesale Ice Cream." The entire neighborhood turned out to see it. It was beautiful! It was very well known all over the streets of Niagara Falls.

So, it was then that the ice-cream truck business started to take on a whole new concept. Dominic started to deliver ice-cream to many stores in Niagara Falls, some of which included, DalPortos Grocery at the corner of Pine Avenue and 21st Street, LaPorto's Grocery and Patsy Christiano's Grocery were also on Pine Avenue. And then there were Louie Trapasso's and Enzinna's grocery stores on 12th Street between East Falls Street and Niagara Street, and Phil Morgante's store at the corner of 19th Street and Ferry Avenue.

After all of her father's hard work in these two businesses it was around 1952 that he blessed their family with a newly built home at 1322 Niagara Street. The home was the whole expanse of the upper floor. On the first floor in the rear of the building was his ice cream business and on the first floor off the street was S'Dao's Furniture Store.

At this point in time, Dominic closed his two stores and devoted all his time, effort and passion to make a very successful ice cream wholesale business, especially during the summer months which enabled him to work fewer hours throughout the winter.

The people that he serviced in the grocery stores in Niagara Falls were not only customers but many became his friends. His operational hours were Monday through Saturday, but Saturday was the busiest day by far as he would start very early in the morning and work till late in the evening which included weekly trips to Lockport to Castle's Dairy loading the truck with all kinds of ice cream until it was full.

Each and every order had to be placed in the truck to his liking so it was easily accessible when delivering to his customers. This is when Viola started to drive the truck for him at the age of 16.

While attending school up to the time of graduation from high school, her second older sister Joan was also a great help to her father working on the truck until she found full-time employment.

Viola, lost in all those memories from years ago could go on and on, because her father's ice cream business touched many establishments all over the City of Niagara Falls....Hyde Park Blvd.; 19th Street; 24th Street; Pine Avenue, and East Falls Street, to name a few. Just for a few cents more for boxes of ice cream, he even supplied customers with ice cream freezers.

Sometime in her early 20's and newly married, Viola returned to help her father as he had become ill. After being away from the business for several years, she didn't realize how much she had learned from her father as carrying out the daily business came back very easily for her. The business continued on until he died in 1968.

Viola told me that she was so glad she did return as he was able to feel comfortable knowing somehow his business was still alive and servicing all his customers/friends. Viola said, "One thing she will always remember is that so many people she didn't know came to his wake to pay their respects. Even though she didn't know them, they certainly remembered her father from when they were young children. That really touched her."

Viola says "she really knew the business well and somewhat sad 'Oh,' how much I wish I could have carried it on through the years, but we all know that in today's world there are so many big competitors who have taken over the little "Mom and Pop" type businesses that "Dominic LoPrete Wholesale Ice Cream" would never have survived."

THE TROMBETTA FAMILY
CAPITAL SWEET SHOP
BY PATRICIA DINIERI

I have enjoyed reminiscing and obtaining most of the information along with the many photos on the Trombetta family businesses from my first cousin Mary Louise Trombetta. Mary Louise is the daughter of my Uncle and Aunt, Peter Trombetta and Arline (Ciambrone) Trombetta. Mary Louise and her brother, James Trombetta, reside in Arizona.

My mother, Amy (Ciambrone) Palumbo is the sister of my Aunt Arline (Ciambrone) Trombetta and over the years we have all talked about the great memories of going to Uncle Pete's ice cream parlor and how it served the best lemon ice in town.

The Trombetta businesses began in 1930 when PETER TROMBETTA's mother, CAROLINE (LaDOTA) TROMBETTA [born about 1894 in Italy and immigrated to Niagara Falls in 1906], and his father, ANDREW TROMBETTA, [born around 1883-85 in Italy who immigrated to Niagara Falls, NY in 1901]. They were proprietors of TROMBETTA'S GROCERY STORE in Niagara Falls, NY.

MAY 1939
1302 Niagara Street
Niagara Falls, NY.

Peter and his brother Frank bought BELMER'S ICE CREAM store located at the 1300 block of Niagara Street on the right side of the Capital Theater.

In 1939 Belmer's was relocated to the left side of the theater at the corner of 13th Street, 1302 Niagara Street and renamed the "CAPITAL SWEET SHOP."

I remember as a child visiting the CAPITAL SWEET SHOP numerous times. They had the best Lemon Ice and it was a great place to go because they had a soda fountain with a long bar on one side of the room that had round stools that turned so you could see the other side of the shop and mirrors behind the bar. The other side of the shop had booths.   Many teenagers would come in after school, and everyone stopped after going to the movies at the Capital Theater.

In 1942 Frank enlisted in the Army. At this time Peter Trombetta and his wife, Arline (Ciambrone) Trombetta became sole proprietors of the Capital Sweet Shop. Arline worked full-time job during the day as well as maintaining the office work during the evenings at the Capital Sweet Shop.

Arline Ciambrone Trombetta and Peter Trombetta, 1940's

In the 1950s Peter and Arline moved to Arizona with their two children: Mary Louise and James.

TROMBETTA FAMILY RESEARCH
PETER J. TROMBETTA –
Date of Birth: December 2, 1915 in the City of: Niagara Falls, State of: New York, in the United States
Date of Death: October 24, 1991
Place of Death: Phoenix, AZ
ARLINE (CIAMBRONE) TROMBETTA –
Date of Birth: May 5, 1916 in Niagara Falls, NY
Date of Death: October 19, 1998
Place of Death: Phoenix, AZ
Date of Marriage: September 8, 1941
CHILDREN:
    1. MARY LOUISE TROMBETTA

Date of Birth: March 2, 1944
Place of Birth: Niagara Falls, NY
Place of Current Residence: Phoenix, AZ

2. JAMES (Jim) TROMBETTA

Date of Birth: January 23, 1950
Place of Birth: Niagara Falls, NY
Place of Current Residence: Phoenix, AZ
PARENTS OF PETER J. TROMBETTA
FATHER – ANDREW TROMBETTA – Emigrated to US in 1901 (at around 18 years old)
Date of Birth: About 1883-1885
Place of Birth: Italy
MOTHER – CAROLINE (LaDOTA) TROMBETTA – Emigrated to US in 1906 (around 12 years old)
Date of Birth: About 1894
Place of Birth: Italy
SIBLINGS OF PETER J. TROMBETTA:
BROTHER –
FRANK TROMBETTA –
Date of Birth: October 18, 1914
Place of Birth: Niagara Falls, New York
Date of Death: October 1977 (63 years old)
Place of Death: Arizona
SISTERS –
THERESA (TROMBETTA) ZASO –
Date of Birth: May 14, 1918
Place of Birth: Niagara Falls, New York
Date of Death: August 17, 1997
Place of Death: _____
JANE (TROMBETTA) ASTORINO
Date of Birth: About 1922
Place of Birth: Niagara Falls, New York
Date of Death: _____
Place of Death: _____
JOSEPHINE (TROMBETTA) ZYKES
Date of Birth: _____
Place of Birth: Niagara Falls, New York

Date of Death: _____

Place of Death: _____

CENSUS RECORDS

1925 – Resided at 1525 Pine Avenue, Niagara Falls, NY

1930 – Resided at 1525 Pine Avenue, Niagara Falls, NY

ANDREW (FATHER) OF PETER TROMBETTA was proprietor of a Grocery Store

1936 – Resided at 1607 Pine Avenue, Niagara Falls, NY

1938 – Resided at 1607 Pine Avenue, Niagara Falls, NY

PETER – Clerk at Belmer's Ice Cream

FATHER – Sanitary Meat Market

1939 – PETER and FRANK – "Capital Sweet Shop" – 1302 Niagara Street, Niagara Falls, NY

FATHER AND MOTHER – TROMBETTA'S GROCERY STORE

1940 – Same as 1939 – "Capital Sweet Shop" – 1302 Niagara Street, Niagara Falls, NY

1951 – 1302 Niagara Street, Niagara Falls, NY – "Capital Sweet Shop"

1955 – Moved to Arizona

Mary Lou and Jimmy Trombetta   Pat DiNieri and Mary Lou Trombetta

THE BATTAGLIA AND MUTO FAMILIES
NEW YORK FISH HOUSE
BY MICHELLE ANN KRATTS

The first Italian-run fish and oyster business in Niagara Falls was operated by the Battaglia family at 612 20th Street, in 1916. Orazio Battaglia was born on April 25, 1864, in Valledolmo, Palermo, Sicily, Italy. He arrived in the United States in 1890. In 1894, Orazio married Maria Carmella Siragusa in Buffalo, New York and made Niagara Falls his home for fifty-four years. Other fish and oyster proprietors (and addresses) included:

Angelo Ponzo and Giuseppino Frada (260 11th Street), Joseph Mucci (307 11th Street), Salvatore Scutari (1107 Falls Street), Andrew Montondo (343 3rd Street), Tony Genova (2209 11th Street), Achille Navarolli (1124 Falls Street), Joseph Santoro (625 18th Street) and Vincent Rossi and Vincent Geracitano (260 11th Street, 1715 ½ Pine Avenue, 734 ½ 19th Street, and 1814 Pine Avenue).

ORAZIO BATTAGLIA

In the 1930 Census and the 1930 Niagara Falls City Directory, the New York Fish Market was first mentioned as being located at 1715 ½ Pine Avenue. By 1949 the fish market was moved to 734 19th Street. In 1960, the New York Fish Market was located at 1814 Pine Avenue. Vincent Geracitano was the owner of the New York Fish Market. Born in Italy around 1880, he married Carolina and raised several children in Niagara Falls. He was known for making fine clay reproductions of famous structures, such as St. Peter's church in Rome, Italy. He would often display his handiwork in the window of the New York Fish Market.

Builds Model of Famous Church

Photo by Frank O. Seed

Vincent Geracitano, of 1715½ Pine avenue, is shown above beside an unusually clever clay model of the famous St. Peter's church in Rome, Italy, which took him two months to build. Geracitano, who has made many other fine clay reproductions of famous structures, is displaying his work in the window of the New York Fish market, of which he is proprietor.

Joseph Santoro opened La Gondola Restaurant at 625 18th Street off of Pine Avenue in June of 1947 which specialized in seafood. Advertisements in the Niagara Gazette also publicized the New York Fish Market at 625 18th Street.

By 1972, Victor J. Muto purchased the restaurant. The New York Fish Market was one of the mainstays of the City Market. Everyone went for Muto's fish on Fridays. Victor Muto had worked in the laboratory at DuPont, alongside my grandfather, Henry Borgatti. Victor was originally from Clairton, Pennsylvania. His wife, Rose, was of the Gara family. She also helped out and worked at the fish market. My grandmother remembers that family meals were important to Victor and Rose. They insisted the family all come together each Sunday for a large family meal after church.

In 1992, two sons of Victor and Rose, Dominick and Vincent, became the owners. They expanded the business and constructed a full dining area. By 2012, James Thomson (a third generation Muto) and Gary Bevilaqua, along with the support of Diane Bevilaqua, began a partnership which remains to this day at 745 E. Market Street in the City Market.

THE NIAGARA FALLS CITY MARKET
BY BEVERLY M. BIDAK

In the US the term public market is often used for a place where vendors meet at the same location on a regular basis. Traditionally public markets were owned and operated by city governments. Three characteristics that distinguish public markets from other types of retail activity are:

1. They have public goals which include attracting shoppers to a central business district, providing affordable retailing opportunities to small businesses, preserving farming in the region, and activating or repurposing public space.

2. They are located in and/or create a public space in the community, where a wide range of people mix and aim to be a heart of the community.

3. They are made up of locally owned, independent businesses operated by their owners. This gives public markets a local flavor and unique experience.

These were the goals of the City of Niagara Falls, NY when by city ordinance established a city market on July 5, 1893 at Linwood Avenue and Main Street. The market began operations on August 11th of that year and ran six days a week at that location for another 13 years. In 1905, after a number of property owners in the area voiced opposition to the Linwood Avenue site, the city began looking for a new location.

The market was temporarily located on Willow Avenue in structures known as "the old car barns" of the International Railway Co. The land was leased from the railway from August 1906 until May 1913, when overcrowded conditions forced the city to once again look for an alternative.

Courtesy Niagara Falls Gazette calendar

The city purchased 6 acres of land on Pine Avenue and 18th Street for $39,400 in August 1912. The New City Market on Pine Avenue was formally opened on May 27, 1913.

Courtesy Niagara Falls Public Library

During and after World War I, the city grew fast. As the population grew so did the retail business at the market. People came in large numbers to get fresh produce and on their way home picked up purchases at stores located nearby. The fact that the market was a great drawing power to get people out helped in centralizing the Pine Avenue business section in the area.

Throughout the ensuing years the city made improvements to the market including paving, parking and construction of the concrete roof shelter for the farmers stall area. Many permanent establishments were constructed along the east and west boundaries of the market (today known as East and West Market Streets.)

In 1964, Amedio Daurizio opened a dairy luncheonette and a clam bar in the enclosed area of the city market. He also owned the Kitchen Restaurant.

Niagara Falls city government set up a market commission, with its own budget, to operate and maintain the city market. The market clerk was the officer in charge. John W. Potter was the market clerk in the early 1920's and was later appointed the first market superintendent in 1928. Included in his duties was to collect the fees from the vendors for the stalls. He held that position until his death in 1934.

Jacob J. Hiller became the next market superintendent and held that position until his retirement in 1957. The last person to hold that title was John Teeto. He remained in that position until the market was sold in the early 1970 s.

Fridays were usually the busiest day at the market because most of Niagara Falls' industrial plants paid their employees on Thursday and housewives chose Friday to stock up for the weekend.

Over the past one hundred plus years the Niagara Falls Gazette has published numerous articles about the city market. Many of the articles have been the source for most of the information in this story.

Today the city market is privately owned and managed by Victor Muto. It is open weekly on Mondays, Wednesdays and Fridays.

When you enter the market today at 18th Street and Pine Avenue, you pass by the Golden Arches of McDonalds. The roofs over the vendor's stalls are gone. The businesses on East and West Market Streets are GAGSTERS, MARKETSIDE, MICHAEL'S COIFFEURES, JAMAICAN RESTAURANT, NEW YORK FISH HOUSE, AMERICAN LEGION POST 1664, PINE PHARMACY, DOLLAR GENERAL, SAVE-A-LOT, BANQUET HALL, GOODFELLOWS, CATARACT FOODS AND DMR HARDWARE. There are many vacant structures.

............Not our parents and grandparents city market of yesteryear.............

MEMORIES OF THE CITY MARKET

"My Grandparents sold cemetery clay pots of flowers there for years"

"Shopping the farmers stands"

"My father went every Friday morning. We had our own garden but he went anyway and bought things he didn't grow. I remember going also in the summer and haggling over prices with him. He would go back and forth to different farmers."

"In the early 1970s, I took my 3 year old son to ride the Ferris Wheel and merry-go-round at a carnival held in the city market."

"Going to the poultry shop in the market with my grandmother to buy chicken. You would purchase a live chicken, it was put in a brown paper bag with its head sticking out of the top. At home she would twirl the chicken around by the head to kill it."

"Remember the students from Mt. Carmel School would go to the market before Halloween so they could pick out their pumpkins."

"I remember getting the yummy cheese chunks there. Oh yes the basket cheese."

"LaSalle girls would cruise up and down Pine Avenue looking for the downtown boys. They would all hang out at the city market showing off their cars and waiting for the carloads of girls to drive by."

"I used to love taking my class there. The vendors always took time to answer any questions my students had."

"I used to sell produce with my uncle out of the back of his truck. He was a farmer from Ransomville."

"The fish market"

"Went with my father, pulling the wagon, to buy bushels of peaches, tomatoes, and other fruits and veggies for canning."

"We went 3 times a day to the city market. First time was to see what was available, second to price goods and the third time to purchase."

"Thanks for your memories"

ITALIAN ROMAN CATHOLIC RELIGIOUS HOLIDAYS:
"THOSE LONG LOST SUNDAYS WITH GRANDPARENTS AND EASTER WEEK"
BY ELEANOR MIGLIAZZO NOVARA

Oh how I loved the week leading up to Easter Sunday. When I was a young girl I remember my father would walk me and my two brothers from our apartment on 12th Street between East Falls and Niagara Street in Niagara Falls, NY, to visit our maternal grandparents, Salvatore Agostino Mariano and Saveria Paonessa Mariano, after the nine o'clock mass at St. Joseph's Church. They lived on the third floor in an apartment house on the corner of 14th Street (since renamed Place) and Walnut Avenue, down the street from the church.

I can still recall how excited I was climbing those stairs and at my first step I took in the aroma of freshly made Italian sauce (not gravy as some Italians living in other parts of America call it) mingled with the smell of a stogie cigar, most likely a Di Nobile, coming from their apartment. Both my grandparents would greet us with the grandest kisses ever. Taking our faces in their hands and with kisses so hard you thought you wouldn't have any face left when they were through. My grandmother with her sweet smile would be preparing the noon day meal, yes, like in almost every Italian family in our neighborhood it was a tradition to eat our Sunday meal at noon consisting of the usual homemade sauce, meatballs and macaroni as we referred to it (not pasta). Grandma's approximate 4' 11" frame was always attired with a pretty apron over her dress; looking so fresh with her beautiful long pure white hair pulled back in a bun. The memory of her frying little *"polpettine"* as a snack prior to eating our noon meal when we got home will live with me forever. I call them *"polpettine"* and hope it is correct. Grandma set aside some of the meatball mixture from her *"polpetta"* (meatballs).

She would take the meatball mixture, form them into small flat oval-shapes and fry them in olive oil till brown and crispy. Now in those days the Catholic Church required that you fast after mid-night in order to receive communion at mass, so this was such a treat as we were famished from not eating breakfast prior to attending mass. While my father and grandfather drank Anisette (a licorice tasting aperitif) poured into strong Italian coffee, we ate our fried *polpettine* and a *polpetta* with sauce and Italian bread for dipping. How sad that this tradition is lost as no one has time today for these little extra greatest gifts of love. After greeting our Uncle Tony and Aunt Betty Mariano and their son, Anthony and daughter Gale as they arrived to spend Easter Sunday with our grandparents, we would then leave for home, as our mother was preparing our family Easter meal.

After returning from our grandparent's house I remember my mother serving her delicious traditional Easter bread for breakfast. We would each get our own individual small loaf festively decorated with a colored egg on top. This was our breakfast and we devoured the bread. This tradition is still alive in our family as my sister Connie Migliazzo Paolone is the only one who keeps this tradition going. My husband Sam and I look forward to her little gift of Easter Bread every year.

The Last Week of Lent–The week leading up to Easter Sunday was filled with a succession of religious days for Catholics. My recollection was of a Holy Week filled with traditions of the church. It is the holiest and greatest of all Christian feasts. Another reason, especially when I was very young, is that it was getting closer to when I no longer had to fast. Actually there was one year that I made a contribution, rather than abstaining from eating something I really loved. I attended early mass every morning prior to attending school. A light breakfast was prearranged in the church hall after the mass and I was one of several of my religious instruction classmates who volunteered to help serve those present.

My recollection of the last week of Lent starts, of course, with Palm Sunday.

Palm Sunday – Palms are passed out at Catholic churches on Palm Sunday. The cross folded from a Palm Sunday palm frond is a tradition that has been around for many years. Folding your palm is said to be a way to express the Easter story. Jesus came into the town walking over the palms laid down by the people, but one week later died on a cross.

After mass I would rush home and present my father with palms. He would spend the afternoon preparing various versions of folded crosses. This was a tradition he learned in Italy. My mother would usually arrange them over a picture on the wall or put them in a vase with pussy willows. They would last forever until the following Easter. Another lost family tradition as no one learned or took the time to learn from him. I guess we think traditions will go on forever – but who will carry them on….? If not us!

Holy Thursday – Considered one of the oldest of the celebrations during Holy Week, it is the day on which Christ celebrated the Last Supper with His disciples, four days after His triumphal entry into Jerusalem on Palm Sunday.

Holy Thursday was a very special day for me during the last week of Lent. One tradition I thoroughly enjoyed was the pilgrimage I made with my friends to seven nearby churches, some of which were a little further away from our neighborhood. Years ago it was a wonderful custom and a great experience to visit the individually beautifully decorated altars. We would set out for the night as if on a mission after Holy Thursday mass and say a few prayers at each altar. Saint Philip Neri and pilgrims are credited with popularizing the Roman practice of a pilgrimage by visiting seven Basilicas in Rome on the same day.

I was always curious why only seven and not 4, 6, etc. I found that there are various theories that account for the significance of number seven with reference to how many churches to visit, such as those below:

- Seven Scripture passages of Christ's arrest and trial

- The Seven Last Words – The Sayings of Jesus on the cross (also called the Seven Last Words from the Cross) are seven expressions traditionally attributed to Jesus during His crucifixion, gathered from the four Canonical Gospels

- Seven Holy Wounds (five wounds plus the Scourge marks and His injured left shoulder)

- Seven first Christian holy sites in Israel

- Seven Deacons of the Twelve Apostles

- Seven ancient basilicas of Rome

I have lost track of this tradition and haven't visited seven churches in years for reasons, it is sad to say, that times have changed and it is not easy to find the churches open during the day or night not even on Holy Thursday.

Good Friday – On this day Catholics commemorate the passion, or suffering, and death on the cross of Jesus Christ. It is a day of strict fasting and abstinence.

Holy Saturday – Holy Saturday is the final day of Holy Week, the final day of the traditional 40 day Lenten Fast, and a part of the Triduum, three days (Holy Thursday, Good Friday, and Holy Saturday) and commemorates Jesus lying in the tomb until His resurrection on the next day, Easter Sunday.

In the evening we sometimes went to the Easter Vigil mass which is considered the most important and longest mass of the year (or maybe it appears that way because the first part of the mass is done while standing, listening and participating in several readings).

The vigil is divided into four parts:

1. Service of Light,

2. Liturgy of the Word,

3. Liturgy of Baptism, and

4. Liturgy of the Eucharist.

It was a long day preparing for the next day's Easter Sunday dinner. My mother was getting the food and her delicious Easter Bread prepared for Sunday which was an all-day chore. After dinner, she prepared our bath as she made sure we were all bathed and our clothes were ready for mass the next morning… then early to bed which was probably around 9:00 p.m., since there were six children in the family.

EASTER SUNDAY – *"Buona Pasqua"* – was a very different celebration of foods from any other we had throughout the year. It was a different type of traditional meal. I guess you could say it was more American in some ways, because my mother's table was filled with a variety of different dishes consisting of baked ham and sweet potatoes along with a different vegetable and, of course a salad. There were some dishes prepared with eggs and cheese that she didn't always make throughout the year. It wasn't the usual meal with her macaroni, sauce and meatballs…maybe that was because we wore our finest clothing and the sauce would have splashed on us. Instead of cookies or pies, she prepared a light dessert.

I've often wondered what the various array of colors of Easter meant and found that, different colors are used at different times in the celebration of Easter and it varies by religion. However, the colors most closely associated with Christianity and Easter in particular are red, purple, black, white, and gold.

BUONA PASQUA!

A *Good* START FOR THE
Easter Parade

"Good Food" will make your Easter a more enjoyable one.

THE FESTA DEI SETTE PESCE
BY MICHELLE ANN KRATTS

Always on "the fringe" of many of the past adventures of my Italian ancestors, I had "heard" about the Festa dei sette pesce….the Feast of the Seven Fishes (yes, it is always said like this). Of course, I didn't care so much for fish back then as I do today, so it was not a custom I ventured to learn more about until now. I asked my grandmother why our family stopped with this ancient Italian tradition of serving seven different fish recipes on Christmas Eve and she told with brutal honesty the horrible truth of the matter. The younger generations were not interested. They were fussy. They didn't like the fish. Too much work. So it stopped. After hundreds of years, and after having survived so many miserable ocean crossings…my generation, and the generation preceding mine, had put a fork in it. I was horrified to learn that the loss of a family tradition was partially my fault.

The Fortuna and Ventresca families celebrating Christmas holidays

There are several stories about the origin and meaning behind the Festa dei sette pesce (also known as La Viglia di Natale, or the Vigil of the Labor of Mary). My grandmother really wasn't sure why her family celebrated it other than the fact it was another chance to have a great dinner with family. Some say that the "seven" represents the Seven Hills of Rome. Others say it honors the seven Roman Catholic sacraments or it could even be an acknowledgement of the seven deadly sins. Still others see it as a representation of the fulfillment of God's promise after creating the universe in seven days. Legend persists that this tradition of the Festa dei sette pesce began in earnest several centuries ago in Southern Italy. This Christmas Eve dinner was tied into the fast which Roman Catholics were obligated to observe as they anticipated the birth of Christ on Christmas Day. The fast would end when they received Holy Communion during Midnight Mass. During a fast, meat is strictly forbidden, however, fish is permitted.

So how did our family celebrate this night of the Festa dei sette pesce? They cooked a lot of fish! And other things, as well. For, along with the fish, there would be a white pizza with olive oil, zucchini and cauliflower dipped in batter and deep fried, Italian salad and one special American tradition…a huge rectangular apple pie made with a lard crust. The first course was usually a Lentil Soup with rice. My grandmother told me of our family traditions, of the seven fish that we served. As for the fish, it was not a fancy meal, as our family did not have the money for expensive varieties of seafood. Sardines were dipped into a batter and deep-fried until they were crispy. Grandma remembers (with a little laugh) that their heads would still be attached! One of our regular family recipes (which was often served on Fridays during Lent) was a tuna dish with sauce and macaroni. First, they would fry up some onions, throw some sauce in and then finally add chunks of tuna fish. This was usually served with an angel hair pasta. Uncle Victor loved this the most. Another dish included the Italian baccala, or the cod fish. This would be soaked for about two weeks at the fish market. When they would bring it home they would continue to soak it and to wash the salt out of it with cold water. This would require continuously changing the water. The cod would then be cut up into pieces, salted and peppered, and fried in olive oil with some onions. It could also be dipped into a batter and deep fried. There was calamari, which was cleaned and deep fried, in a batter as well. The legs would be pulled off and eaten. Sole was another dish that would be served. It was more expensive and delicate. It was my grandmother's favorite. Baked with olive oil, seasoned with salt, pepper and parsley, it was cooked slowly. The anchovies, of course, were another staple of the Festa dei sette pesce. They would often be served with linguini and cooked with fried onions, garlic, fresh parsley and olive oil. The anchovies would be added toward the end after the macaroni had cooked—or else, they would dissolve. Trout would also be served at times. Great grandpa would clean it and scrape off the skin and clean the innards. According to my grandmother, it was so good baked in the oven with only olive oil, parsley and garlic. Years later, other fish such as crab or shrimp would be added to the meal.

However, in the early days, these fish would be considered too expensive.

After learning the mystery of the Festa dei sette pesce, I told my children about this family dinner that used to be held in most Italian houses in our city less than one hundred years ago. I told them of our family recipes with detail. Some of the recipes made their mouths water, and others made them cringe! I am thinking, though, that maybe the time is right to celebrate our own modified version of the Festa dei sette pesce, in honor of this special family tradition that made its way from Italy and into the city of Niagara Falls. And since I was a part of the reason for its (almost) disappearance I would love to be responsible for bringing it back to a new life in a new generation.

SEAFOOD IN SEASON

Lobster
Shad Roe
Soft Shell Crabs
Scallops

DELICIOUS Seafood dishes that are served perfectly because this is the time of the year when they are just right. The season is a short one! Don't put it off. Come in and eat your fill.

LA FESTA DI SAN GIUSEPPE (ST. JOSEPH'S TABLE) BY MARCIA BUZZELLI

La Festa di San Giuseppe, or the St. Joseph's Table, is a Sicilian tradition observed on March 19th each year. Sicilian immigrants brought it to the United States in the late 19th and early 20th centuries. It continues today in many Italian neighborhoods and churches—including within the city of Niagara Falls.

St. Joseph, the foster father of Jesus, has long been the patron saint of workers and the protector of the family in Italy. In southern Italy, it was not uncommon for religious practice to be based upon a close and personal relationship with the local patron saints. San Giuseppe, or St. Joseph, is quite popular in this region.

One of the stories of the origin of the tradition states that many centuries ago, the spring harvest was less than a bumper crop in Sicily. Producing a famine, the villagers prayed to St. Joseph and their prayers were answered. At the end of the famine a great feast of thanksgiving was held and became the tradition we celebrate today. People with plenty would provide a buffet and invite the less fortunate to their homes.

There was also great religious meaning attached to the St. Joseph's Table. People were selected to represent the Holy Family: an elderly man, a young woman and a child. The three would sit at the head table and remain there during the early part of the feast. A priest would bless the food and then the "holy family" would be served first.

The table is seen as symbolic in its shape and decoration. It is prepared in steps. At the highest step is the statue of St. Joseph. White linen tablecloths cover the table. Vigil lights of green, brown and deep yellow representing St. Joseph's attire are placed upon the table. Flowers and palms adorn the table. The food dishes represent the harvest. Breads are baked in the shapes of a staff, a carpenter's implement, a hand, the cross, and animals and arranged on the table.

TRADITIONAL TABLE BLESSED—The Rev. Carl J. Fenice, pastor of St. Joseph's Church, blessed the traditional St. Joseph's table at the Century Club Monday night. Charles Guarino, left, was chairman of the event which was attended by approximately 200 persons. The table is representative of several throughout this city prepared in honor of St. Joseph's name day, a national holiday in Italy, which is celebrated today.— Gazette Photo.

The Fava Bean (vicia fava) plays an important role at the St. Joseph's table. Often served in a frittata or with a garlic sauce—they represent good luck. When dried, roasted and blessed the Fava Bean becomes the "lucky bean." These blessed dried beans are scattered upon the altars along with a piece of blessed bread during the feast. The legend says that if you carry this lucky bean everywhere you go you will never lack money. Some people believe that keeping one in the pantry will ensure that your kitchen will always be with food. Fava Beans also represent fertility as they grow well even in rocky and poor soil. Sicilian farmers would carry one bean from a good crop to ensure another good crop. Some historians believe this myth began in Sicily during a famine period. The bean was typically used as fodder for the cattle. To survive the farmers prepared them for their table.

No meat will be served at the St. Joseph's table. It is strictly vegetarian. Food consists of *minestras* and very thick soups made of lentils, favas and other types of beans, together with escarole, broccoli or cauliflower. Other vegetables such as celery, fennel stalks and boiled and stuffed artichokes are also commonly served. No cheese is eaten on St. Joseph's Day. Pasta with sardines or fennel sauce is sprinkled with a mixture of toasted dry bread crumbs. Dessert is typically a large cream puff filled with ricotta called, Sfinge.

PREPARATIONS — Mrs. Anthony Monteleone, left, helps Mrs. Charles Choppolla Sr. decorate the altar of St. Joseph for the St. Joseph table Mrs. Choppolla will hold Tuesday beginning at noon at her home, 429 20th St.— Gazette Photo.

St. Joseph's Day Table preparation
Co-chairmen from Mt. Carmel Church prepare traditional foods for a St. Joseph's Day Table on Friday in the church hall at 27th Street and Independence Avenue. From left, Joan Erias, Frances Buzzelli and Joan Monti dip broccoli for deep frying later as part of the meatless fare for the Lenten feast, which will also include fettucini marinara, spinach pies and haddock. Mrs. Monti explained that the feast continues a custom from the Middle Ages. People in Sicily prepared a feast for all the people — especially the needy — in thanks to St. Joseph for bringing an end to a terrible drought.

MY GRANDFATHERS' GARDENS
BY MICHELLE ANN KRATTS

If you travelled back in time to the 1920's, the 1930's, the 1940's…and you happened to find yourself at the corner of Forest Avenue and 19th Street… you would be at my great great grandfather, Angelo Ventresca's, garden. Today the kitchen of Fortuna's Restaurant lies over his garden. But in my mind, I can see it, as if it were still there.

Of course, I never saw Angelo's garden, myself, because he died in 1946. But the ghost of his garden has certainly appeared before me. So many times I have asked my grandmother to describe it to me in detail. The garden was a centerpiece in the lives of the Italians for many of these men and women had descended from generation upon generation of paesani, or farmers. Back in Torre dei Nolfi, a little mountain village in L'Aquila, Italy, my great great grandparents worked the land of their ancestors…and loved the land of their ancestors. They were grateful for its bounty. As Angelo was often in America (he had traveled back and forth across the ocean at least fourteen times) my great great grandmother, Adelina, took charge of the family farm. All of the children had special jobs, as well.

Here in America, on a much smaller scale, Angelo kept a spectacular garden. There was a cherry tree, a pear tree and a peach tree. Vegetables included: tomatoes, red and green peppers, string beans, Roman beans, zucchini, lettuce, carrots, basil, parsley and other herbs. My grandmother also remembers the old barrel that was filled with horse manure.

"Don-nah ever stir da barrel!!" was the warning from their grandfather.

My grandmother and her brother, Joseph, were regularly warned of the hazards of stirring that barrel. However, being children, they were curious and could not resist taking a peek inside. The most horrible odor came forth after they removed the cover! They were never going to do that again! But the manure was precious to Angelo. He would throw it around the growing plants and produce tomatoes as large as melons.

When the garden was ready for harvesting, the women would pick the fresh fruits and vegetables. Mostly everything was eaten fresh and whatever was not eaten immediately was canned. Nothing was wasted. Ever. My family canned tomatoes (with bay leaves), peaches, pears, Italian plums and eggplant (they made caponata). The tomatoes were the most important canned good. My family would can their own tomatoes--as well as an additional seven bushels which they would purchase at the city market. They spent the entire summer canning. Even the children were allowed to help.

My grandfather, Henry Borgatti, (born on July 21, 1922, in Welland, Ontario, Canada, to Aldimiro Borgatti and Luisa Govoni) cultivated his own garden on Woodlawn Avenue for as long as I can remember. He loved to be outside just as the sun came up. I remember that he grew: tomatoes, string beans, peppers, lettuce, carrots, zucchini and various herbs. There was a cherry tree and a pear tree. And there were the most delectable grapes I have ever tasted growing on a vine in a little corner in his backyard. He would offer me some that were just picked and tell me that they were special Niagara grapes that were only grown here and in Canada. I loved how they popped out of their skins inside my mouth. They really were delicious.

Grandpa Borgatti gave everyone paper bags full of tomatoes for his garden was always overflowing. I also remember his herbs. He would dry them over a screen in his garage. Or just use them fresh.

Most Niagara Falls Italians kept gardens and found them to be their fondest treasure. There was something special about spending days underneath the sun, working your hands into the dirt, lovingly raising the sprouts and tender shoots from the earth until full bloom, harvesting the bounty, and finally cooking it into the finest dinners. Even today if you drive through the downtown area of Niagara Falls the remnants of the Italian gardens are still visible. Wind-ravaged lattice boards lean against garages as vines entangle themselves into bushes. Wild greens creep through fences. Empty canning jars sit on basement shelves gathering dust. They used to fill the darkness of the basements with beautiful colors, and now only a dead spider or two.

CANNING VEGETABLES

FORAGING FOR DANDELION GREENS (CICORIA) BY MICHELLE ANN KRATTS

Perhaps one of the oldest traditions the Italians brought to America was the practice of foraging. An ancient custom involving searching for and harvesting wild vegetation, foraging is still taken quite seriously in Italy. Even today Italians forage for wild asparagus, berries, anise seeds, truffles, snails and various vegetables and nuts. Many of these items are considered delicacies as they are not regularly sold in stores. Niagara's Italians were also known to take to the fields in search of various foods not found in stores or markets; mainly, the dandelion greens (cicoria).

THE JUNIOR COOK

DANDELION GREENS

The most fun about dandelion grens is the getting of them. With a jolly crowd it is very good fun.

Cut the greens from 1 inch below the ground so some of the white will come up.

Plants that have not gone to seed are the best for eating.

Wash the greens carefully and cut off any leaves that seem old. n ....- Y.. kinR?a

Cut three-inch cubes of salt pork into tiny pieces.

Drop them into a deep frying pan and cook gently till brown.

Pour over them one cup water and bring to a boil.

Drop the dandelion greens into this and again bring to a boil.

Cover well and cook slowly 25 minutes.

Drain, pour into a hot dish, dot with butter and serve at once.

This is a very tasty spring dish

I remember hearing about the cicoria foraging, although, unfortunately, I was never a member of my grandmother's hunting party. Mostly the younger people laughed about the older people rushing off to the countryside in early spring in search of cicoria. What audacity they had! Bending over along highways—bloomers showing—as passers-by drove past puzzled and stunned. As embarrassing as it may have been to the younger generation who had sought to "fit in" with the other Americans...they were not laughing when they were presented the wonderful dishes made with the foraged cicoria.

I am sure the American tradition of hunting down cicoria began out of necessity and because of the sheer abundance of this green in the Niagara area. Many of the early Italian immigrants were poor and welcomed any food, especially if it was free and abundant. Dandelion greens usually spring up during the final weeks of April and early May after warmer temperatures become the norm and light rains have fallen. You do not want to wait too long, however, for once the yellow flowers pop up the leaves become bitter. Although all parts of the dandelion green are edible, Italians usually only eat the leaves. There is a very slim window of opportunity for cicoria foragers. You want to harvest the youngest leaves for they are the most tender and delicious. They are the best in salads, sautéed, steamed or cooked with eggs.

My Uncle Victor would take my great grandmother (Clementina Ventresca Fortuna) and their mother (Adelina Ventresca) to an area off the road near Model City. Others frequented Walmore Road, Swann Road or even areas near Fort Niagara. The cicoria was very plentiful in these remote country-side sections of Niagara County; places not treated with pesticides or frequented by animals. They would bring only sharp knives and straw baskets or bags. To harvest the leaves they would gather a bunch in one hand and then with the other, dig the knife into the root just below the surface of the ground and slice off. This would take the entire head out of the ground (like a head of lettuce).

When they brought the greens home they would require a thorough washing. They would then be tossed with olive oil and vinegar, salt and pepper, and maybe even some anchovies. Other recipes included sautéing the bigger leaves with olive oil and onions or serving them with poached eggs (with some Italian cheese, of course). Easter dinner tables were often graced with recipes donning the sacred dandelion greens, as well, as some cooks baked them into special pizza pies.

To most Americans, the dandelion greens were merely weeds and even today many of us cover our yards with fertilizers and poisons in order to rid ourselves of these flowers. The Italians, however, believed that the dandelion greens were healthful and that they would "clean the blood." It turns out that they are, indeed, extremely healthy foods. They contain high amounts of Vitamins A, B, C, D, E and K, as well as iron, potassium and zinc. It has been found that they aid in cleansing and detoxification. Their nutrients revitalize the liver and potentially reduce the risk of cancer, diabetes, MS, cataracts and heart disease. Perhaps the Italians were right…and this humble little weed may be worth the trouble of foraging its tender shoots and leaves along country roads.

THOSE CARDOONS
BY MICHELLE ANN KRATTS

As I write this piece, the cardoons are everywhere. They are crowding together in fields, hovering against hillsides, bursting through patches of grass on driveways and even alongside highways. Of course, I had seen them before...but I hadn't *really seen them*...or acknowledged their majesty and their history until my friend Lynda La Greca took me to them. They are here, right outside the library, with their giant velveteen leaves and celery stalks. When I held one in my hands, flashes of summer days flooded my mind. When I smelled one, I was back in time. A child again in my backyard.

Those cardoons, which once graced the tables of the ancient Romans, are now mostly left alone with all of the other troublesome weeds. Or destroyed. At one time, in Italy, they were a delicacy. A close cousin of the artichoke family, their delicate flavor resembles its relative...only with a small hint of licorice. The Niagara Italians knew of the cardoons and took every opportunity in mid-May—when they are at their prime—to forage for these delicious greens. They knew exactly where to find them. They grow wild just about everywhere.

Lynda pulled one for me that we had found outside our parking lot at the Lewiston Public Library. She explained how she had just recently gathered some and had gone through all of the usual rigmarole in order to serve them to her grandchildren. The leaves are not used, but the stalks must be meticulously treated before cooking. The stalks are very fibrous and require a great deal of care and cleaning. She showed me how the white velvet coating on each stalk must be scraped away first...leaving black stains on your hands and inside your fingernails. Then the pieces would be chopped and boiled, not once, but twice over. The first time the water is black and must be drained and then the pot must be refilled with fresh water and boiled once again. In the meantime, a batter (similar to a meatball batter) would be prepared. Once the cardoons are well-boiled they are added to the batter, shaped and fried in olive oil.

All of this talk of cardoons brought Lynda back to stories of her own family. As far as she knew, her grandmother, Maria Lena (La Marca) La Greca, had first made the cardoons. Born in Licata, Agrigento, Sicily, back in 1901, she arrived in Niagara Falls as a young girl. Her father was already here. Rosario La Marca was a stone mason and had worked on such local landmarks as Holy Trinity Roman Catholic Church and the historic Old Stone Chimney. Lena met her husband, Calogero La Greca, when she lived in Buffalo. She worked at a grocery store that her sister and brother-in-law owned and one day a cheese and olive oil peddler walked in and stole her heart. This peddler was Calogero La Greca and it was love at first sight. They were married soon after.

Lynda has fond memories of gathering cardoons with her father, Frank La Greca. They grew wild on their own property in Youngstown. In fact, Lynda's brother, who lives there now, recently asked her if she wanted the cardoons that were popping up through the driveway…as he knew how she liked them. They are quite a hardy green! And quite arrogant as they push their way through any landscape.

Lynda's father, Frank, was the one who cooked the cardoons. Her mother did all of the cleaning—which was quite the job! And as one food memory leads to another, the cardoons made way to memories of foraging for mustard greens, as well. They also grew wild and abundantly in fields all over the Niagara area. She remembers how her father loved these, as well. Now things such as cardoons and mustard greens are delicacies. But do we realize that we can gather them ourselves?

The cardoons, perhaps, have gone the way of many things from the past. Yet, there are some, like my friend, Lynda, who keep the traditions alive and well for another generation.

CARDOONS OREGANATO

This is baked, in a covered dish, and it's usually a side dish. The cutlets are often eaten as a main dish.

Sprinkle the bottom of a casserole dish with finely chopped garlic and black pepper. Put parboiled burdock on top and sprinkle with more garlic, grated Parmesan cheese, salt, pepper and oregano. Add sliced or canned tomatoes if you like. Drizzle with olive oil, add enough water to barely cover the bottom of the dish, and add a layer of breadcrumbs. Bake at 350 degrees for 30 minutes.

People who love burdock claim it has all sorts of magical powers -- to purify the blood, rejuvenate the body and even cure acne and build strength. I can't vouch for those claims but I can definitely agree that burdock is a delicious and unusual wild vegetable.

PIZZELLE TRADITIONS
BY MICHELLE ANN KRATTS

When I lived in Texas on an Air Force Base my friends were amazed by my pizzelle. One Halloween I dusted off my pizzelle maker (I actually have two—one was my grandmother's and one was given to me as a wedding gift) and used melted chocolate to "draw" spider webs onto the lacey lines of the cookie. It was a perfect treat for all of my southern friends. *How clever!* They thought. My grandmothers would probably have fainted if they had known I had turned their classic cookie into a ghoulishly fun little tidbit. Or maybe they would be pleased to know I had shared it with some "*mangia cakes.*" (For those of you who do not know...a "*mangia cake*" is a term used to describe non-Italians, specifically WASPS. The literal translation is "*cake eater.*") I grew up eating pizzelle—never realizing they were a mystery to the rest of the world. Nor did I realize that pizzelle are considered by some to be the oldest Italian cookie recipe to survive to this day.

This traditional Italian waffle cookie was made from flour, eggs, sugar, butter and anise or vanilla flavoring. However, some Italians would scoff at the idea of flavoring pizzelle with vanilla! In fact, it was customary to ask those traveling to Italy to bring back jars of anise seeds. Our friend's mother would purchase over $35 worth. This was quite an expense for an Italian-American housewife in the 1930's! But those little black seeds would certainly go a long way.

Historians believe that the pizzelle may have been developed from a Roman cookie, called the "crustulum." The cookies were also called "ferratelle" in the province of Lazio—because they were baked over an open fire with an iron (called a ferro) which was often embossed with the family crest. My great Aunt Phil had once mentioned to me that she had ended up with the Ventresca family iron. It was stamped with a "V" and had been passed through the family for several generations. Unfortunately, when the electric irons came out, she sold our family iron at a yard sale. The pizzelle iron was very heavy and by the time you had made even a few your hands and your wrists were aching. Because they were more complicated to make, pizzelle were usually saved for the fancier occasions and not an "everyday" cookie. It took some skill to master the heat of the iron, the amount of batter to use and how long to keep it over the fire. The pattern on the early pizzelle (made in the iron ferro) was a little different from the patterns made by the electric pizzelle makers. The old style patterns were of an oblong shape and their design was very simple. There were crisscrossing lines (like in a waffle) and then in the middle was a large "V" revealing that these cookies were made by the Ventresca family. Apparently, families had their own designs. Usually the first few cookies would burn until the correct temperature had been reached. And they tasted different from present-day pizzelle, too. They were crispy and crunchy and not as soft. Today's pizzelle are softer and more delicate. They can be dried and shaped into cannoli or cones or little bowls to fill with custard, ice cream or fruit. My friend, Patricia DiNieri, has fond memories of making pizzelle with an old fashioned iron down in her cellar. Her dog would wait patiently for any pieces that would drop to the floor. Patricia still has that old pizzelle iron.

Pizzelle were said to have originated in Abruzzo—specifically in the province of L'Aquila. A legend persists that in about 700 BC snakes had infested Abruzzo. After they were banished, the townspeople celebrated by eating pizzelle. My great grandmother's family was from the province of L'Aquila and, indeed, the pizzelle, was a most important part of our family traditions. Especially at weddings –all of the women would gather to make hundreds of pizzelle. I often wonder if my ancestors were among those celebrating the banishment of the snakes by eating those delectable pizzelle.

There were other cookies that were baked and eaten regularly by Niagara's Italians. The biscotti were served almost daily with our afternoon tea. Biscotti are not a delicate cookie. They can store in a dry place for a very long time without spoiling. We would dunk them into our tea until they melted and then eat them when they were soft. Biscotti is also a generic term for any "cookies" in Italian. The biscotti itself, however, was made from dough which was formed into logs and baked until golden brown. The logs would be sliced and then re-cooked. The biscotti also originated from an ancient Roman recipe.

Pace quickens as Christmas nears

Home-baked cookies are such an endearing token for an Italian. My grandmother's friend, Phyllis Infantino, mentioned that her mother, Mary Rotella Palmeri, would make special cookies that were white with white frosting and package them into little boxes for sick friends. As a young girl, it was Phyllis's job to deliver these boxes.

There were, of course, many other cookies associated with the Italians of Niagara Falls. There was the cuccidati (a Sicilian fig cookie), lemon cookies, cookies made with wine, ricotta-filled cookies, crostoli, and the sesame seed cookies (which the men would dunk into their coffee or into glasses of wine); however, none of them were as important (in my family, at least) as that pretty and dainty pizzelle.

ANTIPASTO ALL'ITALIANA
BY MICHELLE ANN KRATTS

A delicious antipasti is something my husband and I still enjoy preparing for friends and family who happen to be our dinner guests. As a little girl I was always delighted with that colorful dish as it was carried out of the kitchen at my great grandfather's restaurant, Fortuna's. Of course, I knew that it was a portent of glorious things to come—but there was also another reason that I loved this entree. My grandfather's antipasti was a beautiful work of art—a garden, bursting with exuberant flavors and bold colors—it was definitely something to behold. We would pass the platter around the table and gather whatever interested us and then gorge ourselves upon the salty meats, the cheese, the vegetables. As I grew older I would try and stop myself from eating too much of this "pre-dinner" meal and to leave room for the macaroni and the meats that were to come. But it was of no use...what began with tearing into a piece of Italian bread...ended with some caponata and one last olive.

Francesco Fortuna

Antipasto all'italiana is a dish that preceded the main meal. To Americans, it is known as the appetizer. To the French, the hors d'oeuvres. An antipasti is the traditional first course of an Italian meal. It is eaten with your hands, and with gusto. You sip your Chianti and realize how smoothly it attracts the roasted red peppers and the pepperoncini inside of your mouth. It can be a little messy, but everyone knows that manners are not so important during an Italian repast!

All Italians have their preference when it comes to the perfect antipasti. My great grandfather, Francesco Fortuna, had a special way of preparing his at his restaurant. My grandmother, Jean Fortuna Borgatti, recently reminded me of the details. Grandpa would almost always use an oval platter and would line it with chopped lettuce and sliced tomatoes. He would then add thin slices of the traditional cured meats (all imported from Italy): Genoa Salami, Capicola, Prosciutto. Although he had a personal and deep aversion to cheese—he added provolone to the platter, as well. Vegetables included homemade eggplant caponata, roasted red peppers, pepperoncini, cherry tomatoes stuffed with anchovies, and Italian olives. A torn off hunk of chewy bread from the Portage Bakery in Canada... and I had everything I needed in the world—until, of course, the soups and salads were paraded out into the dining room...along with the meats and the steaming macaroni. Oh but what a wonderful prelude my grandfather's antipasti was to a sumptuous feast!

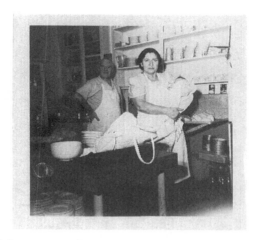

My great grandparents in the kitchen at Fortuna's

POLENTA
BY MICHELLE ANN KRATTS

I was never quite sure what to think of polenta. It was nothing like the steaming plates of macaroni that I was so accustomed to. And I must admit that I had to grow to appreciate it. How strange it seemed to serve this "mush" with sauce and meats! But taking it into my mouth was always a pleasure and I have introduced it to my own family, to their delight.

My grandparents always told us that polenta was what my Grandpa Borgatti's family ate in Italy. His family was from the north—from Emilia-Romagna-- and polenta formed the basis of their cuisine. However, the peasants of Abruzzo (where my grandmother's family hailed from) ate it quite regularly, too.

```
Fried Polenta,
Tomato Sauce
```

By BERTHA E. SHAPLEIGH
Of Columbia University

1 cup cornmeal
1 1-2 teaspoons salt
4 cups boiling water
3-4 cup grated cheese

Into the boiling water sift the cornmeal mixed with the salt, stirring constantly to prevent lumps forming. Cook over the fire 10 minutes, then over water one hour. Add cheese and stir until cheese is melted. Turn into a mold, and when cold cut into slices. Roll each slice in flour and fry in bacon or ham fat until a golden brown. Serve with tomato sauce, made as follows:

3 cups canned or 5 fresh tomatoes
1 slice onion
2 tablespoons lard or bacon fat
3 teaspoons sugar
2 tablespoons flour
1 teaspoon salt
Bit of bay leaf
6 pepper corns (unground pepper)

Fry onion in lard or bacon fat, ad flour and brown slightly. Add tomatoes and seasonings and simmer half an hour. Strain and rub all the tomato to pulp through the sieve. Season more to taste and serve. If bacon has been fried, garnish with the bacon strips.

It is quite likely that most Americans, particularly those who are not of Italian descent, have never heard of polenta. This simple cornmeal dish that has been boiled into a porridge can be eaten directly, baked, fried or grilled. It is said that it emerged from an earlier Roman meal called pulmentum (a gruel or porridge) and formed the center of the diet for Roman soldiers. Before corn was introduced to Italy in the 16th century, polenta was made from farro, chestnut flour, millet, spelt or chickpeas. It was full of healthful nutrients.

Polenta is preferably cooked in a large copper pot called a paiolo with a ratio of about 3:1 of water to cornmeal. It must be stirred constantly as it cooks.

My grandmother explained to me how our family prepared the polenta. This manner of preparation mirrored how her parents and grandparents had prepared it in Italy. A simple sauce was made first, along with several meats, including spare ribs, sausage and meatballs and the drippings would be added to the sauce. After the polenta was fully cooked it would be poured onto a board. I still have the red and white board my family used. It is actually a vintage 1920's sideboard from a table top that belonged to my great grandparents. After being poured out it would then be rolled with a pole (or a couple of wooden spoons) to ¾ of an inch in thickness. The sauce would be added with a soup ladle (a "cupina," according to my grandmother). Cheese would be sprinkled over the top (Romano and Parmesan). Finally, the meats would be placed in the center. The family members would choose a spot and sit around the "board" and cut off pieces to eat. I never did eat polenta like this. By the time I was around, many of these customs had faded into oblivion. Only little crumbs remained for the American great grandchildren. But, interestingly, I have read that "polenta on a board" is actually finding a second life in new generations of Italian-Americans.

My grandmother preparing the dinner table

There is one special family story that I learned of only a few years ago that involves polenta. Always intrigued by our family history, I once asked my little Aunt Phil (who was born Felicetta Ventresca) about her trip to America—never realizing I would get a story about polenta! It was in March of 1928 when Felicetta (age seven), her brother Vittorio (age ten), her sister Antoinette (age seventeen), and her mother Adelina, came across the ocean. Her mother (my great great grandmother) and my Aunt Antoinette were extremely sea-sick throughout the voyage and never left their bunks. Meanwhile, the younger children, Felicetta and Vittorio, had full reign of the ship. There were kindly Italian sailors on board who often amused the children and even took them to dinner. On one particular night, as a polenta dinner was being prepared for the Italian passengers, the sea stirred up a terrible storm. Just as the polenta had been poured out onto the wooden tables a wave picked up the ship and violently tossed it around. People were thrown about and some even came crashing down the stairs. There were serious injuries. In the commotion, a huge sea creature burst through the windows and onto the tables that were set with the polenta, breaking them into pieces and making the polenta inedible. There was screaming and terror from every corner. There was great destruction. I don't believe the passengers had anything to eat that night. Discussions of polenta always reminded my Aunt Phil of that fateful encounter on the ship to America and the night she was not able to eat the delicious polenta.

My Aunt Phil, my great great grandmother and my Uncle Victor
on their way to America

SOPRESSATA
BY MICHELLE ANN KRATTS AND BEVERLY BIDAK

I have been told that my family in Italy made their own version of sopressata, an Italian dry salami, for our name, Ventresca, literally translates as "dressed pork product." In making sopressata, pork is the traditional meat of choice.   Sopressata was most commonly prepared by the Southern Italians from Abruzzo, Basilicata, Apulia, Molise and Calabria.

Preparing sopressata requires drying coarsely ground pressed meat that has been flavored with seasonings. Sometimes hot peppers are added to spice it up. There are many different unique recipes for the meat. After being flavored, the sausage is hung to dry for between three and twelve weeks. Sopressata has a distinct oblong shape as it is pressed between two sheets of linen—on top of which is placed a wooden plank with some weights or heavy stones.

Italian SOPRESSATA
Hot or Sweet
lb. 99¢

Sopressata has been made since the time of the Greek presence in Italy. It was traditionally cured in olive oil. As the Italians settled in Niagara Falls, they brought their own family recipes. Some men actually made their basements into special kitchens specifically for making sopressata. My favorite sopressata was the one my husband would bring home from work. A fellow probation officer, Bob Zambito, would share his wonderful sopressata with his friends at work and inevitably my husband would bring some home for the rest of us. Bob explained to me that the sopressata is made at his friend Joe Sacco's home. When Joe's father built the house they had a special room made in the basement which was made with a sole purpose of producing wine and sopressata.

Making sopressata is serious business to the Italians of Niagara Falls—and especially to Joe Sacco. A group of 26 or 27 men (and one woman) from all over Niagara Falls and Buffalo and from all walks of life work on the sopressata at Joe's home. They have been doing this for a very long time. They are businessmen, professionals and even friends from Joe's youth. They only do this once a year during the second week of January...or about a week before the Super Bowl for it is best to cure the meats during the winter months. All of their ingredients are locally purchased. The recipe includes the following ingredients: 1,400 pounds of pork butt (purchased at Scipione's), 5 cases of gallon Paisano red wine (from the Wedge Liquor Store), and 13 spices including white pepper, black pepper, red crushed cayenne, wine, pecorino cheese, romano cheese, garlic and onion (from

Latina's). The most sopressata they ever had hanging in the basement was 1, 150 pounds. In order to achieve the best results, the room temperature is kept at a frigid level. There are six or seven thermometers that keep the temperature even and it must be checked three times a day to be sure the temperature doesn't get too warm. It also has to be watched to make sure it doesn't freeze. According to Joe, the meats are hung to dry for eight weeks. Some things have changed through the years and adjustments have been made. They used to use sheep's stomach and intestines for the casings but there was too much breakage (and the smell of the casings was not very pleasant). Now they use synthetic casings.

The result is something wonderful! Joe's sopressata is legendary in these parts and hopefully the tradition will continue for many years to come.

MAKING WINE
BY MICHELLE ANN KRATTS

Italians love their vino! Even during the Prohibition Years the Italians were making homemade wine. My great grandfathers were no exception. My great grandfather, Aldimiro Borgatti, from Finale, Italy (in the Emilia-Romagna region) made his own homemade wine in Welland, Ontario. My great great grandfather, Angelo Ventresca, made it in Niagara Falls.

My great grandfather, Aldimiro Borgatti, (far left) and unknown men drinking wine

I have been told that Angelo's wine was one of the best. Everyone would come for a bottle. It was not surprising to my grandmother (his granddaughter), when she visited Italy (many years following his death), to see that his home in the old country was built around a vineyard. In front of the Ventresca family home in Torre dei Nolfi (a small village in the Abruzzo region) was a slope that was filled with grapevines. Behind the home were the olive orchards that went on endlessly. Angelo made wine and whiskey. For the purpose of wine-making in Niagara Falls, special wine grapes would be delivered from Buffalo to their home on 19th Street. The grapes would be taken directly to the cellar. First they would be ground in a machine. Then they would go through the presser. The entire house would carry the scent of the grapes and the wine for quite some time. It was heavenly. My grandmother remembers it well.

After producing the wine (which was always done in the fall), they would bottle it. Gold caps were put on the bottles, one at a time. They had a special machine that would force the cap to be airtight.

Wine was not only drunk by the men and the women. The children were also offered wine.

Some of the Italians made specialty wines. My friend Eleanor Migliazzo Novara's father made cherry wine with a special cherry press.

And the wine-making continues even to this day. Some Italian Niagarans have continued in the family tradition. A Niagara Falls physical education teacher by day, Carmine Bianco's wine-making is celebrated locally. He recently won second place for his homemade rose wine in the Antonacci Annual Wine and Sopressata Contest. Last year he won first place for his homemade rose. In 2008 he won first place for his red wine. He learned how to make wine from his father, Salvatore Bianco. The Bianco family was originally from Naples, Italy. Carmine's other grandparents, John and Beatrice DiCicco, owned and operated D's Best Pizzeria which was in the City Market in the 1950's and 1960's. The DiCiccos were from the Abruzzo region of Italy.

John DiCicco with his famous antipasto and pizza

2014 Wine and Sopressata Contest

Carmine is also the chairman of the Italian Festival, as well as the head of the Pax Romana Commission which is a men's bocce club. Carmine has a dream to revive the city's Italian American heritage by celebrating Italian culture. He plans on making the festival bigger and better each year. The festival is in the tradition of past Italian festivals for they have been held in Niagara Falls on and off for almost one hundred years. The festival includes Italian music and dancing, bocce playing, a spaghetti-eating contest and much more. This year's Italian Festival will take place on August 1st, 2nd and 3rd.

Advice from Carmine: "the more you make, the more you drink, the more you drink...the better it gets...."

"Rocking the wine with the boys..."
Carmine Bianco

A CULINARY HISTORY OF MY GREAT GRANDMOTHER
BY MICHELLE ANN KRATTS

This is a photograph of my great grandmother, Clementina (Ventresca) Fortuna, (far left) displaying a Thanksgiving feast she helped to cook during World War II at Camp Bell. She worked at Camp Bell as an assistant chef. Her main duty was to cook for the airmen and pilots. Beside her in the picture is Ethel Mt. Pleasant Zomont and in the center was the head chef, Jack. The other two men are unknown.

Clementina Ventresca was born on November 16, 1901, in the little mountain village of Torre dei Nolfi, located in Bugnara, Abruzzo, Italy. She lived with her parents, Angelo and Adelina Ventresca, and her sisters and brother on a small farm. The following is an excerpt from a family history written by my uncle, Robert Borgatti, who had gathered this information after interviewing my great grandmother about her life in Torre de Nolfi.

Each day the family would rise to an early morning breakfast which usually consisted of eggs, bacon, homemade sausage, and wine for all—including even the youngest child. The whole family would spend the next several hours in the fields cultivating and/or harvesting such crops as peaches, pears, apples, grapes, walnuts, olives and figs. In addition, chickens, sheep, pigs, goats and cows needed tending. Angelo (Clementina's father) worked for several years as a gate watcher for the village's communal cheese manufactory up in the mountains.

All of the people in the town shared in the making and distribution of not only cheese but olive oil, bread and wine, as well. Fruit and vegetable crops were grown on individual family farms for personal use. Most families, however would cart their produce to the city of Sulmona to be sold in the market place there. The one exception was olives, which were gathered together at a central location in Torre dei Nolfi to be ground into oil for the use of all families. A mule, whose eyes were covered with a cloth to prevent dizziness, would be led around a large mill pulling a heavy grinding stone with which the olives would be crushed.

In mid-afternoon families would take time out for "l'ora di colazione" (lunchtime). Resting under a shady tree, they would lunch on a light meal consisting of cheese, prosciutto, apples and, of course, ever present was "il vino." "L'ora di pranzo" (dinner) would be observed late in the evening and usually consisted of polenta or various types of pasta, and vegetable soups. In Torre de Nolfi families may have been poor, but they always ate well.

Years later, my great Aunt Phil--Clementina's youngest sister--also mentioned a little about the culinary traditions of Torre dei Nolfi. My great grandmother and another one of my aunts usually tended to the sheep. They would take them up into the mountains to graze each morning. She also recalled how the family would tie a cart to a donkey and transport their fruits and vegetables to sell at the markets in Sulmona—which was about an hour's journey by donkey. They would bring Roman beans, celery, tomatoes, Swiss chard, peas, grapes, olives grown in the mountains, walnuts, peaches, apples and cherries. In Sulmona they would always treat themselves to the famous chocolate almond candies.

My great great grandfather, Angelo, made his own prosciutto. In fact, the name "Ventresca" actually translates as "dressed pork product." Perhaps the family was well known for producing meats from the humble pig, which so predominate the little farms that dot this mountainous area of Southern Italy.

Clementina Ventresca left Italy in 1922 (after refusing an arranged marriage) and joined her father, who was already living in Niagara Falls. Even one of her stories of the voyage to America involved food. We always laughed when she mentioned how she had seen a banana for the first time at sea. How shocked she was to figure out that it was actually a sort of fruit! Throughout the trip she was sure that it was an odd-shaped squash.

Clementina married my great grandfather, Francesco Fortuna, on December 12, 1923, at St. Joseph's Church and the culinary traditions continued. She had numerous food industry type jobs before she and my great grandfather opened the Deluxe Restaurant located at 827 19th Street in Niagara Falls. For a time she and several of my aunts worked at a tomato canning factory in Model City. My grandmother, Jean (Fortuna) Borgatti, recalls how this one particular farmer would pick the women up early in the morning in a flat-bed open air truck. Rain or shine. He would take them all to the factory and then bring them all home. When the women returned each evening, they would be soaked in the tomato juice, their hands raw from the acids. She still remembers the smell to this day. The man who drove them would sometimes stop at a bakery or some sort of shop along the way home and they would all buy these wonderfully delicious apple turnovers. My grandmother said she would look so forward to this.

After the war ended, and she was no longer working at Camp Bell, my great grandmother worked in the kitchen at the Cataract House—that beautiful and grand hotel that had at one time stood at the brink of Niagara Falls.   My great grandfather, my grandmother and my uncle Joe would meet her there sometimes and walk her home from work. Just a young girl, my grandmother loved the wraparound porch most of all.

Finally, in 1945, my great grandparents opened the Deluxe Grill at 827 19th Street, in Niagara Falls where she spent most of the rest of her life in the kitchen, creating some of Fortuna's most exquisite dishes.

I love this photograph of my great grandparents on swings at Hyde Park

What I remember most about my great grandmother was sitting in her kitchen with a cup of tea. There was always so much conversation and there were her soups. Lentil, ditalini, and that wonderful family staple, the Chicken Soup (with the little delightful acini di pepe). We would always look forward to diving into these delectable broths. In fact, they were a complete dinner in themselves.

I was fascinated by the kitchen, itself, as it had a restaurant-style stove top with a flat area for frying. And there was a full kitchen in the basement! In fact, the basement was a secret hideaway for my sister and myself. How strange it was to have a kitchen down there. I believe this was how they prepared for so many family weddings…and the baking of the pizzelle. There was also a bar (that was fully stocked). We would sometimes pretend that we were working there. And I have to admit (after all of these years) that we did take a few sips here and there.

So many afternoons, I would stop at their house on Woodlawn Avenue as it was along my walk home from Our Lady of Mt. Carmel School. My great grandmother would always welcome me and bring out the tea and the biscotti, the fruits and the nuts. I would bring a girlfriend along at times. And great grandma would always ask the same question. "Italiano?"

"No, grandma," I would answer. "She's not Italian. She's Polish."

"Oh….," great grandma would sigh. But it was inevitable that she would continue to ask "where" my girlfriend's family had come from *in Italy*. Was she Abbruzzese? Calabrese? Sicilian? My girlfriend and I would laugh and repeat over and over again that she was not from Italy. That her family was from Poland. It was then that I was sure that my grandmother thought that all of the world somehow, someway, originated in Italy.

Great grandpa, my sister, Patty, great grandma and me

MALOCCHIO
BY MICHELLE ANN KRATTS

Many of us live in fear of "malocchio," or the "evil eye," even today. My mother said that our grandmother and our aunts insisted that after I was born (like most of the other newborns of Italian descent that lived in Niagara Falls) I would wear the traditional horns pinned to my undershirt in order to ward off "malocchio." Apparently these horns, which resemble a chili pepper, (also called the *corno, cornuto,* or *cornicello*) saved me from all sorts of evil curses and horrors. I was always curious about this most unusual custom. What was the "evil eye?" And who were these special women who were able to perform these magical spells to break the curse? These women who were healers and magicians…

ITALY MORE CONVINCED THAN EVER THAT GIOLITTI HAS THE "EVIL EYE"

Minister Calissano Dropped Dead While Making Speech at
a Banquet—19th Minister to Die During
Giolitti's Tenure of Office.

An old newspaper article shows the extent of the Italian belief in the "Evil Eye"

Southern Italians are historically very superstitious and many brought these superstitions to America with their luggage. Originating along the Mediterranean and Aegean coastline, the practice usually involves curses and prayers and ceremonies to "break" the spells and curses. Only these special women can remove or "break" the curses of the malocchio. These women are passed on the knowledge on the most sacred night of the year—Christmas Eve—by an older woman already well-versed in the tradition.

The roots of "malocchio" are in Envy. If one looks at a beautiful person (especially a child) without saying "God bless him/her" he or she may inadvertently have cast a curse upon that individual. There was a family story that was passed along in my family about a curse that had been placed upon my mother when she was an infant. My grandmother had been pushing her buggy through the city when a woman stopped to marvel at her. She did not say the required: God bless her. From that moment on, my mother would not stop crying. She screamed for hours. My grandmother could not figure out what was wrong. Her mother told her that there was only one explanation: malocchio. So the baby was brought to a woman who performed the ceremonies to remove the curse. She did her work over the olive oil and the water and my mother stopped crying instantly. The curse had been lifted by this magical woman.

I knew of a few of the magical women. One of my grandmother's good friends is one of them. I hope that one Christmas Eve I can learn the tradition from her…if she is willing. I am wondering how many people actually practice this today in the city of Niagara Falls.

It wasn't until years later that I did learn one of the secrets to lifting the curse. The following is a recipe, or magical spell, to first check for the presence of malocchio, as well as how to remove it.

How to check for the presence of malocchio:

A common way to check is to place three drops of olive oil into a bowl of water. Flick them in with your fingers. If the oils stays together, that is good. If the oil breaks up then a spell has definitely been cast. At this point, the women would pray and perform ceremonies in order to dispel the evil eye curse.

To dispel malocchio:

Pierce the broken olive oil with scissors while reciting prayers.

You can also sprinkle salt around the perimeter of your house.

You will have to continue to check for the presence of malocchio by repeating the olive oil routine until the three drops of olive oil stay together.

MEMORIES OF TIMES PAST
BY BEVERLY BORGATTI BARTHEL

I am a child born post WWII in the middle of the 20th century...1949 to be exact. I was a child of the happy and carefree 1950's. I remember black and white TV, and shows like Howdy Doody and the Mickey Mouse Club. I remember leaving doors on houses and cars unlocked, playing outside till dark and those wonderful old neighborhood stores that were slowly fading away. It was a time when my city, like so many others in America, was slowly transforming from the old and comfortable family friendly ways, pre-WWII, to adapt to the modern age of mass production and huge and impersonal corporations.

Henry Borgatti, little Beverly and Jean (Fortuna) Borgatti

I was a child born into an Italian American family, like most of my friends, with grandparents speaking Italian and adhering to many of the old world ways, and also, my own Mom and Dad who were starting their home and family amid the prosperous 1950's. My generation of kids witnessed, first hand, the demise of the old style, friendly neighborhoods, and mom and pop businesses along with the entry of modern America with its plazas and huge and impersonal corporate stores and super markets. Those were the days when people shopped for everything right within their own neighborhoods.

I remember the old neighborhood delicatessens that had been on most every street corner. They were disappearing ... one at a time. One of my favorite memories is of Sam's Store on 19th street... Sam's little store which was right in front of Trusello's Bakery. I remember it quite well and miss Sam and that little store. Sam, the owner, always made me feel special. When I was a little girl my Dad and I would walk there and Sam would always give me a free bottle of Orange Crush and lift me up to pick out a wonderful Popsicle from the frozen ice cream chest. I don't think orange pop ever has tasted quite the same as that or a Popsicle could be so special ever again to me.

Sam's store was like so many others in Niagara Falls.... the cans stacked neatly on the shelves, the glass counter with cold cuts, the old style cash register, and the wonderful owners with their white aprons. They knew their customers by name and made us always feel welcome. I loved that place. I still dream of it and remember fondly the scent in the air coming from Trusello's which was right behind...another small family run business.

I remember another neighborhood store, this one on 22nd street, Pete's store. I remember my Mom allowing me to shop for the very first time all by myself. I felt so proud but actually forgot the name of the Italian pasta my mother wanted. Pete figured it out and gave me a penny's worth of candy. Great memory.

I remember walking to the City Market as a little girl first, with my Mom and Dad and Grandma Fortuna and then again with my own husband and baby daughters. My grandma would, in good humor, bargain with the farmers for the best price and deal. We'd shop at Latina's and get special imported olive oil and other Italian goodies.

I remember another favorite place on Pine Ave. Trapasso's 5 and 10. It seemed to have everything we needed...and so close to home. I remember Markay's Dress shop where my Mother bought many of my pretty bonnets and dresses... and where I bought a few for my baby daughters too, before it, too, sadly closed. Yes, I feel quite fortunate to have had a wonderful taste of what life was like for my Italian immigrant grandparents and my parents as they were growing up...the good old days, before the progress of the modern age took complete hold. Sometimes I wonder if it really was progress after all.

Sitting on My Grandma's Lap

By Beverly Ann Barthel

Sitting on my Italian Grandma's lap
is something I will always remember
It felt warm and cozy
It felt like love there
I dream of her now and how things used to be...

Her lap was large and welcoming

she hugged me close and kissed my cheeks

I always felt safe and warm there

I was her first grandchild

The daughter of her daughter

I felt special

She WAS special.

Her apron was amazing...

A culinary road map of spots and stains that spoke Italian to me

The scent was a marvel too.... better than Channel, way better

It was her own special perfume

The fragrance of sauce and soup and basil and oregano

I remember ... my grandma's lap was the place for reading

Reading English was a new skill for her

I was learning too

we learned together by sounding words out and feeling proud

I loved my grandma's lap.

It felt like love.

And the memory of it still does...

Ti voglio bene nonna! ♥

THE LADIES IN THE LIBRARY
BY MICHELLE ANN KRATTS

Lucy, Phyllis and Jean

It was a beautiful and sun-filled morning when three lovely ladies visited us at the Lewiston Public Library. The library was not opened yet and we scurried around in the little time we had to make sure the food was ready and to get the flowers in place (thanks to Peggy!). Some of our friends joined us, too: Beverly, Marcia, Ellie, Patricia and Peggy. They brought special treats for the occasion and everyone was full of excitement. We would be talking to these three ladies about the past. What was it like here in Niagara Falls so many years ago? What was it like growing up as first generation Americans? As the daughters of Italian immigrants?

I picked up all three of the ladies myself—as they are not doing much driving these days. First, my grandmother, Jean Borgatti, and then her friend, Phyllis Infantino. I dropped them off at the library and then picked up Lucy Rainville.

Finally, we were ready to begin. But, of course, in the beginning there would be food. I had made a fresh green salad and some Italian Ricotta cake for the dessert. We also had pizza, beautifully colored Mediterranean style vegetable chips, bruschetta, and homemade biscotti. We started to eat and then that was when all of the wonderful stories began to come forth.

All three of our ladies are of Italian ancestry. Their parents had come to America before they were born. My grandmother, Jean Fortuna Borgatti, was born in Niagara Falls to Francesco Fortuna (of Rieti, Italy) and Clementina Ventresca (of L'Aquila, Italy). She grew up deep in the heart of Niagara's, Little Italy, on 19th Street. Her name was originally "Gina", however after much teasing in school a kind-hearted teacher, Mrs. Flint, took her to City Hall one day to change her name to the more American-sounding "Jean Ann." My grandmother will be turning 90 in just a few months. Phyllis Palmeri Infantino, my grandmother's friend, was born in Niagara Falls to Vincenzo Palmeri (of Gimigliano, Italy) and Mary Constance Rotella (whose family was from Calabria). Phyllis grew up on 11th and Memorial Parkway. She is 90 years old. Theresa Lucia Massimiliani Rainville—yet another of my grandmother's friends—was born in Niagara Falls to Giambattista Massimiliani (of La Marche, Italy) and Elvira Orlandi (also of La Marche, Italy). Her father had first gone to Argentina but ended up in Niagara Falls. Like my grandmother, while in school, a teacher also anglicized Lucy's name and took the "i" from the end so she would be called "Massimilian." She said she was often mistaken for an Armenian for that lack of an ending "i." Lucy lived on 19th Street across from my grandmother. Lucy is 92 years old.

Talk was very easy with these ladies. Phyllis, jokingly, said that the "talk is still easy…but the walk is not…for women in their nineties…." They certainly remembered so many things from their childhoods—things that are now history.

We heard stories of the City Market…for it was such an integral part of their lives. Usually Monday, Wednesday and Friday were market days. They would take a little wagon with them to transport their goods. The market was open winter and summer. Their mothers would go through the market three times in one day; first to see what was there, then to price things and finally to buy things. Money was scarce and these women knew best how to stretch a penny. Lucy's mother, Elvira, would often buy the cracked eggs that no one else wanted and she would immediately make homemade macaroni with them. My grandmother wished that she could remember the German farmer who only carried double-yolk eggs! They were delicious! They also spoke of their mothers buying half a pig. There was so much they could make with half of a pig: sausage, capicola, prosciutto, and sopressata. After being prepared, the meats would be hung to dry up in the attic. Some of the meat would be placed into a crock with oils. Then there was the mention of a special bakery called Morinello's that preceded Trusello's. And always those Palermo chickens. Also sold in the City Market, the stench of the chicken cages would hit them immediately. Some said they would buy the chickens while still alive and carry them home with their heads popping out of the top of a paper bag. However, Lucy mentioned that her mother never brought home a live chicken. She would always have it butchered in the shop.

I think we learned the most about their mothers from their stories. It seemed their mothers' work was never-ending. I don't know how I can ever complain again. Monday was probably the most dreaded of all of the days of the week for it was Wash Day. But the children were excited as it was also Chicken Soup Day, for the soup would just simmer on the stove as the women scrubbed the laundry. Phyllis mentioned that she had no idea what time her mother actually started the laundry as she was already hard at work by 5 am. It was such a long and grueling affair doing laundry back in the 1920's and 1930's. Ellie chimed in with a humorous story of her own concerning her mother's laundry days. She would hang the laundry out to dry outside their third floor apartment window. In the winter the clothes would freeze and her mother would bring the frozen laundry back inside and hang the items over a chair to melt. It was nothing like doing laundry today.

It seems the women did most of the work around the home. Many of the men worked long hours on the railroad and in other labor-oriented positions. I was surprised to learn that the women also usually made the sausages—well, at least in these three women's families. They also recalled a special machine to grind the meat. Marcia's family had a funnel that was specifically made with an opening wide enough for a thumb. They also remember how the casings would have to soak. The men, however, usually made the wines. Whether it was legal or not, wines were made in the Italian homes at Niagara Falls. Ellie's father had a cherry press and made wine from the cherries.

We also talked about the cicoria foraging—well, that was mostly in the car, as we kept passing fields filled with the flowers. How delicious the greens are in the perfect recipe! And how this day, of all days, would have been so perfect to pull off the side of the road and pick some.

These lovely ladies were so proud of their heritage and the contributions made by other Italian-Americans in our community. All three of them are professional women—Lucy was a social studies instructor at Niagara Falls High School, Phyllis was the owner and manager of the Mar- Kay Shop on Pine Avenue, and my grandmother was a nurse and a professor of Nursing at Niagara University, as well as the first female Democratic legislator in Niagara County. They worked hard to break through all sorts of barriers—both gender and ethnic— in order to succeed in life. Their world was one that did not encourage women to pursue careers.

Finally I had one more request. After having asked them so many questions I was still so curious to know whatever their secrets were to longevity. What did they do all of these years that allowed them to live so well into their nineties? It was clear that these three women had broken a few other barriers, as well…for most Americans will never live as long as Lucy, Jean and Phyllis.

In unison (and unrehearsed!) they said the same things: hard work and good food. They also added some other things such as: a diet filled with fresh fruits and vegetables, crossword puzzles, reading, spending time with friends and taking naps. I think I liked what Phyllis said best of all, though. She suddenly interrupted everyone and said something very profound: *I have had a love affair with food my entire life.* And we all knew exactly what she meant. Food is not merely sustenance. Food is an expression of our cultural heritage. Food is life.

Funnel used for making homemade sausage
Courtesy Marcia Buzzelli

RICETTE

Prima Colazione

"Simple" Italian Breakfast Recipe (Eleanor Migliazzo Novara)
[A comforting favorite fast breakfast dish]

My father, Rocco Migliazzo and mother, Catherine Mariano Migliazzo didn't drink the actual Italian Espresso Coffee. They made a strong American Coffee. My mother would boil the water for the coffee in a small 2-quart pot and then add the strong coffee and lower the heat. She would strain the coffee into their cups and then with the left over coffee she would save the rest for a simple breakfast for me and my siblings.

[This recipe is an individual serving]

1 slice of Italian bread	1 cup of warm milk
1 teaspoon sugar	½ cup of strong Italian coffee

Break apart the thick slices of Italian bread and place in the milk. Use a hand strainer, pour the strong coffee into the bowl of milk containing the pieces of bread and sprinkle a teaspoon of sugar over the top.

I had forgotten about this breakfast until I visited my cousins in Gimigliano, Calabria Catanzaro, Italy in 2013. The first morning we sat down for breakfast, my cousin Antionetta Paonessa Rocca (my mother's first cousin's daughter on the Mariano side of the family) prepared this for us. It was very emotional because I hadn't had this since I was a child. My parents were forever in my thoughts throughout that day.

Rocco Migliazzo and Caterina (Mariano) Migliazzo
Wedding Photo – September 26, 1928

Antipasto

Prosciutto e Melone (traditional dish of Abbruzzo)

1 cantaloupe seeded and cut into 8 wedges

8 thin slices of prosciutto

Remove the flesh from the rind of the cantaloupe. Wrap the prosciutto around the cantaloupe wedges. Serve cold.

Antipasti (Francesco Fortuna)

Lettuce

Sliced tomatoes

Meats: Genoa Salami, Prosciutto, Capicola

Hard-boiled eggs

Italian olives

Roasted red peppers

Pepperoncini

Stuffed Cherry Peppers (clean out seeds and scoop out, drain oil from canned anchovies, stuff anchovies into peppers with a chunk of mozzarella or provolone cheese)

Eggplant caponata

Chunks of provolone cheese

Italian bread

Line a large oval platter with chopped lettuce leaves (or on individual plates)

Roll up the meats

Place chunks of cheese, peppers, pepperoncini, Italian olives and eggs around the platter

Place the caponata in a smaller bowl and place on the platter

Serve with a loaf of Italian bread

Insalata

Aldo's Own "Caesar Salad" for two (Aldo Evangelista)

4 oz. of La Hacienda Homemade Italian Dressing

1 oz. of Pecorino Romano grated

3 fillet of anchovies or one teaspoon full of anchovies paste

The yolk of a fresh egg or a tablespoonful of pasteurized egg product

One cup of croutons or more if so desired

One head of Romaine lettuce, fresh and crispy

Wash lettuce. Cut into bite-sized pieces. Place into a strainer basket and put aside. Place the dressing in a large bowl, add the anchovy fillets and mash them down with the back of a spoon. Add the yolk of the egg and the grated Pecorino Romano, stir vigorously until all ingredients are well mixed. Add the lettuce and the croutons. Toss until all lettuce is coated with the dressing and serve. Additionally, fresh chopped garlic, fresh ground black pepper or more grated Pecorino Romano can be added if so desired.

Jillian's Salad Dressing (Jillian Kratts, great great granddaughter of Francesco and Clementina Fortuna)

½ cup olive oil

2 tbsp red wine vinegar

Salt to taste

Black pepper to taste

Garlic salt sprinkle

Onion salt sprinkle

Onion powder sprinkle

Garlic powder sprinkle

2 cloves of chopped garlic

½ teaspoon sugar

Juice of half a lemon

Italian seasoning sprinkle

Mix all in a jar and shake.

Verdura

Traditional Recipes for Dandelion Greens (Cicoria), Italian Style

Dandelion Salad

¼ cup extra virgin olive oil

1 tablespoon red wine vinegar (add small amount of sugar to vinegar bottle)

3 large cloves of garlic, chopped

Salt and pepper to taste

Dandelion greens (about 2 cups)

Wash dandelion leaves thoroughly. Remove tender leaves from the tougher stems. Add garlic.

Drizzle with olive oil and vinegar. Salt and pepper to taste.

Sautéed Dandelion Greens

1 large bunch of dandelion greens

1 chopped garlic clove

4 tbsp extra virgin olive oil

Salt and pepper to taste

Dash of red pepper flakes

Rinse greens thoroughly. Squeeze dry. Cut into 3 inch pieces. Add to hot frying pan: olive oil, garlic and greens. Sauté for 8-10 minutes. Add salt and pepper to taste and red pepper flakes.

Dandelion Greens, Eggs

4 eggs—separate whites from yolks, set aside

Parmesan cheese freshly grated

Salt and pepper to taste

Poach eggs in skillet on medium heat with cooked greens (that have been sautéed). Make small wells in the greens. Pour the yolks into the wells to poach. Cover. The steam from the greens will poach the eggs. Whisk and pour egg whites around the edge of the skillet. Add salt and pepper to taste. Top with grated parmesan cheese.

Zucchini Blossoms (Marcia Buzzelli)

With their lovely, delicate flavor and gorgeous orange-yellow hue, zucchini blossoms are an evocative summer treat. Choose plump and fresh ones and use as soon as possible.

They are served battered.

Dip 10 to 12 blossoms in a mixture of 2/3 cup flour, 1 cup club soda, 1 beaten egg, and ¼ tsp salt. Fry in small batches in vegetable oil until golden. Drain on a cooling rack set over paper towels. Serve immediately.

May also be served chopped into an omelet with cheese or stir fried in a wok with other summer vegetables.

Zucchini Fritatta (Jean Fortuna Borgatti)

One zucchini (not too thick, but preferably long)

One onion

Handful of cleaned mushrooms

5 eggs

Italian cheese

Clean and chop up vegetables and fry in olive oil. In separate bowl, scramble eggs well.

Add to vegetables. Once it has begun to cook, add cheese. Cook until firm and mixture is set around the edges.

If using an oven-proof pan, place in oven under broiler to crisp up. If you are not using an oven-proof pan place large plate over the top of the pan and carefully flip over onto the plate and then back into the pan. Mixture will be reversed. Cook other side a few minutes.

Roman String Beans and Potatoes (Jean Fortuna Borgatti)

Roman Beans (1 ½ pounds)

Potatoes (two or three pounds of potatoes)

Olive Oil

Dash of garlic powder

Salt and Pepper

Clean beans and then snap in half. Toss them into boiling water. Cook for 7-10 minutes in boiling water. Throw in the potatoes that have been peeled and cut into large chunks. Cook for an additional fifteen minutes. Drain. Add salt and pepper, drizzle olive oil and a pinch of vinegar (if you would like)

Our family would have this on Fridays with tuna (mixed with onions, olive oil and a dash of wine vinegar).

Cavolfiore dorato e fritto (Clementina Ventresca Fortuna)

1 cauliflower

¾ cup flour

2 eggs beaten

Oil

Salt and pepper

Separate cauliflower into florets. Cook in boiling water until tender but still crisp. Do not overcook. Place in colander to drain. Roll in flour, add salt and pepper. Dip into egg. Heat oil and fry until golden.

Melanzane alla parmigiana (Eggplant Parmigiana) (Jean Fortuna Borgatti)

1 Eggplant

1 Egg

½ cup Flour

Salt and Pepper to taste

2 cups homemade tomato sauce

1 lb ball, fresh Mozzarella

½ cup of freshly grated Parmigiano-Reggiano

Preheat oven to 350.

Cut eggplant into ½ inch slices. Leave skin on. Salt each side. Lay in sink in a large colander for about 30 minutes with something heavy on top to drain bitterness. Rinse salt off. Dry on towels. Dip into egg. Dip into flour sprinkled with salt and pepper. Bake in oven with a little olive oil or sauté on stovetop in olive oil.

Drizzle olive oil on a cookie sheet. Layer sauce, eggplant, slice of mozzarella and sprinkle with Parmigiano-Reggiano. Repeat. Finish with the cheeses on top. Bake until golden brown and bubbly.

Stuffed Artichoke (Clementina Ventresca Fortuna)
One artichoke per person
Pre-made filling (the same as you'd use for stuffed peppers, usually containing cooked rice, tomato, cheese)
Pre-made sauce
Cheese
Peel off outer stems of artichoke. Take out middle section. Cut the bottom so that the artichokes will stand up in pan. Spread the leaves open and drop filling inside. Add sauce to the top of the stuffed artichoke. Put in pan on top of stove that has about an inch and a half of water. Cook about forty minutes.

"Simple" Italian Vegetable Recipes (Eleanor Migliazzo Novara)
These are very comforting dishes I remembered my mother, Catherine (Mariano) Migliazzo, making.

I can't tell you the exact recipe, but I learned to make these vegetable recipes from memory and have enjoyed making them throughout my lifetime.

My mother had a way of combining vegetables that were simply delicious. She never really had a recipe for them, but I found them very easy to remember and make them often. We had this often during the summer months.

Fresh String Beans and Potatoes (Eleanor "Ellie" Migliazzo Novara)
(I call this a one pot and skillet dish)

2 large potatoes (Idaho, Yukon or Russet)

1 pound fresh string beans – trimmed

¼ cup extra-virgin olive oil – you will need more for drizzling over the finished mixture

2 garlic cloves peeled and sliced with salt and freshly ground pepper.

½ onion, peeled and chopped

Several sprigs of Italian parsley chopped

The technique of this recipe is "simple" and fast. You simply -

Peel the potatoes and cut into 1 ½ inch pieces. Pour enough cold water over the potatoes in a large saucepan to cover by about three inches. Bring to a boil over high heat, lower heat to a gentle boil and cook about 8 minutes. Add the string beans and continue cooking until both are tender – about 7 to 8 minutes. Drain the vegetables in a colander. Heat ¼ cup olive oil in a skillet over medium heat. Sauté the garlic and onion and cook until slightly browned, about 1 minute. Slide the drained potatoes and string beans into the skillet, season again (if needed) with salt and pepper and mix together. Drizzle additional olive oil into the vegetables and mix just before serving.

This dish can be served warm or cold. It is simply delicious!!!

Peas and Prosciutto (Eleanor Migliazzo Novara)

[A great side dish]

2 – Tablespoons olive oil

3 – Shallots (or cooking onions), chopped

2 – Garlic cloves, minced

1 – Pound bag frozen peas, thawed

4 – Ounces (about 1/8 inch thick slices) prosciutto or ham, diced

¼ – Cup chopped fresh Italian parsley

Salt and pepper to taste

Heat the oil in a heavy large skillet over medium-low heat. Add the shallots or cooking onions, garlic, salt, and pepper, and sauté until tender, about 1 minute. Add the peas and sauté until heated through, about 5 minutes. Stir in the prosciutto or ham and cook for 1 to 2 minutes. Remove from heat, season with salt and pepper to taste, garnish with parsley, and serve.

Caponata (Frances Buzzelli)
1 ½ to 2 lbs eggplant – unpeeled and cubed
2 large onions
5-6 ribs of celery – chopped into 1 inch cubes
½ cup olive oil
1 can black olives sliced and drained
1 jar stuffed green olives sliced and drained
2 TBSP drained capers
2 sm. cans of tomato sauce
1 medium can crushed tomatoes or 1 lb plum tomatoes skinned and chopped
1 sm. cans tomato paste
½ cup wine vinegar
½ cup sugar
1 tsp Basil chopped
Salt, pepper & red pepper to taste
Sauté onions & celery in oil until soft not browned. Add eggplant, simmer until partially soft.
Add everything else, stir well –

Bring to a slowly to a boil, simmer 30 to 45 min covered until all flavors are blended & consistency is slightly thickened.

Let cool at room temperature covered.

Keeps 3-4 weeks refrigerated or can be frozen

Canned Eggplant (Velma DiMarco)

Cut eggplant into slices (1/4 inch thick); salt and drain overnight. Mix equal parts of cider vinegar and water and bring to a boil. Drop eggplant slices a little at a time in pot. When it comes to a boil again, turn slices for a minute. Remove and place on paper towels to drain when all are cooked. Start to fill jars by putting a little olive oil on bottom of jars. Then layer eggplant. Season every layer with oregano, crushed red pepper, and garlic (a small clove or slices). Fill jars with olive oil and cap. Refrigerate before serving.

Polenta

Polenta with Red Beans (Joseph and Michele Fortuna)

1 ½ cups of cornmeal

4 ½ cups of water

1 teaspoon salt

2 cans red kidney beans (16 oz.)

1 large red onion diced

6 cloves garlic minced

Salt and pepper to taste

Sauté onion and garlic in olive oil until soft. Add kidney beans and sauté about 2 minutes. Boil water in large saucepan. Add cornmeal, water and salt. Then add kidney bean, onion and garlic mixture. (Start the cornmeal mixture by slowly adding the cornmeal to the water continuously stirring with wooden spoon to avoid lumps.) Cook 8 to 10 minutes until you see an oatmeal consistency. Pour mixture into a shallow baking sheet. Cool until firm (10 to 15 minutes). Cut and serve with red sauce.

Zuppa

"Simple Italian Soup Recipe" (Eleanor Migliazzo Novara)

[A comforting favorite fast soup dish especially when we were sick with a cold. This was always soothing and comforting. -Some call this Egg Drop Soup-]

1 – Quart of Water   1

– slightly beaten egg

1 – Tablespoon Italian Parsley chopped

Salt & Pepper to your taste

1 – Bouillon cube (or ½ cup chicken soup stock)

Grated Italian cheese of your choice

½ – Cup pastina (macaroni), (either Acini di Pepe or Rosa Marina)

In a saucepan, boil your pastina in a quart of water. When the macaroni is al dente, strain in a colander and return it to the same pan. Add a quart of water, bouillon cube (or chicken broth) and salt and pepper to taste. Bring to a boil and let simmer about 5 minutes, and keep stirring the beaten egg so that it doesn't coagulate.

Serve with a sprinkle of Italian parsley and some grated Italian cheese.

Brodo di polo (chicken broth) (Jean Fortuna Borgatti)

One 3 pound chicken (washed with cold water)

2 or 3 celery ribs

1 large carrot

1 onion, peeled

Fresh parsley

1 bay leaf

Salt and pepper to taste

Place all ingredients in stockpot. Add enough cold water to cover by 2 inches. Boil over high heat, reduce to low, simmer half-covered for about three hours. Intermittently skim off the fat that boils to the top. Remove the chicken after one hour. Cool the chicken. Remove skin. Pull meat from bones. Discard the skin but return the bones to the pot. Reserve the chicken meat for another use. Continue simmering the broth for about two more hours. When done, strain the broth.

Italian Wedding Soup (Jean Fortuna Borgatti)

Head of endive

Chicken broth (already made)

Prepare ahead—cook ½ box (about 8 oz) of rosamarina or acini di pepe pasta (or other small pasta). Boil pasta in plenty of hot water. When cooked, drain and run cold water through in a colander. Set aside in a bowl.

Boil water. Add washed endive leaves. Boil for around ten minutes. Drain. When cool, squeeze into a ball. Cut with knife both ways.

For meatballs:

½ lb pork

½ lb veal

½ cup regular bread crumbs

Small sprinkle of nutmeg

½ teaspoon salt

Sprinkling of black pepper

½ cup Parmigiano-Romano cheese

½ tsp fresh or dried parsley

1 or 2 eggs (depending on size)

Add more bread crumbs if mixture is too soft.

Mix all ingredients together.

Place 2 tbsp oil in a small bowl.

Rub oil on your hands. Periodically add more oil to your hands and to meatballs as you roll the mixture into tiny balls.

Place meatballs on cookie sheet. Bake at 350 degrees for just long enough to firm meatballs. About 5 minutes. Set aside to cool. Add to hot chicken broth. Then add endive, pastina and diced carrots. Cook 10-12 minutes.

Lentil Soup (Phyllis Ventresca Tecchio)

Olive oil

1 pound lentils

1/2 cup barley

1 onion, chopped

Clove of garlic, diced

2 ribs of celery, chopped

2 large carrots, chopped

Half a pound of chopped pancetta

Salt and pepper to taste

Italian cheese

In sauce pan, sauté onion, garlic, celery and pancetta in olive oil.

Add the lentils and sauté for about 3 minutes.

Add 8 cups of water. Add chopped carrots. Cook for about an hour. Add four more cups of water. Add 1/2 cup of barley. Simmer an additional two hours on very low heat. Add more water as needed. Add salt and pepper to taste. Top with Italian cheese. Serve with crusty Italian bread and a green salad.

Beans and Greens Soup (Jean Fortuna Borgatti)

2 cloves garlic, chopped (do not cook garlic too long, it will become bitter)

1 onion, chopped (cook until soft)

2 cups chicken stock

Cleaned and chopped greens (spinach, endive or escarole)

Italian cannellini beans (if in a can, drain and rinse)

Crushed red pepper

Dash of white wine

Italian cheese

Sauté onion in olive oil. Then sauté garlic in olive oil. Add chicken stock. Boil. Add chopped greens. Add Italian white beans. Cook through. Sprinkle with crushed red pepper. Add a dash of white wine and simmer. Add cheese before serving.

Ditalini Soup (Jean Fortuna Borgatti)

¼ lb pancetta, chopped

Chicken broth (8 cups)

Ditalini

Cannellini beans (one can drained and rinsed)

Celery, chopped (two)

Onion, chopped

Potatoes, chopped (two)

Carrots, chopped (two)

Pureed Tomatoes (one can)

Fry up chopped pancetta until golden brown. Add broth and all vegetables. Bring to a boil. Add ditalini and cook until done.

Salsa

A Basic Italian Sauce (Jean Fortuna Borgatti)

Olive oil

Onion, chopped

Garlic, chopped

Can crushed tomatoes (my grandmother prefers Red Pack brand, or Marzano)

Tomato paste

Fresh chopped parsley and basil (a handful)

Salt and pepper to taste

Sauté onion first. Add garlic (just until soft). Add tomatoes. Cook for about an hour. Add tomato paste. Simmer on stove for several hours. Stir periodically to prevent burning sauce.

You can also add meat drippings to this sauce.

Carne

Marina Chicken (Felix and Clara Palermo)

Cut up fryer

Paprika

Oil

Salt and Pepper

Mint leaves

Clove garlic, minced

½ glass sherry, dry

½ cup diced celery

1 diced green pepper

Dip the chicken pieces in paprika mixed with oil, then place in roasting pan. Add the other ingredients, and place in cool place overnight. When ready to cook, place in 325 degree oven, adding a little oil. Bake for 1 ½ hour.

Add tomato sauce and bake for an additional 20 minutes.

Meatballs (Jean Fortuna Borgatti)

Olive oil

Chopped onion

Chopped garlic

Egg

Fresh parsley

Stale Italian bread (about two slices)

Milk or water (enough to make bread soggy)

1 pound ground beef

½ pound ground pork

½ pound ground veal

Salt and pepper to taste.

Preheat oven to 350 degrees.

Soak bread until soggy. Squeeze out liquid. Add to meat mixture.

Add onions, garlic, herbs, and an egg. Salt and pepper to taste.

Drizzle olive oil over baking sheet. Shape meatballs in your hands to whatever size preferred.

Bake in olive oil for about a half hour. Then put meatballs in sauce. Some Italians just place freshly rolled meatballs right in sauce to cook.

Augie's Homemade Sausage Recipe from Dec. 1993

15 lbs of course ground once pork

1 oz course black pepper

2 oz salt

½ oz red pepper flakes

¾ oz fennel seeds

8 oz water

Mix together; fry a small amount to taste. Than make patties or stuff casings.

Brasciole (Joseph and Michele Fortuna)

6 oz. salami (chopped)

6 oz. capicola (chopped)

6 oz. prosciutto (chopped)

9 oz. Romano Cheese

.8 oz dry rosemary

½ cup chopped parsley

5 lbs pork loin (sliced thin and pound out)

2 cups bread crumbs

4 cloves fresh garlic minced

4 oz pine nuts

4 eggs hardboiled, then quartered

Mix salami, capicola, prosciutto, cheese, rosemary, parsley, bread crumbs, pine nuts.

Add a little bit of water to mixture to make moist.

Lay out 4 inches by 8 inches pieces of pounded pork. Spread a layer of mixture about ¼ inch thick on each pieces of pork. Put ¼ egg at the end and roll it up and tie with a string. Brown with olive oil all sides when browned. Set aside. Put in roasting pan and cover with red sauce. Cover and put in oven at 375 degrees for 45 minutes to an hour.

Veal Parmigiana (Velma DiMarco)

1-1/2 lbs veal cutlets

Put in bag:

1 cup bread crumbs

½ teaspoon salt

¼ teaspoon pepper

½ teaspoon garlic powder

1 tablespoon parmesan cheese

1 egg, beaten

Spaghetti Sauce

Mozzarella Cheese

Salt very lightly and sprinkle flour on both sides of veal. Beat 1 egg with 1 teaspoon water and dip veal. Let drip and shake veal in bag of crumbs. Fry slowly until brown and drain on paper towel. Put veal in shallow pan. Cover each piece with spaghetti sauce. Bake covered for 20 minutes at 350 degrees. Then shut off oven. Place a slice of mozzarella cheese on each cutlet and cover pan again. Let pan remain in hot oven until cheese is melted.

Italian Meat Sauce (Velma DiMarco)

½ lb ground chuck

½ lb ground pork

1 medium onion, minced

2 garlic cloves, minced

Olive oil

1- 6 oz can tomato paste

1 cup water

2 -29 oz cans tomato sauce

1 teaspoon crushed basil

1 bay leaf

Salt

Sugar

¼ cup parmesan cheese

Heat olive oil in sauce pan. Sauté onion and garlic for 2 minutes. Then add ground chuck and pork. Cook until brown. Add tomato paste and water. Stir until dissolved. Add tomato sauce, crushed basil, bay leaf, salt to taste, and a pinch of sugar. Simmer, uncovered, all ingredients for about 2 hours or until thickened. If sauce becomes too thick, add more water. When done, stir Parmesan cheese into sauce and use sauce as needed.

Chicken Cacciatore (Velma DiMarco)

1 ½ lbs boneless chicken*, cut into bite-size pieces

1 large onion, cut into thin wedges

1 large green pepper, thinly sliced

½ lb fresh mushrooms, sliced

Olive oil

1-14-16oz can stewed tomatoes

1-8 oz can tomato sauce

1 cup water

Salt, pepper, garlic powder to taste

8 oz thin spaghetti

Heat olive oil in large fry pan. Saute onion, green pepper, and mushrooms for about 5-7 minutes. Remove from pan and add chicken to fry pan. Cook chicken for about 5 minutes or until lightly brown. Return vegetable mixture to pan and add stewed tomatoes, water, and tomato sauce. Season with salt, pepper and garlic powder to taste. Simmer until sauce thickens enough to pour over spaghetti. Cook spaghetti according to package directions. Drain and place on a warm platter. Top with chicken cacciatore mixture and serve.

*1 ½ lbs stewing veal may be substituted for chicken

Frutti di mare

Seven Seas Christmas Stew (Barbara Coppock)

As the number of "cooks dwindled I was trying to make my life easier as I "inherited" Christmas Eve. I came across this recipe which allowed me to spend one day in the kitchen (instead of one week)!

2 tablespoons olive oil or salad oil

3 cloves garlic, minced

1 can (28 oz.) Italian plum tomatoes

2 bottles (8oz each) clam juice

1 teaspoon dried parsley flakes

1 teaspoon dried basil leaves

½ teaspoon ground black pepper

¼ teaspoon crushed red pepper

2 dozen littleneck clams

1 dozen mussels

¾ pound large shrimp

½ pound sea scallops

½ pound cleaned squid

¼ pound flounder fillet

¼ pound cod or scrod fillet

1 loaf Italian bread

About 1 ½ hours before serving:

In 8-quart Dutch oven or saucepot over medium heat, in hot olive or salad oil, cook garlic until tender but not browned. Stir in tomatoes with their liquid, clam juice, parsley flakes, basil leaves, black pepper, and crushed red pepper; over high heat, heat to boiling. Reduce heat to medium-low; cover and simmer 30 minutes, stirring occasionally.

Meanwhile, with stiff brush, scrub clams and mussels under running cold water to remove any sand; remove beards from mussels. Shell and devein shrimp; rinse with running cold water. Rinse scallops with running cold water to remove sand from crevices. Cut squid crosswise into ½ inch thick slices. Cut flounder and cod into 1 inch chunks.

After sauce has simmered 30 minutes, add clams and mussels to Dutch oven. Over medium-high heat, cook, covered, until shells just begin to open, stirring occasionally, about 5 minutes. Stir in shrimp, scallops, squid, flounder, and cod. Over medium-high heat, heat to boiling. Cook 1 minute or until fish flakes easily when tested with fork and shrimp and scallops turn opaque throughout.

To serve, spoon stew into 6 large bowls. Serve with Italian bread.

Note: In honor of the Italian tradition of serving 7 kinds of seafood on Christmas Eve.

Stuffed Clams / Clams Casino (Marcia Buzzelli)

(Como recipe given to my mom by a waitress from Como Barbara Salerno)

Sauce

2 quarts of tomatoes

1 cup tomato paste

3 cloves of garlic, brown in oil

1 onion

2 bay leaves

Use part of sauce for topping at end

Cook together

2 cans of anchovies

3 cans chopped clams

Oregano

1 ¼ cup cooked rice place in sauce

Add

1 ½ cups of bread crumbs, 2 eggs, grated cheese, parsley and stuff clam shells than top with sauce, mozzarella cheese and bake until hot.

Baccala (Dominick Muto)

1 1/2 pounds of salted cod, soaked for three days in cold water, changing the water each day (or buy already soaked and frozen. Then thaw under stream of cold water.)

1 cup olive oil

2 medium Spanish onions, chopped

2 tablespoons dried pepper flakes

1 tablespoon black pepper

2 tablespoons paprika

Parmesan cheese to taste

In a deep frying pan pour oil into pan until it's about a quarter-inch deep. Add onions and pepper flakes, pepper and paprika. After onions are browned add fish, and add about two inches of water into the pan. Simmer about two hours until fish breaks into small slivers. Serve over cooked pasta, garnished with parmesan cheese

Pasta

Chitarra (guitar) Spaghetti (Marcia Buzzelli)

In the Abruzzo region of Italy one of the specialties is Chitarra pasta. They have been handmade in the region since 1800. Durable stainless-steel wires can be adjusted for tension to ensure precise, even cutting. The Chitarra is usually double sided. It cuts two different widths of pasta through wires suspended in a beechwood frame. A sheet of dough is placed on the wires and using a special beechwood rolling pin over the dough; it is pressed through the wires to cut the pasta. Mine is only one sided and I use a regular rolling pin.

Recipe:

Ingredients: slightly over 1 pound of semolina flour, 4 eggs, water, oil, and salt

Make a fountain with half the flour on the kitchen table, put all the ingredients into the center and mix thoroughly, add a little water and slowly the rest of the flour. Work the ball for some minutes, and then let rest for an hour. Roll out the dough in 1/8 inch (2 mm) thick to a size which should not exceed the size of your chitarra unit. Then put the pasta slice on the wires and press with a rolling pin.

Spaghetti L'Amatriciana (Francesco Fortuna)

About a half a pound of salami, prosciutto or bacon

Two onions, sliced and chopped into small pieces

Garlic cloves, chopped

Sauté onions and when almost done add garlic. Do not overcook onion and garlic.

Cut meat into chunks. Fry in olive oil. Cook macaroni (spaghetti). Toss cooked macaroni into pan with fried meat. Add Italian cheese (although my grandfather did not add cheese).

Eat with a lettuce salad containing chunks of tomatoes and cucumbers. Cook pasta al dente.

Gnocchi (Velma DiMarco)

3 medium size potatoes, cut in quarters

1 ¾ cups sifted flour

3 quarts water

Italian meat sauce

2 tablespoons parmesan cheese

Wash, pare, and cook potatoes in boiling, salted water for about 20 minutes or until tender. Dry cooked potatoes over low heat. Mash or rice potatoes; keep hot. Measure sifted flour into a bowl. Make a well in center of flour; add hot mashed potatoes. Mix well to make a soft, elastic dough. Turn dough onto lightly floured surface and knead. Break off small pieces of dough and roll into strips equal to pencil thickness. Cut into pieces about ¾ inch long. Curl each piece by pressing lightly with index finger and pulling the finger along the piece of dough toward you. Boil water in large sauce pan. Gradually add Gnocchi, about ½ at a time. Cook, uncovered about 8-10 minutes or until tender and come to surface. Drain. Mix Gnocchi with Italian meat sauce and grated parmesan cheese. Serve immediately.

Manicotti (Velma DiMarco)

4 eggs

¼ cup water

¾ cup unsifted flour (fork stir to aerate before measuring)

¼ teaspoon salt

Spaghetti sauce

In small mixing bowl, beat together all ingredients until smooth. Place in skillet with a rounded bottom (8 inches across top) over low heat until a few drops of water evaporate. For each pancake, lightly brush skillet with melted butter, margarine, or salad oil; pour batter from ¼ cup measuring cup filled a little over half full (2 ½ tablespoons) into hot, greased skillet, lifting and rotating as you pour batter in order to spread batter over entire pan. If batter is too thick, stir in a little water. Cook just long enough to set—about 20 seconds. Turn pancakes and cook long enough to set other side. As pancakes are cooked, stack them on a plate. Put some spaghetti sauce into bottom of shallow dish. Fill each manicotti and place side by side in dish. Cover each manicotti with spaghetti sauce. Cook at 300-325 degrees for 20 minutes.

Filling:

1-15 oz container ricotta cheese

¼ teaspoon salt

¼ teaspoon pepper

¼ teaspoon garlic powder

¼ teaspoon crushed basil

Parmesan cheese to taste

2 eggs

Shredded mozzarella cheese

Beat together all ingredients till fluffy. Spoon heaping tablespoon into middle of pancake. Sprinkle with shredded mozzarella cheese. Fold end and roll to close.

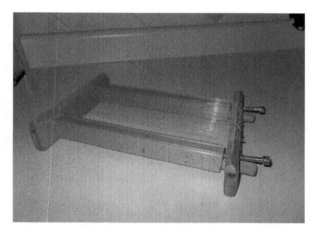

A Chitarra

(Courtesy Marcia Buzzelli)

Formaggio

Homemade Ricotta (Cathy Peuquet)

1 gallon whole milk

1 quart buttermilk

½ teaspoon salt

1 pint of heavy cream

(You can halve recipe.)

Line a large sieve with cheesecloth, place over a large bowl. In a large saucepan slowly bring the milk, heavy cream, buttermilk and salt to a gentle simmer on medium/low heat. Stir now and then until little bubbles form on the surface, about ten minutes. Let bubble gently without stirring, until temperature reaches 170 degrees on an instant read thermometer, about 5 minutes. Curdles will begin to form. Remove from heat, let sit out without stirring for 10 minutes. Pale green whey will separate from the mixture. Then, gently pour the mixture into the lined sieve, including the bits on the bottom. Let drain until all of the liquid runs off, but the cheese is still moist. (I lift the cheesecloth and squeeze gently to remove liquid faster after about 30 minutes. Draining process takes about an hour. Chill ricotta covered until ready to serve. Will firm up in the refrigerator. Will last in refrigerator for at least 4-5 days.

Ravioli Filling (Jean Fortuna Borgatti)

You can also use this for lasagna or to stuff into shells.

2 containers Ricotta Cheese

Parsley

Garlic Salt

Minced onion

Rum

Sherry

Anisette

2 eggs

Mozzarella Cheese

Romano Cheese

Dolce

Old Style Pizzelle made with iron over a fire

7-8 cups flour

6 eggs

2 cups of sugar

¼ cup baking powder

1 stick of butter

2 ounces of anise seeds

Sift flour and baking powder. Melt butter. Set aside. Beat eggs until foamy. Add sugar to eggs and beat. Add cooled butter and anise to egg mixture. Slowly add flour mixing by hand until dough doesn't stick to hands. About 7-8 cups flour. Make balls a little smaller than golf balls. Heat both sides of hand held iron on medium flame until water beads off of iron. Use 3 balls placing them towards center of iron. Squeeze tightly for about 30 seconds on each side. They should fall off when the iron opens, or you can ease off with a knife.

Pizzelle made with electric iron

1 ½ cups flour

1 tsp baking powder

3 eggs, beaten

¾ cups of sugar

¾ cups butter, melted

2 tsp pure vanilla extract

1 tsp anise seeds

Powdered confectionary sugar

Preheat pizzelle baker. Red light will flash on and off when it is ready. In bowl, sift flour and baking powder. Lightly spray the pizzelle grids with nonstick spray or brush with vegetable oil. Beat eggs, sugar. Add melted butter, vanilla extract, anise seeds. Add the flour mixture. Beat until smooth. Add by teaspoon (or use cookie scoop) and drop on griddle. Close lid and secure. Should only take between 25-30 seconds. Your first few may be "practice" cookies. Open up lid and they will fall off. Or you can push off with a butter knife. Cool on kitchen towel. You can cut away the edges if you want to make them all alike in appearance. Then stack on a plate. This recipe makes about 25-30 pizzelle.

Biscotti (Jean Fortuna Borgatti)

3 cups sugar

3 cups Crisco

12 eggs

2 cups milk

8 tsp baking powder

12 cups flour

8 tsp vanilla

4 oranges (juice and rind)

Add flour and baking powder and vanilla

Bake at 375 degrees for 10 minutes.

Do not let them get too brown. When the cookies are cool enough to handle, slice each 1 crosswise into 1/2-inch slices. Place the slices cut side up back onto the baking sheet. Bake for an additional 6 to 10 minutes on each side. Cookie slices should be lightly toasted.

Frosting:

Juice of one orange

Juice of one lemon

1 box of confectionary sugar

Ricotta Cheese Pie (Buzzellis)

Pastry Crust:

2 cups of flour

2/3 cup shortening

6 Tbsp very cold water

2 Tbsp sugar

Mix as for pie crust and roll out a little thick. Put in glass 10 inch pie pan.

Filling:

4 eggs

1 cup sugar

¾ cup light cream

3 cups whole milk ricotta

4 Tbsp flour

1 lemon, use rind and juice

Pinch of salt

Beat eggs, add sugar, and a pinch of salt. Add lemon juice, rind, ricotta, flour and cream. Beat thoroughly. Pour into crust.

Bake at 350 degrees for one hour. Turn off the temperature and leave in oven with door open to cool.

Sesame Cookies (Ciccilani) (Velma DiMarco)

¾ cup Crisco

¾ cup sugar

2 or 3 eggs (depending on size)

3 to 4 cups flour (if possible use only 3)

2 teaspoons baking powder

1 teaspoon vanilla

Dash salt

Sesame seeds

Cream together Crisco and sugar. Add eggs, one at a time. Sift together flour, baking powder, and salt; then add to creamed mixture. Add vanilla. Place mixture in refrigerator for ½ hour. Then roll small amounts into strips about 6 inches long. Roll strips over seeds and cut into 1 inch pieces. Bake at 375 degrees until brown.

Cuccidati (Carmela Tosetto)

2 eggs

¼ cup shortening

¾ cup sugar

1-3 teaspoons salt

3 tablespoons baking powder

Grated rind of one lemon

1 cup flour

½ cup evaporated milk

2 ½ to 3 cups of flour

Beat eggs with electric mixer. Add and blend shortening, sugar, salt, baking powder. Gradually add lemon rind and 1 cup flour. Add evaporated milk. Gradually blend in 2 ½ o 3 cups of flour to make pastry dough. Chill until ready to use.

Filling:

1 cup cut up figs

1 cup dates

1/3 cup raisins

¾ cup walnuts

1 whole orange cut up (including rind, remove pits)

¼ teaspoon nutmeg

¼ teaspoon cinnamon

¼ teaspoon ground cloves

¼ teaspoon allspice

Juice of one lemon

2-3 cups honey

2-3 cups water

¼ teaspoon salt

Put first six ingredients through food chopper. In a large pan add to these ingredients spices, lemon juice, honey, water and salt. Cook over medium heat until a soft thick paste. Two tablespoons of rum flavoring may be added at this time.

Roll strips of pastry 3 inches by 10 inches. Fill center and roll up sides to make a 10inch long roll about 1 ½ inches for diameter.

Cut into bars and back at 350 degrees on greased cookie sheets for about 15 minutes.

When cool, frost with butter frosting and decorate with colored sprinkles.

Wine Cookies (Amy Ciambrone Palumbo)

1 cup butter

2 cups sugar

2 egg yolks

5 cups sifted flour

Pinch of salt

2/3 cup sweet wine

1 egg white

Chopped nuts

Mix butter and sugar with yolks until smooth. Add sifted dry ingredients alternating with wine. Mix well. Chill. Roll on floured board and cut into 2 inch rounds. Brush with slightly beaten egg white and sprinkle with nuts. Bake at 325 degrees for ten minutes.

Makes 8 dozen.

Italian "S" Cookies (Velma DiMarco)

5 cups sifted flour

2 tablespoons baking powder

1 teaspoon salt

1 cup sugar

Rind of 1 orange chopped fine

1 cup shortening

3 eggs

1/3 cup orange juice

¼ cup milk

Sift together flour, baking powder, salt, sugar, and orange rind. Cut in shortening as for pie dough. Beat eggs until very fluffy and then add orange juice and milk to eggs. Mix all together and then turn out on floured board. Knead lightly and cut and shape into "S" on greased cookie sheets. Bake at 400 degrees for 8 to 10 minutes.

Cassata (Sicilian Cream Cake) (Patricia DiNieri)

1 sponge cake

1 lb ricotta

½ cup sugar

2 ounces of chocolate, chopped

½ cup brandy

4 ounces candied mixed fruits

Cut cake into three layers, add sugar to cheese and beat. Add orange or apricot brandy. Set aside ½ of filling, to remainder, add chocolate and fruit. Mix well. Spread ½ chocolate mixture over cake. Cover with the second layer. Sprinkle with liquor and spread with the rest of the chocolate and cheese. Set remaining layer on the top and press together firmly. Spread reserved cheese over the top and sides. Decorate with glazed fruit.

Easter Bread (Emily Voelker)

1 pound butter

3 cups sugar

5 envelopes yeast (3 if doing ½ of recipe)

2/3 cup milk

5 pounds flour (7 or 8 cups)

1 tsp salt

1 dozen eggs

1 bottle anise flavoring (2 ounces)

Dyed Easter Eggs (uncooked)

Beat eggs until fluffy (about 15 minutes).

Scald milk—butter—sugar—salt—and cool.

Melt yeast in ½ cup warm water

Put half of the flour in a large pan. Make a well in the flour. Add everything else. Begin kneading. Adding flour as you go. Turn onto board and knead until smooth.

Put in a warm place, covered, and allow to rise until double in bulk.

Knead again. Make braided rolls, etc., and put on a greased sheet. Allow to double in size. Optional: place a dyed (but not cooked or hardboiled) Easter egg in the center of the braided rolls. Bake at 300 degrees for about 50 minutes. The eggs will cook with the bread.

Brush with whole egg before putting into the oven.

Struffoli--Fried Sweet Dough Balls with Honey (Barbara Coppock)

Served on New Year's Day.

4 cups all-purpose flour

½ cup plus 1 tablespoon sugar

Finely grated zest of 1 lemon

Finely grated zest of 1 orange

¼ teaspoon ground cinnamon

Pinch kosher salt

4 large eggs

1 teaspoon vanilla extract

2 tablespoons unsalted butter, cut into small pieces

2 cups honey

Vegetable oil, for frying

Sprinkles, for garnish

Pulse together the flour, 1 tablespoon sugar, the lemon zest, orange zest, cinnamon, and salt in a food processor. Whisk together the eggs and vanilla in a separate bowl. Pour the egg mixture into the food processor with the motor running, and then drop in the butter pieces. Process until a smooth dough forms, about 30 seconds. Knead the dough on a counter a few times, then wrap in plastic and let rest at room temperature for 1 hour.

Make the syrup: Combine the honey, the remaining ½ cup sugar, and 1/3 cup water in a medium skillet over medium heat. Bring to a boil, and cook until syrupy, about 6 to 7 minutes.

In the meantime, heat 1 inch of vegetable oil in a pot or straight-sided skillet to about 365 degrees F, or until a piece of dough sizzles on contact. Pinch off a golf-ball-sized piece of dough, and roll into a rope about ½ inch wide. Cut the rope of dough into pieces the size of a hazelnut and roll into balls. Repeat until all the dough is used.

Fry the struffoli in batches until puffed and deep golden, about 3 to 4 minutes per batch. Drain on a paper-towel-lined baking sheet, and repeat with the remaining struffoli.

Toss the struffoli in the hot honey syrup, in batches, as many at a time as you can fit without crowding. Roll the struffoli in the syrup until well coated, then scoop them up with a slotted spoon or strainer, and drain off the excess syrup. Stack the struffoli in layers on a plate to form a cone, sprinkling each layer with the sprinkles as you stack. Repeat until all the struffoli are coated in the honey syrup and covered in sprinkles. Drizzle the completed stack of struffoli with any remaining syrup, if you wish.

White Cake (Frances Buzzelli)

¾ cup shortening

1 teaspoon vanilla

¾ teaspoon salt

2 cups sugar

3 cups sifted flour

3 teaspoons baking powder

½ cup milk

½ cup cold water

6 egg whites

Cream shortening, sugar and salt, add dry ingredients alternately with milk and water. Last fold in egg whites which have been beaten stiff but not dry—fold in mixture. Bake at 350 degrees for 35 minutes.

VARIOUS FAMILY SAYINGS (AND THEIR MEANINGS)

There were those little sayings…often a mixture of Italian and American English…that somehow made their way into our family vocabulary. Often they are derogatory, or slang terms. In this chapter we tried to remember some of those "sayings" from our own Italian-American families.

Alcuni sono Calabrese e alcuni sono dialetto Sicilian
Some are Calabrese and some are Sicilian dialect – Spoken by the Migliazzo/Mariano/Novara families

Che cosa e? - What is it? (kay-koh-za-eh)

Che su dice? - What are you saying? (kay-su-dee-chay)

Chi succede? - What's happening or slang for who gives? (kee-su chee-day)

Che fai? - What are you doing? (kay-fay)

Che vuoi? - What do you want? (kay-vwoy)

E Che posso fare? – What can I do? (kay-pah-soh-fah-ray) – Chi pochema fare figlio mio? (Sam's mother said it this way in Sicilian dialect)

Perche mi? – Why me? (pehr-keh-may)

Ascoltami! – Listen to me! (ay-scol-ta-mee)

Non dimenticato! - I don't remember or I forgot! (non-dee-mehn-tee-kah-toh)

Aiutami! - Help me! (ay-oo-tah-mee)

Tuo pazzo! - You're crazy! (too-ee-paht-zoh)

E' Puzzi! - It smells! (ee-poot-zee)

Vieni qui adesso! – Get over here now! (vee-yehn-nee koo-ee ah-deh-soh)

Sta' zitto! - Keep your mouth shut! (stah zee-toh)

Ti faccio il malocchio. – I'll put the evil eye on you. (tee fah choh eel mahl och kee oh)

Un po'! – A little bit! (oon poh)

Aspetta uno momento! – Wait a minute! (ah speh tah oo noh mee noo toh)

Salute, per cent' anni! – Cheers, to a hundred years! (sah loot ay, a chehnt ahn nee)

Piano, piano. – Slow down. (pyah-noh Pyah-noh)

Adesso basta! – Enough is enough! (ah-deh-soh Bah-stah)

Ancora! – Again, Still, Yet, More – (an-cho-rah)

Piangia, Piangia! – Cry, Cry – (pee-an-jah) - or - Chonga-chonga! – (chee-on-jah, chee-on-jah)

Scolapiatto – Macaroni strainer! (sco-la-pia-tah) - or scula Pasta (scu-la pa-sta)

Ma peen! - Dish towel! (ma-peen)

Cosi e cosi – So, so - (koh-zee koh-zee)

Mensa e mensa. – half and half. (men-za eh men-za)

Abbruzzese dialect from the Ventresca and Fortuna Families

A banja crook (ah-banjah-crook): "a bunch of crooks," the concluding remark from my great grandfather, Frank Fortuna, to any conversation about politics, politicians, taxes, and the government in general would inevitably be: "All a banja crook!"

Agiada (ah-gia-dah): "butterflies in your stomach"

Brusiata (broo-zhata): a chafing, or burning sensation of the skin (as in a diaper rash)

Chiavalatone (shee-ah-vah-la-tone): a sloppy person

Chooch (ch-oo-ch): from "ciuccio," meaning jackass, dummy, idiot or moron

Coccharilles (coke-uhh-rilles): My great grandmother always said this meaning "knick-knacks"—"dust collectors"

Dondied (done-deed): a dull or stupid person

Facce brute (fah-chay-broo-tah): ugly face

Fuliarille (foo-yah-rille): one who makes decisions or takes action without considering the possible consequences

Goomba (goom-bah): a stereotypical Italian male

Ice-a-box-a (ice-uh-box-ah): refrigerator (ice box)

Junkarille (junk-uh-rille): trinkets

La massa (la-mah-sa): when you over-do something, extravagance

La Donna (la-doh-nah): a beautiful lady

La Monica (la-monicah): a woman, or girl, who keeps to herself; actually means "the nun"

La pranza (la-prahn-zah): large feast accompanying a funeral or wedding

Mala femme: (mahla-femme): a sexy and "bad" woman

Mangia-cake (mahn-jah-cake-a): a non-Italian, meaning one who eats little cakes, or cookies, small appetite

Marone (mah-rrohn): the Madonna (usually used in a derogatory manner)

Mingia (meen-gyah): "holy cow!" or worse...

Power-halls: overalls

Putana: (poo-tah-nah) a lady of the evening

Scustamatta (skoo-stah-mah-tah): generally refers to someone who has no manners

Sfruscione (sss-froo-shone): also generally refers to someone who is lazy or sloppy

Sporcacione (spor-kah-shone): a dirty person

Sta zito (sta-zee-toe): "shut your mouth!"

Testa dura (testa doo-rah): a hard-headed person

From the LaGreca Family

Agiatu (ah-gia-too): indigestion

Chi cha lia? (chee-cha-lee-ya): who is hungry? Who wants some?

Ia (ee-yah): I am!

Disgraziana (diz-gratz-ee-ah-na): disgraceful

From the Nicolla Family

Afunabla (ahh-fah-nah-blah): "aw, forget it!"

From the Interisano Family (Sicilian dialect)

Puta (pooh-tah): a lady of the evening

Stunad (stooh-nahd): a stupid person

From the Buzzelli Family

Zingara (zing-ah-ra): gypsy

From Beverly Bidak

Here is a proverb to remember on a cold winter day.

Sette cosa fa la zuppa. Cura fame, e sette attuta, empie la ventre, netta il dente, fa dormire, fa smaltire, e la quancia la colorire.

Soup does seven things. It appeases your hunger, quenches your thirst, fills your stomach, cleans your teeth, makes you sleep, helps you digest and colors the cheeks.

Made in the USA
Middletown, DE
29 June 2015

IN VIVO MEASUREMENT OF
BODY COMPOSITION IN MEAT ANIMALS

A workshop in the EEC Programme of Coordination of Research on Animal Production, held at the Agricultural and Food Research Council's Meat Research Institute, Langford, Bristol, UK, on 30 November and 1 December 1983

Sponsored by the Commission of the European Communities, Directorate-General for Agriculture, Coordination of Agricultural Research

IN VIVO MEASUREMENT OF BODY COMPOSITION IN MEAT ANIMALS

Edited by

D. LISTER

*Agricultural and Food Research Council, Meat Research Institute,
Langford, Bristol, UK*

ELSEVIER APPLIED SCIENCE PUBLISHERS
LONDON and NEW YORK

ELSEVIER APPLIED SCIENCE PUBLISHERS LTD
Ripple Road, Barking, Essex, England

Sole Distributor in the USA and Canada
ELSEVIER SCIENCE PUBLISHING CO., INC.
52 Vanderbilt Avenue, New York, NY 10017, USA

British Library Cataloguing in Publication Data

In vivo measurement of body composition in meat animals.
1. Meat inspection—European Economic Community countries
I. Lister, D.
636.08′83   TS1975

ISBN 0-85334-319-5

WITH 57 TABLES AND 51 ILLUSTRATIONS

© ECSC, EEC, EAEC, Brussels and Luxembourg, 1984

Publication arrangements by: Commission of the European Communities, Directorate-General for the Information Market and Innovation, Luxembourg.

EUR 9001 EN

LEGAL NOTICE

Printed in Great Britain by Galliard (Printers) Ltd, Great Yarmouth

PREFACE

This publication contains the proceedings of a Workshop held at the Agricultural and Food Research Council's Meat Research Institute, Langford, Bristol, UK, during 30 November and 1 December 1983, under the title **'In vivo Measurement of Body Composition in Meat Animals'**. This meeting was held as a coordination activity of the Commission of the European Communities' Agricultural Research Programme. This activity was the third of its kind. The first, organised by Dr B. Bech Andersen of the National Institute of Animal Science, Copenhagen, was concerned primarily with reviewing techniques (mainly ultrasonic) for describing the carcass characteristics of meat animals (Publication 524, Beretning fra Statens Husdyrbrugsforsøg, Copenhagen). Subsequently a report on the application and evaluation of ultrasonic techniques was commissioned for the CEC Beef Research Programme (Publication EUR 7640 EN).

The meeting reported here was arranged to consider the latest techniques, eg X-ray Computed Tomography, Nuclear Magnetic Resonance Spectroscopy and Neutron Activation Analysis, which are becoming increasingly important as diagnostic aids in human medicine. Much of the experience and expertise in these fields comes, consequently, from the medical world and the CEC is extremely grateful for the substantial contribution made to the meeting by medical colleagues.

In addition to enlisting such help it was hoped to have appreciable involvement from various commercial organisations responsible for the manufacture or sale of appropriate equipment, for it is known that several Member States are actively considering the purchase of suitable equipment. Unfortunately, only two companies responded positively to invitations to take part in the Workshop. Oxford Research Systems Ltd provided demonstration material and active participation via Mr Randal Rue; Siemens Ltd provided a display stand. Potential purchasers of the equipment discussed herein may recognise that applications in animal science represent a secondary and relatively small market which may not attract an appropriate interest from suppliers who will look primarily to the vast potential market in clinical medicine.

The programme was planned by Dr D. Lister and Dr C.A. Miles of the Meat Research Institute, Langford and Dr B. Bech Andersen of the National Institute of Animal Science, Copenhagen. The meeting was organised and the proceedings edited by Dr D. Lister.

The CEC wishes to thank all those who took responsibility for the organisation and running of this Workshop, who chaired sessions, prepared papers and posters, and took part in the discussion.

vii

CONTENTS

SESSION I

INTRODUCTION

Chairman: David Lister

REVIEW AND UP-DATING FROM PREVIOUS MEETING IN COPENHAGEN

B.Bech Andersen

National Institute of Animal Science

Research Center Foulum

Postboks 39, 8833 Ørum Sønderlyng

Denmark

One of the important research objectives drawn up by the CEC Beef Production Commitee has been estimation of body composition in beef. A CEC workshop titled "In Vivo Estimation of Body composition in Beef", was held in Copenhagen 15-16th December, 1981. In total 32 scientists representing research disciplines of genetics, nutrition, carcass quality and electrotechnics participated.

The workshop was divided into three sessions. The presented papers and the concluding discussion were published in the report no. 524 from The National Institute of Animal Science.

1.Practical use and experimental results of in vivo techniques.

The reviews presented demonstrated, that the use of in vivo techniques varied **greatly** between the EEC countries.

In the performance- and progeny tests of bulls subjective scoring for conformation and fleshiness is done routinely in Belgium, France, Holland, Germany and Great Britain. In Great Britain additional fat area measurements are taken with Scanogram ultrasonic equipment. Only in Denmark **is fleshiness** measured routinely by use of Danscanner measurements of M.longissimus dorsi areas.

In most countries experiments have been carried out in the field of in vivo estimation of body composition in beef, and a great number of results were summarized at the meeting.

Also,results from a CEC supported ultrasonic trial in UK and DK were presented. Five ultrasonic machines were compared in that experiment. It was concluded that the repeatability of the scanning results was highest at the 1st lumar vertebra position and higher for fat than muscle measurements. Correlations between ultrasonic measurements and corresponding carcass cut face measurements at 1st lumar vertebra ranged from 0.52 to 0.81 for fat area and from 0.53 to 0.71 for area of M. longissimus dorsi. The percentage of lean in the carcass was best correlated with fat measurements, whereas muscle area was best correlated with dressing percentage and lean/bone ratio. Between the machines there was only a small difference between the correlations averaged over interpreter, location and origin of cattle. Among the operators, however, there was a preference for the "Danscanner" and "Scanogram", which are specifically constructed for use on farm animals.

It was pointed out that those starting scanning work should know the anatomy of the relevant parts of the animal, receive training in the use of the equipment, ensure a good back-up service and arrange periodic checks of the accuracy of their measurements.

2. Potential use of in vivo techniques and their limitations.

Two papers on the potential use of in vivo techniques for breeding purposes were presented. Dr. King grouped in his paper the discussion of alternative prediction methods under the headings:i) practicability, ii) portability, iii) cost and iv) public acceptability. Dr. King also discussed two alternative methods to performance testing comprising sib testing or individual testing followed by gamete storage. Bech Andersen presented results on the use of ultrasonic measurements in a performance test selection, and he discussed the expected difference in long term responses by selection for subcutaneous fat layer vs muscle area.

Dr. van Es discussed the precision needed in nutrition experiments and Dr. Robelin presented results of estimation of body composition by dilution techniques in nutrition experiments.

Finally in that session Dr. Kempster discussed the use of in vivo techniques and their limitations for commercial management and selection of cattle for slaughter.

3. Review of in vivo techniques for possible future use.

The session was concentrated on ultrasonic, computerized tomography and dilution techniques.

H.Skjervold told about the use of Computerized Tomography (CT scanning) in Norway. In a pilot experiment it was possible to describe 85% of the variation in energy content of living pigs. A Siemens CT scanner is now in use in Animal Science in Norway.

Peter Levin concluded in his paper, that the recent advances in ultrasonic imaging seems to be applicable to in vivo evaluation of body composition in beef. However, the new methods discussed, require extensive development before they can be applied to obtain valuable information relevant to animal research.

J.Robelin presented results from French experiments with dilution techniques, and he concluded that this method of measurement of body water is fairly good as long as enough blood samples and body weight recordings are made.

In a reviewing paper C.A.Miles assessed the potential and limitations of some methods not covered in previous present- ations, namely density measurements, dielectric methods, X-ray or gamma radiation, hormone measurements, nuclear magnetic resonance, Potassium-40 and neutron activation analysis.

4. Concluding discussion

The participants in the Copenhagen meeting made the following conclusions:

"The papers presented in the workshop demonstrated very rapid technical development in the area of in vivo tech- niques. The development seems to go in two directions. One for relatively robust and simple equipment easy to apply under farm conditions; and the other for more advanced techniques to be used on testing and research stations. Examples of techniques in the first direction of develop- ment are visual assessments, body measurements and ultra- sonic scanning using machines based on a relatively simple technique. Examples of more advanced techniques are dilution space of D_2O, real-time ultrasonic scanning and computerized tomography from X-ray transmission data.

6

New in vivo techniques have great potential use in several
areas in nutrition, breeding and management. However, objectives and problems can be different. In breeding the
more advanced in vivo techniques can be used in indirect
selection for dressing percentage and carcass quality a-
mong performance tested young bulls. It is not unlikely
that technical development will make it possible in the
future to follow the development of various vital organs,
the deposition of energy and the reaction on different
fasting/refeeding systems. If this proves possible, it
will increase the importance of in vivo techniques drastically. In nutritional experiments there is a great need to
obtain more information on growth and development, including the possibility of being able to follow the continuous changes in histological and chemical body composition
during feeding experiments. A fully developed in vivo
technique could possibly be a substitute to the very
costly procedure of serial slaughtering.

In testing and comparisons of various in vivo techniques,
emphasis must be concentrated on factors like their value
in predicting the components of interest, as well as their
repeatability and reproducibility. The reference basis in
such comparisons will depend on the objective of the technique. Preliminary analyses have shown that some techniques have very favourable cost/benefit ratios and that
considerable investment in equipment can sometimes be
justified. However, further analyses are necessary, based
on various assumptions.

Further development and experiments with in vivo techniques should be given high priority in the near future.
However, development and testing is expensive and, since
the results are of general interest in many countries,
close co-ordination and co-operation between countries
is recommended. When new techniques are tested, it is considered important to build in comparisons with one or
more previously established in vivo methods. It is also
important to follow very closely developments in human
medicine.

The workshop recommends that a seminar is arranged on the
use of in vivo techniques in breeding and nutrition experiments. Such a seminar could give further progress in the
area and also add to the international co-ordination. It
was agreed that a multidisciplinary seminar would be the
most appropriate. The seminar should concentrate especially on further elucidation of problems and prospects of in
vivo techniques in relation to breeding and selection,
and of the role of in vivo techniques in relation to physiological studies and also on cost/benefit analysis. Experts on the use of in vivo techniques in human medicine
should be invited to take part in the seminar and give a
review and evaluation of the use of the techniques in
their field".

In the last two years promising results have been obtained both in the technical development and in the practical application of various techniques to use in animal science. Among experts in genetics, nutrition etc., we can see an increasing interest in use of in vivo techniques as tools in the experimental work. It means that the topic on the program today and tomorrow is very timely, and therefore we are looking forward to a lively discussion and a fruitful exchange of ideas and new knowledge at this Langford CEC Workshop.

THE MEASUREMENT OF BODY COMPOSITION -
OPPORTUNITIES AND REQUIREMENTS IN ANIMAL PRODUCTION

P. Glodek
Institut fur Tierzucht und Haustiergenetik der Universitat
D 3400 Gottingen, F.R.G.

ABSTRACT

Such new techniques as Computed Tomography and Nuclear Magnetic Resonance Spectroscopy have been shown to measure body composition in live animals with much greater accuracy than all other methods applied presently in animal breeding. Extremely high costs, limited mobility and suitability for larger farm animals of the equipment presently used in medicine require a close consideration of potential future applications in animal production, before large investments are suggested. I conclude that the new techniques would have great potential in future animal breeding programmes if
(1) their higher accuracy leads to substantially greater heritabilities for live animal measurements,
(2) live animal measurements could replace all sib and progeny carcass informations completely,
(3) applied by large enough centralized breeding programmes which can distribute costs and additional progress over a large pyramid of customers.
In the face of such prospects it seems to be highly advisable to set up a few pilot research units in the EEC in order to find out whether the above expectations are realistic and how the techniques can most efficiently be applied in routine animal breeding programmes.

INTRODUCTION

Exact measurements of body composition require such expensive machinery that at present it is only applied in human medicine. It has, however, been shown that such methods as Computed Tomography (CT) and Nuclear Magnetic Resonance Spectroscopy (NMR) in principle could just as successfully be used to measure body composition in smaller farm animals (SKJERVOLD et al., 1980). More progress reports will be presented here and it may be possible to examine soon large farm animals, such as cattle and even horses, if that seems to be desirable. On the other hand enormous costs are still involved and one cannot see how these could ever be reduced into amounts which animal breeders would be prepared to invest for measuring body composition. Before investing a lot of experimental and financial resources into adapting the new methods to animal breeding purposes - and that would certainly be necessary if they are to be effectively utilized in animal breeding routine work - we should very carefully discuss the following questions:

9

(1) Where in animal breeding or production are the additional accuracy in
    measuring body composition and possibly more complicated morphological
    and physiological parameters useful and desirable?
(2) Does the present infrastructure of animal breeding or production allow
    an economically acceptable utilization of the new techniques or could
    the structure be developed to meet their requirements?
Despite the fact that many of the more sophisticated applications of the
new devices in farm animals are not yet sufficiently investigated, and
hardly anything is published so far, I have tried to collect some actual
facts and figures from the present industry, which may be relevant for
answering the above questions. In agreement with the Organizers I see my
main function here in stimulating the discussion between the assembled
experts in the new techniques and animal breeders.

GENERAL USE OF BODY COMPOSITION MEASUREMENTS IN ANIMAL PRODUCTION
    I can see three major applications for accurate body composition
measurements in animal production:
(1) in animal breeding programmes, particularly for meat production
(2) in scientific experimentation on metabolic efficiency, growth and
    carcass quality characters
(3) in market classification of live animals and their carcasses.
There will certainly be other specific applications, such as selection for
specific anatomical conditions (pelvis dimension, digestive tract in cows,
leg deformities in horses, cattle, pigs and poultry, bone distribution in
fish etc.), veterinary diagnostics of internal bone and muscle disorders
etc., but these will not further be considered in this discussion.
    By far the most extensive application would be in grading market
animals and carcasses but, since this has to be done at many different
market places on very large numbers of animals and carcasses, high speed
and low costs are more important than accuracy. As long as in some
countries (eg. W.Germany) even the very simple objective grading devices
already meet stiff opposition from the trade, I do not see much hope for
the manifold more expensive devices, we are concerned with here.
    Utilization in scientific experimentation, on the other hand, would
not require large strategic discussions, because it can to some extent
already be done on the available medical instruments and these will certainly become much more available in University hospitals everywhere.

Nevertheless, would it be very helpful if such facilities could be installed at a few large research institutes in the EEC, in order to study
potential applications in the farm animal industry with concentrated pilot
investigations under much more favourable conditions.

The predominant discussion here should, however, concentrate upon the
potential application of the new techniques in our routine breeding programmes for farm animals. A very obvious application here is the estimation of body composition on live animals as an alternative to carcass
evaluation tests on relatives in all breeding programmes for meat production.
In the following I will restrict myself to cattle and pig production
although most conclusions would also apply to sheep and other species.

OPPORTUNITIES AND REQUIREMENTS IN PRESENT CATTLE AND PIG BREEDING
PROGRAMMES

In vivo estimates of body composition with the present methods are in
most farm animal species of fairly poor accuracy as the following Table 1
demonstrates.

Coefficients of determination (r^2) for lean content, lean-fat or
lean-bone ratios reach generally only the order of 20-50%. Subjective
conformation scores and body measurements are even worse than that, and
only the most sophisticated ultrasonic B-scan-techniques have, in pigs,
given slightly better predictors. The latter methods, however, have not
achieved wide distribution in practical breeding programmes, because their
application is considered to be complicated.

Another problem with ultrasonic measurements is that their accuracy to
some extent depends on the mean and standard deviation of the measurements
taken. Therefore, fat measurements were originally much better in pigs
than in cattle or sheep. Successful breeding over twenty years seems to
have reduced the values for pigs almost to those for cattle as Table 2
indicates. Means and standard deviations of ultrasonically measured backfat thickness in North German auction boars have been halved over 20 years.
Because the technical accuracy of the machine has not improved much the
repeatability of measurements and their predictive value must be reduced.

In consequence in most farm species, sibs or progeny have to be tested
and slaughtered to provide additional information on body composition from
their carcass assessment. This does not only occupy much expensive station
test capacity (eg. 10 progeny per bull in cattle and 2 - n full and half
sibs in pigs) but requires also very costly carcass dissections, because

Table 1: Accuracy of Present Live Animal Measurements of
Body Composition (Selected Literature Examples)

Spe-cies	Live Animal Measurements	Body Compo-sition Trait	Correlat. r_p	Source
C A T T L E	Subjective Confor-mation Scores } :	% L + B (Pist.)	.14 - .21	1
		% Internal Fat	.15 - .33	1
	Body Measurements :	dto.	0 - .19	1
	US-Muscle Area	{ % Lean in Carc.	.31 - .32	2
	US-Musc./Fat Area :	{ Lean-Bone-Ratio	.53 - .32	2
	US-Muscle Area	{ Muscle Area Carc.	.35 - .63	3
	(1. + 5.Lumb.Vert.) :	{ % L + B (Pist.)	.37 - .53	3
P I G S	US-Fat (A-Scan) :	% Lean in Carc.	.52 - .68	4
	US-Muscle (A.Scan) :	—— " ——	.22 - .44	4
	US-Musc.Area (B-Scan):	—— " ——	.36 - .50	4
	US-Fat Area (B-Scan):	—— " ——	.50 - .58	4
	US-Fat (A-Scan) :	% Lean Cuts	.54 - .64	5
	US-M + F Areas (B-Scan) :	—— " ——	.59 - .79	5
	US-M + F (A + B-Scan) :	% Lean in Carc.	.50 - .90	6
	US-M + F-Areas (B-Scan) :	—— " ——	.74	7

Sources:
1   LANGHOLZ und JONGELING, 1972   (n = 733 bulls)
2   BECH-ANDERSEN, 1975   (n = 213 bulls)
3   ERNST et al., 1981   (n = 37 bulls)
4   KALM et al., 1983   (n = 230, 530 pigs, 6 lines)
5   BLENDL et al., 1980   (n = 534, 300 DL-MPA-pigs)
6   KEMPSTER et al., 1979 (n = 143, 38,27 CPE-pigs,
                                       3 wts, 2 reg.)
7   BECH-ANDERSEN et al., 1970   (n = 99 Dän.LR-MPA-
                                              pigs)

Table 2: Ultrasonic Measurements on Live Auction Boars in the DL-Pedigree Population (Lüneburg 1960 - 63 and 1981)

Traits	1960 - 63 $\bar{x}$	1960 - 63 s	1981 $\bar{x}$	1981 s
Number of Boars	1 529		1 693	
Live weight (kg)	127.6	15.3	138.8	11.6
BFT (Mean 3 pts) (mm)	27.6	4.8	15.3	2.5
BFT$_c$ (corr. 120 kg) (mm)	26.9	4.4	13.4	2.2
MT$_c$ (corr. 120 kg) (mm)	60.6	4.2	65.0*	
BF : M - Ratio	.453	.077	.192*	
Source of Data	GLODEK, 1964		GROENEVELD, 1982	

BFT / MT = Backfat-/Muscle thickness, Mean 3 pts 6 cm lateral

* figures on 1 955 boars (Annual Report 1978 - 80, EGZ Uelzen

the cheap whole carcass measurements or scores are not sufficiently accurate.

EAAP-study groups have in recent years tried to count available station testing capacities in member countries by questionnaires (BECH-ANDERSEN et al., 1981; SMITH, 1978). I have put together in Table 3 what they found out for 8 included EEC-countries.

The cattle figures are only performance test stations, where all animals undergo some live body measurements or judgement for estimating the carcass merit. Progeny testing facilities at stations as well as in the field were not available for all EEC-countries, but I will come back to them later with the 1982 F.R.G.-capacity figures. In pigs, however, all progeny test and CPE-capacities are occupied by slaughter animals and even varying proportions of the performance test station capacities are reserved for sibs to be slaughtered for carcass information. Here the same EAAP-study provides figures on the numbers of boars and gilts tested in most EEC-countries, which are given in Table 4.

All the progeny testing capacity (41117 animals) and half the performance test station capacity (over 20000 animals) in the seven EEC-countries was devoted to slaughter animals in order to improve the carcass information of performance tested boars. If body composition and, particularly important at present, meat quality (and/or stress susceptibility) could accurately be measured on live animals in the 55 testing stations, four times as many boars as 1978 could be performance tested in the same capacity (nearly 80000).

These figures are of interest if one notes that in 1981 in the seven EEC-countries 4.925 000 sows and 329000 boars were kept for breeding. With annual replacement of 45 % boars there hould be 148000 selected replacement boars per annum. which could, of course, never be station tested all together. Rough estimates show, however, that there would certainly be no more than 4000 boar breeding herds and they could recruit from this capacity 2 station tested boars with a selection of 1 : 10 per annum.

As it is not likely that the new measuring devices could also be used in on-farm or auction testing, these tests would be less valuable without information from slaughtered sibs. But with sensible elite schemes the overall genetic progress could be much higher than with the present slaughter schemes.

No EEC-figures were available for cattle, therefore as an example, the situation in the F.R.G., using the data of Table 5 on 4 Dual Purpose Breeds

Table 3: Station Test Capacities for Cattle and Pigs in EEC-Countries
(EAAP-Survey 78)

EEC-Country	Perf. Test Stat. Cattle (BECH-ANDERSON et al., 1981)			Perf. and Prog. Test Stat. Pigs (D.H. SMITH, EAAP-study 1978)			
	no.	Station Places all	% Beef	no.	No. Station Places Prog. Test	Perf.Test	CPE
B	2	700	43	(2)	(400)	(800)	•
DK	5	725	14	17	4 000	300	100
F	13	1 341	21	14	1 480	2 840	1 480
FRG	10	1 630	13	11	3 500	500	732
IRL	3	146	66	2	80	1 600	-
I	6	485	48	•	•	•	•
NL	4	437	0	4	2 560	-	1 344
UK	6	760	100	5	-	2 400	1 300
Σ (8)	49	6 224	1 985	55	12 020	8 440	4 956

( ) own estimates, because no data in EAAP-study

Table 4: Tested Boars and Sows by different Testing Methods in EEC-Countries
(EAAP-Survey 78)

EEC-Country	Progeny Testing		approx. no. progeny	Performance Testing at Stations		Performance Testing in the Field	
	Sires	Dams		Boars	Gilts	Boars	Gilts
B	306	300	1 224	2 435	2 142	0	12 010
DK	1 000	4 000	16 000	300	0	5 000	32 000
F	50	0	400	6 040	.	9 200	25 800
FRG*	(2 000)	9 591	19 182	1 336	0	61 653	34 651
IRL	34	0	136	1 504	0	.	.
NL	200	2 075	4 175	4 175	0	18 000	13 000
UK	0	0	0	3 500	1 000	10 000	60 000
Σ (7)	3 590	15 966	41 117	19 290	3 142	103 853	177 461

* Data for 1981; ( ) own estimate

Table 5: Performance- and Progeny-Test-Situation of AI-Bulls in
4 DP-Breeds in the F.R.G. 1982 (ADR-Ann.Rep. 1982)

Breed	No. AI-Bulls		No. Stationtested Bulls		No. Field-Progeny Tested Bulls
	Total	Testbulls	Perform. T.	Progeny T.	
SB	2 345*	575	127	252	240
RB	1 065	372	40	100	110
FV	1 660	973	409	547	68
BV	263	159	10	142	10
Σ (4)	5 744	2 194	647	1 057	428

Herdbook Population: 16 571 Bulls and 1.5 million Cows (16 Breeds)

Station Test Capacity: 1 937 Places in 6 Progeny Test. Stations
                       1 690 Places in 10 Perform. Test. Stations

* double countings included (ca. 1 600 Bulls with $\geq$ 1 owner)

(96.5% of all cows) will be discussed here.

The available station capacity would allow 200 progeny and 1700 performance tested bulls, annually, which is much less than the number of test bulls in the 4 breeds. The progeny test capacity, however, cannot be transformed into performance test capacity as easily as for pigs, so that in cattle breeding completely new testing schemes would have to be developed. However, in order to select all testbulls on their body composition at least least 1 : 2, the present capacity would have to be tripled and that would - if at all - only be feasible with performance testing. The milk situation in the EEC and recent scientific recommendations support more emphasis of meat performance at least in "Dual Purpose" cattle (DGfZ, 1982).

What could be gained in accuracy of selection for meat with the new techniques? It can easily be shown (FLOCK and HAUSSMAN, 1970), that the accuracy of an individual measurement determines the gain one could reach with additional informations or more precise measurements. If, for example, the correlation of a live body measurement to the real body composition could be increased from .4 to .7 then the new individual measurement alone would already be better than any feasible number of additional sib - and up to 25 progeny informations. Very important for such calculations is, however, what heritabilities could be reached for the live body composition measurements in comparison to the present auxiliary traits.

In summarizing the opportunities for the new measuring techniques under the present cattle and pig breeding conditions in the EEC one could conclude:

(1) The accuracy in measuring body composition exceeds all present live animal testing methods. It may be expected that this results in subsequentially higher heritabilities for the new traits.

(2) Slaughtering of sibs and progeny for carcass evaluation could completely be abandoned, especially if the new methods also provided sufficient information on meat quality traits, which are at present particularly important in pig breeding.

(3) If the techniques could be applied in all testing stations, and present progeny- and sib capacities would be converted to additional performance test capacities, the expected selection intensity and genetic progress in body composition traits could be much greater than at present.

NECESSARY ADAPTATIONS OF BREEDING PROGRAMMES TO THE NEW TECHNIQUES

As it is most unrealistic that CT- or NMR- facilities could be installed in or moved around between 100 EEC-testing stations routinely, the obvious advantages of the new techniques cannot generally be utilized with the present structure of animal breeding in the EEC. The very expensive equipment can only be installed at places where its maximal technical capacity can be utilized and, in addition, the measurements can effectively be transferred into large scale genetic progress. I can see at present only two possible ways of meeting such conditions:

(1) Very large Performance Test Stations

If one station is large enough, or several stations cooperate in the utilization of a central measuring unit by transporting their test animals, there may be a way of keeping the testing costs per animal within limits acceptable to individual breeders. Unfortunately, even approximate figures can only be given if the fixed and running costs of such units and their throughput per unit of time are known; another good good reason for a pilot project. Routine measuring units, however, can probably never be provided by public test stations as a service to individual breeders. They will always require a rather large and well organized breeding programme behind them, in order to distribute the central costs over a large pyramid of customers.

(2) Large Breeding Programmes with own Central Test Facilities

There are some large (even worldwide operating) AI-programmes in cattle, which may adopt their own centralized bull testing- (if not breeding-) scheme. Should beef characteristics or other specific body composition parameters become more important in our large Dairy and Dual Purpose Breeds, there may well be some organizations to make use of a central test facility. If Multiple- Ovulation-Embryo-Transfer-Breeding Programmes (NICHOLAS and SMITH, 1983) should ever become popular in practice, they would also be potential customers.

We know already of some Pig Hybrid Programmes which are large enough not only to afford, but could probably also make optimal use of accurate live body composition measurements in their central Nucleus Units if they then could avoid sib or progeny testing and carcass dissections completely.

The general pattern is obvious; more concentration in breeding programmes supports the new techniques. However, if they turn out to provide superior test results, they may also support the concentration of breeding programmes. The future impact of the new techniques on animal production, and that is my general conclusion, depends largely upon the superiority of the data output in routine applications. In order to find out as soon as possible, a few pilot research units for animal production purposes should be built in the EEC, even if money is scarce. The poten tial scope of the technique is so great, that even large investments are much more justified than most of the milk subsidies in the EEC.

REFERENCES

ADR (1982). Rinderproduktion in der Bundesrepublik Deutsch-
    land.
ADS (1981). Schweineproduktion in der Bundesrepublik Deutsch-
    land.
Appel, W. (1980). Die Bestimmung des Schlachtkörperwertes am
    lebenden Rind mit dem dänischen Ultraschallgerät "Dan-
    scanner". Diss. Kiel, 1980.
Bech-Andersen, B., Pederson, O.K., Busk, S.A. and Jensen, P.
    (1970). Ultraschallmessungen bei Rindern und Schweinen.
    Fleischwirtschaft 22, 843 - 846
Bech-Andersen, B. (1975). Recent Experimental Development in
    Ultrasonic Measurement of Cattle. Livestock Prod. Sci. 2,
    137 - 146.
Bech-Andersen, B. et al. (1981). Performance Testing of Bulls
    in A.I.: Report of a Working Group of the Commission on
    Cattle Production. Livestock Prod. Sci. 8, 101 - 119.
Blendl, H.M., Horst, P. and Petersen, J. (1980). Vergleichende
    Untersuchungen zur Aussagefähigkeit der Ultraschall-A-
    und B-Scan-Verfahren über den Schlachtkörperwert am le-
    benden Schwein. 1. Mitteilung. Züchtungskd. 52, 444 - 455.
DGfZ (1982). Grundsätze zur Berücksichtigung der Fleischlei-
    stung in der Zucht des Zweinutzungsrindes. DGfZ-Ausschuß
    Genet. Stat. Meth. (Vors. Fewson). Züchtungskd. 54,
    315 - 317.
EGZ im Verband Lüneburger Schweinezüchter. 3. Jahresbericht
    1978 - 1980.
Ernst, E., Appel, W. und Claus, J. (1981). Erfahrungen mit
    dem Danscanner zur Schätzung des Fleischanteils am le-
    benden Rind im Rahmen der Eigenleistungsprüfung. Tier-
    züchter 33, 92 - 94.
Flock, D.K. und Haussmann, H. (1970). Tabellen für die Zucht-
    wertschätzung bei landwirtschaftlichen Nutztieren. DGfZ-
    Ausschuß Genet.Stat. Methoden (Vors.Lauprecht), Polykopie.

Glodek, P. (1964). Über ein unter praktischen Verhältnissen an-
    wendbares Verfahren zur Abschätzung des Fleischbildungs-
    vermögens lebender Schweine mit Ultraschall. Züchtungskd.
    36, 356 - 370.
Groeneveld, E. (1982). Erfahrungen mit der Indexselektion 1981.
    n. publ. Arbeitspapier.
Kalm, E. und Mitarbeiter (1983). n. publ. Arbeitspapiere.
Kempster, A.J., Cuthbertson, A., Owen, H.G. and Alliston, J.C.
    (1979). A Comparison of Four Ultrasonic Machines for Pre-
    dicting the Body Composition of Live Pigs. Anim. Prod.
    29, 175 - 181.
Langholz, H.J. and Jongeling C. (1972). Untersuchungen zum ge-
    netischen Aussagewert der stationären Nachkommenprüfung
    auf Mastleistung und Schlachtkörperwert beim Rind. Züch-
    tungskd. 44, 368 - 384.
Nicholas, F.W. and Smith, C. (1983). Increased Rates of Gene-
    tic Change in Dairy Cattle by Embryo Transfer and Split-
    ting. Anim. Prod. 36, 341 - 353.
Skjervold, H., Gronseth, K., Vangen, O. and Evensen, A.(1980).
    In vivo estimation of body composition by computerized
    tomography. Z. Tierz. u. Zübiol. 98, 77 - 79.
Skjervold, H. and Vangen, O. (1981). Die Computertomographie -
    ein neuer Weg zur Schätzung der Schlachtkörperzusammen-
    setzung und des Energieansatzes am lebenden Tier. Tier-
    züchter 33, 368 - 372.
Smith, D.H. (1978). Interim Report on European Pig Production.
    pres. at EAAP-Pig Commission Meeting Stockholm, 1978,
    pp. 65

DISCUSSION

In this session, the discussion considered the indications for and practicalities of using the newest techniques for measuring body composition. It was felt (Kempster) that applications in progeny and performance testing were not mutually exclusive and use in livestock markets was a distinct possibility. Glodek felt that the large breeding companies would be the most likely users and that livestock markets were not good sites; abattoirs even less. Whatever the ultimate application there was an urgent need for pilot trials to assess usefulness and identify potential applications of the techniques on offer.

There was a distinct need to reduce scanning times which, other things being equal, would cause a many fold increase in the potential uses and market for the equipment (Steane). Attention was drawn (Wells and Boddy) to the possibility of using mobile scanners, thereby increasing the range of applications and consequently the marginal costs of operating the equipment.

SESSION II

BODY COMPOSITION MEASUREMENTS IN MAN

Chairman: J.W.B. King

INTRODUCTION TO IMAGING TECHNOLOGY

P.N.T. Wells

Department of Medical Physics
Bristol General Hospital
Bristol BS1 6SY, UK

ABSTRACT

Some of the technologies used in medical diagnostic imaging are already being applied to the measurement of body composition in meat animals, and others may be transferable to this area. Radionuclide imaging, computed tomography, ultrasonic imaging, digital radiography, nuclear magnetic resonance, thermographic imaging, diaphanography, microwave imaging and electrical impedance mapping are reviewed, and the role of digital picture archiving and communication is discussed.

INTRODUCTION

During the last decade, the horizon of medical imaging has expanded beyond conventional X-radiography to include in routine clinical practice techniques using new X-ray detectors, computed tomography, radionuclides and ultrasonics. These imaging methods have vital roles in the diagnosis of many different disease processes in man, in the management and treatment of patients, and in screening. Generally they are complementary to each other; rarely does a new method render an old one fully obsolete. They do compete with each other, however, in the sense that choices have to be made in terms of cost-effectiveness.

Besides the imaging methods which are already of established value, new techniques, such as imaging by nuclear magnetic resonance, are being developed. These techniques, based on phenomena previously unexploited in medical diagnostics, will doubtless have new and complementary roles. Supporting developments are also being made in image processing, analysis, storage and display.

Innovations in diagnostic imaging technology can be judged to be successful when they give improvements in one or more of the following:

- Reducing the 'invasiveness' of the examination
- Reducing the dose of ionising radiation, or obtaining more information with the same dose
- Increasing the flexibility and convenience of the investigative technique

· Increasing the yield of information

· Improving the cost-effectiveness of the examination.

In this paper, imaging technologies are examined in the context of their applications to medical problems. Some of the techniques are already being applied to the measurement of body composition in meat animals and some of the other technologies may now be appropriate for transfer to this area.

RADIONUCLIDE IMAGING

The instrumentation used for routine radionuclide imaging is now quite mature. Modern gamma cameras often have data processing computers; these are particularly useful for dynamic studies in, for example, cardiology. Some systems have tomographic capability.

It seems unlikely that positron emission techniques will have any significant impact in medical practice in the UK if only because of the need for extremely expensive cyclotrons to produce the required short-lived radionuclides.

During the last few years, and in parallel with the development of new instrumentation for radionuclide imaging, progress has been made in radiopharmaceuticals. Currently the radionuclide most commonly used is technetium-99m. Iodine-123 and indium-111 have important roles.

A promising new approach is based on the use of highly specific carriers to target the radionuclides to the site being studied. In principle, such carriers include tumour-associated antigens (currently much research is being devoted to their development) and tumour-specific radiosensitisers.

COMPUTED TOMOGRAPHY

CT scanners are now available for a whole range of different applications. Extremely high resolution is possible, with good tissue discrimination, and scanning speeds and processing times are fast enough for all but real-time cardiac studies. At the other end of the scale, relatively inexpensive instruments are available when either speed or spatial resolution are not of vital importance.

There is much scientific interest in very high speed CT, capable of imaging the heart in real-time in three dimensions. Instruments capable of this performance will undoubtedly be very expensive, however, and for medical applications in the UK they will inevitably have a lower priority than those using radionuclide, digital radiographic and ultrasonic approaches.

ULTRASONIC IMAGING

There are three main reasons for the growing importance of ultrasonic imaging:
* Ultrasonic imaging equipment technology has developed to a stage where instruments are easy and satisfying to use
* The information obtained by ultrasound, particularly in dynamic studies, cannot be acquired by any more convenient or cost-effective technique. It should be noted, however, that the low cost of the instrumentation is often overshadowed by the high cost of manpower
* Ultrasound is apparently free from hazard at the exposure levels used in imaging.

The demand for ultrasonic systems is currently the most rapidly growing in the diagnostic imaging market. Being a relatively inexpensive technology, it is possible for hospital-based departments still to make substantial research contributions to the understanding of the scientific basis of the subject and to the evolution of new instruments. Special-purpose ultrasonic scanners have been developed for dedicated applications in such areas as breast, prostate, interventional and intraoperative imaging.

Ultrasonic diagnostic techniques now extend beyond the traditional role of morphological imaging as the following capabilities are becoming available:
* Doppler blood flow imaging and measurements, either alone or in duplex with real-time imaging
* Tissue characterisation.

DIGITAL RADIOGRAPHY

'Digital radiography' is the term used to describe the process of high-speed acquisition, manipulation and display of X-radiographic information. Digital radiography has become possible because of recent developments that have taken place in the following technologies:

- Large area transducers (image intensifiers or scanned detectors) for X-ray-to-electronic signal conversion
- Wide dynamic range, high spatial resolution, solid state two-dimensional image stores, capable of rapid input and output rates
- Computers capable of processing digital image data at high speed.

The potential advantages of digital radiography are as follows:

- Real-time image processing is done while the patient is being examined
- Visualisation of blood vessels, and particularly arteries, with intravenous (as opposed to intra-arterial) injection of contrast medium and temporal subtraction; the technique is called 'digital subtraction radiography' (DSR)
- More efficient and cheaper interventional techniques for the demonstration of specific arteries (such as the popliteal artery)
- Tissue differentiation by X-ray energy discrimination; by this means, it is possible, for example, to 'subtract' the bone shadows from a chest radiograph thus improving the perceptibility of soft tissue lesions.

The most common real-time image processing algorithms are mask mode subtraction, time interval difference imaging and dual averaged subtraction. The possible post-storage processing algorithms are much more numerous and include videodensitometry, gray level manipulation, smoothing, edge enhancement and so on.

NUCLEAR MAGNETIC RESONANCE

The basic physics underlying nuclear magnetic resonance (NMR), although complex, is well understood. Developments in magnet technology and high speed computers have extended an essentially analytical tool into diagnostic devices capable of imaging the structure and measuring some of the functions of the body.

Nuclear magnetic resonance imaging

An NMR imaging machine consists of a magnet (permanent, resistive electromagnetic, or superconducting electromagnetic) with a central opening large enough to accommodate a patient. This magnet applies a strong, uniform magnetic field to the patient. This field tends to align the nuclei of atoms in the patient which have an odd number of protons, or an odd number of neutrons, or both. Such nuclei are slightly magnetic; the most abundant of them in the body is the nucleus of the hydrogen atom, which consists of a single proton. The concentration, distribution and properties of the protons in the body can be explored by measuring the electromagnetic signals which they radiate in response to slightly changing magnetic fields superimposed on the main field by electric currents passed through subsidiary coils enclosing the patient.

NMR imaging does not use ionising radiation and is apparently completely harmless.

Clinical trials currently in progress have already confirmed that NMR imaging has the following capabilities:

· Images can be generated corresponding to intrinsic parameters, the so-called relaxation times, of the protons in the tissues; these parameters represent gross chemical characteristics such as the state of hydration, fat content and the presence of paramagnetic compounds administered as contrast agents

· A finite time is required for NMR signals to be registered; this makes the technique relatively immune to movement artifacts, and offers the possibility of flow measurement

· There are no moving parts in an NMR scanner, and any scan plane – transverse axial, coronal, sagittal or oblique – can be obtained merely by changing the electrical operating conditions; moreover, it is possible to collect information from the whole of a volume of interest, and subsequently to extract and display two-dimensional images of any desired plane within the volume

. Images of moving structures can be made by time-gating or by the so-called echo-planar method.

NMR scanners should not be thought of as being replacements for CT scanners. The demand for CT scanning is enormous, and will continue to be so. The potential value of NMR imaging rests in the ability of the technique to characterise tissues, to investigate biochemical processes and to measure flow. Although in practice a range of morphological studies may turn out to be able to be carried out with more or less equal effectiveness using either CT or NMR imaging, when both methods are available the choice of which to use will be most likely to be based on consideration of the experience and acquired skills of the radiologist and the relative costs of the techniques in terms of financial resources, radiation exposure and the need for contrast media.

Topical magnetic resonance

The nuclear magnetic resonance technique is sensitive to many other nuclei in addition to protons. The nucleus of the phosphorus atom is one of these, and it is of great interest because of the role of phosphorus in metabolic processes. Phosphorus is not nearly so abundant as hydrogen in the body, however, and so high-resolution NMR images of phosphorus nuclei cannot be made in practicable scanning times. The chemical characteristics of the phosphorus in a volume of a few millilitres of tissue can nevertheless be determined by measuring the NMR signals from the tissue when located in an extremely uniform magnetic field. A magnetic field of the necessary strength can only be produced by a superconducting magnet. To distinguish the process from NMR imaging, it is called 'topical (nuclear) magnetic resonance' (TMR).

The potential clinical applications of TMR are extremely important. For example, it can be used to study muscle disease, the viability of muscle prior to reconstructive arterial surgery, the viability of donor kidneys prior to transplantation, and brain function following ischaemia. A recent development has been the combination of NMR imaging with the measurement of TMR characteristics from localised regions of interest.

OTHER IMAGING TECHNIQUES

Thermographic imaging

Recent developments in the pyroelectric vidicon television camera may lead to the wide use of thermography, since the device is simple and reliable and does not require a supply of liquid nitrogen.

Clinical applications of thermography traditionally include detection of breast cancer (but it is not reliable when used alone, although it may have a role for follow-up after initial multi-modality tests). Other proposed applications are in the diagnosis and management of cerebro-vascular disease, deep vein thrombosis, perforating veins, rheumatoid arthritis, and burns.

Diaphanography

'Diaphanography' is the term used to describe transillumination imaging, and in the past it has been used in medical diagnosis for imaging fluid in the newborn skull, in the breast and in the scrotum, and for assessing the state of sinuses. All these applications used visible light.

During the last thirty years, there has been an increasing interest in the potential particularly of infrared diaphanography for the detection of breast cancer. Intense light sources have been developed which do not heat the area of contact with the skin. The shadow image can be visualised either photographically or through a television system.

Realists agree that diaphanography alone is not a reliable method for breast cancer screening or detection. Used in conjunction with other methods, such as palpation, fine needle aspiration cytology, mammography, ultrasound and thermography, however, it may turn out to be extremely useful in managing patients with suspected or known breast disease.

Microwave imaging

Microwaves in the region of 2 GHz are being used for transmission imaging. Although the wavelength is relatively long, careful design of antennae gives resolution of the order of a centimetre. The properties visualised include dielectric constant and loss factor. The method is still very much in the research stage.

Electrical impedance mapping

By measuring the electrical currents between an array of electrodes placed on the surface of the body, it is in principle possible to reconstruct an image based on the three-dimensional spatial distribution of tissues according to their electrical impedances. If research at present being undertaken solves the image reconstruction problem associated with indirect electrical current paths without the need for impracticably large computers, this method of imaging may become extremely important.

DIGITAL PICTURE ARCHIVING AND COMMUNICATION

In principle, all images can be transmitted, stored and processed in digital form. Radionuclide scanners, gamma cameras, CT scanners, ultrasonic scanners, digital radiographic systems and NMR scanners already operate with digital images. This leads to the concept of digital picture archiving and communication systems (PACS) which offer three important capabilities:

* Inexpensive storage of images
* Rapid and reliable access to stored images, and rapid communication between imaging systems and viewing stations
* Communication between imaging systems and image processing computers.

Within a few years, large radiology departments could be virtually 'silverless'. The efficiency and effectiveness of radiologists could be enormously increased as they learn to use viewing centres, like those currently used for CT scans, at which they can speedily call up not only images of every kind, but also physiological data, laboratory reports and patient records.

CONCLUSIONS

Presently the two imaging techniques which are attracting most interest in the medical field are digital radiography and nuclear magnetic resonance. This excitement should not be allowed to eclipse the importance of developments in ultrasound and radionuclides. Moreover, conventional radiography will remain the primary imaging method for the forseeable future. Computed tomography is meanwhile enjoying something of a resurgence. Diaphanography, thermography and microwave imaging show promise in specialised applications. Electrical impedance mapping is a newcomer which may prove to be significant. The increase in digital picture information has resulted in the new and important technology of picture archiving and communication.

TO PROBE FURTHER

Hamilton, B. (Ed.). 1982. Medical Diagnostic Imaging Systems. (F&S Press, New York).

Wells, P.N.T. (Ed.). 1982. Scientific Basis of Medical Imaging. (Churchill Livingstone, Edinburgh).

THE ASSESSMENT OF BODY COMPOSITION BY
NMR IMAGING

B.S. Worthington

Division of Academic Radiology, Queen's
Medical Centre, Nottingham, England.

ABSTRACT

   NMR imaging is a new method of mapping the internal
anatomy of the human body. It has the advantages of avoiding
completely the use of ionising radiation and it appears to be
unassociated with any significant hazard.

   NMR is an extremely complex phenomenon and whilst this
confers a remarkable versatility when applied to imaging there
is also great scope for confusion. NMR imaging uses
radiofrequency radiation in the presence of a magnetic field
to produce high quality cross-sectional images of the body
in any plane which portray the distribution density of
hydrogen nuclei and parameters relating to their motion in
cellular water and lipids (Hinshaw et al, 1978). As with
CT, the display of soft tissue detail is at a premium and
with NMR there is the added advantage of being able to
manipulate the contrast between different tissues in order
to highlight pathological changes by altering the pattern
of RF pulse which is applied. These pulse sequences produce
images whigh are weighted differently by the parameters,
proton density, flow and the T_1 and T_2 relaxation times.
Whilst with CT there is an invariant grey scale covering the
tissues of the body with established normal ranges of
Hounsfield numbers the pixel values of NMR can vary widely
for a given tissue and the grey scale ordering of tissues
is not constant. In the abdomen (Fig. 1) and pelvis (Fig. 2)
the principal solid organs can be identified; deposits of fat
give a high signal and in the retro-peritoneal space this
allows the kidneys and adrenal glands to be clearly outlined
(Moore et al, 1981). The walls and lumen of the principal
blood vessels are readily identified on flow dependent
sequences and the spinal column and paravertebral muscles

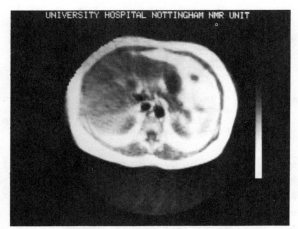

Fig.1   Transverse NMR scan through the upper abdomen

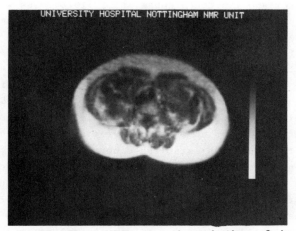

Fig. 2   Transverse NMR scan through the pelvis

are well shown. More significantly the spinal cord can be
displayed without the use of intrathecal contrast media. In
the thorax the major vessels and airways of the central
mediastinum can be clearly resolved and mass lesions can be
well demonstrated. In self-gated images of the heart the
chambers are clearly defined (Moore et al, 1981). High
resolution scans of a restricted portion of a body section
can be obtained by increasing the applied field gradients.

It has long been a goal of animal breeding research
to find a practical new technique which would allow the
estimation of body composition in living animals.
Extrapolating from human experience NMR could well provide
an additional in vivo method for assessing the meat/fat
ratio; but more than this may give information relating
to the chemical composition of the tissues.

I would like to thank Mr. John Williams and
Dr. Gordon Higson of the Department of Health and Social
Security for their continued advice and encouragement.

REFERENCES

Hinshaw, W., Andrew, E.R., Bottomley, P.A., Holland, G.N.,
    Moore, W.S. and Worthington, B.S. 1978. Display of
    cross-sectional anatomy by Nuclear Magnetic Resonance.
    Br. J. Rad. 5.
Moore, W.S., Hawkes, R.C., Holland, G.N., Roebuck, E.J. and
    Worthington, B.S. 1981. Nuclear Magnetic Resonance
    (NMR) tomography of the Normal Abdomen. J. Comput.
    Assist. Tomog. 5, 613.
Moore, W.S., Hawkes, R.C., Holland, G.N., Roebuck, E.J. and
    Worthington, B.S. 1981. Nuclear Magnetic Resonance
    (NMR) Tomography of the Normal Heart. J. Comput. Assist.
    Tomog. 5, 605.

MEASUREMENT OF BODY ELEMENTS AND THEIR METABOLISM

K. Boddy
Regional Medical Physics Department,
Newcastle General Hospital,
Newcastle upon Tyne, NE4 6BE.

Body composition and metabolism are notoriously difficult to study. Often recourse is made to indirect methods whose interpretation requires considerable caution and an understanding of their limitations. However, adoption or adaptation of modern technology has provided techniques which are more directly quantitative and meaningful.

The analysis of the elemental content or administered radioactive tracer in plasma, serum or blood cells is generally attractive for its overall simplicity. However, the results are usually expressed as a concentration, which may be subject to homeostatic control, and fail to reflect total body composition and its relation to body habitus. However, in some cases, measurement of administered radioisotopes in blood can be of diagnostic value, such as estimating the oral absorption of labelled vitamin B_{12} or of oral calcium-47 when calcium-45 is administered parentally at the same time to account for blood clearance.

Isotope dilution is a potentially powerful technique and is commonly used in medicine to determine exchangeable body potassium and sodium, total body water, blood and plasma volume etc. However, care is required to ensure that equilibration is either complete or sufficiently well defined. For instance, there is evidence that an equilibration period of 24 hours is probably adequate for the determination of exchangeable body electrolytes in healthy subjects. In contrast, an equilibration period of up to 72 hours is required in some pathological conditions, measurements during a shorter period artifically indicating "depletion" compared with controls. Nevertheless, the method is widely applicable, being used for

elements such as zinc and magnesium, and requires only
readily available equipment.

Radioactivity within the living human body can be
measured using whole-body counters. Conventional whole-body
counters employ a shielded room, constructed from 10 cm lead
or 15 cm steel, in which the detectors, usually of sodium
iodide, are housed in order to reduce the background counting-
rate due to cosmic rays and natural radioactivity in
building materials, the earth and atmosphere. The system,
functions well but has the disadvantages of substantial
weight, some 40-100 tonnes, relatively high cost, a few
hundred thousands of pounds and isolation of the patient
from attendant staff. Shadow-shield whole-body counters, on
the other hand, employ a specially arranged partial shield
confined largely to the detector(s). The weight is, therefore,
substantially reduced to about 2-8 tonnes and the cost also
by about an order of magnitude. If a single detector is
used, the patient passes beneath it while lying on a motorised
couch, supine and then prone. When opposed detectors are
used, above and below, the patient passes between them. The
shadow-shield counter can attain sensitivities matching
those of most shielded room counters. Total body potassium
can be measured directly by detection of the 1.46 MeV gamma
rays from the naturally radioactive isotope potassium-40
which is a constant fraction of body potassium. Absorption
and long term retention (or turnover) of various elements
and compounds can be determined following administration of
an appropriate radioactive tracer, such as iron-59, zinc-69m,
calcium-47, iodine-131, ^{58}Co or ^{57}Co - vitamin B$_{12}$. The
uncertainties, inaccuracies and unpleasantness of excreta
collection and assay are thus avoided.

Although potassium is the only essential body element
that is naturally radioactive, by exposing the body or the
relevant organ or region of it to a small dose of neutrons,
radioactivity may be induced IN VIVO in other body elements.

The induced radioisotopes are measured by external or whole-body counting. By comparing the spectra and counting-rates with those obtained from anthropomorphic phantoms containing dispensed amounts of relevant elements, a quantitative multi-element measurement is obtained by the IN VIVO activation analysis procedure. To date calcium, phosphorus, sodium, chlorine, potassium, nitrogen, hydrogen, oxygen, carbon, aluminium and silver have been measured in the whole-body. In organs or relevant regions of the body, iodine, calcium, phosphorus, cadmium, and iron are among the elements measured. It will be apparent that determination of potassium, nitrogen and carbon can be combined to provide estimates of lean mass, fat and protein. The method yields fair precision of about 1-3%, is reasonably rapid but the technology is costly involving a neutron irradiation facility as well as a whole-body or organ counting system.

DISCUSSION

Tang Sorensen enquired about the problem of overcoming 'noise' from gastro intestinal tract in CT scanning. Wells recognised the problem and commented on the better discrimination of NMR. In reply to King's question on image resolution, Wells pointed out that the resolution of ultrasound images was limited by wavelength and was worse when large animals were being scanned. When X-rays are used, the problem is scatter and, additionally, in CT the size of the X-ray beam. With NMR a major problem is signal to noise ratio (which, however, is a common limitation amongst the various techniques). CT and NMR provide for multidimensional appraisals but, data accumulation, storage and handling can be overwhelming.

In answer to a question on test procedures to compare performance against specification of equipment Wells replied that these had been conducted for CT scanners and had shown differences both within and between the different types of machine. As yet there were no similarly comprehensive reports comparing NMR equipment.

Lister enquired about the likely future costs of equipment. Wells and Rue felt that prices were likely to be maintained but the equipment would have greater flexibility and sophistication. The possibility existed for the development of simpler equipment for specialist application.

Gibson wondered whether clinical applications required the same degree of precision and possible quantification as are envisaged for animal science. Wells and Rue pointed out that 'non-invasive histology' and chemical analysis of tissues in vivo were increasingly sought by clinicians. It is already possible to measure changes in intra cellular pH using phosphorus spectra and hydration using proton spectra by NMR. Rue envisaged the analysis of whole bodies by NMR in milliseconds though the costs were likely to be very high.

In discussion, Worthington drew attention to the use of NMR in food applications. With imaging times of 2-4 minutes, it is possible to map the protein content in a slice of meat. He considers that there are many potential applications in relation to food quality as a general rule. NMR is as good as CT for quantitative investigations and better for qualitative assessments and the T_2 image was of particular value. King asked how the T_2/T_1 image was weighted and Worthington agreed that, for the most part, this was done subjectively on the basis of the observed image quality.

SESSION III

USE OF COMPUTED TOMOGRAPHY IN FARM ANIMALS

Chairman: E. Kallweit

ESTABLISHMENT OF CT FACILITY FOR FARM ANIMALS.

Nils Standal
Department of Animal Genetics and Breeding
Agricultural University of Norway
Box 24, 1432 As-NLH, Norway

INTRODUCTION

The Department of Animal Genetics and Breeding, the Agricultural University of Norway has during a long period been involved in experiments and ultization of methods for evaluating body and carcass composition in live animals. The ultrasonic equipment for backfat measurements in live pigs was tested and put into practical use by 1958-60. (Skjervold et al, 1960; Standal, 1962). Later we have investigated blood volume and other blood parameters for prediction of carcass composition (Aulstad, 1970) and some dilution methods have also been investigated without much success (Tveit, 1977).

The prime objective for the department has been to use equipment and methods as tools in selection for carcass composition. With accurate methods for estimation of body or carcass composition on live animals, many other types of studies will be possible. From a breeding research point of view, studies of growth and tissue deposition rates in different breeds or selection lines, of compensatory growth and of tissue mobilization during fasting might be mentioned. With a Computer Tomograph available, such and other studies seem to be possible.

X-RAY TOMOGRAPHY FOR BODY COMPOSITION

CT had been used for many years for diagnostic purposes in humans when it was realized that it might be a valuable tool in prediction of body composition. The first results from a small trial with 23 pigs was rather promising (Skjervold et al., 1981), and constituted part of the basis for the procurement of an X-ray CT for the

Agricultural University of Norway.

The principle of X-ray CT for prediction of body composition has been reviewed (Skjervold, 1982), therefore only a very short description will be given here.

An X-ray tube is placed on a big wheel with the object, the animal or human, in the center of the wheel. 180° relative to the X-ray tube, special detectors for X- ray beams are placed. The X-ray tube and the detectors rotate 360° around the object during the scanning operation. The detectors are connected to a computer and this makes it possible by use of the attenuation of the X-rays, to calculate the density in each of up to 65,000 small squares or cubes (called pixels) which make up the cross section image of the object. The densities are set to vary from -1000 for air through 0 for water to +1000 for hard bone. These densities are usually called CT values.

Based on these densities the equipment reconstructs an image of the cross section on the monitor. This image is used for diagnosis.

When the scans are to be used for prediction of body or carcass composition, the density matrix (which is the basis for the image) has to be used in a quantitative manner. This will be demonstrated by some of the later papers. I will only mention that we produce a frequency distribution of the CT values of each scan. Fig 1 demonstrates two such frequency distributions, one of a fat selection line pig and one of an ordinary Norwegian Landrace pig, both fed ad. lib., and with the same live weight. The percentage of pixels in each class (class width 6 C.T. values) is given on the ordinate. The figure demonstrates that the fat line pig has a much higher percentage of its pixels in the "fat area" of the CT range (from about -160 to -40) than the normal pig. The opposite is true for the "muscle area" of the CT range (from about +30 to about +90).

The information in the frequency distribution may be utilized to predict the body or carcass composition as will be shown in later papers at this workshop.

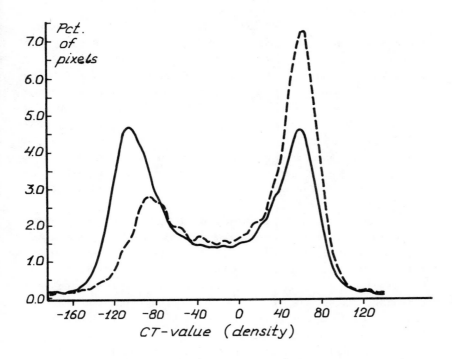

Frequency distribution of CT-values for the average of two scans of a Fat Line pig _____ and a normal Norwegian Landrace pig _ _ _ _ of equal live weight. Class width 6 CT values.

THE PROCUREMENT OF A CT FACILITY

Some fund money, meant to promote meat production, became available for the purpose of establishing a CT facility for agricultural and veterinary research in Norway. Other advanced equipment were also briefly discussed, e.g. N.M.R., but it was concluded that for prediction of body composition the X-ray CT would have the best chance of success.

At the stage when the procurement became a possibility there were several CT facilities available on the market and today there are even more types. CT's from only two companies were seriously considered because both of them already had

service units established in Norway, as well as CTs in
operation at hospitals in Norway.

Our choice was a SOMATOM II from Siemens, Germany.
There were three main reasons for the choice. Firstly the
density matrix of the SOMATOM covers the entire area of the
gantry opening of the CT, and any object passing through the
hole may be scanned. The alternative was a CT in which the
density matrix covered a square contained within the opening
of the gantry. This gives an effective size of the SOMATOM
II equal to the gantry opening (diameter 530 mm), while the
other option had an effective diameter of 420 mm with a
gantry diameter of 600 mm. The difference seems small, but
may be critical for scanning pigs and sheep of usual market
size.

Secondly, SIEMENS promised to deliver software to make
it possible to take out regions of the image and substract
one region from the whole image or from another region.
This is necessary in order to make frequency distributions
of CT-values of specific regions and the difference between
regions. These may be extemely important options e.g. in
order to exclude the intestines from the image, if one wants
to predict carcass composition.

It turned out that SIEMENS were not able to fulfill
these promises. We had to develop the software ourselves,
which was quite a formidable task. On the other hand none
of the other companies we have been in contact with provides
this type of software either.

The third reason for choosing the SOMATOM II was that
the image processing is ready immediately (3 seconds) after
the scan is taken. This is important in order to decide if
a new scan has to be taken due to movements and reflections
in the picture. If one has to wait for 20-60 seconds for
each picture to be processed this will slow down the
operation considerably.

I want to stress here that our requirement for a
CT-scanner for animal body composition prediction is
different from what the companies are used to from their
"hospital market". They were also not able to give us

adequate information on what we would need. When we deviated from the original "package" for a hospital we got units (operation systems, disc drives, tape stations) which were not compatible, or did not work efficiently together with the basic unit.

We have learned a lot about requirements we should have made and how to write contracts. On the other hand we could not have done very much better at the time because the right advisers were simply not available.

The set up we have, or would like to have consist of:
The SOMATOM II with consol and 2 floppy disk drives.
Extra programming terminal for program development.
Users library (necessary for program development).
Tape station for storage of images and programs.
Disk stations, preferably two, in order to be able to rearrange images efficiently (200 images each).
One operating system which can handle the SOMATOM, the tape station and the image manipulation.

FUTURE USE OF CT

1. Research and development

Up to now we have been concerned mainly with develop-ment of prediction equations for pigs and lambs of ordinary slaughter weights. The results of these experiments will be presented in other papers of this workshop. We also have some investigations under way to look at prediction equations for pigs of live weights of about 30 kg.

I believe the results of the present work may show that we will be able to predict carcass composition with about the same accuracy as with slaughter and dissection procedures. This opens great possibilities for many types of studies. I have already mentioned studies of growth and tissue deposition curves for different breeds or lines. I also mentioned studies of compensatory growth at different stages.

Another field is certainly nutritional studies with estimation of net energy of different feeds or feeding levels. We already have some investigations under way where we combined fasting metabolism in respiration chambers with the energy mobilisation data estimated by the CT.

As you will hear later, studies of fat accretion and mobilization during growth and lactation in goats has been carried out.

I would think that the dream of any nutritionist might be, to start with experimental animals of accurately estimated composition as to tissues and energy and to follow the development of these components during the experimental period. I think this will be possible with the CT.

Up to now we have not been using injection of contrast medium except for a small study of the distribution of an anaesthetic drug in the spinal duct. Use of contrast medium is very common in many kinds of medical studies. It is likely that use of such contrast also might improve our information for some purposes. Studies of development and mineralization of the skeleton with different nutrition might also be done with the aid of CT, but up to now has not been attempted.

We have made one study with halothane reactors and normal pigs to look at the changes in muscles during malignant hyperthermia (Frøystein et al., 1983). We observed changes in the density of the muscles. Whether changes in muscles in PSS pigs under less severe stress may be observed is not known. It is also not known if muscles of PSE-prone pigs differ from normal pigs under non-stress conditions.

2. CT for practical breeding purposes

A. Pig breeding

The place for, and the use of CT in pig breeding will vary from country to country, and with the breeding program presently in operation.

In Norway we have a national cooperative breeding program with centralized station and on farm boar performance testing combined with station sib test. The yearly cost of the sib test is about 2 mill Norwegian kroner

(200000 £). With CT information on the station tested boars, the selection for carcass composition may be much improved compared to a situation with only ultrasonic information. This may make it possible and efficient to terminate the sib test stations, and use the money to increase the capacity of the performance test stations and to include CT information as an aid to selection.

More hypothetically it might be speculated on the possibility to reduce the testing period in the performance test. If it can be shown that tissue- or energy mobilization during fasting may be recorded with CT, the next step would be to test if this might be correlated to maintenance requirement or maybe to feed efficiency during normal test. If this is the case, one or two 4-6 fasting periods combined with CT evaluation might replace the performance test.

B. Sheep breeding

One would think that selection for carcass composition on live ram lambs would be of at least the same value as for boar selection, since ultrasonic testing of lambs are of much less value relative to pigs. In the Norwegian breeding program we have an efficient progeny testing scheme for growth and carcass quality. The CT might then possibly be utilized as a tool for preselection of test rams. Even more valuable would the CT be when used in a sire line or breed. Selection for growth of lean in such a line would probably be much improved by the use of CT.

C. Poultry breeding

I know too little of poultry breeding to have many good points on the use of CT there. I understand that fat carcasses are a problem and this may certainly be recorded on live chicken with CT. It is also possible that some aspects of egg, and egg shell quality may be recorded and selected for.

USE OF CT IN FIELDS OTHER THAN ANIMAL SCIENCE

There has been only limited time for disciplines other

than animal science to try other possible uses of CT. Some other items have however been scanned. The most extensive program is a cheese making project by the Department of Dairy Science, to study the maturation of cheese when different manufacturing procedures have been imposed. The density, hole setting and salt concentration may be studied without cutting or damaging the cheese.

Some soil scientists have used CT to study root development in different growth medium and with different watering and fertilization systems. Also the quality of root crops like celery may be studied without cutting. If this will be of any use in selection for root quality I do not know.

To indicate the variety of uses of the CT facility, I may mention that it will be used in a program to evaluate bore cores from the oil fields in the North Sea.

I think there are a lot of possible uses of this equipment in science and industry if we have the imagination to try. Almost any kind of non-destructible investigations on material softer than bones may be conducted with the X-ray CT.

REFERENCES

Aulstad, D. 1980. In vivo estimation of carcass composition in young boars. I. The use of blood volume characters. Acta Agr. Scand., 19, 181-188.

Froystein, T., Gronseth, K., Nostvold, S.O. and Standal, N. 1983. Changes in muscle density in pigs during malignant hyperthermia syndrome measured by computerized tomography. Zeitschr. Tierzuchtg. Zuchtgsbiol. In press.

Skjervold, H. 1982. Estimation of body composition in live animals by use of computerized tomography. (CEC Workshop Copenhagen 15-16 December 1981).

Skjervold, H., Indroebo, T. and Odegard, A. 1960. Registrering av ryggspekkelsen pa levende svin. Meld. Norges Landbr.-h.skole. Nr. 4 1960. 8 pp.

Skjervold, H., Gronseth, K., Vangen, O. and Evensen, A. 1981. In vivo estimation of body composition by computerized tomography. Z. Tierzchtg. Zuchtgsbiol., 98, 77-79.

51

Standal, N. 1962. A scoring system for pig selection base on performance testing for backfat thickness and rate of gain. Meld. Norges Landbr.h.skole. Nr. 4 1962. 8 pp.

Tveit, B. 1977. Muligheter for maling av energiinnholdet hos levende dyr. Husdyrforsoksmotet. 1977. Statens Fagtjeneste.

X-RAY TOMOGRAPHY OF PIGS
SOME PRELIMINARY RESULTS

Paul Allen [1] and Odd Vangen
Department of Animal Genetics and Breeding
Agricultural University of Norway
1432 As-NLH, Norway

[1] Permanent address: Meat Research Department,
Agricultural Institute, Dunsinea Research Centre,
Castleknock, Co. Dublin, Ireland

ABSTRACT

Prediction equations for side weight and its components and for chemical components of the bacons side, subcutaneous fat and m. longissimus dorsi were developed for a group of boars and gilts. Four types of model were used and the residual standard deviations compared. Models including weight and sex alone accounted for between 24.0 and 81.7 percent of the variation in the dependent variables. Models including lean and fat areas and/or CT means reduced by varying amounts the proportion of the total variation unexplained by weight and sex . In no case was there a large advantage from using CT means rather than lean and fat areas in prediction models. Single model and within-sex models were also compared. Possible ways of improving data collection from images and more sophisticated ways of utilizing CT absorption information were discussed.

INTRODUCTION

Computerised X-Ray Tomography (CT) is a relatively new branch of technology developed for use as a diagnostic tool in human medicine. As recently as 1977, Houndsfield and M'Cormack received the Nobel Prize for their contribution to its development. Its potential contribution to animal science as a tool for measuring body or carcass composition in the live animal was soon recognised in Norway and a small trial with 23 pigs was conducted (Skjervold et.al. 1981). In 1982 a Siemens Somatom II scanner was acquired by the Agricultural University of Norway and a trial was begun to evaluate its potential for predicting carcass composition of pigs of end-of-test weight (around 100 kg).

In assessing the utility of a new technique to animal science many factors must be taken into consideration, and the assessment must be relative to techniques currently available to be of maximum use in decision making. The best way to compare different techniques is in parallel trials. In the absence of these, residual standard deviations (RSDs) of predicted variables from separate trials may indicate the relative merit of different techniques. Even so, caution is needed since the RSDs will be influenced by the procedures employed, and the level of skill of the operators.

The most obvious technique for comparison with CT is ultrasonics, and in particular the more advanced ultrasonic machines such as the Scanogram and Danscanner, which allow the measurement of fat and muscle linear and area measurements (Kempster et al. 1979). The authors believe that a parallel trial would be desirable once prediction equations have been developed for CT and procedures have been simplified and improved. In the meantime an attempt has been made to analyse the present data in such a way as to indicate the relative merits of using area measurements and/or CT means. This could not be considered a comparison of ultrasonic and CT techniques, since no information is available on their relative accuracy and repeatability for measuring lean and fat areas. However, it should indicate the utility of employing CT means to predict compositional traits rather than fat and lean area measurements.

Boars and gilts were used in the trial but single prediction equations were developed with sex included in the models. In most practical applications, particularly in animal breeding, the objective will be to rank individuals of one sex. For this reason and also because there were important differences between the two samples, equations were also developed within each sex and the RSDs will be compared to those achieved with a single model.

MATERIAL AND METHODS

Experimental Animals

Data will be presented from an experiment designed to generate equations for predicting carcass composition and energy content in live gilts and boars at around the end-of-test weight (approximately 100 kg). Data were available on 207 individuals, 113 gilts and 94 boars. Gilts were from the University herd and ranged in liveweight from 59 to 120 kg. All boars had been through the Norwegian Central Test Station and ranged in weight from 85.4 to 114.6 kg..

Scanning and Image Data Collection

Feed was withheld from pigs on the afternoon before and the morning of scanning. Pigs were scanned on a Monday or Tuesday in batches of 4 to 13. In turn, each pig was given a tranquilizing injection of Afiperon* in the ham muscle (approx. 1 ml/10 kg of a 40 mg/ml solution). Ten to 15 minutes later Thiopentone(approx. 1 ml/10 kg of a 50 mg/ml solution) was administered intravenously with immediate effect. The pig was then placed on its belly (prone) in a plexiglass cradle and weighed. This was then positioned on the scanner table and a topogram taken. From this the positions of the mid-point of the last thoracic (13th) and first lumbar vertebrae were noted (from 7 to 9 other locations were also used, but data presented here are limited to two positions). Scans were then taken at each location with the following settings:-

    Slice thickness, 4 mm
    Projections, 360 (5 sec)
    Voltage, 125 kW, 230 mAs
    Zoom, 1.0 to 1.5

Scans were retaken if animal movement resulted in a poor quality image. Using software developed in the Department the following regions were superimposed on the left side of the image and frequency histograms covering the entire range of absorption values were automatically recorded then truncated as indicated:

* A/S Farmaceutisk Industri, Oslo

1. Bacon side (BS) region - from the mid-point of the belly to a point mid-way between the edge of m.longissimus dorsi and the dorsal tip of the outermost abdominal muscle, skin excluded but including the fat layer at the abdominal cavity (range= -160 to +120 HU).

2. Longissimus dorsi (LD) region - the outline of the muscle was described by a line drawn to the muscle side of the fat/muscle and fat/bone boundaries (range= -20 to +120 HU).

3. Subcutaneous fat (SCF) region - from the mid-point of the back to a point at the skin defined by a line drawn normal to the surface to the dorso-lateral tip of m. longissimus dorsi (range= -160 tp -20 HU).

Each of the three regions was superimposed on the images taken at the 13th thoracic and 1st lumbar vertebrae and all data are the average of the two. The mean absorption value (CT-mean) was calculated for each region, and LD and SCF areas were calculated in cm2.

Slaughter and dissection procedures

On the Monday morning following scanning pigs were transported to a meat factory in Oslo, slaughtered, dressed and chilled overnight. The left side of each carcass (head, feet, kidneys and kidney fat removed) was weighed before separation into its component parts. Samples of BS, LD and SCF were taken in the region of the last rib. The remainder of the SCF and large intermuscular fat depots were removed and weighed to obtain dissected fat wegiht. The larger muscles were trimmed of fat and weighed to obtain dissected lean weight. Weights were also obtained for the remaining soft tissues and bone. Each of the three soft tissue components was thoroughly mixed, ground and sampled for analysis. Water, fat and protein (Nx6.25) content of BS, water content of the SCF and fat content of the LD samples were determined.

Statistical analysis

Data were analysed using the Statistical Analysis System (SAS 1982). The General Linear Models Procedure was used to develop prediction equations. For each dependent variable a base model (Model I) was fitted with sex as a class variable and liveweight as a main effect. Lean and fat area measurements and/or CT means were added to the base model (Models II, III, IV). All interaction effects were first included then sequentially dropped out due to non-significance. The liveweight x sex term was either just significant at the 5% probability level or approached this. In the interests of simplicity of presentation of results and ease of interpretation, it was excluded in all cases. Quadratic terms for CT-means were also fitted and for protein content of the bacon side this was significant and was retained.

RESULTS

Side weight and its soft-tissue components

Relevant means and coefficients of variation are shown in Table 1 for the 113 gilts and 94 boars. Not surprisingly, boars had more "lean" and less "fat" than gilts though coefficients of variation were similar in the two sexes. However, gilts had considerably more variation in live, side and total soft tissue weights.

TABLE 1. Means ± standard deviations and coefficients of variation for liveweight left side weight and its soft tissue components, areas and CT means for 113 gilts and 94 boars.

| | Gilts | | | Boars | | |
Variable	Mean		CVx100	Mean		CVx100
Live wt (kg)	93.4	11.6	12.4	102.5	5.7	5.6
Side wt (kg)	34.0	4.8	14.1	36.4	2.3	6.4
Fat wt (kg)	5.49	1.76	32.1	2.60	0.89	34.2
Lean wt (kg)	6.00	1.05	17.5	7.87	1.42	18.0
Soft tissue wt (kg)	27.5	4.2	15.1	28.5	2.0	6.9
LD area (cm^2)	34.5	5.7	16.6	43.7	4.9	11.3
SCF area (cm^2)	13.2	4.6	34.8	52.8	3.3	62.0
LD CT mean (HU)	57.4	4.8	8.4	58.8	4.6	7.8
SCF CT mean (HU)	-80.8	10.3	12.7	-56.7	13.1	23.1
BS CT mean (HU)	-14.0	12.1	-	19.0	12.2	-

Applying the four types of model (methods section) to the dissection data yielded the R^2 values and RSD s in Table 2. Side weight was predicted by the base model (RSD = 1.73) almost as accurately as by models including areas and/or CT means (RSD for model IV = 1.61). For all three dissected components Model IV gave the highest R^2 and lowest RSD but the improvement over the beter of the models including only areas or CT means (models II and III) was marginal. Only for weight of dissected fat did the model with CT means (Model III) give a better prediction than that with areas (Model II), but in

TABLE 2. Prediction of side weight and its components from base model and models including areas and/or CT means.

| | | Dependent Variables (all kg) | | |
| | Side | Fat | Lean | Soft |
Model	wt	wt	wt	tissue wt
I Base Model				
R^2 x 100	81.7	63.7	54.6	75.8
RSD (df=204)	1.73	1.22	1.04	1.66
II Base Model + areas				
R^2 x 100	83.9	77.6	61.9	79.8
RSD (df=200)	1.62	0.96	0.96	1.52
III Base Model + CT means				
R^2 x 100	82.8	79.0	57.9	78.8
RSD (df=194)	1.68	0.92	1.00	1.56
IV Base Model + areas + CT means				
R^2 x 100	84.3	81.3	62.1	80.5
RSD (df= 192)	1.61	0.86	0.95	1.49

[1] Factors included in models as follows:

    I Liveweight, sex
   II Liveweight, sex, LD area, SCF area
  III Liveweight, sex, LD CT mean, SCF CT mean, BS CT mean
  IV Liveweight, sex, LD area, SCF area, LD CT mean,
    SCF CT mean, BS CT mean

all cases differences were small. Relative to the means shown in Table 1, the RSD s are somewhat disappointing for dissected fat and lean weights. However, this probably reflects a lack of precision in the dissection technique. Better results are anticipated when prediction equations are developed for chemical component weights and calorific values of the soft tissues.

Chemical components of the bacon side

Data from a subset of gilts and boars were available. Relevant means and coefficients of variation are shown in Table 3. The higher water and protein and lower fat content for boars was entirely expected and was reflected in a higher CT mean. The greater than twofold increase in the coefficient of variation for the fat content of boar samples is a little surprising but is probably due to the inclusion of some extremely lean individuals.

TABLE 3. Means+standard deviation and coefficients of variation for liveweight BS content of water, fat and protein, areas and CT means for 89 gilts and 79 boars.

	Gilts		Boars	
Variables	Mean	C.V.x100	Mean	C.V.x100
Live wt (kg)	93.0 11.8	12.7	102.6 5.8	5.6
BS content(g/100 g):				
water	52.2 4.6	8.9	65.9 4.7	7.1
fat	32.5 5.9	18.2	14.8 5.8	39.1
protein	14.1 1.7	12.3	18.3 1.2	6.7
LD area (cm^2)	34.8 6.0	17.3	43.9 4.8	11.0
SCF area (cm^2)	13.0 4.6	35.4	4.7 3.0	63.5
BS CT mean (HU)	-13.4 12.5	-	21.5 11.9	-

Table 4 shows the results of predicting the three components from the four models. Of the three, protein was predicted by all four types of model with least accuracy. The regression of protein content on CT mean appeared to be curvilinear and when added to models III and IV the quadratic term for CT mean was significant ($P<0.001,< 0.02$ respectively). Perhaps this needs further investigation to find the best description of the relationship. The base model explained

TABLE 4. Prediction of the BS chemical components from base model and models including areas and/or CT means.

Model [1]	Dependent variables (all g/100g)		
	Water	Fat	Protein
I Base Model			
R^2x100	71.0	71.5	67.1
RSD (df=165)	4.46	5.66	1.48
II Base Model + areas			
R^2x100	83.1	84.8	80.2
RSD (df=162)	3.40	4.13	1.13
III Base Model + CT means			
R^2x100	87.2	88.4	84.1
RSD (df)	2.97(160)	3.60(160)	1.02(159)
IV Base Model + areas + CT means			
R^2x100	87.9	89.3	85.2
RSD (df)	2.89(157)	3.45(157)	0.97(256)

[1] Factors included in models as follows:

  I Liveweight, sex
 II Liveweight, sex, LD area, SCF area
III Liveweight, sex, BS CT mean (+(BS CT mean)^2 for protein)
 IV Liveweight, sex, LD area, SCF area, BS CT mean (+(BS CT mean)^2 for protein)

between 67 and 71.5% of the variation in content of chemical components. Fitting partial regressions for LD and SCF areas explained a further 12.1 to 13.3% of the variation, compared to 16.2 to 17.0% for fitting the CT mean of the BS Using information about mean tissue density rather than muscle and fat areas therefore accounted for an additional 4% of the variation in the content of water, fat and protein. A further but marginal improvement was achieved by including areas and the CT mean as covariates. Relative to sample means and standard deviations presented in Table 3, the RSDs for models II and IV are quite encouraging. Fat content was the most variable component and was also predicted with least accuracy. Nevertheless, the sample standard deviation was reduced threefold by the best model.

Water content of the subcutaneous fat sample (SCF).

Plots of water content of the SCF sample against mean CT value of the SCF region revealed some extreme outliers, all of which were boars. These were probably the boars which had so little SCF in this region that extreme difficulty was encountered in obtaining a large enough sample for analysis and in drawing the region on the image. These were therefore dropped from the data set. Relevant means and coefficients of variation are presented in Table 5. On average boars had twice as much water in the SCF, though coefficients of variation were similar. Sex differences in the water content of SCF have previously been noted for boars and castrated males (Allen et al., 1981, Wood and Enser, 1982), and has been reported for a subset of the present data by Allen, 1983.

TABLE 5. Means+standard deviation and coefficients of variation for liveweight, SCF water content, area and CT mean for 113 gilts and 83 boars.

	Gilts		Boars	
	Mean	CVx100	Mean	CVx100
Live wt (kg)	93.5 11.6	12.4	102.5 5.4	5.3
Water content of SCF (g/100g)	11.9 3.0	24.9	21.8 5.5	25.1
SCF area (cm^2)	13.2 4.6	34.5	5.7 3.2	56.3
SCF CT mean (HU)	-80.7 10.2	12.6	-55.1 12.9	23.4

RSD s and R^2 values for the prediction of water content of SCF samples by the four-types of model are presented in Table 6. The base model accounted for 59.1% of the variation in water content and yielded a RSD of 4.12 percentage units of water. Fitting the partial regression coefficient for SCF area explained a further 17.4% compared to 22.8% using the CT-mean rather than the area. No further improvement was achieved by using SCF area and CT-mean as covariates. The RSDs although representing a large reduction from the sample standard deviation are a little disappointing considering the mean water content of 16.1% (Table 5). Possible ways of improving data collection from the images will be discussed later.

TABLE 6. Prediction of SCF water content (g/100 g) from base model and models including SCF area and/or CT mean.

	Model[1]			
	I Base Model	II Base Model + area	III Base Model + CT mean	IV Base Model + area+CT mean
R^2x100	59.1	76.5	81.9	81.9
RSD(df)	4.12(193)	3.13(191)	2.75(191)	2.75(190)

[1] Factors included in models as follows

   I Liveweight, sex
  II Liveweight, sex, SCF area
 III Liveweight, sex, SCF CT mean
 IV Liveweight, sex, SCF area, SCF CT mean

Fat content of m. longissimus dorsi (LD).

    Relevant means and coefficients of variation are presented in Table 7. Boars had less intra-muscular fat than gilts, but more variation. The actual range in fat content was from 0.14 to 3.45% , with about one third of individuals having 1% or less. These are very low levels of intramuscular fat and may cause concern about meat quality.

TABLE 7. Means±standard deviations and coefficients of variation for liveweight LD fat content, area and CT mean for 113 gilts and 94 boars.

	Gilts		Boars	
Variable	Mean	CVx100	Mean	CVx100
Live wt (kg)	93.5 11.6	12.4	102.5 5.7	5.6
Fat content of LD (g/100 g)	1.71 0.56	32.8	1.13 0.43	38.1
LD area (cm^2)	34.5 5.7	16.6	43.7 4.9	11.3
LD CT Mean (HU)	57.4 4.8	8.4	58.8 4.6	7.8

    Table 8 shows R^2 values and RSD s for the prediction of LD fat content of four models. The R^2 values are quite low (0.24 to 0.30) though all models were highly significant. Fitting the LD CT mean did not improve the precision. LD area explained a further 5.4% of the variation remaining after fitting the base model but only marginally reduced the RSD. Using CT-mean and area as covariates did not further reduce the RSD.

TABLE 8. Prediction of the intramuscular fat content (g/100g) of LD from base model and models including LD area and/or CT mean.

		Model [1]		
	I Base model	II Base model + areas	III Base model + CT means	IV Base model + areas + CT means
$R^2 \times 100$	24.0	29.4	25.0	30.2
RSD (df)	0.50(204)	0.49(202)	0.50(202)	0.48(201)

[1] Factors included in models:

    I Liveweight, sex
   II Liveweight, sec, LD area
 III Liveweight, sex, LD, CT mean
  IV Liveweight, sex, LD area, LD CT mean

Water, fat and protein content of BS and water content of SCF were predicted within sex by models including weight only (base model), and by models including weight, plus all the covariates used in model IV for the between sex predictions (model II). RSDs and R^2 values are presented together with the equivalent values from the between sex models in Table 9.

Since the variation within sex is smaller than when sexes are combined comparison of R^2 values is not valid, but the RSDs may be used to indicate the relative merits of between and within sex models. For the reason just outlined, within sex R^2 values are considerably lower than when a single model is used for both sexes, especially for the base models. Furthermore, and for the same reason R^2 values are higher for gilts than boars. The effect of predicting dependent variables within sex is to greatly increase the contribution of the areas and CT means, a consequence of their covariance with sex. Within-sex RSDs are comparable to those achieved with the single model for both sexes and in some cases lower for one or both sexes.

TABLE 9. Prediction of chemical components by a single model and by models fitted within sex.

Deependent variables		Sex		Overall
		Gilts	Boars	
BS content of:				
Water:				
I Base Model	R^2x100	25.5	6.4	71.0
	RSD (df)	4.00(87)	4.50(77)	4.46(165)
II Full Model	R^2x100	59.9	59.1	87.9
	RSD (df)	2.93(85)	2.99(73)	2.89(157)
Fat:				
I Base Model	R^2x100	23.6	9.2	71.5
	RSD (df)	5.17(87)	5.51(77)	5.66(165)
II Full Model	R^2x100	62.9	61.5	89.3
	RSD (df)	3.55(85)	3.63(73)	3.45(157)
Protein:				
I Base Model	R^2x100	19.2	19.5	67.1
	RSD (df)	1.57(87)	1.11(77)	1.48(165)
II Full Model	R^2x100	58.3	52.3	85.2
	RSD (df)	1.10(84)	0.86(75)	0.97(156)
SCF content of water:				
I Base Model	R^2x100	34.4	9.3	59.1
	RSD (df)	2.40(111)	5.22(81)	4.12(193)
II Full Model	R^2x100	56.8	65.4	81.9
	RSD (df)	1.96(109)	3.22(80)	2.75(190)

Factors included in models as follows:

   I Liveweight (+ sex for single model)
  II As per model IV in Tables 4 and 6 (sex excluded for within sex models).

DISCUSSION

The RSDs for the dissected lean and fat weights are a little disappointing. CT means were less accurate than SCF and LD areas in predicting dissected lean weight and only marginally better for dissected fat wieght. This is confirmed by examining the simple correlation coefficients (Table 10) However, the dissection procedure did not aim to totally separate fat and lean tissues and more than 60% of the soft tissues fell into the 'remainder' category. The accuracy and

64

repeatability of this procedure is questionable and will set
lower limits to the RSD s Furthermore, a very simple approach
to utilizing CT absorption information was used. Better
results might be anticipated when absorption data from 11
different anatomical cross sections per pig are used to
optimise the accuracy of prediction.

TABLE 10. Simple correlation coefficients between carcass
components and liveweight, areas and CT means.

	Side wt	Fat wt	Lean wt	Soft tissue wt
Liveweight	0.94***	0.69***	0.68***	0.93***
LD area	0.75***	0.49***	0.70***	0.73***
SCF area	0.69***	0.74***	0.24**	0.70***
LD CT mean	0.00	-0.18	0.06	-0.01
SCF CT mean	-0.56***	-0.60***	-0.14	-0.57***
BS CT mean	-0.57***	-0.68***	-0.18	-0.60***

With the exception of intramuscular fat which will be
discussed separately, the prediction of the soft tissue
chemical components was more encouraging. This probably
reflects the greater accuracy and repeatability of the sampling and chemical analysis relative to the tissue separation
and the fact that all dependent variables and covariates were
recorded at one anatomical location (in the region of the last
rib). In all cases, CT means explained more of the variation
after removal of weight and sex effects than did areas.
Inclusion of areas and CT means in the same model did not
explain any more of the variation, suggesting high correlations among these. An examination of the simple correlation
coefficients indicates that the high correlations between SCF
area and its CT mean (-0.84, P<0.001) and the CT mean of the
BS (-0.77, P<0.001) are responsible for this (Table 11).

TABLE 11. Simple correlation coefficients between areas and CT means.

	CT Mean		
Area	LD	SCF	BS
LD	0.08	0.43***	0.53***
SCF	-0.15*	-0.86***	-0.88***

LD and SCF areas were more highly correlated with weights of dissected fat and lean, respectively than were any of the CT means (Table 10) and, as simple and easily obtained parameters of high predictive value, ought not to be overlooked in future work to develop CT for prediction of soft tissue components. Standard software supplied by Seimens may be used to obtain these areas immediately after scanning, and it is likely that the accuracy could be improved by reconstructing the image from the raw data using a larger zoom factor and targetting on the region to produce a higher resolution image of the muscle and fat. This may be done immediately after a scan and would take less than one minute, or at a later date if the raw data files were stored. Expansion of an area of a stored image is also possible but does not improve the resolution and is of limited use. However, this may be of value for measuring SCF area in some of the very lean boars included in the present trial.

The results for the prediction of fat content of LD are very disappointing but were not unexpected. The problem is that at such low levels of intramuscular fat content errors in determining the CT mean and content of intramuscular fat are much greater than the effect of variation in fat content on the mean. This can be illustrated from first principles. Assuming a mean value of -60 HU for muscle and -90 for fat, the effect of a 1% increase in fat content (approx. twice the standard deviation) would be to reduce the mean density of muscle by 0.7 units. An alternative approach would be to predict fat content from the relative number of pixels within the muscle that lie in the fat range (say -160 to -20 HU). Unfortunately the intramuscular fat deposits are almost certainly beyond the resolution of the scanner. The effect of increasing intramuscular fat content is therefore to skew the distribution in the lean range towards zero, as more and more pixels contain some fat. Use of the approach outlined above to reconstruct areas of images with maximum zoom and obtain histograms for regions of interest may improve the prediction of intramuscular fat content if suitable parameters are found to describe this skewness.

REFERENCES

Allen, P. 1983. Sex differences in fat composition (C.E.C. Workshop on Fat Quality in Lean Pigs, Brussels 20-21 September, 1983).

Allen, P., Riordan, P.B., Hanrahan, T.J. and Joseph, R.L. 1981. Production and quality of boar and castrate bacon. I. Pig Production, in factory processing and carcass value. Ir. J. Fd. Sci. Technol, 5, 93-104.

Kempster, A.J., Cuthbertson, A. and Owen, M.G. 1979. A comparison of four ultrasonic machines (Sonatest, Scanogram. Ilis Observer and Danscanner) for predicting the body composition of live pigs. Anim. Prod., 29_, 175-181.

SAS Institute Inc. 1982. SAS User's Guide: Basics, 1982 Edition. Cary NC: SAS Institute Inc., 923 pp.

Skjervold, H., Grønseth, K., Vangen, O, and Evensen, A. 1981. In Vivo estimation of body composition by computerized tomography. Z. Tierzchtg. Zuchtgsbiol. 98, 77-79.

Wood, J.D. and Enser, M. 1982. Comparison of boars and castrates for bacon production 2. Composition of muscle and subcutaneous fat, and changes in side weight during curing. Anim. Prod., 35, 65-74.

COMPUTERIZED TOMOGRAPHY OF SHEEP

Erling Sehested
Department of Animal Genetics and Breeding
Agricultural University of Norway

ABSTRACT

293 ram lambs of the Dala breed were scanned live in a computer tomograph, slaughtered, dissected and soft tissue chemically analyzed. R^2 values of the prediction equations at constant live weight for kg protein, kg fat, kg fat-free lean, energy (MJ) and kg carcass weight were .56, .73, .58, .70 and .57, respectively.

INTRODUCTION

A computer tomograph is an X-ray based instrument, which reconstructs an image of a cross-sectional slice of the body examined. Use of CT in prediction of carcass composition of live pigs has shown promising results (Skjervold et al. 1981). A similar experiment with sheep was therefore carried out to evaluate the utility of CT-measurements for prediction of compositional traits. The main objective of this experiment was to develop prediction equations. Such equations could be utilized in sheep research e.g. feeding experiments and growth studies. Ranking of breeding animals in a selection scheme is another potential field. Some preliminary results will be presented in this paper.

MATERIAL AND METHODS

There are several options concerning settings of the computer tomograph. The effect of different settings on machine error was investigated in a pilot experiment. The setting which gave least machine error was chosen as a standard.

293 ram lambs of the Dala breed, sired by 32 test rams, were sampled from 2 ram-circles. The lambs were fasted for a 24 hour period before scanning. They were laid on their back in a plexiglass cradle with legs strapped down. This fixation made anesthesia unnecessary. The lambs were then weighed and introduced into the tomograph. A topogram was then

68

taken. The topogram gave a picture of the skeleton and was used for detection of the standard positions where the cross-sectional scans (tomograms) were to be taken. The standard positions were:

1. 11th Thoracic vertebra
2. 13th   "   "
3. 2nd Lumbar vertebra
4. 4th   "   "
5. 6th   "   "
6. The narrowest point on the pelvic limb (mid. pelvis)
7. Head of femur
8. Hind edge of pelvic limb (leg)

One to three days after scanning the lambs were slaughtered. Carcasses were split and right halves cut down to bone and soft tissue. The soft tissue was ground, and chemically analyzed for dry matter, fat and protein. Contents of chemical components in the carcasses were then calculated. Fat-free lean was calculated as weight of soft tissue minus weight of chemical fat. The means and standard deviations of live weight, carcass weight and compositional traits are given in table 1.

TABLE 1. Means and standard deviations of liveweight, carcass weight and carcass content.

	$\bar{X}$	sd.
Liveweight, kg	41.701	6.384
Carcass weight, kg	18.451	3.436
Weight of protein, kg	2.542	0.454
Weight of fat, kg	2.242	0.948
Weight of fat free lean, kg	11.492	2.041
Energy, MJ	147.618	45.677

Construction of predictors

A tomogram is a matrix with 256x256 elements, each element representing a CT-value (density). For prediction purposes, this large amount of information had to be reduced drastically. The first step in this process was to remove the elements that did not represent carcass. This was done by drawing a region along the boundary between the carcass and its surroundings (air, organs, etc,). The elements within the region were then summarized as a histogram of CT-values.

An example of such a histogram is shown in figure 1.

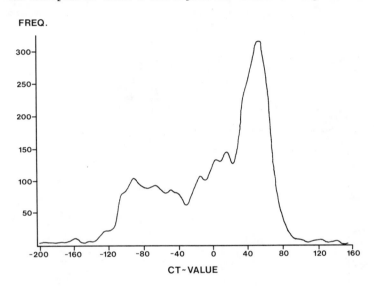

Figure 1.   Distribution of CT-values of a carcass at 4th Lumbar vertebra.

Predictors could now be constructed in two different ways:
1. As frequencies of CT-intervals
2. As distribution parameters: mean CT-value and total sum of elements (composition and size).

RESULTS AND DISCUSSION

Various models for prediction of amount of protein, fat, fat-free lean, energy and carcass weight were fitted. Results from models of frequencies in CT-intervals as predictors, showed that decreasing the width of the interval improved

70

prediction. This can be explained by examining figure 2. The histogram in this figure is obtained by subtracting histograms of two lambs from each other, one fat (3.6 kg fat) and one lean (1.6 kg fat) lamb. Both lambs had carcass weights of 21 kg. In the CT-value range from 30 to 70, differences between the two lambs would not be discovered if CT-intervals are too wide.

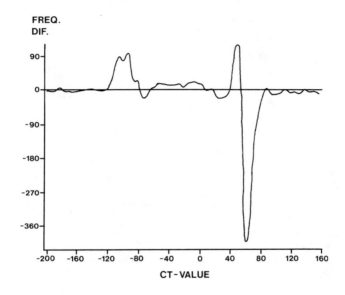

Figure 2: Difference between histograms of a fat and a lean lamb.

Other main trends from initial analyses are:
1. Relative frequencies do not give as good prediction as actual frequencies within CT-intervals.
2. Frequencies are better predictors than mean CT-value + total sum of elements.
3. Image quality was subjectively scored on a 1 to 3 scale. Excluding bad quality images (scores 1 and 2) did not improve prediction. In this context, it should be

mentioned that images of unacceptable quality were never included.

4. Using single positions as source for predictors gave this ranking

a) 13th Thoracic, 4th Lumbar

b) 2nd Lumbar

c) 11th Thoracic

d) 6th Lumbar

e) Mid pelvis, head of femur

f) Leg

Results from analysis of 3 types of models **are now** presented in more detail.

Model 1: $Y = \beta_o + \beta_1 \cdot LW + e$

where LW = Liveweight

Model 2: $Y = \beta_o + \sum_{i=1}^{21} \beta_i P_i + \beta_{22} \cdot LW + e$

where P_i = Frequency in ith CT-interval

CT-interval width = 10 CT-values

Position: 4th Lumbar vertebra

Model 3: $Y = \beta_o + \sum_{j=1}^{8} \sum_{i=1}^{7} \beta_{ji} P_{ji} + \beta_1 \cdot LW + e$

where P_{ji} = Frequency in ith CT-interval from jth position

CT-interval width = 30 CT-values

Traditional regression analysis methods were used. The stepwise procedure was used to select predictors. Results are presented in Table 2.

TABLE 2. Prediction of carcass composition of live lambs.

Content of	Model 1 R^2	rsd	Model 2 R^2	rsd	DFM	Model 3 R^2	rsd	DFM	no. pos
Protein, kg	.81	.200	.89	.149	7	.92	.128	12	6
Fat, kg	.64	.571	.88	.325	5	.90	.300	9	5
Fatfree lean, kg	.83	.837	.92	.599	7	.94	.523	13	7
Energy, MJ	.74	23.415	.91	13.821	8	.92	12.689	14	8
Carcass weight, kg	.88	1.174	-	-	-	.96	.753	14	8

rsd = residual standard deviation.

DFM = number of estimated parameters.

no.pos. = Number of positions entered in the prediction equation.

By expressing dependent variables as amount of protein, fat, etc., there is an automatic correlation between the dependent variable and live weight. This is very clear from the results of model 1. An evaluation of the tomograph should therefore be based on prediction at constant live weight. Table 3 shows squared partial correlations between observed and predicted values on a constant live weight basis.

TABLE 3. Prediction of carcass composition on live lambs at constant live weight.

	Protein	Fat	FFL	Energy	CW
r^2	.56	.73	.58	.70	57

r= partial correlation coefficient.

The results seem to be better than those previously achieved with ultrasonic equipment as reviewed by Leymaster et al. (1983).

The residual variation in the models can partly be

explained by sampling and chemical analysis errors. On 21 lambs, two independent samples of soft tissue were taken. Rough estimates of sampling errors can therefore be calculated. Repeatability between chemical analysis of the independent samples was .95 (dry matter, fat, protein). In addition, a scale error is involved. To quantify this, the standard error stated by the manufacturer of the scale was used. This was estimated to be 20 grams. Equation (1) shows how amounts of fat and protein were calculated :

$$(1) \quad Y_i = C(1 + \frac{V_2}{V_1}) \cdot DM \cdot PY_i$$

C = weight of soft tissue, right half
V_1 = weight of right half carcass
V_2 = weight of left half carcass
DM = % dry matter
PY_i= % fat, protein respectively

In equation (1) both products and ratios are involved. In estimation of total error variance due to sampling, chemical analysis and scale errors, equations (2) and (3) were used (Kendall & Stuart 1977).

$$(2) \quad Var(\frac{X}{Y}) \approx (\frac{\mu_x}{\mu_y})^2 \cdot (\frac{VarX}{\mu_x^2} + \frac{VarY}{\mu_y^2})$$

$$(3) \quad Var(X \cdot Y \cdot Z) \approx (\mu_y \mu_z)^2 \, VarX + (\mu_x \mu_z)^2 \, VarY + (\mu_x \mu_y) \, VarZ$$

Covariances between errors of the components in equation (1) were assumed to be zero. There are approximations involved in each step leading to estimates of total error. The estimates presented in Table 4 therefore are of limited reliability. (See Footnote, next page).

TABLE 4: Approximate standard deviations due to errors in chemical analysis, sampling and weight measurements.

Content of	sd
Protein, kg	·076
Fat, kg	.071

74

Possibilities of improving prediction

Repeated chemical analysis of independent samples would probably reduce the residual variation. It is questionable though, whether repeated samples would alter the prediction equations.

Statistically there are several possibilities of improvement. Only traditional regression analysis has been tried up to now. This approach is probably not the most efficient on these data. The tomograph data are characterized by enormous amounts of information and colinearity. New approaches such as the partial least square regression procedure will be tried.

Alternative use of the computer tomograph may give better results. Attention should here be paid to settings of the machine and methods of removing non-carcass components from images. A suggestion on the latter issue is to try contrast mediums. If contrasts could highlight the internal organs, they could easily be removed by truncating the histograms. The advantage of this is that results will become independent of the drawing ability of the operator.

REFERENCES

Kendall, M. and A. Stuart. 1977. The Advanced Theory of Statistics Vol 1 (4th Ed.) pp. 243-262. Griffin & Company Limited, London & High Wycombe.
Leymaster, K.A., H.J. Mersmann and T.G. Jenkins. 1983. Variation among Suffolk ram lambs in carcass and offal chemical components. 3. The utility in estimation of compositional and depositional traits. Anim. Prod. (submitted).
Skjervold, H,. K. Grønseth, O. Vangen and A. Evensen. 1981. In vivo estimation of Body composition by computerized tomography. Z. Tierzüchtg. Züchtgsbiol. 98 (1981) 77-79.

Footnote

A better approach is probably to ignore the scale precision component which is of minor importance compared to the sampling and chemical analysis component. By this route the maximum achievable R^2 for the two predictions are:

Content of	sd	Max R^2 *)
Protein, kg	.049	.98
Fat, kg	.097	.98

*) Max $R^2 = (1 - \frac{\sigma^2_e}{\sigma^2})$ where σ^2_e = error component
σ^2 = sample variance

COMPUTERIZED TOMOGRAPHY OF GOATS DURING PREGNANCY AND LACTATION

Martin Tang Sørensen
National Institute of Animal Science
Rolighedsvej 25, DK-1958 Copenhagen V, Denmark

ABSTRACT

Four goats were CT-scanned eight times at ten different locations during pregnancy and lactation. CT-measured trend in adipose tissue volume followed the expected one, i.e., increase until late pregnancy, decrease during late pregnancy, decrease during early lactation and increase with advancing lactation. Fat balances based on CT-scannings, net energy uptake/expenditure balances and weight changes were calculated for part of the lactation period. The three sets of calculations did not give the same results, thus untenable assumptions were introduced. For the CT-measured fat balances to be accurate, it is necessary to have equations relating CT-measurements to the fat content of the animal.

INTRODUCTION

Knowledge of the mechanisms, which regulate production of milk, egg and body tissues will increase the possibilities to manipulate and thus control this production. It is essential to get information on the yield of the products as a response to various treatments in order to gain knowledge on regulating mechanisms. With respect to egg and milk production there are no difficulties in measuring the production. However, with respect to body tissues difficulties arise, because weight changes do not give reliable information on changes in the various tissue pools. These difficulties might be remedied by computerized tomography (CT), a technique which can distinguish between and measure body tissue pools.

It is the purpose of this paper to present and discuss preliminary results from an experiment in which changes in the adipose tissue pool of goats during pregnancy and lactation were measured by means of CT-scanning.

MATERIALS AND METHODS

Four goats born in February 1982 were CT-scanned three

times during their first pregnancy and five times during the subsequent lactation. Each time they were scanned at 10 adjacent location, i.e. at the 13th and 12th thoracic vertebrae, at the six lumbar vertebraes, at the narrowest part of the ilium and at the hip joint. Before scanning they were anaesthetized, weighed, put on a stretcher and tied with their forelegs streched forwards and their hind legs streched backwards. The CT-scannings were carried out between morning and afternoon feedings.

The animals were in a feeding experiment during the first 14 weeks of lactation. During this period feed consumption were recorded daily and milk production were recorded weekly (average of two successive days). Samples of feeds were taken every week for chemical analysis. The digestibility of the feeds were determined on two rams fed at maintenance level. During the 14-week period the goats were scanned four times, thus three periods with recordings of energy uptake and expenditure were available.

The volume of the adipose tissue pool was calculated as the area (average from the 10 adjacent CT-scanns) of pixels (i.e., the units into which the CT-scanned slice is divided) with CT-values between -160 and -41 HU (Houndsfield Units) multiplied with the length between the 12th thoracic vertebrae and the hip joint, i.e. the two outermost CT-scann locations. The choise of this length is rather arbitrary, and a change in the length will of course affect the calculated volume.

The CT-range between -160 and -41 HU can also comprise "noise", i.e., gastro-intestinal content, border areas between air and skin and border areas between lungs and surrounding tissue. By means of a photographic pen and developed CT-software it is possible to draw a region of interest on the CT-picture, or, in other words to exclude a region, which is not of interest. In the data presented in this paper, the rumen was excluded, but the CT-range which comprise the adipose tissue pool will still comprise pixels with intestinal content and skin-air border areas.

Thus, because of the arbitrary estimated "length" and the "noise", the calculated adipose tissue volume is not an

accurate measure of this tissue pool. However, the change
in the pool size between CT-scanning days should give an accurate estimate of relative changes in the pool size, provided
that the amount of "noise" is relatively constant.

RESULTS AND DISCUSSION

Figure 1 shows calculated volumes of the adipose tissue
pools of the four goats during pregnancy and lactation. The
trend in adipose tissue balance follows the expected one,
i.e., increase until late pregnancy, a fall in late pregnancy,
a fall during early lactation and an increase with advancing
lactation. Thus the trend seems reliable.

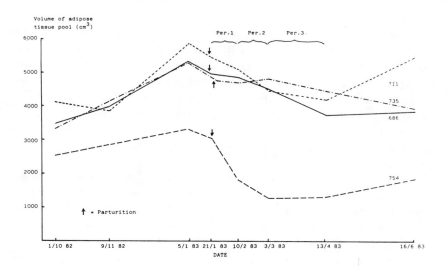

Fig. 1   CT-measured size of the adipose tissue pool of four
          goats during pregnancy and lactation.

The calculated size of adipose tissue pool is, as previously mentioned, affected by the amount of "noise" and the "length" of the included part of the animal. However, the calculated sizes do appear realistic. If it is assumed that adipose tissue contains 80% fat on a wet weight basis, and that fat has a specific gravity of 0.875, one cm^3 adipose tissue will contain 0.8 x 0.875 = 0.7 g of fat. With the adipose tissue volumes shown in figure 1, this means that the three fattest goats contained 9-9.9% fat and the leanest goat contained 6.5% fat at the start of period 1, while at the end of period 3 the three fattest contained 6.8-7.5% and the leanest contained 2.9% on a live weight basis. Even though the figures appear realistic, it is not known how far they are from true values.

Table 1 shows the average daily gain in CT-measured adipose tissue volume, daily weight gain, live weight and daily milk yield in the three separate periods during the feeding experiment.

Table 2 shows the net energy balance calculated on the basis of net energy uptake and expenditure for milk production and maintenance. The energy uptake was measured in fattening feeding units (FFU), which is a net energy unit. The requirements for milk production is 0.4 FFU per kg 4% milk (FCM), and as 1 kg FCM contains 3.14 MJ (Vermorel, 1978), 1 FFU will contain 3.14 MJ x 2.5 = 7.85 MJ net energy. Thus in table 1, the energy uptake is converted to MJ by means of this coefficient.

The net energy requirement for maintenance is calculated from the equation 0.273 x $W^{0.75}$(MJ) given by INRA (1978), and the net energy requirement for milk production is calculated from the energy content of the produced milk, i.e., 3.14 MJ per kg FCM (Vermorel, 1978).

On the basis of these uptake/expenditure relationships it is seen that the goats were in negative energy balance.

Table 3 shows the fat balances of the goats calculated in three different ways, i.e., from the CT-scannings, from the net energy balances and from weight measurements.

The column derived from CT-scannings is based on the

TABLE 1   CT-measured gain in adipose tissue volume and some other para-
          meters of goats during the first app. 80 days of lactation

Goat no	Per.[1]	Length of per. (days)	Ave. weight (kg)	Weight gain (g/day)	Adipose tissue vol.[2] gain (cm^3/day)	Milk yield (Kg FCM /day)
686	1	20	39.0	5.0	−6.8	2.00
	2	21	39.6	28.6	−17.1	2.30
	3	41	39.1	−26.8	−17.8	2.31
711	1	20	39.6	90.0	−18.3	2.26
	2	21	40.4	−9,5	−30.0	2.34
	3	41	40.2	−7.3	−6.6	2.10
735	1	16	38.1	200.0	−4.8	2.13
	2	21	40.6	80.9	4.8	2.25
	3	41	41.4	−2.4	−8.8	2.25
754	1	19	31.9	−94.7	−64.9	2.65
	2	21	31.9	81.0	−24.8	2.84
	3	41	32.3	−22.0	0.9	2.84

1) Period 1 = from 0-2 days post partum to February 10th
   "   2 = from February 10th to March 3rd
   "   3 = from March 3rd to April 13th

2) Adipose tissue volume calculated as the area (average of 10 adjacent
   scans) of pixels with CT-values between −160 and −41 HU multiplied
   with the length from 12th thoracic vertebrae to the hip joint.

TABLE 2   Net energy uptake, expenditure and balance of goats during the
first app. 80 days of lactation

Goat no	Per.[1]	Net E uptake (MJ/day)	Net E expend. for maint. (MJ/day)[2]	Net E expend. for milk prod. (MJ/day)[3]	Net E balance (MJ/day)
686	1	10.42	4.26	6.28	−0.12
	2	10.36	4.31	7.22	−1.17
	3	10.28	4.27	7.25	−1.24
711	1	9.78	4.31	7.10	−1.63
	2	10.50	4.37	7.35	−1.22
	3	10.75	4.36	6.59	−0.20
735	1	9.86	4.18	6.69	−1.01
	2	9.17	4.39	7.07	−2.29
	3	8.68	4.46	7.07	−2.85
754	1	9.58	3.66	8.32	−2.40
	2	9.82	3.66	8.92	−2.76
	3	8.59	3.70	8.92	−4.03

1) See foot note at table 1
2) $0.273 \times W^{0.75}$ (MJ) (INRA, 1978)
3) 3.14 MJ per kg FCM (Vermorel, 1978)

TABLE 3   Fat balance of goats during the first app. 80 days of lactation calculated by means of CT-scanning, net energy balance and weight changes.

Goat no	Per.[1]	Fat balance (g/day) calculated from:		
		CT-measured adipose tiss. volume gain (from tab.1)[2]	Net E balance (from tab.2)[3]	Weight gain (from tab.1)[4]
686	1	−4.8	−3.3	3.0
	2	−12.0	−32.5	17.0
	3	−12.5	−34.4	−15.9
711	1	−12.8	−45.2	53.5
	2	−21.0	−33.8	−5.6
	3	−4.6	−5.5	−4.3
735	1	−3.4	−28.0	118.8
	2	3.3	−63.5	48.1
	3	−6.1	−79.0	−1.4
754	1	−45.5	−66.6	−56.3
	2	−17.4	−76.6	48.1
	3	0.6	−111.8	−13.1

1) See foot note at table 1
2) Assuming 0.7 g fat per cm^3 adipose tissue (see text)
3) Assuming that (a) mobilized energy is converted to milk energy with an efficiency of 84% (Moe et al. 1971), (b) one kg mobilized body tissue contains 25.5 MJ (Gardner and Hogue, 1964); with a water:protein ratio of 4:1 and an energy content of 23.85 kJ/g protein and 39.66 kJ/g fat, one kg mobilized body tissue will contain 594 g fat.
4) Assuming 594 g fat per kg weight change.

values of adipose tissue volume gain listed in table 1, and assuming that one cm^3 of adipose tissue contains 0.7 g fat.

The column derived from net energy balances is based on values listed in table 2, and assuming that mobilized body tissue is converted to energy in produced milk with an efficiency of 84% as found in lactating cows (Moe et al., 1971). Likewise it is assumed that one kg of mobilized body tissue contains 25.5 MJ as found in sheep (Gardner and Hogue, 1964); with a water:protein ratio of 4:1 and energy contents of 39.66 kJ/g fat and 23.85 kJ/g protein one kg mobilized body tissue will contain 594 g fat, 81 g protein and 325 g water.

The column derived from weight gain is based on values listed in table 1 and assuming a content of 594 g fat per kg weight change.

The three columns of results in table 3 should be alike. Obviously they are not. This means that sources of error and untenable assumptions have been introduced. It is not possible to give a qualified evaluation on assumptions and possible errors based on these limited data. However, the trends appearing from figure 1 provide some confidence in the CT-measured fat balances. The fat balances based on net energy balances suffer from the fact that the equation for maintenance, feed digestibility, and utilization of digested and mobilized energy cannot take account of individual differences. Apart from that, the results based on net energy balances appear rather low compared to the results based on CT-scannings or weight gains. The results would have been even lower, if a conversion efficiency of 63%, as calculated by Robinson (1978) for lactating ewes, had been used instead of the 84% found by Moe et al. (1971). The results based on weight gains are bound to be rather inaccurate, one of the reasons being that they are based on single weighings which were not performed at fixed intervals from feeding or at fixed hours of the day.

In conclusion the trend in CT-measured fat balance appear reliable. However, equations relating CT-measurements to the amount of fat in the animal **are** required in order to calculate accurate balances.

83

REFERENCES

Gardner, R.W. and Hogue, D.E. 1964. The effect of energy in-
    take and number of lambs suckled on milk yield,milk com-
    position and energetic efficiency of lactating ewes.
    J.Anim.Sci. 23:935-942.
INRA, 1978. Alimentation des Ruminants. INRA Publications,
    Versailles, 597 pp.
Moe, P.W., Tyrrel, H.F. and Flatt, W.P. 1971. Energetics of
    body tissue mobilization. J.Dairy Sci. 54:548-553.
Robinson,J.J. 1978. Response of the lactating ewe to variation
    in energy and protein intake. In: J.G. Boyazaglu and
    T.T. Treacher (Eds.): Milk Production of the Ewe. EAAP
    Publ. No. 23, pp. 53-65.
Vermorel, M. 1978. Feed evaluation for ruminants. II. The
    new energy systems proposed in France. Livestock Prod.
    Sci. 5:347-365.

ACKNOWLEDGEMENT

Personnel at the Institutes of Animal Science, The Norwegian University of Agriculture are thanked for the use of
CT-equipment, developed CT-software, experimental animals
and records on milk production and feed consumption.

EVALUATION OF BODY COMPOSITION OF
LIVE ANIMALS BY X-RAY AND NUCLEAR MAGNETIC
REASONANCE COMPUTED TOMOGRAPHY

E. GROENEVELD, E. KALLWEIT, M. HENNING and A. PFAU

Institute of Animal Husbandry and Animal Behaviour, Mariensee

3057 Neustadt 1, Holtystr. 10, Federal Republic of Germany

Introduction

The evaluation of body composition on live animals in its present state is unsatisfactory. This is partly due to the measures being only linear, while what has to be estimated is three dimensional. SKJERVOLD (1981) presented X-ray computed tomography as a possible solution to this problem. PFAU (1982) suggested another approach by nuclear magnetic reasonance (NMR) computed tomography. The difference between the two systems lies in how the body itself is analysed. In X-ray CT the absorption rate of ionizing radiation is measured: to take extremes, calcified bones will not be penetrated, whereas long tissue is no barrier to highly energetic photons. NMR-CT operates with a strong static magnetic field and pulsed radio waves which induce reasonance of protons in the measured body. The signals emitted are in fact a reaction of the body to the high frequency disturbance. Therefore they are a product of the matter itself, with intensities depending on the proton spin densities and molecular structures. The NMR signal does not continue indefinately: environmental influences cause the individual flipped magnetic moments to get "out of phase", and return to the orientation they held prior to the application of the radio frequency (rf) pulse. The time needed to establish original conditions again have been defined as spin-lattice relaxation time T1 and spin-spin relaxation time T2. Procedures to determine T1 are known as inversion recovery and for T2 as spin-echo methods.

Both systems produce a data matrix of the size 128*128 or 256*256 which contains in X-ray CT the normalized Hounsfield units, ranging from -1000 (air) to more than 1400 (compact bone), and in NMR-CT, at present non standardized values with respect to magnitude depending on the presetting of the tomograph. The data matrices are the basis for further evaluation. The first step is a reconstruction of an image. There are several ways to produce images: on a device with 7 colours the total data space in a matrix is subdivided into seven regions, each region representing a colour. This method will be satisfactory if the information in the matrix is spread uniformly, or if the number of colours is large relative to the number classes to be discriminated. The first requirement is obviously not met with the normalized Hounsfield scale: tissues are represented by rather well defined values, lean assumes values around +90 with a standard deviation of 5, while fat shows values at -60 with a standard deviation of 14. Accordingly the matrix is mapped onto the colours. But since the main tissues we are interested in are fat, lean, bone and perhaps connective tissue, these 3 groups always show up if the total data space is mapped onto 7 colours.

Four series of experiments were run:
1. X-ray CT on a live pig (german landrace, 50kg)
2. NMR CT on half a carcass (15 kg)
3. NMR CT on a mini pig (20 kg)
4. NMR measurements to estimate in vitro the proportion of meat and fat

For X-ray CT a SIEMENS Somatom SF at the Medical School in Hannover, for NMT-CT a BRUKER BNT 1000 resistive magnet system and for the NMR measurement on small samples a BRUNKER Minispec pc 20 were used. For the NMR-CT spin-echo technique was applied to obtain information on proton spin density and spin-spin relaxation time T2 only. For the NMR measurements in vitro both the spin-lattice relaxation time and the spin-spin relaxation time T2 were determined. For experiments 1 to 3 data were moved via tape from the computer tomograph to our computer for reconstruction of the images. To compare the reconstructed images with reality, the bodies were cross sectioned after deep freezing at the same positions, where the images were taken.

For experiment 4 lean to fat ratios were estimated and correlated with the true proportions.

Results
Both X-ray- and NMR-CT are able to discrminate between fat and lean.

However the 3. series of scans did not produce as good results as the X-ray- and the first NMR-CT on the carcass. This is probably due to suboptimal preadjustment of the tomograph on this occasion.

Contrary to X-ray CT, which yields the absorption coefficients in one matrix, NMR CT may produce three parameters: T1, the "spin-lattice relaxation time", T2, the "spin-spin relaxation time" and the proton spin density. One scan produced 8 matrices, which represent 8 echos, each taken at time interval of 12 msec. They are different, as indicated above, by the rate the signal decays. The first image reflects (almost) the proton spin density, while on the image, based on the last echo, only those areas show up, which still send some signal at that point of time.

The eight images reconstructed from the respective echos reveal different structures within one and the same morphological area. Since different tissues may be different with respect to the proton spin density as well as the rate of the signal decays, there are many ways to optimize the images depending on what the experimenter wants to analyse.

Addition of the first 5 echos seems to produce best results with regard to fat/lean discrimination.

The T2 values vary greatly with temperature, also T2 values seem to be different between live and dead brain grey matter (RATZEL, 1983). This indicates a sensitivity for this parameter to biochemical reactions, which might open a new, interesting field of research.

Table 1. shows the matrix values and standard deviations for some tissues (for NMR CT from the first echo from a cooled carcass):

Table 1

	X-ray CT		NMR-CT	
	$\overline{x}$	s	$\overline{x}$	s
fat	-62.8	14.1	17060	2229
muscle	88.9	5.4	42798	1994
bone	444.3	41.8	29722	1728
spinal marrow	41.4	7.8		

To assess the ability to discriminate between various tissues, the difference between them was calculated in terms of standard deviations. The results in table 2 show higher values for X-ray CT, but even a difference of 6 standard deviations between the means guarantees no overlap, so that for practical purposes both systems should be equivalent.

Table 2

difference between	in standard deviations	
	X-ray CT	NMR CT
fat-lean	16	12
fat-bone	15	6

The images can be further improved by employing methods well known in the area of digital image processing. For instance filtering removes high frequency noise, giving a clearer impression of the image. Edge detectors are the first step for automatic analysis of data matrices: after edges between fat and lean have been determined, it is fairly straight forward to calculate the eye muscle area. If more images are taken along the spinal cord it is possible to calculate the volume and thus the weight of the eye muscle or other morphological parts of the body. In an animal breeding context such evaluation system, which goes directly from digital input (data matrix) to digital output (e.g. kg lean) seems to be much more efficient and straight forward, than producing from digital input an analog image, which has to be evaluated manually to get the digital result, e.g. eye muscle area. Automization of the whole process, seems to us to be one of the main advantages of this technique.

For imaging the NMR system usually takes 120 'shots' in a circle around the body. This procedure requires around 5 minutes plus some time to perform the necessary calculations. If, however, only the relative proportion of certain tissues is of interest, e.g. fat and lean, a much shortened and simplified procedure can be used. From both T1 and T2 the lean to fat ratios can be estimated. In experiment 4 a series of samples with defined proportions of fat and lean, ranging between 30 and 70%, were prepared. T1 measurements took 30 seconds, for T2 5 seconds were needed. The output from this system is a series of data, which plotted against time, give an exponential decay curve. With two phases (fat and lean) in the sample the resultant curve is the sum of two exponential curves. From the shape of this curve the proportion of the constituent parts can be estimated. Table 3 shows the correlation between the true content and the estimate, the regression of estimates on true value and the residual standard deviation.

Table 3

tissue	n	T1			T2		
		r	b	s y.x	r	b	s y.x
backfat : lean	18	.97	-.44	.01	.98	.45	.01
kidneyfat : lean	18	.97	-.52	.02	.98	.36	.01

The next step will be to verify the in vitro results in vivo. However some problems have to be overcome before: the present magnet has an aperture of 15 millimeters. Therefore a new one has to be developed to take a whole pig.

Conclusions

Both, X-ray and NMR CT allow non invasive evluation of body composition, X-ray CT uses ionizing radiation, while NMR is based on magnetic fields and ratio waves with no known detrimental effects. Furthermore NMR differentiates soft tissue better than X-ray does as is known from the medical literature. Deviating tissue, such as tumours, can be detected by NMR. This fact might help to follow up metabolic disorders, as are reflected in e.g. problems with meat quality.

A system that would estimate body composition on the basis of relaxation time is fast enough to become a viable solution to the problem of carcass evaluation, both on live animals and in the slaughter line.

PFAU, A. (1982), personal communication
RATZEL, D. (1983), personal communication
SKJERVOLD, H.; GRONSETH, K.; VANGEN, O.; EVENSEN, A. (1981)
  In Vivo estimation of body composition by computerized tomography
  Zeitschrift fur Tierzuchtung und Zuchtungsbiologie 98, p. 77-79.

* Paper presented at EAAP, Madrid, 1983.

DISCUSSION

In response to several questions of a practical nature, Standal commented that in the initial stages of the research it has not been possible to establish what were the running costs or the likely breakdown rate for routine operation of the equipment. It was necessary to calibrate the instrument every 2h for after this period artefacts appear on the images. Experience so far had suggested that the equipment chosen for the Norwegian facility had the necessary performance for the present applications and those envisaged. It was likely that, in future, simpler methodology eg. fewer scans, could probably be employed without an unacceptable loss of precision. As yet no separate predictive equations had been established for different sexes, breeds or strains of animals. King drew attention to the value of imaging in allowing the contribution of the various tissues and organs to the whole body to be calculated. For example killing-out percentage is a widely used indicator in livestock trading which can vary appreciably from animal to animal. The proportion of the empty carcass to liveweight (i.e. killing-out percentage) can readily be established by CT or NMR.

Kempster congratulated Allen and the Norwegian workers for reporting results which for the first time allowed comparisons to be drawn with measures of body and c-rcass composition obtained by other means eg dissection. Allen explained that there was every intention of extending the work to include more full dissections of cadavers.

Sehested, commenting on questions relating to the precision of his observations, acknowledged that problems of sampling frequently led to the poorer correlation coefficients. Prediction equations were calculated from information collected at different times and from different breeds and types of animal. These inherent variations in the condition of the animals at the time of scanning were of greater consequence than the variation in operational characteristics of the instrument.

Demeyer and Butler-Hogg expressed concern about the problems of identifying the sources of the substrates used in the net energy balance described by Tan Sørensen. Gibson noted that there would be different densities of fat amongst animals of different body types and states of fatness. These would have to be accommodated in assessments obtained via CT scanning.

Kallweit was also concerned that the topography of the animal body was apparently not considered. Wells commented that in medical applications scanners are built not especially for accurate CT value, but for image quality and adjustments made for body profile. A different optimisation might be appropriate for scanning livestock. Improved resolution may be achieved by varying the voltage which permits reduced scan times but may increase X-ray dosage. |Short (eg 5 sec) scans will also reduce noise but some information may be lost| I don't understand why?

Standal agreed that more specialist CT expertise was needed for applications in animal science, especially to obtain better machine performance relative to resolution.

SESSION IV

SHORT MISCELLANEOUS PAPERS

Chairman: Paul Allen

NEW EQUIPMENT FOR MEASURING THE SPEED OF ULTRASOUND AND ITS APPLICATION IN THE ESTIMATION OF BODY COMPOSITION OF FARM LIVESTOCK

C.A. Miles, G.A.J. Fursey, R.W.R. York

Agriculture and Food Research Council, Meat Research Institute
Langford, Bristol, BS18 7DY, UK

ABSTRACT

New equipment is described for estimating carcass composition from measurements of the speed of ultrasound through the live animal. The equipment, built to MRI specification by Wells Krautkramer Ltd. has been undergoing field trials since April, 1982. Two ultrasonic transducers, one acting as a transmitter, the other as a receiver are held in line and facing one another at predetermined points on opposite sides of the animal using a specially designed frame. An electronic system automatically carries out a standard sequence of operations to obtain a valid measurement of the mean reciprocal speed $(\overline{1/V})$. It measures the time of flight (τ) of an ultrasonic pulse from one side of the animal to the other, records the distance (d) separating the transducer faces and computes the ratio $\tau/d = \overline{1/V}$. The three parameters are displayed by the unit and are available on an RS232 line for external logging and printing. The precision of the measurements is discussed. The field trials have confirmed on female cattle a highly significant and useful correlation between ultrasonic measurements of the live animal and the composition of the carcass, determined by dissection, supporting earlier findings on steers and bulls.

INTRODUCTION

Previous papers have described and examined the accuracy of a method for estimation of carcass fatness based upon measurement of the speed with which ultrasound is transmitted through the soft tissues of the live animal (1-3). The method was developed to overcome some of the problems of the ultrasonic pulse-echo technique used hitherto. The method:

(a) is quick, painless, safe and capable of being used by non-scientific staff under farm conditions

(b) gives a digital reading which may be used to yield a fatness prediction on the spot, requiring neither subjective interpretation by experienced judges nor lengthy analysis of photographs and

(c) responds equally to subcutaneous, inter- and intra-muscular fat.

The purpose of this paper is to describe equipment for measuring the speed of ultrasound in farm livestock. Part of the equipment was built to our specification by Wells-Krautkramer Ltd. and the rest was built at the

MRI. The whole system has been undergoing field trials since April, 1982 and this paper includes some of the findings of those trials.

PRINCIPLE OF THE METHOD

The principle of the method has been described in detail elsewhere (1) and it is therefore necessary to summarise only those aspects that are essential for understanding the basis of the equipment.

The method relies on the fact that, in general, the speeds (V) of ultrasound in muscle and fatty tissue at body temperature are correlated with the volume fraction of fat (Y) which the tissues contain, via the equation:

$$Y = (b/V) + a \qquad \text{(equation (1))}$$

where a and b are constants (4)

Consequently if the muscles and fatty tissues are arranged in an arbitrary number of parallel layers, the mean volume fraction of fat in the mixture is given by:

$$\bar{Y} = b\ (\overline{1/V}) + a \qquad \text{(equation (2))}$$

where $(\overline{1/V})$ is the transmission time that a pulse of ultrasound takes to travel through the tissues, divided by the tissue thickness, characteristics that can be measured directly (1-3, 5-7).

If, in a live animal, $(\overline{1/V})$ is determined through a region comprising adipose tissue and muscle only (such as the soft tissues of the limbs), the mean volume fraction of fat in the tissues through which the beam passed may be estimated via equation (2). However it is important that the measurement of $(\overline{1/V})$ be made precisely since at body temperature $(\overline{1/V})$ for lipids is only about 14% higher than that for fat-free tissues. By defining measurement sites on the animal so that different animals may be measured at one or more corresponding sites, it is possible to rank animals in order of predicted fatness at these sites (1,6) and to correlate the data with tissue proportions in the carcass (2,3,6).

MEASUREMENT EQUIPMENT

The determination of $(\overline{1/V})$ requires a measurement of the time of flight of an ultrasonic pulse across the animal and a measurement of the tissue thickness. These are measured on an animal using a specially designed frame as shown in Figure 1. This frame holds two transducers, one a transmitter and the other a receiver, in line and opposite one another at pre-determined points on opposite sides of the animal. The distance

95

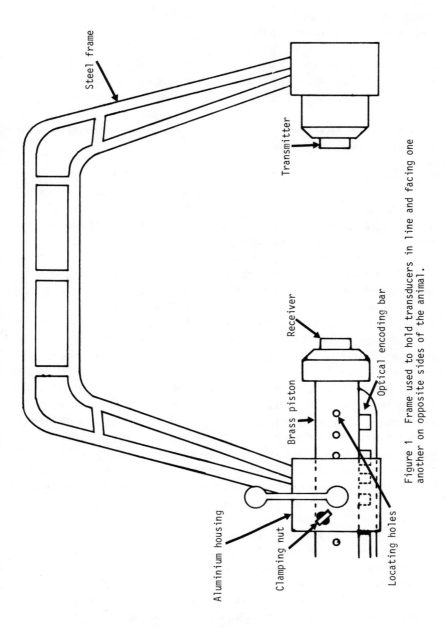

Figure 1   Frame used to hold transducers in line and facing one another on opposite sides of the animal.

between the faces of the transducers can be adjusted in discrete steps to accommodate various sizes of animal.

An electronic system automatically carries out a standard sequence of operations to obtain a valid measurement of $\overline{(1/V)}$. It measures the time of flight (τ) of an ultrasonic pulse from one side of the animal to the other, records the distance (d) separating the transducer faces and computes $\overline{(1/V)} = \tau/d$.

These three parameters are displayed by the unit and are available on an RS232 line for external logging and printing.

MEASUREMENT OF THE TIME OF FLIGHT (τ)

The whole system is microprocessor controlled but the basic acoustic system for measuring the time of flight consists essentially of a pulse generator, pre-amplifier, amplifier with automatic gain control, comparator threshold detector and timer (Fig. 2).

At a rate, determined by a front panel control, the timer is started and simultaneously a pulse generator produces a high voltage pulse of short duration which is applied to the transducer acting as transmitter. This emits a pulse of ultrasound which travels through the tissue of the animal. After a delay, dependent upon the thickness of the tissue and the speed of sound, the pulse is received on the other side of the animal by the receiving transducer which reconverts it to an electrical pulse. This pulse passes through a pre-amplifier and is rectified, shaped and its amplitude adjusted by an amplifier with automatic gain control so that its amplitude is between 8 and 9 volts. This is fed to a threshold detector which, at a predetermined level on the rising edge of the pulse, generates a new sharp pulse to stop the timer. The threshold level, which may be adjusted, was set at 1V for work described in this paper.

The time recorded by this measurement (τ_m) does not equal the required time of flight because it includes a system delay (τ_0) which has to be predetermined and subtracted from the reading:

$$\tau = \tau_m - \tau_0$$

The system delay depends on such factors as the choice of trigger level threshold and the transducers employed. For measurements of mature cattle, 1MHz transducers, 25.4 mm in diameter were found to be suitable, and at a trigger threshold of 1 volt, τ_0 happened to be 1.50 ± 0.05 µs for our system. This was determined at intervals during the trial and showed no discernable drift away from the adopted value over a six month period.

Fig. 2   Simplified Block Diagram

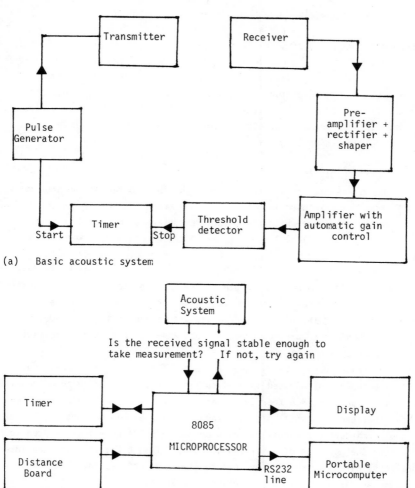

(a)   Basic acoustic system

(b)   Role of the microprocessor control system

τ_0 was determined in preliminary measurements of the pulse transit time across various lengths (d) of water, τ_0 being the intercept of the regression of τ_m against d (Table 1) since

$$\tau_m = (d.V_w) + \tau_0$$

where V_w = the speed of ultrasound in water.

Tap water was used routinely for this work but glass-distilled water was used to obtain the data given in Table 1. The residual standard deviation of the regression, 0.025 µs, is comparable with the resolution of the timer (.02 µs, since it is based on a 50 MHz oscillator). Errors in the distance measurement also contributed to the scatter of the data about the regression line.

MEASUREMENT OF DISTANCE

The ultrasonic transducers are held in line and facing one another using the frame sketched in Figure 1. One transducer was fixed to one side of a steel frame while the other transducer was attached to the end of a brass piston which slid within an aluminium housing, fixed to the other end of the frame. A spring-loaded tapered pin mounted in the aluminium housing, could be located in any one of a number of holes drilled at equal intervals along the length of the brass piston. Once the transducers were at the desired separation, with the pin located in the appropriate hole, the piston was clamped with a wing nut, the frame was carefully positioned around the animal and a switch operated to initiate the measurements.

An optical coding bar is used to record the transducer separation. The encoding bar is divided into 64 sections, each section being of equal width. A section is either left open or blanked off to provide a unique coding pattern. A metal block, attached to the aluminium housing, houses 6 photo emitters and receivers which produce a 6 bit code that is used to identify the position of a particular hole. This 6 bit code is then interpreted by circuitry within the unit to give a direct reading of the inter-transducer distance with a resolution of 0.01 cm.

Repeated re-location of the piston at a particular hole showed that the standard deviation of the distance between the faces of the two transducers was .002 cm and equal to the resolution of the vernier calipers used to make the measurement. This showed that desired transducer separations could be achieved with a satisfactory level of reproducibility.

The rigidity of the frame was tested by hanging masses on it in such a way as to pull the transducers apart along a line joining the centres of their faces. On application of the force, the transducer separation increased by approximately 6 µm/N, so that if, with reasonable handling, the maximum force exerted in testing animals was 10 N (say), the transducer separation would be increased by 0.006 cm only.

Rough measurement of the temperature coefficient of the transducer separation in its fully open position (50 cm spacing) yielded a value of $1.0 \pm 0.3 \times 10^{-5}$ K^{-1} over the temperature range 2 to 18°C. This agreed with the linear coefficient of expansion of steel, quoted by Kaye and Laby (8) to be ~1.1×10^{-5} K^{-1}. In the fully closed position (30 cm spacing), one would expect a slightly higher temperature coefficient because of the increased contribution of the brass piston.

It was concluded that the maximum error in the distance measurement would be approximately .03 cm at a spacing of 50 cm. This was calculated on the extreme basis of the frame being subjected to a force of 10 N, a temperature change of 30°C and that these and all other errors were cumulative.

DETERMINATION OF $\overline{T/V}$

The microprocessor (Figure 2b) is used to check the stability of the amplitude of the received signal and, if this is acceptable, to take the time of flight and distance readings, compute $\overline{T/V}$, display the results and send the data to an RS232 line for external logging and printing. If the received signal is not sufficiently stable, or too high or too low, the display and output are suppressed and new data requested.

The standard error of the slope of the regression $(1/V_w)$ reported in Table 1, represents an error of approximately 0.01% and indicates the order of magnitude of the ultimate limit of the precision of the equipment for speed measurements through samples of about 40 cm in thickness, since it appears to be determined largely by the finite resolutions of the time interval and distance recordings (0.02 µs and 0.01 cm respectively). This precision was obtained under laboratory conditions and it is emphasised that for measurements on animals much larger errors arise, as we shall see below.

Table 1

Linear regression analysis of pulse transit time (τ_m) recorded
by the equipment against path length (d) in glass-distilled water at
25.2°C
The equation $\tau_m = \dfrac{d}{v_w} + \tau_o$ applies

	This work	Previous work
slope $1/V_w \pm$ SE µs/cm	6.6820 ± 0.0007	6.6834 (1) 6.6776 (2) 6.6808 (3)
Intercept (τ_o) ± SE µs	1.49 ± 0.04	
Residual standard deviation µs	0.025	

Measurement (this work) at 1 MHz, and a mean path length of 37.3 cm.

(1) Kaye and Laby, 1973.
(2) Greenspan and Tschiegg, 1957.
(3) American Institute of Physics Handbook, 1963.

MEASUREMENT ON ANIMALS

In order to rank animals on the basis of the transmission measurements,
it is necessary to define positions on the animal that can be located
reproducibly from animal to animal and from one occasion to another. Sites
on the hind limbs were defined relative to the position and size of
skeletal features as shown in Figure 3 and the short-term repeatability of
the ultrasonic measurements determined by measuring the animals twice, the
two measurement sessions being separated by a period ranging from 4 hours
to 14 days. At each session at least four measurements were made at each
of the two sites and the site-means used to compute an overall mean which
was used for all subsequent analysis. The within-animal standard
deviation of the data (Table 2), a measure of the repeatability, represents
about 0.06% to 0.11% of the measured values, or expressed in terms of predicted lipid content averaged over the two sites, 4.3 to 7.8 ml lipid/litre
tissue.

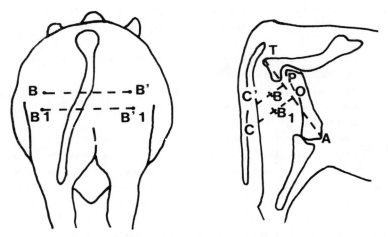

Fig. 3   Sites where transmission measurements were made.
A: lateral ridge of the trochlea of the distal end of the femur.
T: caudal extremity of the ischiatic tuber.   AT follows contour
of buttock.   OT = AO, AP = 2PT.   PC' and OC perpendicular to AT.
C and C': caudal points of the buttock.   PB = BC' and $OB_1 = B_1C$
(these are medial plane projections).

Table 2:

Repeatability[†] of the measurement of the reciprocal of the speed
of ultrasound* in groups of living cattle.   Data are residual
standard deviations, expressed in μs/cm

	Number	Residual standard deviation μs/cm
Dairy cows (from Herd A)	10	.0056
Dairy cows (from Herd B)	10	.0042
Hereford bulls	68	.0069

[†]short term, measurements repeated within a period of 4 hrs to 14 days.

*measured by transmission through the hind limbs and averaged over
 two sites (B and B_1), defined in Figure 3.

Comparison of the data in Tables 1 and 2 will show the uncertainty of the speed measurements of cattle was about 6 to 11 times larger than the error quoted for water. Several factors contribute to the loss in precision:

(a)   the limited precision with which the measurement sites could be located on animals;

(b)   small additional errors in the measurement of distance (see above) due to the effect of stress on the frame and its finite coefficient of thermal expansion;

(c)   additional errors in the measurement of transmission time due to phase cancellation effects caused by tissue inhomogeneities, perturbing the shape of the leading edge of the received pulse.

Uncertainties due to (a) might be reduced by averaging measurements over more sites and those due to (c) might be reduced by increasing the frequency (f) of the sound since these errors should fall as 1/f.

During the course of the field trials some cattle were measured immediately prior to slaughter and dissection at the MRI. There had been a particular interest in measuring the body composition of female cattle during the period of the trials and we were able to accumulate enough data to examine correlations. A report of these experiments will be given elsewhere, and it is necessary to note here only some of the results.

(a)   there was a strong positive correlation between measurements of 1/V made with the equipment on 51 live female cattle and adipose tissue proportions in their carcasses determined by physical dissection (Figure 4).

(b)   the slope and form of the regression of carcass fatness against reciprocal speed was similar to that observed previously with other equipment on steers (6) and bulls (2). However, there appeared to be a slight shift of the calibration curve, such that in these data, carcasses were slightly fatter at the same speed of sound.

(c)   the precision of the correlation was acceptable for some practical applications and about the same as that observed previously on steers and bulls (2,3,6). 1/V significantly ($P<.001$) improved the precision of the prediction made on the basis of live mass (M) alone, and the residual standard deviation, after regression on 1/V and M, was 19.2 g adipose tissue/kg carcass. This compared with 40.9 g/kg after regression on live mass alone.

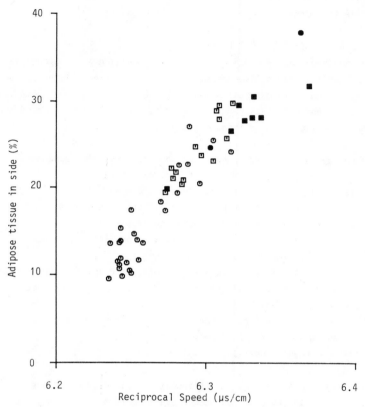

Fig. 4: % Adipose tissue in the side against 1/V
Correlation between the reciprocal of the speed of ultrasound in
the hind limbs of live female cattle and the proportion of adipose
tissue in the carcass determined by dissection.   Circles represent
heifers, squares represent cows.   Open symbols represent British
Friesian; closed, Hereford.

PRACTICAL ASPECTS

The equipment allows the above measurements to be made at a rate of
about 10-20 animals per hour and the major consumable is acoustic couplant:
we used liquid paraffin at a rate of about 25 ml/animal.   Data may be
logged automatically using an external microcomputer.   We used an Epson
HX-20, which printed the data on site and retained the data in its memory

after it was switched off at the end of measurement sessions.   The data was recalled on return to the laboratory and loaded automatically via an RS232 line to another computer for further processing.

POTENTIAL AND LIMITATION OF THE METHOD

The equipment described in this paper has considerable potential for practical application in live animal evaluation.   As one of the purposes of the symposium is to make assessments of the advantages and limitations of various techniques it is perhaps useful to end by listing some of the pros and cons of ultrasound transmission:

Pros

1.   it employs portable equipment, suitable for making measurements on farms.   The method is quick, safe and painless;

2.   it is suitable for measurement of large farm animals;

3.   the method can be used by non-scientific staff, since it gives a direct digital reading, requiring no subjective assessments;

4.   the method yields an 'on the spot' fatness prediction, requiring no subsequent lengthy analysis of photographs;

5.   it responds equally to subcutaneous, inter- and intra-muscular fat;

6.   it is probably more sensitive at low fat levels than measurements of subcutaneous fat thickness;

7.   the regression equations appear to be less sensitive to breed differences than ultrasonic pulse-echo techniques;

8.   it has low running costs.

Cons

1.   perhaps the most serious limitation is that it depends on the accuracy of the relation between a small section of the body and overall carcass composition;

2.   it gives no information on the way the fat is distributed among the different depots;

3.   the relationship between ultrasound speed and fatness is indirect;

4.   the transducer assembly is cumbersome, because the method requires that the transducers are held in line and facing one another on opposite sides of the animal;

5.   it relies on passing the beam through muscle and fatty tissue only. This severely restricts the areas of the body available for measurement.

ACKNOWLEDGEMENTS

The basic electronic system described in the paper was designed and
built to MRI specification by Wells-Krautkramer Ltd. The distance
encoding device was designed and constructed at the MRI. Mr J. Alexander
constructed the mechanical system from our rough sketches. The dissection
data for the female cattle were made available to us by Dr J. Wood. The
following are thanked for their interest and for allowing us to measure
their animals: Mr J. Wray of Bridget's Experimental Husbandry Farm:
Dr J. Roberts of the Institute for Research into Animal Diseases;
Mr R. Baker, Mr. M. Gibb and Mr E. Charmley of the Grassland Research
Institute, Mr J.S. Tavernor of the Animal Breeding Research Organisation.

REFERENCES

1. Miles, C.A., Woods, M.O. & Fursey, G.A.J. 1982. In vivo technique
    for the estimation of body composition in beef: note on ultrasound
    transmission. In 'In vivo estimation of body composition of beef '
    edited by B. Bech Andersen (1982) published by 1 Kommission los
    Landhusholdningsselskabets forlag, Rolighedsvej 26, 1958 Copenhagen
    V, pages 139-147.
2. Miles, C.A., Fursey, G.A.J., Fisher, A.V. & Brown, A.J. 1983.
    Predicting carcass composition from the speed of ultrasound in live
    Hereford Bulls. (Abstract) Anim. Prod. 36, 526.
3. Miles, C.A., Fursey, G.A.J. & Pomeroy, R.W. 1983. Ultrasonic
    evaluation of cattle. Anim. Prod. 36, 363-370.
4. Miles, C.A. & Fursey, G.A.J. 1977. Measurement of the fat content
    of meat using ultrasonic waves. Fd. Chem. 2, 107-118.
5. Miles, C.A. & Fursey, G.A.J. 1974. A note on the velocity of
    ultrasound in living tissue. Anim. Prod. 18, 93-96.
6. Woods, M.O. Ph.D. Thesis. University of Bristol (in preparation).
7. Ludwig, C.D. 1950. The velocity of sound through tissues and the
    acoustic impedance of tissues. J. Acoust. Soc. Am. 22, 862-866.
8. Kaye, G.W.C. & Laby, T.H. Tables of Physical and Chemical constants
    and some Mathematical Functions. Longman, London and New York.
9. Greenspan, M. & Tschiegg, C.E. 1957. Speed of sound in water by a
    direct method. J. Res. NBS 59 (4), 249-254.
10. American Institute of Physics Handbook. 1957. 2nd edition, pages
    3 - 79, McGraw-Hill Book Co. Inc., New York.

PREDICTION OF BODY COMPOSITION IN VIVO
BY DILUTION TECHNIQUE

J. Robelin

Institut National de la Recherche Agronomique
Laboratoire de la Production de Viande
Centre de Recherches Zootechniques et Vétérinaires
Theix, 63122 CEYRAT, France

ABSTRACT

The prediction of body composition in living animals by dilution technique has been extensively studied for many years. Several reviews have already been published on this topic; so this paper only recalls some basic knowledge on this method, and presents the more recently published results. The two main concepts involved in this method are 1) the fact that body composition is well related to the water content of the body and 2) the possibility to measure body water by dilution of a tracer. After a short description of the practical conditions of the measurement of dilution space, the equations of prediction of body lipids and proteins observed recently in various kinds of animals are presented. Their coefficients are quite similar whatever the authors and the type of animals. The standard deviation amounts to 8 to 15% of body lipids and 2 to 5% of body proteins. It is concluded that this method is a powerfull tool for prediction of body composition in experimental conditions. It is fairly accurate and its cost is rather low in smaller animals.

INTRODUCTION

There is an acute need for in vivo techniques of estimation of body composition in many aspects of animal or human research. Several methods have been developed more or less successfully, such as specific gravity, ^{40}K counting, various measurements of subcutaneous fat (skinfold, ultrasonic, adipose cell diameter), dilution methods, and, more recently, computerized tomography. Among all these methods, measurement of the dilution space of water tracers has received considerable attention in domestic animals.

Several reviews have been published on the use of this method (Robelin, 1973; Hwai-Ping and Huggins, 1979). The author has presented detailed results on this method in a previous EEC Workshop (Robelin, 1982a and b). The main principles of this method and examples of its application are briefly presented in this paper. Special emphasis is given to its usefulness and accuracy.

BASIS OF THE METHOD

This method is based on two concepts : 1) the fact that the chemical
composition of the body is fairly well related to its water content and
2) the possibility of **measurement in vivo** of body water by dilution of
water tracer.

Relationships among the chemical components of the body

Half of a century ago,Moulton (1923) described a statistical
relationship within body components (water, lipids, proteins and ashes).
He showed that in various domestic species (pigs, sheep, cattle) the water
and protein content of the fat free body (empty body - lipids) was fairly
constant in growing animals after "chemical maturity". The composition of
fat free body has been recalculated on the basis of a large number of
animals and more accurate figures for cattle, sheep and pigs were published
by Reid et al. (1968). The percentage of water in fat free body (FFB)
ranged from 73% in cattle to 75% in sheep and 77% in pigs, whereas the
respective percentages of **protein** were 22, 20 and 19%.

These relationships have been reanalysed recently and allometric
equations were proposed for growing cattle (Robelin and Geay, 1978).

$$\text{Proteins (kg)} = 0.1259\ FFB^{1.096} \quad (RCV = 2.8\% \text{ proteins})$$
$$\text{Water \quad (kg)} = 0.8477\ FFB^{0.974} \quad (RCV = 1.1\% \text{ water})$$

These relationships are very accurate from a statistical point of
view. The residual coefficient of variation (in relative value to the
dependent variate) is lower than 3% for proteins and nearly 1% for water.

A more direct relationship between the water and lipid content of
empty body weight (EBW) has also been established in growing cattle and
sheep (Robelin and Theriez, 1981).

Cattle Water % EBW = 74.7 - 0.824 Lipids % EBW   (SYX = 0.97% EBW)
Sheep   Water % EBW = 77.4 - 0.866 Lipids % EBW   (SYX = 1.5 % EBW)

On the other hand, proteins have been shown to represent a practically
constant proportion of fat free empty body, approximately 80% -81% in sheep
and 83% in pigs (Reid and al., 1968; Robelin and Theriez, 1981). Such
relationships have also been observed in a very wide range of types of
animals, in the growing rabbit (Vigneron, Baron and Dauzier, 1971), the
chicken (Delpech, 1966), as well as in mature ewes (Tissier et al., 1983)
and cows (Robelin, Chilliard and Lestrade, in preparation).

On the basis of these relationships, it is theoretically possible to evaluate the lipid weight and the protein weight of the body from the measurement of body water. These relationships are expressed on an empty body basis (body weight minus gut content). From a practical viewpoint, only full body weight and total body water can be measured _in vivo_. This discrepancy has already been widely discussed previously (Robelin, 1982b).

Measurement of body water by dilution technique

This measurement is based on the principle of tracer dilution in body compartments. A known amount (Q) of water tracer is infused into the body. After equilibrium , the tracer is supposed to be distributed homogeneously in all body water compartments. If there were no losses of tracer during the equilibration period, the volume (V) in which the tracer was equilibrated, is represented by the ratio between the dose infused (Q) and the concentration (C) of the tracer in body water : $V = Q/C$.

Such idealistic conditions are not met in practice. There is a loss of tracer during equilibration due to the water turnover. The theoretical concentration of the tracer in body water must be determined mathematically.

PRACTICAL MEASUREMENT OF DILUTION SPACE

In practical conditions, the most commonly used tracers are deuteriated or tritiated water. They are generally infused into the jugular vein, and blood samples are taken during the 24–48 h following injection in order to observe the changes in the concentration of the tracer in body water. All details about the conditions of infusion, blood sampling and the determination of the D_2O content of blood water have been published previously (Robelin, 1982b; Robelin, 1982c).

The change with time after infusion in blood concentration of D_2O in cattle is represented in figure 1. During the first 6-9 hours after injection, the concentration decreases very rapidly because the tracer infused into the blood mixes with all the water compartments of the body when equilibrium is reached. The concentration of the tracer decreases at a fixed rate in logarithmic scale; this rate correspondsto the turnover rate of water, approximately 0,33% of total body water per hour in growing cattle (Robelin, 1982b).

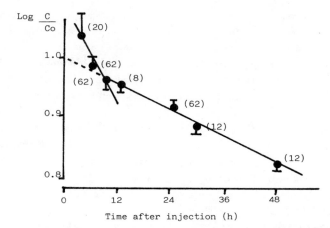

Fig. 1 Relative changes of blood concentration of tracer with time after injection in cattle (the number of data are indicated between parenthesis) (from Robelin, 1982b).

As stated before, the volume of dilution of the tracer (V) is represented by the ratio between the dose of tracer infused (Q) and the theoretical concentration of the tracer in body water (Co) at the time of injection if the equilibrium has been immediate : V = Q/Co. Three methods have been used to determine the concentration Co.

The first one consists of measuring blood concentration (Ce) after equilibrium (5-7 hours after infusion) and to postulate that Ce is similar to Co. As it is the most simple, this method has been widely used even recently (Chigaru and Holness, 1983). Obviously, it leads to an overstimation of the dilution space because Ce is always lower than Co. The calculated dilution space is generally 10 to 15% greater than the measured body water.

With the second method, serial measurements of C, the concentration of the tracer in blood water, are made during the 24 to 48 hours following infusion, and the concentration Co is calculated by extrapolation of the dilution curve (fig. 1) to the time of infusion. With this method, the calculated dilution space is still greater than body water, but by 3 to 5% only (Robelin, 1982b, c).

The third method is similar to the second from a practical viewpoint, but it differs in the statistical analysis of the dilution.

110

A two-compartment model is used (Robelin, 1977) and the calculation of total body water (the sum of the two compartments) is made according to more sophisticated equations. It does not lead to any significant improvement of body water estimation. Byers (1978) has shown that the volume of these two compartments was similar to that of empty body water and alimentary tract water in cattle. However this similitude has not been confirmed recently in pigs (Shields, Mahan and Byers, 1983).

Whatever the method used, there is generally a good statistical relationship between dilution space and total body water (even though the slope is not one), and the residual standard deviation, the accuracy of prediction of body water, amounts to 2 to 4% of body water only.

ESTIMATION OF BODY LIPIDS AND PROTEINS

The equations between body lipids (L) body weight (BW) and water space (WS) (L = bo BW + b1 WS + b2) for various kinds of animals are presented in table 1.

TABLE 1   Equations of prediction of body lipids (L, kg) and proteins (P,kg) from body weight (BW, kg) and water space (WS, kg) in various types of animals.

Animals (n)		Equations	RCV %[1]	References
Growing pigs	(81)	L = 0.934BW-1.316WS-0.22	7.9	Shields et al (1983)
Growing cattle	(42)	L = 0.769BW-0.943WS	13.8	Robelin (1982a)
Mature ewes	(38)	L = 0.904BW-0.913WS-6.0	12.8	Tissier et al (1983)
Mature cows	(20)	L = 0.903BW-1.135WS	8.7	Chilliard et al(1983)
Mature cows	(18)	L = 0.828BW-0.904WS-15.1	14.8	Chigaru et al (1983)
Growing cattle	(42)	P = 0.124BW+0.058WS	4.7	Robelin (1982a)
Mature ewes	(38)	P = 0.048BW+0.076WS+1.055	2.3	Tissier et al (1983)
Mature cows	(20)	P = 0.088BW+0.075WS	2.5	Chilliard et al(1983)

(1) RCV = residual coefficient of variation in percentage of the mean of dependant variable.

The comparison of estimates given by these equations is not realistic due to the variability of body size and conditions between these different sets

of results. However, there is a remarquable agreement in the values of the
coefficients between authors and whatever the types of animals. They show
that for a given body weight, the body lipid   decreases by 0.9 to 1.3 kg
when the water space decreases by 1 kg. The accuracy of body lipid's
prediction is fairly good, as the residual standard deviation of these
equations amounts to a mean value of 10% of body lipids.

Similar equations for prediction of body protein are also presented
in table 1. The coefficient of water space is greater than zero,indicating
an increase in body protein for increasing water space. The accuracy of
prediction amounts to 2.5 to 5% of body protein

We have already discussed in details elsewhere (Robelin, 1982a,
Chilliard and Robelin, 1983) the consequences of this residual standard
deviation on the accuracy prediction of body lipid and protein deposition
in growing and mature cattle. For a group of 4 animals, it is possible to
put into evidence a body lipid deposition of approximately 8-10 kg and a
protein retention of 3-4 kg. These values indicate clearly the limits of
such a method of investigation. This accuracy has been shown to be closely
related to the determination of body weight during the period of measurement
(Robelin, 1982a,b).

CONCLUSION

On the basis of this rapid survey of this method of prediction of
body composition, we might stress the following points: 1) This method is
easy to manage in experimental environment, but not in farm conditions;
2) It is based on powerfull relationships between body components and so
it is not sensible to the type of animals; 3) It gives a good estimate of
body lipids and proteins as far as care is taken to the various measurements
and particularly the determination of body weight; 4) Its cost is relatively
high, 0.25 ECU/kg body weight. So its use is better justified in smaller
animals.

REFERENCES

Byers, F.M. 1978. Fed. Proc. 37, 410 (Abstr.)
Chilliard, Y. and Robelin, J. 1983. IVth Symp. Protein Metabolism and
    Nutrition. Ed. INRA Publ., 1983, II (Les Colloques de l'INRA, N°16)
    pp. 195-198.
Chigaru, R.N. and Holness, D.H. 1983. J. Agric. Sci., 101, 257-264.
Delpech, P. 1966. C.R. Acad. Sci., Paris, 263, 1735-1738.
Hwai-Ping, S. and Huggins, R.A. 1979. American J. Clin.Nutr., 32, 630-647.
Moulton, C.R. 1923. J. Biol. Chem., 37, 79-97.

Reid, J.T., Bensadoun, A. and Bull, L.S. 1968. in "Body composition of
    animals and Man", N.A.S. pub n° 1598, pp. 19-41.
Robelin, J. 1973. Ann. Biol anim. Bioch. Biophys., 13, 285-305.
Robelin, J. 1977. Ann. Biol anim. Bioch. Biophys., 17, 95-105.
Robelin, J. 1982a. Beretn. Stat. Husd. forsog, 524, 107-117.
Robelin, J. 1982b. Beretn. Stat. Husd. forsog, 524, 156-164.
Robelin, J. 1982c. Reprod. Nutr. Develop., 22, 65-73.
Robelin, J. and Geay, Y. 1978. Ann. Zootech· , 27, 159-167.
Robelin, J. and Theriez, M. 1981 . Reprod. Nutr. Develop., 21,335-353.
Shields, R.G., Mahan, D.C. and Byers, F.M. 1983. J. Anim. Sci., 57,66-73.
Tissier, M., Theriez, M., Purroy, A. and Bocquier, F. 1983. Reprod. Nutr.
    Develop., 23, 693-707.
Vigneron, P., Baron, R. and Dauzier, L. 1971. Ann. Biol. anim. Bioch.
    Biophys., 11, 669-679.

POSSIBILITIES FOR APPLICATION OF VIDEO IMAGE ANALYSIS IN BEEF CARCASS CLASSIFICATION

Svend Erik Sørensen

Danish Meat Research Institute
Maglegårdsvej 2, DK-4000 Roskilde, Denmark

ABSTRACT

With the aim to introduce more objectivity into beef carcass classification, and to supplement the conformation and fatness grading with carcass composition estimates, the feasibility of video image analysis for automatic grading of beef carcasses is being investigated. As a background for this, the relationships between conformation, body composition, and commercial cutting yield is discussed, and it is concluded that for young bulls only lean/bone-ratio but not lean/fat-ratio can be predicted by conformation. Among various body composition traits, lean/bone-ratio is shown to have the highest correlation to commercial cutting yield and value. Preliminary objective carcass shape measurements and their relationships to carcass composition and conformation are presented. A short description of the VIA principle being developed for classification is given.

INTRODUCTION

Routine measurement of carcass composition for grading purposes have in Denmark been introduced many years ago for pigs, whereas grading of beef carcasses is still based on subjective assessments. There are many reasons for this, among which are the lack of uniformity of carcasses, the distribution of killings on many small slaughterhouses, and problems in getting consistent measurements of the thickness of the warm, soft fat. Moreover, the conformation of beef carcasses is still regarded by the industry as been the trait of highest importance, and grading for conformation is now compulsory in the newly introduced EUROP grading system.

It is, however, well known that the ability of conformation score to predict carcass composition is limited (Andersen et al., 1977; Sornay, 1982). Of more predictive value for carcass composition is the fatness score, which in the EUROP-system is based on the assessment of external fat covering.

To ensure objectiveness and reproducibility in carcass grading, there is a potential need for automated methods which minimizes the human factor in the grading process and thereby reduces the potential risks for variation over graders, slaughterhouses and time. Also, an important task for such methods would be a description of body composition, which ideally should be the best method for prediction of yield and to some extent quality of the carcass.

PRINCIPLE OF VIDEO IMAGE ANALYSIS

With the above mentioned background, the Danish Meat Research Institute has commenced a feasibility study for possible methods for objective beef carcass grading. One part of this study is investigations over the possible use of video image analysis (VIA) as replacement for or supplement to the subjective visual assessment of shape and fat covering.

The basic principle of video image analysis is probably well known. A video image, obtained by a normal video camera, is through an analog/digital converter converted to a numerical array of gray values, which is stored in a computer and can be further manipulated by the appropriate software. This basic principle is in different configurations now widely used in research (e.g. microscopy), production control (pattern recognition) and for automation of production processes (robotics).

Thus, the application of VIA for carcass grading based on visually measureable traits is theoretically just to expand well known principles to another application. In relation to carcass grading, it is furthermore an advantage that the method is non-destructive and there is no physical contact between the object and the measuring system, which eliminates the risks of contamination through carry-over.

In practice, the application of VIA for carcass grading is far from simple. Of the potential problems to be considered are:
- development of image analysis procedures with optimal correlation to carcass anatomy and carcass composition.
- technical problems associated with daily use of electronic equipment in the harsh slaughterhouse environment.
- standardisation of the video inspection process (relative position of the object, background contrast, lighting, etc.).
- development of software with ability to handle carcasses with large variations in size, varying dressing procedures, split or non-split carcasses, etc.

DEVELOPMENTS ABROAD

In several countries the VIA principle is being developed and tested for grading purposes. In UK, the VIA principle is now commercially used to measure visible lean in fabrication beef (Anon, 1981a), and research concerning the use for body composition measurements in carcasses is being carried out at Langford (Anon, 1981b). In Sweden, a version of the system called Electronic Scanning Planimetry has been developed and tested for prediction of carcass composition in pigs (Malmfors, 1981). In the US, very promising results have been published by Cross et al. (1983) on a survey using a VIA prototype for beef grading. Both the Swedish and

US systems are based on image analysis of a cut surface, and ribbing of the carcasses is thus required before grading.

The research reported on VIA-applications for carcass shape or conformation measurements seems limited. In Germany, the principle is used in the SKG-system for measurements of ham and waist breadth and ham angle in pigs, and results have been published by Sack (1983). For beef carcasses, no publication regarding use of VIA for conformation grading has come to our attention. An objective shape measuring device is being developed in France (Auge, 1981), but based on mechanical measuring probes rather than VIA. In UK, a feasibility study using VIA for conformation score seems to be considered (Anon, 1981a).

DANISH INVESTIGATIONS

At this point, no results directly obtained through the use of automated VIA have been produced in Denmark, although investigations are progressing. Some basic features concerning this method have, however, been investigated and reported. This research, which has been concentrated on young bulls, has mainly been intended to answer the following questions: 1) Which carcass composition traits can be predicted by grading based on conformations, and how do these correspond to commercial carcass yield and value. 2) Which objectively defined carcass dimensions will be suitable for prediction of carcass composition and conformation.

Concerning the first point, it seems rather clear from previous experiments that for young bulls at constant weight the conformation score is most closely correlated to bone content and lean/bone ratio (Andersen et al., 1977; Lykke, 1978). This has later been verified in a comprehensive study consisting of carcass data pooled from many years' Danish experiments, as shown in Table 1.

It should be noted, that the experimental error may be rather high in these data as the experiments are carried out over a 15-year period, and no correction is made for differences over time. This may to some extent account for the generally low R^2-values found. However, the results clearly demonstrate that only the bone content and the lean/bone ratio can be predicted from conformation alone, and that any prediction of meat and fat percentage cannot be made without considering the fatness of the carcass.

116

TABLE 1   Prediction of carcass composition by commercial grading. Calculated from dissection data of 2,246 young bulls of 122-411 kg
carcass weight

Description by:	Conformation	Conformation + carcass weight[1]	Conformation + carcass weight[1] + fatness score
		R^2 values	
% lean	.04	.10	.19
% fat	.01	.21	.33
% bone	.28	.50	.52
lean/fat	.00	.21	.32
lean/bone	.28	.37	.37

1) linear + quadratic regression

It is, however, important to consider, to what extent the dissection data for carcass composition reflects the commercial value of the carcass, i.e. the yield of saleable meat and the value of the produced cuts and trimmings. This has lately been investigated in a smaller experiment, where standard dissection on one half of the carcass has been compared with commercial deboning and trimming on the other half of the carcass (Sørensen, 1983). In the experiment, which was carried out on 43 young bulls of 190 kg carcass weight, an estimate of commercial wholesale value was calculated using standard prices for the individual cuts and trimmings. Some of the results are shown in Table 2.

TABLE 2 Partial correlation coefficients (constant carcass weight) between dissection data, commercial cutting yield and value, and conformation

	Commercial cutting	
	% saleable meat	Wholesale value (D.kr./kg)
Carcass composition		
% lean meat	.51***	.57***
% fat	-.27	-.37*
% bone	-.53***	-.44**
lean/fat	.36*	.46**
lean/bone	.64***	.60***
Conformation (EUROP)	.55***	.49***

It can be seen from the results, that the lean/bone ratio based on dissection has given the best prediction of commercial yield and value, whereas the lean/fat ratio is less strongly correlated to these traits. This reflects, of course, that a considerable amount of fat (in this experiment 60%) of the dissectable fat is included in the commercial cuts, and consequently is sold at "meat price". Thus, it seems important to emphasize that the content of lean meat is not necessarily the most important yield predictor, and that the lean/bone ratio is indeed of considerable importance in this respect. For older animals, this finding doesn't necessarily hold, due to the much higher level and variation in fat content in these animals. It can also be seen from Table 2 that the conformation score is relatively well correlated to the commercial yield, which of course reflects the correlation between conformation and lean/bone ratio.

Concerning the other aspect we have investigated in relation to objective conformation measurements by VIA, namely in which way to define objective carcass measurements to be taken for optimum predictive value, our results are based on manual measurements on standardized carcass photographs taken according to the EAAP-standard, position C (De Boer et al., 1974). The measurements have been concentrated on the conformation of the thigh, which is of highest importance in carcass grading.

118

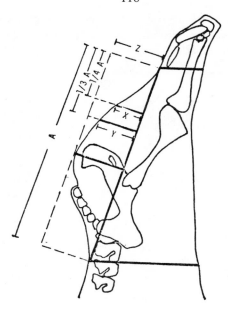

Fig. 1. Procedure used for objective measurements of thigh conformation in young
bulls

The procedure is schematically shown in Figure 1. As it can be seen, the
measurements taken (X, Y, and Z) give information about the muscularity in the
posterior part of the thigh, and the ratios between these measurements - e.g. X/Z
has, together with the carcass length (EAAP-method) and weight given good
correlation to carcass conformation, bone content and lean/bone-ratio, as shown in
Table 3. Results produced by rather similar methods have been published by Bass et
al., 1981.

In conclusion, it seems clear that measurements of body length and of thigh
widths or ratios between these can serve as useful predictors of lean/bone-ratio
(and thereby cutting yield), as well as conformation score.

Based on the described philosophy and results, a simple VIA system has been
built, and development of image analysis procedures is now ongoing. The principles
of the system are outlined in Figure 2.

In the preliminary system, only step 1-4 are carried out on location,
whereafter data is stored on a floppy disk and step 5-13 carried out at a remote
computing centre.

An example of the pictures obtained is shown in Figure 3.

TABLE 3 Prediction of conformation and carcass composition by two-dimensional carcass measurements. 105 young bulls of 320-560 kg live weight

R^2-values obtained by:	Carcass weight EAAP-carcass length Weight/carcass length Thigh measurements X/Z
% lean	.19
% fat	.26
% bone	.64
lean/fat	.26
lean/bone	.59
conformation score	.74

It is yet too early to evaluate results from this, as a thorough optimization of the developed analysis procedures used is required. One important point to consider, however, is that the existing procedure gives only possibilities for two-dimensional measurements. For optimal performance, the next step may have to be inclusion of the third dimension and thereby give possibilities for estimates of carcass volume etc.

120

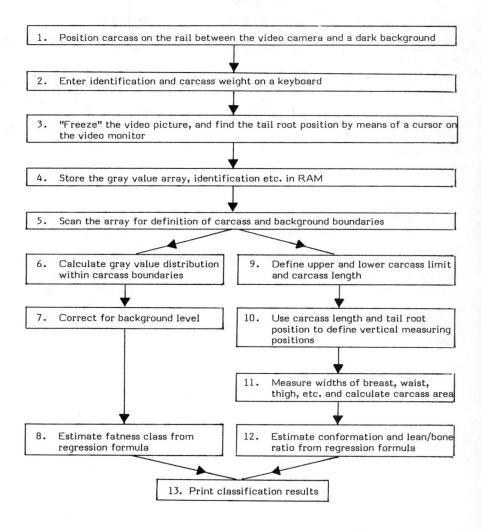

Fig. 2. Schematic overview of the Danish experimental VIA classification system

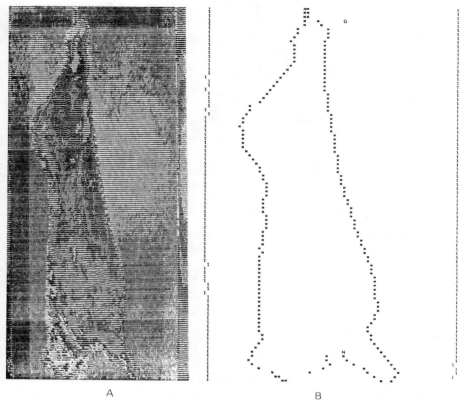

A   B

Fig. 3. EDP-prints of raw video image with 16 gray levels (A) and after calculation
of carcass boundaries (B), the latter in half resolution.

REFERENCES

Andersen, B.Bech, Lykke, Th., Kousgaard, K., Buchter, L., & Wismer-Pedersen, J.
1977. Growth, feed utilization, carcass quality and meat quality in Danish
dual-purpose cattle. 453. Beretning, Statens Husdyrbrugsforsøg, Copenhagen.

Anon. 1981a. Video fat measurement - a new way of guaranteering meat quality.
Meat, 54, 14-15.

Anon. 1981b. Meat Research Institute Biennial Report 1979-81, Langford, Bristol,
pp. 48-51.

Augé, J 1981. Appareil pour la mesure des caractéristiques de classification et la classification des animaux de boucheries abattus. European Patent Application EP 0 046 704 A2.

Bass, J.J., Johnson, D.L., Colomer-Rocher, F., & Binks, G. 1981. Prediction of carcass composition from carcass conformation in cattle. J. Agric. Sci., Camb. 97, 37-44.

Cross, H.R., Gilliland, D.A., Durland, P.R., & Seideman, S. 1983. Beef carcass evaluation by use of a video image analysis system. J. Anim. Sci. 57, 908-917.

De Boer, H., Dumont, B.L., Pomeroy, R.W., & Weniger, J.H. 1974. Manual on EAAP reference methods for the assessment of carcass characteristics in cattle. Livest. Prod. Sci. 1, 151-164.

Lykke, Th. 1978. Investigations concerning carcass quality in cattle with special reference to carcass classification. Thesis, Royal Vet. and Agri. Univ., Copenhagen.

Malmfors, G. 1981. Pig carcass evaluation by use of an electronic scanning planimeter, ESP. Thesis, Sveriges Landbruksuniversitet, Uppsala.

Sack, E. 1983. Using instruments to grade pork sides. Fleischwirtsch. 63, 372-379.

Sornay, J. 1983. Variation between carcasses in economic terms, considering either carcass composition or market prices. In "Comperative retail value of beef carcasses" (Ed. A.V. Fisher). Commission of European Communities, Report EUR 8465, pp. 106-117.

Sørensen, S.E. 1983. Sammenligning af forsøgs- og handelsopskæring samt klassificering af ungtyre. Rapport nr. 01.641, UNGTYRE - SLAGTEKVALITET. Danish Meat Research Institute, Roskilde.

NUCLEAR MAGNETIC RESONANCE IMAGING OF PIGS

M. F. Fuller*, M. A. Foster, J. M. S. Hutchison**

*Rowett Research Institute, Bucksburn, Aberdeen, Scotland
** Department of Biomedical Physics and Bioengineering,
University of Aberdeen, Scotland

ABSTRACT

The Aberdeen NMR imaging machines, MkI operating at 0.04 Telsa and 1.7
MHz, MkII at 0.08 Telsa and 3.4 MHz, are briefly described. They have
been used to produce images of the water proton density and of the water
proton spin-lattice relaxation time (T_1) in cross sections of living and
dead pigs. Tissues taken from the dead pigs were also examined at 2.5
MHz. Subcutaneous fat in vitro gave values of T_1 or 0.13 s, compared
with 0.10 s for perinephric fat. Skeletal muscle gave values of 0.19 s.
Highest T_1 values in vitro were 0.32 s for lung and 0.40 s for kidney
medulla. Values of T_1 for subcutaneous fat in vivo at 3.4 MHz varied
little from a mean of 0.140 s (SE 0.0013). For muscle in vivo at 3.4 MHz
the mean T_1 was 0.243 s (SE 0.0019). Potential developments to improve
resolution of fat and its interface include higher static field strengths,
pulse sequences optimized for this purpose and the detection of changes
associated with chemical shift.

INTRODUCTION

The principles of NMR imaging have been described by Hutchison (1976,
1979) and in other contributions to this volume. The development of
whole-body NMR imaging has been directed primarily towards clinical,
particularly diagnostic, applications, and its potential in the nutritional
and agricultural sciences has been as yet little explored. Whereas the
clinician is primarily interested in visualizing the size and location of
particular normal or pathological tissues within body sections, the
interests which led to the present study are far more concerned with
visualizing the amount and distribution of fat and muscle and, ultimately,
with the estimation of the total volumes of these tissues in the whole body.

NMR proton imaging visualises the hydrogen nucleus (a single proton)
but only when the T_1 and T_2 relaxation times of the nucleus are long. If
the hydrogen atom forms a part of a large molecule, the correlation time
is very long since it is held in a fairly rigid position in relation to
its surroundings. Both energy- and spin-interchange, therefore, are rapid
among a population of such protons. If, however, the proton is part of a
water molecule, it is normally able to move much more freely in the cell
or tissue. Hence the correlation time is shorter and T_1 is longer.
The freedom of motion which the water molecule experiences is related to

the molecular and ionic composition of its environment since both ions and large organic molecules are able to bind layers of water molecules over their surface. This reduces the motion of the water molecules and hence reduces the expected T_1 below that of unstructured water. The T_1 value obtained from a tissue, or a protein solution, is a weighted average of all the T_1 values one might expect from all the degrees of restriction of movement of the water molecules. (It may also be influenced by the presence of paramagnetic materials in the tissue).

The only other type of proton which is "seen" in an NMR image is that from free lipid in a cell. Membrane lipids are held in a fairly rigid structure and the protons of their $-CH_2$ groups do not contribute to the NMR image but if the lipid is free, as in adipose tissue, then the relaxation time of its protons can be sufficiently long to affect the NMR signal from the tissue. These lipid relaxation times are always shorter than those of the water protons and in the imaging process, which produces only a single value to represent the mean relaxation time in the image pixel, they can reduce apparent relaxation time. Hence adipose tissue shows as a fast-relaxing tissue whilst muscle, with very little free lipid, has a much longer T_1 relaxation time. The actual concentration of observable protons in adipose tissue, however, is higher than that of low-fat tissues.

On examination of a fully plotted set of T_1 relaxation information the difference between the fast-relaxing lipid protons and the slower relaxing water protons is easily seen in the bi-exponentiallity of the curve obtained for tissues with a high fat content (Foster, 1983).

The Mark I Aberdeen NMR imaging system (Fig. 1) has been described by Mallard et al. (1979) and by Hutchison et al. (1980). It uses the principle of spin warp imaging (Edelstein et al., 1980; Mallard et al., 1980) to provide images of the density of water protons and of their spin-lattice relaxation time (T_1).

Examples of images of human subjects obtained with this machine have been published by Smith and Mallard (1982).

INSTRUMENTATION

Images were obtained on both the Aberdeen MkI and MkII NMR proton imaging systems and in vitro T_1 values were obtained from a non-commercial spin echo NMR spectrometer operating at 2.5 MHz.

Fig. 1   The Aberdeen MkI NMR imaging machine (January 1979).

The MkI NMR imager is illustrated in Fig. 1. Both NMR imaging
systems use 4-coil resistive magnets, MkI producing a static field of 0.04
Tesla (operating frequency 1.7 MHz) and MkII of 0.08 Tesla (operating
frequency 3.4 MHz). In the Aberdeen systems the coil configuration is
vertical and the subject to be imaged is placed in a non-conducting tube
between the inner coils of the magnet. This limits subject size to 0.3 m
in the MkI and 0.5 m in the MkII imager. Gradient coils, producing the
three orthogonal gradients needed for the Spin Warp Imaging technique
(Johnson et al., 1982) are wrapped onto the patient tube along with the
R.F. coil. In MkI the y-gradient coils are separate. R.F. interference
is eliminated by a Faraday shield surrounding the entire magnet assembly.

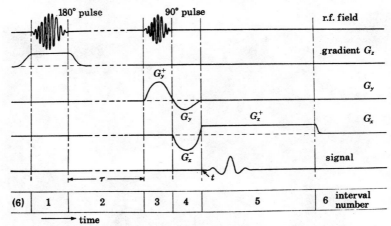

Fig. 2   The main features (diagrammatic) of the R.F. pulse and
magnetic field gradient basic sequence, divided into six intervals
(not to scale).

The Spin Warp pulse sequence is illustrated in Fig. 2. This consists,
for a transaxial slice, of the delivery of a shaped 90° R.F. pulse in the
presence of the selective y-gradient. This, along with the subsequent
reversed y-gradient for re-phasing, selects the slice along the body of the
subject and defines slice thickness. The 90° pulse is followed by the
application of a z-gradient of programmable size and direction. This
gradient induces the spin warp - i.e. the phase of spins from top to
bottom of the selected slice - hence defining the spin packages along the
vertical axis. The readout gradient, G_x, is applied in one direction at

the same time as the z-gradient and is then reversed to allow the spins first to fan out in the x-direction and then to re-align to produce a spin echo. This spin echo (the S1 signal) with its side structure contains all the information required for a two-dimensional Fourier transform of its frequencies to produce a 2-D image of spin distribution through the selected slice.

Every second 90° pulse is preceded, by 200 ms, by an inversion of the spin magnetisation, by means of adiabatic fast passage. This sequence yields the S2 signal. The S1 and S2 signals can be used to produce various displays. S1 alone gives the image referred to as "proton density". Since the signal is obtained after only a 90° pulse it contains information about the size of the total spin population with only a small effect from T_1 and T_2 relaxation. The S2 signal, displayed as "inversion recovery" is strongly T_1-weighted. The T_1 image is calculated from a combination of S1 and S2 signals by means of the following formula:

$$\frac{S1}{S2} = 1 - 2 \exp \left(-^{t}/T_1\right)$$

This yields an accurate T_1 value provided that the adiabatic fast passage is completely efficient - i.e. full inversion is always achieved.

The final type of display is the difference image (D image) which is that of S1 - S2. This again is a T_1-weighted image but with a larger proton density component than the S2 alone.

The processed data (after Fourier transformation) is stored on magnetic floppy disc and displayed in either grey scale or colour. The grey scale (or hot metal scale) is a direct display with the variation from black through grey (or red) to white being a direct function of the signal intensity. The colour display is coded so that each chosen range of signal values is represented by a particular colour. This can assist in enhancement of certain features but can lead to loss of fine detailed information within a single set of values expressed as one colour.

The fast scan images were achieved using a saturation recovery pulse sequence. This takes the form of a train of 90° pulses (with selection, warp and readout gradients) at a time interval which is comparable to the T_1 relaxation time of most wet tissues (200 ms for the present images). The fast images are, therefore, T_1 weighted due to the lack of recovery of signal in the short inter-pulse interval.

In vitro studies were made of small (0.5 g) samples of a variety of tissues. These studies were performed on a home-built NMR spectrometer based on a Watson-type permanent magnet with an operating frequency of 2.5 MHz. The T_1 values were obtained by the measurement of signal intensity using an inversion recovery/Hahn spin echo sequence (Farrar and Becker, 1971) and making a plot from a minimum of 10τ-interval values. Linear regression analysis of this plot yielded the time constant of the exponential which was the T_1 value of the water and   lipid protons in the tissue. Observation of the plot showed whether it was simple or multi-exponential. In general it was found that tissues such as kidney or muscle yielded single exponentials whilst fatty tissues produced more complex plots. In these latter cases the quoted values are weighted averages of the various components. All in vitro samples were measured at room temperature, approximately $18^{\circ}C$, and within 5 hours of the death of the animal.

IN VITRO MEASUREMENT OF SPIN-LATTICE RELAXATION TIME (T_1)

Studies of normal rabbit tissues in vitro showed a 3.5-fold range in T_1 from 0.141 to 0.463 seconds (Ling et al., 1980), but that study did not include adipose tissue. Our own studies (shown in Table 1) of tissues excised from pigs show a smaller range, with minimum values of 0.10 s for perinephric fat, a higher value of 0.13 s for subcutaneous fat, up to 0.40 s for the kidney medulla.

TABLE 1.   (T_1, seconds) at 2.5 MHz of pig tissue samples studied.

	$1/T_1$	SD	T_1	Average correlation coefficient
Subcutaneous fat (loin)	7.78	0.21	0.129	0.967
Subcutaneous fat (shoulders)	7.70	0.22	0.130	0.962
Perinephric fat	10.33	1.34	0.097	0.957
Skeletal muscle	5.33	0.28	0.188	0.987
Cardiac muscle	3.87	0.18	0.259	0.989
Lung	3.16	0.02	0.316	0.993
Kidney medulla	2.51	0.05	0.399	0.992
Kidney cortex	3.85	0.06	0.260	0.990
Liver	6.35	0.28	0.158	0.986
Spleen	3.74	0.04	0.268	0.990

The correlation coefficient indicates the degree of homogeneity of the water protons being imaged: in the adipose tissue samples the lower correlation coefficients indicate two components, the more tightly-bound lipid protons and the slower-relaxing water protons in the adipose tissue.

IMAGING LIVING AND DEAD PIGS

Three pigs have been examined. In each study the animal was continuously anaesthetized and strapped onto a tray consisting of a softwood frame glued to a plywood base with plastic runners. Images were obtained at nine sites along the body, three each at the shoulder, midback and rump. The animal was then killed by an overdose of barbiturate and the images were repeated. The carcass was then frozen and sectioned at the 9 chosen locations. The cut surfaces were photographed for comparison with the tomographic NMR images. Figs. 3 and 4 show the NMR images of sections through the thorax and rump together with the corresponding photographs of the carcass cross sections.

An alternative approach to characterizing fat and muscle in terms of their T_1 values is made by examining the T_1 value of single pixels of the image chosen from within areas of subcutaneous fat or muscle. This is readily obtained from the digital record of the image which allows individual pixels to be identified within the matrix of 256 x 256 pixels which comprise the image. A series of such estimates for fat and muscle in several body regions are given in Tables 2 and 3. Mean values of T_1

TABLE 2. Measurements of T_1 (milliseconds at 3.4 MHz) in living and newly-dead pig adipose tissue at different sites.

Site	Alive	SEM	Dead	SEM
Shoulder 1	135	1.8		
" 2	139	1.7	135	2.3
Thorax	138	1.6		
Midback 1	142	1.7		
" 2	138	2.7	137	1.9
Loin	148	3.3	132	3.3
Rump	155	2.5		
All sites	140		135	SED 1.9
	Inner backfat		Outer backfat	
	140		135	SED 1.5

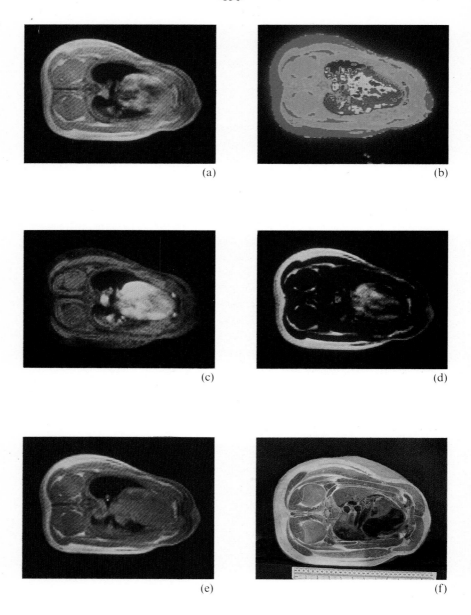

Fig. 3.   Images obtained from a live pig, using the pulse sequences
described in the text, and the corresponding anatomical cross-section
of the carcass: a, proton density; b, T_1; c, difference image; d,
inversion recovery; e, fast sequence; f, carcass cross-section.

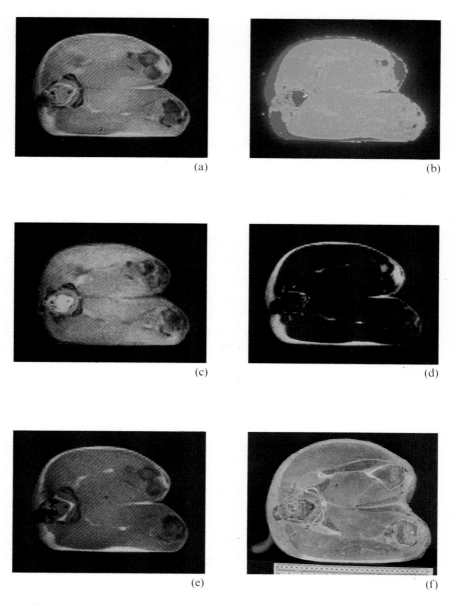

(a)

(b)

(c)

(d)

(e)

(f)

Fig. 4. Images obtained from a dead pig, using the pulse sequences described in the text, and the corresponding anatomical cross-section of the carcass: a, proton density; b, T_1; c, difference image; d, inversion recovery; e, fast sequence; f, carcass cross-section.

132

TABLE 3.   Measurements of T_1 (milliseconds at 3.4 MHz) in living and
newly-dead pig muscles.

Muscle	Alive	SEM	Dead	SEM
Triceps	245	3.5	241	3.5
Superspinatus	288	5.0		
Trapezius	260	5.0		
Longissimus dorsi				
at thorax	236	2.2		
at last rib	233	2.5		
at loin	234	2.2	232	7.1
Psoas	246	7.1		
Rectus femoris	235	3.5		
Biceps femoris	238	3.5	239	3.5
Semimembranosus	239	4.1		

for subcutaneous fat and muscle differ by a factor of 1.5, offering the
potential for good discrimination.   These indicate higher T_1 values for
fat than those obtained from excised tissue, with small, though
significant variation from one site to another.   Values for living muscle
are more variable, though whether this reflects differences in the
composition of muscle from different sites remains to be established.
Because the animals underwent prolonged anaesthesia lying on one side it
is possible that the upper and lower sides of the body were unequally
perfused with blood.   Measurements of T_1 in muscles from the lower side
of the body were 6.7 milliseconds (SED 2.4; $p < 0.01$) longer than in the
contralateral upper muscles.

Future developments

      This seems to be the first attempt to use NMR imaging to examine the
distribution of adipose tissue in farm animals.   There are no major
problems in its use with immobilized animals, and machines of the size of
the Aberdeen MkII imager would easily accommodate pigs up to 100 kg.

      In future work, five potential developments are worth examining.
First, later machines, such as the Aberdeen MK2 imager, use more powerful
magnets: instruments with superconducting magnets having static field
strengths an order of magnitude greater than those obtained with resistive

equipment are now available. These will allow either faster imaging or enhanced resolution (more line scans) in the same operating time.

Second, little work has yet been done to develop the best combination of field gradient and pulse sequence for imaging body fat and its interfaces. There is evidence from the MKII to suggest that this can be greatly improved by these adjustments.

Third, there is evidence that chemical shift can be detected with sufficient precision to contribute to the discrimination of fat and lean.

Fourth, work so far has concentrated on producing images of either proton density or T_1. Signal processing programs which combine this information, perhaps including also chemical shift information, may be expected to produce better images of particular aspects of the body's composition.

Lastly, estimation of whole-body adipose tissue volume will require serial scans along the body and computer integrations. Programs to do this have been developed in X-ray CAT systems but not so far in NMR imaging.

REFERENCES

Edelstein, W.A., Hutchison, J.M.S., Johnson, G. and Redpath, T.W. 1980. Spin warp NMR imaging and applications to human whole-body imaging. Phys. Med. Biol., 25, 751-756.

Farrar, T.C. and Becker, E.D. 1971. Purse and Fourier Transform NMR, p.24. New York: Academic Press.

Foster, M.A. 1983. Magnetic Resonance in Medicine and Biology, Chapters 7 and 7. Oxford: Pergamon Press.

Hutchison, J.M.S. 1976. Proc. 7th L.H. Gray Conference, Medical Images (Leeds), pp. 135-141. Bristol: Wiley/Institute of Physics.

Hutchison, J.M.S. 1979. IEE Med. Electron. Monogr., nos. 28-33 (Ed. B.W. Watson). (Peter Peregrinus, London). pp.79-93.

Ling, C., Rosemary, Foster, Margaret, A. and Hutchison, J.M.S. 1980. Comparison of NMR water proton T, relaxation times of rabbit tissues at 24 MHz and 2.5 MHz. Physics in Medicine and Biology 25, 748-751.

Mallard, J., Hutchison, J.M.S., Edelstein, W., Ling, R. and Foster, M. 1979. Imaging by nuclear magnetic resonance and its bio-medical implications. J. Biomed. Eng. 1, 153-160.

Mallard, J., Hutchison, J.M.S., Edelstein, W.A., Ling, C.R., Foster, M.A. and Johnson, G. 1980. Phil. Trans. R. Soc. Lond. 289, 519-533.

Smith, F.W. and Mallard, J.R. 1982. Whole body nuclear magnetic resonance tomographic imaging - imaging method and human atlas. Journal of Medical Imagings Vol. 2 Special Issue, 1-23.

THE POTENTIAL OF IN VIVO NEUTRON ACTIVATION ANALYSIS FOR BODY
COMPOSITION MEASUREMENTS IN THE AGRICULTURAL SCIENCES

B.W. East, T. Preston and I. Robertson

The Scottish Universities Research and Reactor Centre,
East Kilbride,
Glasgow G75 OQU,
U.K.

ABSTRACT

A description of the methodology of 14 MeV in vivo neutron activation
analysis (NAA) of humans adapted and used for body composition measurements of rats, sheep and pigs is given together with some conclusions and
general observations on the potential of NAA for animal studies.

INTRODUCTION

Recent practical experience of the adaption of human total body in
vivo NAA using 14 MeV neutrons and shadow-shield whole-body counting for
animals indicates that in principle, body composition data are obtainable
for specimens ranging from 50g up to 80 and probably 100kg if suitable
methods of handling live animals and calibration at the top end of this
weight range can be devised. Subject to the availability of 14 MeV neutron
sources, which can be costly, activation with neutrons of this energy
would appear to be ideal and have good potential for even larger animals.
A key issue here is however the design of suitable body counting equipment
(Lohman, 1970).

14 MeV NEUTRON ACTIVATION

The 14 MeV NAA facility at East Kilbride (Williams et. al., 1978a) has
been used for many hundreds of clinical analyses of the total body elements
N, Na, P, Cl and Ca and the associated whole-body counter also measures
total body potassium via the natural ^{40}K activity. Total body oxygen
measurement (Williams et. al., 1978b), using the 7.1 second ^{16}N activity,
is also routinely done. Whole-body counting is accomplished in a scanning-
bed counter (Boddy et. al., 1975) comprising two 29cm diameter x 10cm thick
NaI(Tl) detectors mounted above and below the subject within a 10cm thick
Pb shadow-shield (Figure 1a). Simultaneous bilateral scanning irradiation
is conducted in an adjoining facility which uses two 14 MeV sealed-tube
neutron generators (3 x 10^{10} neutrons second^{-1} each) housed in a massive
concrete shield and mounted above and below a moving bed giving similar

geometry to the counter (Figure 1d). This equipment has been extensively
used for sequential investigations of bone minerals, electrolyte balance,
protein and lean body mass in various clinical disorders such as renal
disease, bone disease, hypertension and heart disease.

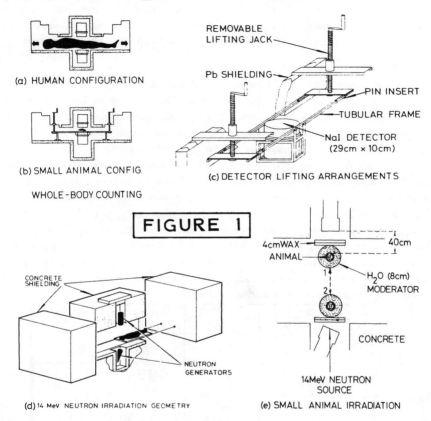

(a) HUMAN CONFIGURATION

(b) SMALL ANIMAL CONFIG.

WHOLE-BODY COUNTING

REMOVABLE LIFTING JACK

Pb SHIELDING

PIN INSERT

TUBULAR FRAME

NaI DETECTOR (29cm × 10cm)

(c) DETECTOR LIFTING ARRANGEMENTS

FIGURE 1

CONCRETE SHIELDING

NEUTRON GENERATORS

(d) 14 MeV NEUTRON IRRADIATION GEOMETRY

4cmWAX
ANIMAL
40cm
H_2O (8cm) MODERATOR
CONCRETE
14MeV NEUTRON SOURCE

(e) SMALL ANIMAL IRRADIATION

Our interest in the agricultural application of NAA has led to the
development of a static small animal counting and irradiation arrangement
within the existing facility. The live animal (fully conscious rat) is
activated near the target of each neutron generator in turn, while sur-
rounded by a hydrogenous premoderator to optimise the neutron flux
(Figure 1e). It is then counted with the lower detector of the counter
raised to give greater sensitivity and nearly 4π counting geometry
(Figures 1b and 1c). A closely similar procedure is used for subsamples

of carcass homogenates. Data for large animals up to about 80kg (exempli-
fied by pig carcasses) are obtained without significant modification of the
existing facility, although live animals would clearly require caging and
probably anaesthetising. Analysis time for a full elemental investigation
is typically just over an hour and usually includes a 20m background study,
a 5m irradiation and up to 4 post-irradiation counts or groups of scans,
with durations matched to the half-lives of the radionuclides of interest.

RESULTS AND DISCUSSION

   Table 1 shows NAA data from a range of animal and human studies. Mean
elemental contents are quoted for rats of 55-550g studied _in vivo_ and by
carcass analysis, 1.5kg homogenates of 41kg lamb carcasses, whole pig carcasses (64kg gilts) and _in vivo_ analysis of humans (males of 75-95kg). The
method thus spans a wide range of sample types and a range greater than 2g
to 2kg nitrogen. These type of data are very useful for sequential studies
and for comparing differences between populations (e.g. bone minerals in
pigs are much less than in humans), but can show a large spread within a
population (e.g. nitrogen content of field reared sheep, 20% C.V., n = 8)
Radiation dose effects are unlikely to affect sequential studies even in
small animals (Preston _et. al._, 1984). Further breakdown and discussion of
these elements bringing out their potential usefulness for expressing body
composition in terms of fat, water, protein and mineral contents can be
found in Preston, East and Robertson (1983a).

	RATS n=16	SHEEP n=23	PIGS n=3	HUMANS n=21
MEAN WT. (Kg)	0·28	41	64	85
N	8·67	1166	1953	2046
Ca	2·14	589	553	1108
P	1·58	332	384	614·9
K	N.D.	113·7	151·3	151·9
Na	0·27	49·1	72·3	85·8
Cl	0·25	38·7	66·8	68·7

COMPARATIVE ELEMENTAL CONTENTS (g) BY NEUTRON ACTIVATION ANALYSIS.

TABLE 1.

SOME CONCLUSIONS AND GENERAL OBSERVATIONS

1. The application of the methods described here to animals larger than
100kg requires much more detailed study. Attenuation of neutrons and
gamma photons by body tissue, while acceptable in 80kg humans may
limit the technique unless combinations of irradiation and counting
geometries can be devised to overcome the tendency of bias towards
surface tissues.

2. The potential applicability of in vivo NAA depends on a clear definition of the exact requirements of the user. The technique would appear
to complement other methods of tissue distribution assessment. In the
specific case of nitrogen, detection of changes in body content of a
few percent can provide a useful reference baseline for metabolic
measurements, such as ^{15}N protein turnover studies. A preliminary
study of the simultaneous use of these methods has been completed
(Preston et. al., 1983b).

3. Extension of the technique to enable other elements to be measured
routinely would be an advantage. Total body carbon analysis by neutron
inelastic scatter gamma rays (Kyere, 1982) would allow more direct
estimation of body fat and carcass energy than at present.

4. NAA studies have largely been on a collaborative basis between
specialised groups with the equipment and expertise and other life
sciences departments, so that problems such as inconvenient access have
often been encountered. It is likely that this situation will continue
for the development of animal studies but there might be some scope for
the use of sealed tube 14 MeV neutron generators, radioactive neutron
sources such as ^{252}Cf, ^{238}Pu-Be and ^{241}Am-Be (Boddy, 1973) and mobile
or semi-portable equipment (East, 1983) in "non-nuclear physics"
establishments.

5. Depending on specific requirements, some procedures, particularly for
smaller animals or partial body analysis might be adaptable for rapid
throughput, either for analysis of single animals or in batches.

ACKNOWLEDGEMENT

One of us (T.P.) gratefully acknowledges the award of an MRC/ARC
earmarked research fellowship which enabled this work to be carried out.

REFERENCES

Boddy, K. (1973). Neutron sources, energy, flux and moderation in the body. In: In vivo neutron activation analysis, 49-64, IAEA, Vienna (IAEA-PL-493/13).

Boddy, K., Elliott, A., Robertson, I., Mahaffy, M.E. and Holloway, I. (1975). A high sensitivity dual-detector shadow-shield whole-body counter with an "invariant" response for total body in vivo neutron activation analysis. Phys. Med. Biol., 20, No. 2, 296-304.

East, B.W. (1983). In vivo nitrogen analysis using ^{241}Am-Be neutrons - a feasibility study for a mobile facility. Clin. Phys. Physiol. Meas. 4, No. 2, 217-221.

Kyere, K., Oldroyd, B., Oxby, C.B., Burkinshaw, L., Ellis, R.E. and Hill, G.L. (1982). The feasibility of measuring total body carbon by counting neutron inelastic scatter gamma rays. Phys. Med. Biol. 27, No. 6, 805-817.

Lohman, T.G., and Twardock, A.R. (1970). Large animal counter. In: Directory of whole-body radioactivity monitors. International atomic energy agency, Vienna, STI/PUB/213.

Preston, T., East, B.W., Robertson, I. (1983a). Body composition measurements of rats, sheep, pigs and humans by neutron activation analysis. In: CEC Workshop: in vivo measurement of body composition in meat animals, Bristol, November 1983. - this volume.

Preston, T., East, B.W., Robertson, I. (1983b). Simultaneous measurement of body protein and protein turnover in humans and animals. Proceedings of SAC 83 Edinburgh. In press (Analyst).

Preston, T., Reeds, P.J., East, B.W. and Holmes, P.H. (1984). A comparison of body protein determination in rats by in vivo neutron activation and carcass analysis. To be published.

Williams, E.D., Boddy, K., Harvey, I. and Haywood, J.K. (1978a). Calibration and evaluation of a system for total body in vivo activation analysis using 14 MeV neutrons. Phys. Med. Biol. 23, No. 3, 405-415.

Williams, E.D. and Boddy, K. (1978b). Measurement of whole-body oxygen in living humans by neutron activation analysis. Int. J. of App. Radiat. and Isotopes, 29, 281-283.

PROPOSALS FOR A "PORTABLE" FACILITY FOR IN VIVO PROTEIN
DETERMINATION AND CARCASS QUALITY PREDICTION IN FARM
ANIMALS BY NEUTRON ACTIVATION ANALYSIS

T. Preston, B.W. East and I. Robertson
The Scottish Universities Research and Reactor Centre,
East Kilbride,
Glasgow G75 0QU,
U.K.

ABSTRACT

The design of a low-cost facility for measuring body protein in farm animals by neutron activation analysis is discussed. Particular emphasis is placed on the choice of neutron sources and gamma detectors needed for in vivo prompt gamma analysis.

INTRODUCTION

Neutron activation analysis (NAA) appears to have much potential as a method of in vivo body composition determination in the agricultural sciences. Clinical experience suggests that NAA could be used for multi-elemental body composition measurements in animals up to 100kg (East et al. 1984). Many of the elements measured by delayed NAA (e.g. N, Na, P, Cl and Ca) can also be measured in much smaller animals (e.g. Rats, Preston et al., 1984). It is argued that a central research facility specifically designed for animal work would be the most cost effective method of examining the full potential of multielemental NAA in farm animals up to and beyond 100kg, as this could be equipped with apparatus designed for high precision measurements (2-4%) in a range of animal sizes, e.g. 14 MeV neutron generators, prompt and delayed counting arrangements (East et al., 1984).

It is possible however, to carry out in vivo body composition measurements by NAA using more modest equipment, especially if multielemental analysis is not required. Rapid sample throughput might also be achieved if lower precision (5-10%) were acceptable. A potentially important example of this approach is body nitrogen determination by prompt gamma analysis. Nitrogen data are readily converted to protein content which is a useful index of tissue quality. A suitable choice of irradiation and counting geometry could possibly allow bias away from the viscera and provide an index of carcass quality from the living body (see below). In this contribution we consider some of the practicalities of nitrogen analysis in relation to the provision of "portable" or similar facilities.

DISCUSSION

The thermal neutron capture reaction ^{14}N (n,γ) ^{15}N has a low cross
section (80 m barns), but as nitrogen is abundant in animal tissue and the
gamma photons produced are energetic (10.8 MeV) and clear from interference, it is suitable for nitrogen measurement (Vartsky et al., 1979).
Apparatus required to observe this reaction consists of a collimated source
of neutrons, shielded from the operators, and gamma ray detectors placed to
count photons emitted as the animal is being irradiated.

Fast neutrons are preferred, relying on premoderators and moderation
by body tissue to provide a suitable thermal neutron flux throughout the
animal. Radioactive sources (e.g. ^{241}Am-Be) or 14 MeV sealed tube
generators would appear to be the most suitable neutron sources, cyclotrons
being out of the question for this application on economic grounds. Both
these types of neutron sources have been proposed for portable facilities,
the major field of use being geological survey (Clayton and Wormald, 1983).
14 MeV neutron generators are considerably more expensive than small
radioisotope sources, but can provide higher neutron fluxes. If speed of
analysis is critical, the minimum practical neutron flux may well neces-
sitate a large radioactive neutron source or an array of several sources
in order to give a neutron flux comparable to a single neutron generator.
Fast neutron outputs of $> 10^8$ n s^{-1} are attainable with small neutron
generators costing about U.S. \$37K (1983), a neutron output of 1.8×10^8
n s^{-1} from an array of 4 x 740 G Bq (80 Ci, in total) ^{241}Am-Be sources
would cost about £39K (1983). Neutron generators are more economical at
higher outputs, however lower neutron fluxes will cost proportionately
less for the radioactive sources.

14 MeV neutrons have better tissue penetration, and therefore give
greater sensitivity at depth (important for large animals); sources are
easier to handle and transport as the generators can be switched off,
although radioactive neutron sources last much longer and do not have
maintenance problems. Shielding to reduce the radiation dose to the
operators would be a problem for both types of fast neutron sources, but
shielding during transport would be an extra cost for radioisotope sources.
An additional benefit of many neutron generator designs is that their
output can be pulsed. A detection system for thermal neutron capture
gamma analysis could be gated to avoid counting during the few micro-

seconds of each fast neutron pulse, providing a useful increase in signal-to-noise ratio.

In clinical applications, where whole body protein analysis by the ^{14}N (n, γ) ^{15}N reaction has been developed, radiation dose to the subject has on ethical grounds, been kept as low as possible, typically 0.25-1 mSv (25-100 m rem) per measurement. These standards can probably be relaxed in an agricultural application, allowing use of greater neutron fluxes rather than greater detector volumes (possibly the more costly option) to minimise analysis time. Measurement speed and precision will be very important factors in the design of apparatus as they will greatly influence equipment cost, perhaps the major consideration in an agricultural application.

The choice of detectors is an important factor in the planning of an NAA facility. NaI (Tl) detectors have much greater sensitivity and considerably lower cost than semiconductor detectors, however the latter have much better gamma energy resolution and can therefore give superior signal-to-noise ratios. A 15cm diam x 10cm NaI (Tl) detector gives comparable performance in this context to a 25% (relative to a 7.5 x 7.5cm NaI detector) semiconductor detector. A hyperpure n-type Ge detector (more resistant to neutron damage) of this size costs about £25 K (1983) including electronics in comparison with £5 K including electronics, for the NaI detector. Another limitation to field use of semiconductor detectors is their need for liquid nitrogen cooling. It is therefore of no benefit to use semiconductor detectors for single element prompt gamma analysis unless interference from similar gamma energies is severe. Semiconductor detectors have however, shown great promise for multielemental NAA in the field, in geological applications (Clayton and Wormald, 1983).

An important requirement for NAA facilities in the clinical sciences has been the need to achieve an acceptably uniform neutron flux throughout the body and "invariant" detector response thus giving uniform sensitivity to evenly distributed elements. An advantage of prompt gamma analysis is that information on the hydrogen content of the body is also obtainable simultaneously. The thermal neutron capture reaction on hydrogen, ^{1}H (n, γ) ^{2}H, emits a gamma photon of 2.23 MeV which is the most prominent in the spectrum of irradiated tissue. This reaction is induced by neutrons of the same energy as that of nitrogen and as both elements are evenly distributed in body tissue, hydrogen can act as an internal standard to correct for body shape and positioning. Indeed, it is conceivable that exploitation of this reaction would permit the design of a simple walk-

142

through apparatus, not needing the most uniform sensitivity but measuring
a body nitrogen-to-hydrogen ratio. This would simplify the procedure with
some sacrifice of precision. A prediction of carcass protein, fat, water
and mineral could be made from the known nitrogen and hydrogen stoichio-
metry within these compartments together with an average lean body composition (protein/water/mineral ratio). Using this basis, each measured
nitrogen-to-hydrogen value would have a unique protein-to-lean mass ratio.
Only experimentation will show whether this simple approach is adequate
for predicting carcass quality from a measurement of the living animal.

Interestingly, it would be possible to bias the measurement towards
the muscle mass, away from the viscera. Figure 1 shows models of irradiation and detection geometries which demonstrate this possibility. The
models are far from accurate, especially in the surface tissues nearest
the neutron sources, where premoderator depth will greatly influence the
thermal neutron flux. Tissue half thicknesses used were 32cm, 8.9cm and
5.7cm for 10.8 MeV photons, 14 MeV neutrons and ^{241}Am-Be neutrons respectively. Detector- and source-to-subject distances are to scale, with the
cross section of the subject being 30cm in diameter in each example.
Figure 1 as shows the rather uniform response of a system with a single
14 MeV neutron generator and a single detector opposite, a geometry which
is similar to a clinical NAA facility (Vartsky et al., 1979). Figs. 1 b)
and c) demonstrate possible arrangements that bias the measurement in a
"horseshoe" shape to represent the carcass. Method b) is achieved with an
array of ^{241}Am-Be sources and a single detector, method c) with a single
14 MeV neutron generator and two detectors. It may well be acceptable for
this application, to assume that the animal is symmetrical about its dorsal
axis and investigate a single side or pass the animal through the apparatus
in both directions. For the 14 MeV neutron generator system in Fig. 1c)
this would further reduce complexity, apparatus and shielding costs in
allowing the use of a single neutron source and a single detector.

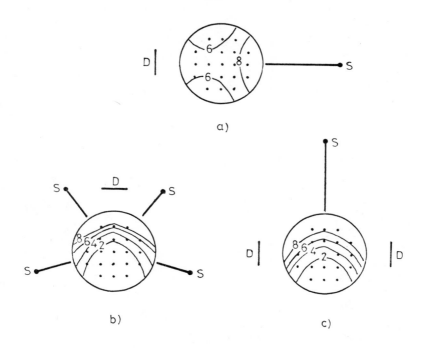

FIGURE 1   PROMPT GAMMA GEOMETRIES
(See text for details; contours relative sensitivity;
S, source   D, detector)

REFERENCES

Clayton, C.G. and Wormald, M.R. (1983). Coal Analysis by Nuclear Methods. Int. J. Appl. Radiat. Isot., 34, (1), 3-22.

East, B.W., Preston, T., Robertson, I. (1984). The potential of in vivo neutron activation analysis for body composition measurements in the agricultural sciences. In: CEC Workshop: in vivo measurement of body composition in meat animals. Bristol, November 1983. - this volume.

Preston, T., East, B.W., Robertson, I. (1984). Body composition measurements of rats, sheep, pigs and humans by neutron activation analysis. In CEC Workshop: in vivo measurement of body composition in meat animals. Bristol, November 1983.

Vartsky, D., Ellis, K.J., Cohn, S.H. (1979). In vivo measurement of body nitrogen by analysis of prompt gammas from neutron capture. J. Nucl. Med., 20, 1158-1165.

SESSION V

POSTERS

Chairman: P. Walstra

HERITABILITY OF SOME IN VIVO MEASUREMENTS AND CONFORMATION SCORES, AND GENETIC CORRELATIONS WITH POST MORTEM DATA IN YOUNG ITALIAN SIMMENTAL BULLS.

G. Bittante and G. Guidetti

Instituto di Zootecnica Universita degli studi di Padova
Via Gradenigo, 6 - 35131 Padova, Italy

ABSTRACT

A research programme, carried out on 327 young Italian Simmental bulls sired by 23 A.I. bulls utilized in three cycles of progeny test for meat production, was used to examine the possibility of indirect selection for carcass quality based on in vivo measurements and judgements.

Generally speaking the descriptive conformation scores presented medium-high heritability (h^2) and positive genetic correlation (r_G) with growth rate, dressing percentage, lean percentage and muscle-fat ratio, while the live animal measurements and the body conformation indexes appeared scarcely heritable and thus their r_G with growth rate and carcass composition would have no practical value. The alternative "phenotypic" indirect selection route does not seem to be practicable because of the lower phenotypic correlation (r_p) with the productive parameters.

The substitution of a performance test for the progeny test to estimate the genetic value for beef production of A.I. bulls from dual purpose breeds requires an improvement of the in vivo evaluation of the carcass composition.

INTRODUCTION

The genetic improvement of the Italian Simmental (Pezzata Rossa Friulana) is based mainly on the progeny testing of the A.I. bulls, both for meat and milk production. Substituting performance testing for "in station" progeny testing for meat production, could increase the overall selection efficiency, and also reduce costs. The major limit for this approach is the in vivo estimate of the post-mortem traits (Bech Andersen, 1982;) and a research programme has been carried out to study the heritability of various measurements, indexes and descriptive

148

judgements of the live animals and their genetic correlations with the
productive parameters. These included growth rate, dressing percentage,
lean meat percentage in the carcass and muscle/bone ratio (Figure 1).

FIGURE 1 - DIRECT AND INDIRECT SELECTION FOR CARCASS QUALITY

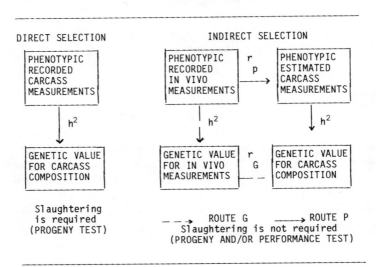

h² = HERITABILITY

r_p = PHENOTYPIC CORRELATIONS
GROWTH RATE

r_G = GENETIC CORRELATIONS

CARCASS MEASUREMENTS:
- DRESSING %
- LEAN MEAT %
- FAT %
- BONE %
- MEAT/BONE
- HIGH QUALITY JOINTS

IN VIVO MEASUREMENTS:

- DESCRIPTIVE CONFORMATION
  SCORE
- BODY MEASUREMENTS
- BODY CONFORMATION INDEXES
- METABOLIC PROFILE
- ENZYMATIC PROFILE
- HORMONAL PROFILE
- ULTRASONIC MEASUREMENTS
- RADIOGRAPHY
- COMPUTED TOMOGRAPHY
- NUCLEAR MAGNETIC RESONANCE
- DILUTION TECHNIQUES
- BIOPSY TECHNIQUES

TABLE 1 – HERITABILITY OF SOME IN VIVO MEASUREMENTS AND CONFORMATION SCORES AND GENETIC COR-
RELATIONS WITH POST-MORTEM DATA.

	h^2 ±s.d.	Genetic correlation (r_G ±s.e.) with			
		weight gain	dressing %	lean %	muscle/bone
Stature score	.41+.19	.89+.03	.30+.10	.32+.08	.39+.08
Partial scores:					
– head	.26+.16	.22+.20	.54+.09	1.00+.00	.93+.02
– shoulder	.10+.12	–	–	–	–
– back	.42+.19	.03+.16	.39+.09	.60+.06	.37+.08
– thorax	.27+.16	.24+.19	.08+.13	.42+.09	.18+.11
– abdomen	.17+.14	–	–	–	–
– loin	.41+.19	.51+.12	.34+.09	.89+.02	.61+.06
– rump	.61+.23	.34+.12	-.04+.09	.73+.04	.58+.05
– round	.78+.26	.00+.12	.69+.04	.76+.03	.75+.03
– legs-feet	.30+.17	.10+.19	.07+.12	.90+.02	.78+.04
– skin	.56+.22	1.00+.00	-.21+.09	.66+.04	.88+.02
Total score	.67+.24	.34+.11	.30+.08	.86+.02	.69+.04
Body measurements:					
– Height at withers (HW)	.36+.18	-.78+.07	-.40+.09	-.55+.07	-.66+.05
– Height of thorax (HT)	.12+.12	–	–	–	–
– Heart girth (HG)	.09+.11	–	–	–	–
– Length of trunk (LT)	.08+.11	–	–	–	–
– Length of rump (LR)	.00+.00	–	–	–	–
– Width of hip (WH)	.04+.10	–	–	–	–
– Width of pelvis (WP)	.18+.13	.78+.10	-.52+.12	.14+.14	-.21+.13
– Width of rump (WR)	.21+.14	.18+.22	-.55+.10	-.48+.10	-.45+.10
– Circum. of cannon (CC)	.07+.11	–	–	–	–
Conformation indexes:					
– HT/HW	.13+.12	–	–	–	–
– HW/LT	.22+.14	-.49+.17	-.37+.12	-.38+.11	-.51+.09
– HT/LT	.23+.15	-.36+.19	-.62+.09	-.29+.11	-.56+.08
– LR/LT	.06+.11	–	–	–	–
– CC/HG	.12+.12	–	–	–	–
– LT/HG	.24+.15	-.09+.21	.70+.07	-.04+.12	.10+.12
– HG HG/HW	.10+.12	–	–	–	–
– HT WP LT/10^4	.02+.10	–	–	–	–

NOTE: The genetic correlations of variables with a low heritability ("sire" effect not
significant for P=.05) are not reported.

MATERIAL AND METHODS

The study was carried out on 327 young Italian Simmental bulls. The progeny of 23 sires over three progeny testing cycles. The animals were bred, slaughtered and controlled by the "Associazione Nazionale Allevatori di bovini di razza Pezzata Rossa Friulana" at the "Centro Genetico per il miglioramento della razza P.R.F." in Fiume Veneto (PN) following a technique described in previous papers (Bittante et al, 1980a and 1980b).

The data, covaried with the fat content of the carcass, were analyzed according to a model of analysis of variance including the cycles, the sires and the between half-sibs source of variation. The expected value of the sire component was utilized to estimate the hertability "h^2" of the traits controlled and the matrix of their phenotypic (r_p) and genetic (r_G) correlations (Pirchner, 1969). The muscle/bone ratio was also employed as the dependent variable in a phenotypic step-wise multiple regression analysis with the in vivo data as independent variables (Pirchner, 1982).

RESULTS AND DISCUSSION

Table 1 reports the main results of the trials. With the exceptions of those relative to the shoulder and the abdomen, the descriptive conformation scores presented a medium-high heritability. Moreover, these traits generally showed positive genetic correlations with the productive parameters. These two facts indicate the possibility of introducing conformation scores in an indirect selection programme following the "route G" of figure 1.

On the other hand, the live animal measurements, and the derived body conformation indexes, appeared scarcely heritable and thus their r_G with the productive parameters have no practical value. The only exceptions were (a) the height at withers (b) the widths of the pelvis and of the rump, the indexes formed by (c) the ratios of the height at withers and (d) of that of thorax on the length of the trunk and, (e) that obtained by dividing (d)^2 by the height at withers (compactness index). Contrary to the results for the conformation scores, the r_G of the measurements were generally negative, indicating that the "compact" animals should be preferable and this is confirmed by the data relative to the body conformation indexes.

The penotypic correlations generally fell lower than the genetic ones, indicating the difficulty of following the "route P" of figure 1. In fact the step-wise multiple regression analysis between the muscle/bone ratio (Y) and the in vivo measurements, indexes and conformation scores (Xi) furnished the following equation:

$$Y = 2.13 + .00098X_1 + .0.23X_2 - .042X_3 + .061X_4 + .016X_5 + .040X_6 \pm .251 \quad R^2 = .228$$

where: X_1 = weight gain (g/d); X_2 = height of thorax/height at withers (%); X_3 = circumference of cannon (cm); X_4 = stature score (0-9); X_5 = length of rump/length of trunk (%) and X_6 = thorax score (0-9).

CONCLUSIONS

Examination of the results indicate the following conclusions:
(i) the descriptive conformation scores presented a medium-high heritability and positive genetic correlations with carcass quality;
(ii) body measurements and conformation indexes generally seemed to be scarcely heritable and the few significant genetic correlations were almost all negative;
(iii) the phenotypic correlations were lower than the corresponding genetic ones;
(iv) an improvement of the in vivo evaluation of carcass composition is required to increase the efficiency of indirect selection, thus permitting the substitution of performance for progeny testing for meat production in the beef and dual purpose breeds.

REFERENCES

Bech Andersen R.B. 1982. In vivo estimation of body composition in beef. CEC Workshop, 15-16 December 1981. Copenhagen.
Bittante G., Guidetti G. and Xiccato G. 1980a. Valutazione genetica dell'attitudine alla produzione della carne di tori Pezzati Rossi Friulani. La Pezzata Rossa, XIII, 2-3.
Bittante G., Guidetti G. and Xiccato G. 1980b. Prove di progenie su tori Pezzati Rossi Friulan per la produzione della carne. Risultati del terzo ciclo di prove. La Pezzata Rossa, XIII, 11.
Pirchner F. 1969. Population genetics in animal breeding. Ed. Freeman & Co. S. Francisco.
Pirchner F. 1982. Personal communication.

PREDICTION OF EWE BODY COMPOSITION
AT DIFFERENT PHYSIOLOGICAL STATES

F. BOCQUIER AND M. THERIEZ

Institut National de la Recherche Agronomique
Laboratoire de la Production Ovine
Centre de Recherches Zootechniques et Veterinaires
Theix, 63122 Ceyrat, FRANCE

ABSTRACT

Deuterium oxide was used on 43 ewes at different physiological states in order to establish relationships to predict body composition.

Back extrapolation to calculate deuterium oxide space was not affected by the physiological state of the ewe, early lactation, mid-lactation and dry.

Relationships between fat and measured or estimated water (W or D) were both modified by physiological state, probably due to variations in udder weight.

An accurate prediction of ewe body composition is possible with different equations.

INTRODUCTION

The prediction of body composition "in vivo" is possible with the deuterium oxide dilution technique (RO-BELIN, 1977). This method has been satisfactorily applied to dry or growing animals. But, there have been conflicting results as to the ability of D_2O-space to predict body fat in lactating ewes. COWAN et al. (1979, 1980), found that this method was not adapted to predict body fat, although TISSIER et al. (1983) showed that it was possible to use it.

This experiment was conducted to confirm these last results and to improve the suitability of prediction equations for the physiological state.

MATERIALS AND METHODS

Animals and feeding

43 ewes of four different breeds were used : Limousine, Romanov X Limousine, Ile de France and Frison X Sarde X Lacaune.

Ewes were at three phsyiological states :

- State 1 : early lactation, + 3 days, n = 11
- State 2 : mid-lactation, + 42 days, n = 13
- State 3 : dry, n = 19

Ewes were individually penned and had free access to water. Fresh food was offered each morning "ad libitum" except in the morning of slaughter day.

Ewes were weighed just after infusion i.e. : live weight at infusion (LWI) and before slaughter (LWS).

Deuterium oxide space (D) :

D_2O was infused as described by ROBELIN (1977) ; the weight of D_2O infused was about 0.6% of body weight.

Blood samples were taken at 4, 6, 23 and 24 hours after infusion.

D_2O in blood water was determined with infrared spectrophometry (TISSIER et al., 1978).

D_2O-space was calculated by back extrapolation (Co method).

Slaughter

Before slaughter, ewes were clipped and weighed. Body parts were weighed and stored as described by TISSIER et al. (1983) before chemical analyses for dry matter, nitrogen, ash and energy. Fat was determined as the difference between D.M. weight and ash plus protein. These data were verified by comparison of directly measured and calculated energy.

RESULTS

Main results on weight live, body components and chemical analysis are given in Table 1.

TABLE 1 :

CHEMICAL COMPOSITION AND CHARACTERISTICS OF EWES : MEAN (SD)

PHYSIOLOGICAL STATE	EARLY LACTATION	MID-LACTATION	DRY
NUMBER	11	13	19
BODY WEIGHT INFUSION (KG)	62.1 (11.9)	55.6 (10.0)	58.4 (11.2)
UDDER (KG)	1.693 (0.79)	1.194 (0.36)	0.82 (0.52)
TOTAL BODY WATER (KG)	36.2 (5.40)	35.6 (4.5)	34.7 (4.3)
GUT WATER (KG)	8.3 (1.5)	8.4 (1.7)	9.0 (2.2)
FAT (KG)	11.4 (4.8)	7.9 (5.1)	12.6 (7.5)
PROTEIN (KG)	7.3 (1.2)	6.6 (0.8)	6.7 (1.0)
ASH (KG)	2.2 (0.4)	1.9 (0.1)	1.8 (0.2)

Ewe body weights did not differ according to physiological state, except for udders weights, which decreased from early lactation (1.693 kg) to the dry period (0.820 kg). Gut water content did not differ between lactating ewes, but was higher in dry ewes. Chemical compositions were identical between three groups except for total fat in mid-lactation (state 2). These ewes, which had the lower fat content, were also taller.

Relationships between body components and "in vivo" estimation of water.

Water
___

Estimation of body water (W, kg) by D_2O space (D, kg):

(1) W = 0.772 D + 6.340 R.S.D. = ± 1.34

% VAR = 0.917

Fat
___

Physiological state had no significant effect on the body water estimation.

A good relationship (figure 1) was noted between body water (W % LWS) and fat (F % LWS).

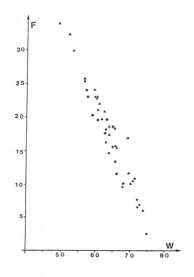

FIGURE 1

RELATIONSHIP BETWEEN FAT (F)
AND TOTAL BODY WATER (W)
AS PERCENTAGE OF SLAUGHTER WEIGHT

▲   DRY EWES (19)

*   EARLY LACTATION (11)

●   MID-LACTATION (13)

The relationship between body chemical fat (F, kg) and body water, either measured (W, kg) or estimated (D, kg) :

(2) $F = 0.932 LWS - 1.113 W + S***R.S.D. = \pm 0.557$

% VAR = 0.993

State = S1 = - 3.316, S2 = - 2.750, S3 = - 2.507

(3) $F = 0.854 LWI - 0.827 D + S***R.S.D. = \pm 1.501$

% VAR = 0.950

State = S1 = - 9.027, S2 = - 8.457, S3 = - 7.167

Physiological state had a highly significant effect on both equations (2) and (3).

The relationship on an empty body weight basis (EBW, kg), which removes the variations in gut content and water gut content (WG, kg) was set up as follows :

(4) $F = 0.947 EBW - 1.777 (W-WG) + S***R.S.D. = \pm 0.673$

% VAR = 0.989

State : S1 = 2.370, S2 = -1.740, S3 = -1.530

This remaining state effect could be due to udder weight differences.

Protein
</u>
Relationship between body proteins (P, kg) and body water estimated (D, kg).

(5) P = 0.048 LWI + 0.070 D + 1.361 R.S.D. = ± 0.431
% VAR = 0.820

There was no significant effect of physiological state, even if a slight (P<0.05) effect was observed with measured components (W).

Energy
Relationship between energy (E, Mcal) and body water estimated (D, kg)

(6) E = 8.28 LWI - 7.33 D + S*** R.S.D. = ± 13.36
% VAR = 0.960
State : S1 = - 78.21, S2 = - 74.34, S3 = 61.10

As for fat, physiological state had a highly significant effect.

DISCUSSION AND CONCLUSION

Even if water turnover is very different between ewes in early lactation as opposed to the dry state; the back extrapolation method for calculating D_2O space is not significantly affected by physiological state. This is in contrast with the D_2O space calculated by the equilibration method (COWAN et al., 1979, 1980).

The biological relationship between body fat, live weight and body water varies with physiological state (equation 2). This agrees with a previous paper (TISSIER et al., 1983), but not with COWAN'S results (1980). This 'state' effect may be due to udder weight variations and udder water content, not to the gut content because it is still significant when gut content is not taken into consideration (equation 4).

The present prediction relationship with D_2O space is also affected by physiological state, because its estimation of body water (W) by D_2O space (D) is fairly accurate.

In these conditions, three different equations have been proposed for body fat and energy estimation, but only one for body protein estimations.

These relationships are suitable for normally fed and watered ewes, weighed at infusion time undergoing blood sampling at different times (4, 6, 28 and 32 hours after).

REFERENCES

COWAN R.T., ROBINSON J.J., GREENHALCH J.F.D., McHATTIE I., 1979. Body composition changes in lactating ewes estimated by serial slaughter and deuterium dilution. Anim. Prod., 29, 81-89.

COWAN R.T., ROBINSON J.J., McHATTIE I., FRASER C., 1980. The prediction of body composition in live ewes in early lactation from live weight and estimates of gut content and total body water. J. Agric. Sci. Camb., 95, 515-522.

ROBELIN J., 1977. Estimation "in vivo" de la composition corporelle des agneaux à partir de l'espace de diffusion de l'eau lourde. Ann. Biol. Anim. Bioch. Biophys., 17, 95-105.

TISSIER M., ROBELIN J., PURROY A., GEAY Y., 1978. Extraction et dosage automatique rapide de l'eau lourde dans les liquides biologiques. Ann. Biol. Anim. Bioch. Biophys., 18, 1223-1228.

TISSIER M., THERIEZ M., PURROY A., BOCQUIER F., 1983. Estimation "in vivo" de la compositin corporelle de la brebis par la mesure de l'espace de diffusion de l'eau lourde. Reprod. Nutr. Develop., 23(4), 693-707.

IMPROVED DANSCANNER FOR CATTLE, PIGS AND SHEEP

Hans Busk
National Institute of Animal Science
Rolighedsvej 25, DK-1958 Copenhagen V, Denmark

ABSTRACT

Since 1972 ultrasonic measurements have been part of the animal breeding programmes in Denmark, and from 1976 these measurements have been taken by the DANSCANNER equipment.

To obtain reliable ultrasonic measurements it is necessary, to educate the person, who use the equipment, to obtain a good routine, always to control the equipment and results, and to have a good service on the equipment.

There are still some difficulties with ultrasonic measurements, and an experiment was carried out to test, whether effects of intermuscular fat and wrong sound velocity could be some of the reasons, However, the experiment showed that none of those effects could cause the difficulties.

A flexible multielement transducer has been constructed, but because of difficulties with the membrane, this transducer cannot yet be applied.

The DANSCANNER has been improved with grey-scale in addition to the dots. This improved equipment has been used on a few animals. The preliminary results show that the correlations between ultrasonic measurements and cut face measurements are the same as for the old DANSCANNER in cattle and a little higher in pigs.

INTRODUCTION

Measurement of slaughter quality on live cattle and pigs with ultrasound began in Denmark in 1972, and since 1976 the DANSCANNER equipment has been used. It is possible with the DANSCANNER to measure area of m. longissimus dorsi and fat area or fat thickness,

The DANSCANNER is a real-time scanner with multielement transducer. Two multielement transducers have been designed, one for cattle and one for pigs, in order that the transducer can fit as well as possible to the different species. Both transducers can be used for sheep.

Reliable results can only be achieved if a great deal of attention is paid to some basic factors. However, there are still some difficulties in measuring with ultrasound, some of which will be discussed. The DANSCANNER is reconstructed and improved in an attempt to overcome some of these difficulties. Results from experiments with the improved DANSCANNER will be presented.

IMPORTANT FACTORS WHEN MEASURING WITH ULTRASOUND

Because the DANSCANNER is delicate equipment it is necessary to stress the following basic factors:

1. Education: In Denmark 1-2 months are used to **instruct the person.**
2. Routine: It is important to measure many animals in order to acquire the routine.
3. Control: It is important to control **both operator and** equipment. It must be done both visually and by statistics.
4. Service: Service of the equipment is very important. In Denmark the **machines** are often brought together on a testing station and compared, and if necessary a technician from the firm will be present.

DIFFICULTIES WITH ULTRASOUND MEASUREMENT

Some animals are more difficult to measure than others. There are difficulties between breeds and within breeds. Some of the difficulties could be due to effect of 1. Intermuscular fat, 2. The Shape of the multi-element transducer and 3. Sound velocity in different tissues.

Also there is an effect of measuring day. Until now, it has not been possible to find the reason.

Some experiments designed to test the 3 mentioned effects have been carried out, and some of the results are presented below.

INTERMUSCULAR FAT

No correlation was found between the amount of intermuscular fat and picture quality or sound velocity.

FLEXIBLE MULTIELEMENT TRANSDUCER

The multielement transducer used on the DANSCANNER is built up in three blocks with fixed angles. A new multielement transducer, where the angles between the blocks are adjustable has been constructed. There have been problems in finding a suitable membrane to put in front of the multi-element transducer. Until now about 30 animals have been tested, and the test will continue.

MEASUREMENT OF SOUND VELOCITY

Two weeks before slaughter the sound velocity was measured in skin, fat and m.long.dorsi on live animals. One hour and 24 hours after slaughter the measurement was repeated on reheated probes. The results are shown in table 1.

TABLE 1 Mean velocity values (m/s) measured in beef cattle and pigs.

	Beef cattle			Pigs		
	Muscle	Fat	Skin	Muscle	Fat	Skin
In vivo	1604	1471	1591	1579	1426	1503
1 hour post mortem	1612	1493	1589	1591	1428	
24 hours post mortem	1612	1399	1597	1603	1444	

In addition the velocity in dual-purpose cattle compared to beef cattle is 40 m/s lower in muscle, the same in fat and 50 m/s higher in skin.

The results show that there are some differences in sound velocity, but not so big that it is necessary to change it from 1560 m/sec. as used now.

GREY-SCALE

The DANSCANNER has been reconstructed so that there are both grey-scale and 4 times more dots on the picture (fig.1). Some animals are measured with both the old and the improved DANSCANNER, and results are presented.

The effects of these modifications will be investigated soon so see if they can eliminate part of or the whole measuring day effect.

RESULTS WITH IMPROVED DANSCANNER

Cattle

Until now only 25 animals from a cross-breeding experiment have been measured two days before slaughter. They were slaughtered at a live weight of 470 kg. The carcasses were dissected at the carcass evaluation centre. Therefore, we were able to compare the ultrasonic measurements to the dissection results.

The preliminary results are shown in table 2.

TABLE 2   Repeatability between two measurements and correlations between ultrasonic measurement and cut face area.

| Equipment | Repeatability | | Correlations ultrasound x cut face | | | |
| | | | Without adjustm. | | Adjusted for day effect | |
	Old	Impr.	Old	Impr.	Old	Impr.
Area MLD	0.99	0.96	0.72	0.71	0.86	0.87
Fat area	0.94	0.92	0.83	0.83	0.86	0.89

Even if there are few animals in the calculation, it can be seen that the correlations are high and at the same level for the old and the improved DANSCANNER.

PIGS

58 pigs from the progeny test were measured 3 days before slaughter. Control measurements of area of m.long.dorsi and sidefat thickness were taken at the carcass evaluation centre. The results are shown in table 3.

TABLE 3   Repeatability between two measurements and correlations between ultrasonic measurements and cut face measurements

| Equipment | Repeatability | | Correlation (ultra.x cut face measm.) | |
	Old	Impr.	Old	Impr.
Area of MLD	0.93	0.95	0.76	0.80
Sidefat thickn.	0.98	0.98	0.91	0.93

The correlations are high, and a little better for the improved DAN-SCANNER than for the old one.

Sheep

Until now, we have not been able to measure sheep, which were slaughtered afterwards. Therefore, there are no correlations to carcass measure-

162

ment.

In table 4 the repeatability between two measurements on 98 sheep is shown.

TABLE 4 Repeatability between two measurements

Equipment	Repeatability	
	Old	Improved
Area of MLD	0.93	0.92
Fat area	0.95	0.95

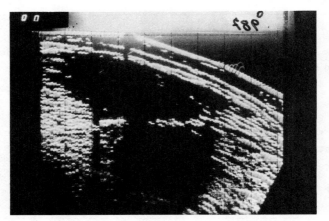

Fig. 1 Ultrasonic scan, produced by the improved DANSCANNER

CONCLUSIONS

Reliable results can only be achieved if attention is paid to education, control and service.

Only a few animals have been measured with the improved DANSCANNER, and therefore, it is too early to give a final conclusion. The results obtained until now show that measurements from the improved DANSCANNER are as good as those from the old one in cattle, and a little better in pigs.

IN VIVO ESTIMATION OF LAMB CARCASS COMPOSITION AND
LEAN TISSUE GROWTH RATE

A Cuthbertson, D Croston, D W Jones

Meat and Livestock Commission
PO Box 44, Queensway House
Bletchley, Milton Keynes, MK2 2EF

ABSTRACT

Alternative in vivo predictors of carcass lean content and lean gain per day were examined in rams of two Suffolk flocks. None of the predictors achieved a consistent improvement over the simply measured combination of final liveweight and age when added in trivariate regression. Alternative approaches are sought.

INTRODUCTION

An important objective in within breed selection is to identify and then to use sires with superior lean tissue growth rate. MLC implemented a test on rams of the Suffolk breed to assess the precision with which this can be done. This breed is the dominant terminal sire in Britain and contributes some 35% of genes in the slaughter population.

MATERIALS AND METHODS

Two Suffolk flocks were selected with a total of 105 rams available for test. A wide range of assessments were made on each ram at an average age of 22 weeks in one flock and 24 weeks in the other. In addition to recording weight and age at time of assessment, a series of scores and linear measurements were taken on the live rams. The measurements included tactile assessments of fatness, and length and body width measurements. Three types of ultrasonic equipment were tested - a simple A-mode unit (Meritronics) and two scanners - Danscanner and Scanogram. These were used to provide estimates of fat and muscle depths and areas.

From each flock, a group of 20 rams was selected at random for slaughter and detailed carcass assessment down to tissue separation into lean meat, fat and bone. This allowed the determination of carcass composition and lean tissue growth rate (LTGR) of each ram, and the results were used to assess the value of alternative predictors of both carcass composition and LTGR.

RESULTS

These relate to the 20 rams from each flock which were slaughtered and the results have been pooled within birth type/rearing type groups.

Table 1 shows for each flock the means and standard deviations for a range of assessments. As expected, the two flocks showed different mean liveweights and ages at assessment, but there was rather more variation in these characteristics in Flock 1. The extent of variability in lean content was low compared with results of other MLC lamb cutting work.

The simple correlations found for each flock between a number of the assessments and both carcass lean content and lean gain/day are shown in Table 2. Some of the correlations were quite good, but those found in Flock 2, particularly for lean content, tended to be lower, due partly to the rather lower variability in leanness of that flock. In predicting lean content, liveweight and age, both easily measured characters were good in Flock 1; the other potential predictors were not generally as good and probably did little more than provide a measure of body size or weight. In Flock 2, several other measurements were as good as liveweight.

So far as lean gain/day is concerned, liveweight at 22 or 24 weeks was the best single predictor. The good correlation found for one of the eye muscle area assessments in Flock 2, probably reflects the relationship which existed in this sample between muscle size and weight.

Correlations are frequently used when reporting results of this type of study, but they need to be treated with caution as they can be misleading and give unjustified confidence in certain predictors. In Table 3 an alternative method of presentation has been adopted. The residual standard deviation (RSD) of carcass lean content and lean gain/day achieved using the easily measured characters of final weight and age are given together with the RSD required for significant improvement. A range of other variables are then examined in trivariate regression with weight and age. It is apparent that, so far as lean content is concerned, none of the measurements provided an improvement except fat area by Danscanner in Flock 2. With lean gain/day knowledge of eye muscle area reduced the RSD in Flock 2 only.

CONCLUSIONS

Since the residual standard deviation of carcass lean content or lean gain per day cannot be reduced consistently below that achieved by liveweight and age, it can be argued that different approaches are needed. However, it may be unrealistic to expect the techniques used to provide greater discrimination at this level. Perhaps attempts should be made to increase variation in breeding schemes by, for example, measuring rams at a later stage of growth when there is likely to be greater variability in fatness. In these circumstances, other predictors than weight and age might contribute to a greater extent. In any event, the sheep breeding industry would welcome the opportunity to evaluate any fresh, promising approach which might be offered by developments in the medical field.

TABLE 1   Means and standard deviations for a range of assessments in each flock (20 rams per flock)

	Flock 1 Mean	SD	Flock 2 Mean	SD
Final liveweight (kg)	47.6	6.9	50.9	6.1
Age at assessment (days)	155	10	168	6.5
Fat score * - dock	2.33	0.54	2.40	0.60
- rib	2.28	0.53	2.38	0.48
Blockiness score **	2.43	0.63	2.95	0.60
Buttock width (mm)	240	16	231	10
Length (mm)	684	27	694	26
Hook width (mm)	172	8.3	168	9.8
Cannon bone length (mm)	131	8.5	133	5.0
Fat depth (mm) ≠ - Meritronics	2.23	1.2	2.33	0.91
- Danscanner ≠≠	5.94	1.4	6.34	1.7
- Scanogram	1.85	0.56	2.43	0.57
Fat area over eye muscle - Danscanner ≠≠ (sq. cm) ≠≠≠	3.89	0.75	3.89	0.88
- Scanogram	1.33	0.51	1.80	0.56
Eye muscle area (sq. cm) - Danscanner	10.5	1.2	12.2	1.2
- Scanogram	12.0	3.4	11.9	2.1
Carcass weight (kg)	20.6	3.9	20.8	3.0
% Lean in carcass	64.5	2.7	59.9	2.5
% Fat in carcass	16.8	3.6	21.8	3.3
Lean gain (g) per day	85	12	74	9.3

*	5 point scale: 1 = very lean, 5 = very fat
**	5 point scale: 1 = very poor, 5 = very good
≠	3.5 cm from the midline at 12th rib
≠≠	includes skin
≠≠≠	at 12th rib between midline and 6 cm from midline over M.longissimus

TABLE 2 Simple correlations of a range of assessments with carcass lean percentage and lean gain per day

	Flock 1 % Lean	Flock 1 Lean gain/day	Flock 2 % Lean	Flock 2 Lean gain/day
Final liveweight (kg)	-0.72	0.81	-0.56	0.82
Age at assessment	-0.82	0.17	-0.45	-0.21
Fat score - dock	-0.34	0.52	-0.48	0.57
- rib	-0.52	0.65	-0.40	0.54
Blockiness score	-0.50	0.68	-0.31	0.61
Buttock width	-0.47	0.42	-0.54	0.69
Hook width	-0.66	0.25	-0.59	0.47
Cannon bone length	-0.22	0.36	-0.50	0.57
Fat depth - Meritronics	-0.68	0.58	-0.53	0.54
- Danscanner	-0.70	0.60	-0.62	0.47
- Scanogram	-0.47	0.74	-0.31	0.57
Fat area - Danscanner	-0.69	0.60	-0.61	0.45
- Scanogram	-0.47	0.75	-0.57	0.67
Eye muscle area - Danscanner	-0.04	0.37	+0.45	0.33
- Scanogram	-0.64	0.67	-0.37	0.86

TABLE 3 Improvement in prediction of carcass lean content and lean gain (g)/day over final weight and age from addition of other variables in trivariate regression (RSDs)

	Flock 1 % Lean	Flock 1 Lean gain/day	Flock 2 % Lean	Flock 2 Lean gain/day
Final weight and age	1.42	3.84	1.92	4.24
RSD required for significant improvement	1.29	3.48	1.74	3.84
Fat score - dock	1.36	3.94	1.96	4.36
- rib	1.40	3.92	1.98	4.20
Blockiness score	1.44	3.84	1.96	4.26
Buttock width	1.44	3.66	1.94	4.34
Hook width	1.34	3.92	1.92	4.08
Cannon bone length	1.42	3.96	1.79	4.38
Fat depth - Meritronics	1.46	3.96	1.91	4.30
- Danscanner	1.45	3.74	1.83	4.36
- Scanogram	1.45	3.82	1.97	4.24
Fat area - Danscanner	1.44	3.66	1.68	4.38
- Scanogram	1.45	3.78	1.94	4.02
Eye muscle area - Danscanner	1.34	3.92	1.79	3.54
- Scanogram	1.46	3.86	1.91	3.82

PIG CARCASS EVALUATION BY LINEAR MEASUREMENT AND FAT 'O' MEATER

B. Desmoulin

INRA Station de Recherches sur L'Elevage des Porcs
Saint-Gilles, 35590 L'Hermitage, France

Summary

In order to assess its value in EEC grading, the fat 'O' Meater (FOM) device (SFK, Hvidoure, Denmark) has been used to measure fat and muscle thickness on 537 pig carcasses. The hams and backjoints (see Fig. 1) of 200 of these carcasses in the weight range 70-95 kg were also dissected and shown to have a mean lean content of 49.0 ± 3.1% (RSD = 0.73%).

Various programs for the FOM have been tested previously and used in this experiment. Of these, the Danish prediction equation overestimated lean content by 2.9% whilst the German equation gave a value of 49.4%. There was agreement with EEC grading on 72.5% of all the carcasses examined.

A new program was developed in the light of the dissection results and to accommodate various line speeds in slaughterhouses. A complete equation which included weight and 3 measurements gave an RSD of 1.76% lean. A simplified equation using 2 measurements only and no reference to weight showed an RSD of 2.11% lean. The estimates of lean showed agreement with EEC grading in 74.5 and 68% of carcasses respectively.

Fat content could be estimated with greater accuracy than lean content when weight was not included ($R^2 = 0.82$). The combination of weight and carcass length with FOM measurement, correlates well ($R^2 = 0.77$) with muscularity (weight of muscle/carcass length).

Correct EEC grading is possible with objective measurements showing an RSD below 2% lean. The scoring of muscularity requires the establishment of further combinations of linear measurements and fat and muscle thickness.

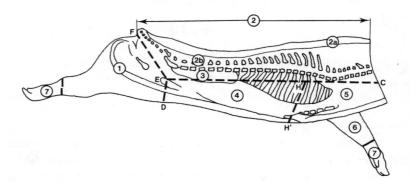

Fig. 1. System for carcass cutting.
1 - Ham, 2 - Backjoint (2a Backfat; 2b Loin), 3 - Leaf fat, 4 - Belly,
5 - Fore end, 6 - Prime, 7 - Feet.

MUSCLE FIBRE NUMBER; A POSSIBLE TRAIT IN SELECTION FOR MEAT PRODUCTION?

E. Kanis*, H.A. Akster**, T.G.H. Boumans*

Agricultural University, P.O. Box 338
6700 AH WAGENINGEN, The Netherlands
*Department of Animal Breeding
**Department of Experimental Animal
Morphology and Cell Biology

ABSTRACT

The effects of environmental and genetical factors on muscle fibre number in pigs were studied. From 72 pigs out of 16 litters, fattened at 3 feeding levels in 3 housing systems and slaughtered at 3 weights, the fibre number in the musculus flexor digiti V brevis was counted. After slaughtering carcases were dissected to determine carcase composition.

There was no effect of feeding level, housing system or weight at slaughter on fibre number. The effect of litter was significant but the additive genetic variation was probably small. Correlations between muscle fibre number and meat production traits were low.

It was concluded that it does not seem to be worthwhile to try to improve meat production by selection on fibre number in the m.flexor digiti V brevis.

INTRODUCTION

The availability of accurate predictions for meat production characteristics of animals, early in life, would be of great importance in animal breeding work. Most current methods estimate body composition at the time of measuring and do not predict any future body composition. Physiological parameters like hormone levels were sometimes suggested for this prediction, but without much success (Kempster et al. 1982). Stickland and Goldspink (1973, 1975) suggest the use of a number of muscle fibres in an indicator muscle (m.flexor digiti V brevis) as a possible predictor for future muscularity in pigs and as a possible trait in selection of young animals. This suggestion is based on the following assumptions: a) the muscle is indicative of other muscles in the animal with respect to fibre number. b) It can be removed in young animals without impairing the locomotion. c) The ultimate size of a muscle under normal conditions depends mainly on its fibre number. d) The total number of fibres in a muscle is genetically determined and already fixed at, or near birth. Nevertheless Stickland and Goldspink (1975) conclude that, although there exists a significant correlation between muscle fibre number and several meat production characteristics, the method is not accurate enough for selection purposes, but it provides the basis for future work.

An experiment was carried out to study the effects of environmental and genetical factors on muscle fibre number and its relation to carcase composition.

MATERIAL AND METHODS

At about 25 kg live weight, 72 pigs (male castrates from the cross Dutch Yorkshire times Dutch Landrace), out of 16 litters, have been divided over 3 housing systems (individual housing in a pen or in a balance cage and group housing in respiration chambers) and 3 feeding levels (ad libitum and approximately 85 and 74% of ad libitum). Animals were slaughtered at 3 weight classes (about 65, 85 and 105 kg live weight) and dissected according to the IVO standard method (Bergstrom and Kroeske, 1968). After slaughtering, the musculus flexor digiti V brevis was removed from the right foreleg. Images of stained, 10 μm transverse sections from the muscle belly were projected on a table and the number of muscle fibres was counted with an electric pen counter. In 18 slides the muscle fibre number was counted 3 times to calculate the repeatability of the counting method.

RESULTS

The average fibre number in all 72 animals was 5632 with a standard deviation of 1488. Compared to many other traits this variation is very large. The repeatability was .98 indicating a fairly accurate counting procedure.

The statistical analyses showed no effect of housing system, feeding level or slaughter weight on the fibre number in the m.flexor digiti V brevis. The only significant (P = .07) effect was the litter effect. From a one-way analysis an intra litter correlation of .14 was calculated, resulting in a heritability estimate based on full sib analysis of .28 ± .08. There was a non significant (P = .10) tendency for a higher fibre number in large litters. Correction for litter size gave a heritability estimate of .14 ± .12.

No significant correlations between muscle fibre number and growth rate, feed intake or feed conversion ratio were found. Also correlations between fibre number and meat % or fat % in the carcase were not significantly different from zero (r = -.15 and r = .14 respectively).

DISCUSSION AND CONCLUSIONS

The large variation in muscle fibre number within a species and the absence of environmental effects during the fattening period confirm the general conclusions in the literature as reviewed by Hegarty (1971). The significant differences in fibre number between litters are in agreement with the results obtained by Stickland et al. (1975). The heritability of .28, based on those differences, does not only reflect additive genetic differences between litters, but also differences in epistatic factors and in pre- and post-natal common environment within litters. Correction for litter size probably removes part of the common enviornmental effects. The resulting heritability of .14 ± .12 indicates that additive genetic variation in fibre number in the m.flexor digiti V brevis is low.

The correlations between muscle fibre number in the m.flexor digiti V brevis and carcase composition traits are much lower than those found by Stickland and Goldspink (1975). The reason for this discrepancy may be the fact that the present correlations are based on the proportion of meat and fat in the carcase, while those from Stickland and Goldspink (1975) are based on absolute measurement like muscle weights and muscle depths. Together with the low additive genetic variation it leads to the conclusion that in order to increase meat production in the population, it does not seem to be worthwhile to select on muscle fibre number in the m.flexor digiti V brevis.

REFERENCES

Bergstrom, P.L. and Kroeske, D. 1968. Methods of carcase assessment in research on carcase quality in The Netherlands. I Description of methods. Proc. E.A.A.P. conf. Dublin.

Hegarty, P.V.J. 1971. Muscle fibre growth and development. Proc. 24th Annual Reciprocal Meat Conference. National Live Stock and Meat Board, Chicago, pp. 319-344.

Kempster, A.J., Cuthbertson, A, and Harrington, G. 1982. Carcase Evaluation in Livestock Breeding, Production and Marketing (Granada, London).

172

Stickland, N.C. and Goldspink, G. 1973. A possible indicator muscle for the fibre content and growth characteristics of porcine muscle. Anim. Prod., 16, 135-146.

Stickland, N.C. and Goldspink, G. 1975. A note on porcine skeletal muscle parameters and their possible use in early progeny testing. Anim. Prod., 21, 93-96.

Stickland, N.C., Widdowson, E.M. and Goldspink, G. 1975. Effects of severe energy and protein deficiencies on the fibres and nuclei in skeletal muscle of pigs. Br. J. Nutr., 34, 421-428.

DIRECT MEASUREMENT OF CARCASS COMPOSITION
IN BREEDING ANIMALS

J.W.B.KING

ARC ANIMAL BREEDING LIAISON GROUP
WEST MAINS ROAD
EDINBURGH

ABSTRACT

For breeding purposes two special methods for assessing carcass composition are of potential value. The first is gamete storage in which sperm or ova are collected and preserved before the donor animal is slaughtered and assessed in whatever detail is required. The second alternative is to produce identical genotypes by micro-manipulation of developing ova so that one individual can be slaughtered and assessed while its clone is retained for breeding purposes. Both procedures allow measurements in a detail not feasible by alternative methods.

INTRODUCTION

The search for in vivo methods of measuring body composition has diverted attention from simpler direct methods of potential value. These are the methods of gamete storage and the production of identical genotypes made possible by various reproductive techniques.

GAMETE STORAGE

The prototype method has been used in bulls (Magee et al, 1968). It is simply to collect semen from young bulls, to preserve the sperm by deep freezing, slaughter the bulls and then dissect the carcasses. After evaluation of the results, the preserved sperm from the bulls of choice can be used.

Up-dated technology allows this to be carried out with cows also. Potential breeding females can be super-ovulated and their ova preserved by deep freezing. (At present only fertilised ova can readily be kept in this way but methods for the preservation of oocytes and unfertilised eggs are on the horizon.) After slaughter and carcass dissection, ova from chosen cows can be transplanted into surrogate mothers.

Why are these methods not used?

a)   Collection procedures may disturb routine management and affect carcass composition.

b)   These procedures are not cheap.

c)   Carcass appraisal at desired (low) body weights may not be possible.

d)   Carcass dissection is itself expensive.

PRODUCTION OF IDENTICAL GENOTYPES

Some of the difficulties with gamete storage can be overcome by
producing pairs of identical genotypes and sacrificing one of each pair
for carcass appraisal.

Although the study of naturally occuring monozygotic twins has shown
the potentialities of such genotypes, routine application is dependent on
producing these twins to order. Such a method was first described by
Willadsen (1979) for sheep. His method used blastomeres at the 4-cell
stage but involved complicated technology and a much simpler method has
been evolved using morulae or early blastocysts. Good quality embryos are
held on the end of a pipette by suction and cut in two with a microknife.
One of the halves is moved into an empty zona pellucida, and both halves
can then be transferred into recipient cows [Willadsen et al (1981),
Ozil et al (1982)]. The microsurgery involved can be carried out in 15-20
minutes so the costs over and above those of embryo transplantation are
small. Although embryonic mortality reduces the numbers of surviving twin
pairs, the method does offer a method which might be used in a routine
manner. For beef bulls to be in AI the dissection of an identical twin
could provide a final selection step with high cost effectiveness.

This method can be claimed as the most realistic prospect for the
improvement of killing-out percentages and organoleptic qualities of meat.

CONCLUSION

Along with physical methods of assessing body composition in vivo,
consideration should also be given to gamete storage or the production of
identical genotypes as alternative means of achieving the same ends for
breed improvement purposes.

REFERENCES

Magee, W.T., Bratzler, L.J. and Merkel, R.A. (1968) Direct selection for
    carcass traits in beef cattle. J.Anim. Sci 27, 1756.
Ozil, J.P. Hevman, Y. and Renard, J.P. (1982). Production of monozygotic
    twins by micromanipulation and cervical transfer in the cow. Vet
    Rec 6, 126.
Willadsen, S.M. (1979). A method for culture of micromanipulated sheep
    embryos and its use to produce monozygotic twins. Nature, UK 277,5694
Willadsen, S.M. Lehn-Jensen, H. Fehilly, C.B. and Newcomb, R (1981). The
    production of monozygotic twins of preselected parentage by micro-
    manipulation of non-surgically collected cow embryos. Theriogenology,
    15, 23.

MAMMARY DEVELOPMENT IN GOATS MEASURED NON-INVASIVELY
USING NUCLEAR MAGNETIC RESONANCE (NMR) IMAGING

Christopher H. Knight,
Margaret A. Foster* & J. Ewen Rimmington*
Hannah Research Institute, Ayr KA6 5HL
and * Department of BioMedical Physics and BioEngineering,
University of Aberdeen, Foresterhill, Aberdeen AB9 2ZD

ABSTRACT

The Aberdeen NMR imager produces cross-sectional body
images of tissue water content (proton density) or the T_1 relaxation time of the tissue water protons (Hutchison, Edelstein
& Johnson, 1980). T_1 images were used to monitor mammary
development during the first (n=2) or second (n=2) pregnancy of
goats. Serial images, spaced 2 cm apart, were taken through
the udder of each goat on six occasions during gestation (weeks
5, 9, 13, 16, 18 and 20). All four udders increased considerably in size and in content of presumptive secretory tissue
during the course of gestation, particularly from week 13
onwards. The appearance of the tissue did not change appreciably during gestation. The two second gestation goats were
lactating when first imaged; milking ceased immediately after
this imaging. One lactating gland of each goat was imaged
"empty" (milked), the other "full". The empty gland appeared
to be a homogeneous mass of secretory tissue, while the full
gland was dilated with secretion. The milk storage areas
(teat and gland cisterns) were clearly delineated. Between
then and the second imaging both udders decreased in size and
fluid content during post-lactational involution.

REFERENCE

Hutchison, J.M.S., Edelstein, W.A. and Johnson, G. (1980).
J. Phys. E. 13, 947-955.

NMR IMAGING OF GOAT FETUSES <u>IN UTERO</u>

C.H. Knight & Margaret A. Foster*
Hannah Research Institute, Ayr KA6 5HL
and *Department of BioMedical Physics and BioEngineering,
University of Aberdeen, Foresterhill, Aberdeen AB9 2ZD

ABSTRACT

Proton density NMR cross-sectional images were obtained
through the uterus of pregnant goats during weeks 13 (n=4) or
20 (approximately 14 days pre-partum, n=6) of gestation. The
Aberdeen Mk 1 NMR imager was used, in addition one other goat
was imaged during week 20 using the Mk 2 imager which generates
longitudinal sections (sagittal and coronal) as well as cross-
sections. Fetal structures were clearly visible in all of the
images obtained. They appeared white (high proton density) in
extreme contrast to amniotic fluid which, for technical reasons
related to its extremely long T_1 relaxation time, appeared
black. Fetal head, long-bones, pelvis, heart, lungs and
kidneys were all identified in different images obtained at 20
weeks. The uterus of one goat was imaged serially at 2 cm
intervals, and individual fetal structures and the orientations
of the twin fetuses were clearly observed. Six of the seven
goats carried twins. No problems were encountered with partur-
ition, and all twelve kids were, and still are, healthy and
apparently normal. The seventh goat carried triplets, one of
which was still-born. Post-mortem examination revealed normal
development up to two weeks pre-partum. A second kid was
killed neonatally and appeared normal on post-mortem examination, the third kid is now nine months old and healthy.

GROWTH RATE EVALUATION 'IN VIVO' IN FOUR CATTLE BREEDS

USING AN ULTRASONIC TECHNIQUE

D. Matassino, L. Ramunno, E. Cosentino

Istituto di Produzione animale, Università di Napoli.
Facoltà di Agraria, 80055 Portici, Italy.

ABSTRACT

The study was carried out on 144 cattle of 4 genetic types in order to identify the relationship between the variation of live weight and that of eye muscle area. The regression equations demonstrated that eye muscle area, measured ultrasonically, could be a good index to identify the readiness of the animals for slaughter and showed at the same time, the different rates of maturity among genetic types.

INTRODUCTION

In vivo evaluation of beef cattle always presents a problem. In genetic improvement schemes, the estimate of the genetic value of a given sire for meat production, cannot be based on parameters requiring measurements on the carcass because the potential sire itself has to be slaughtered. This would be overcome if his semen could be stored but this would increase the cost of improvement. Therefore the most economic means of estimating the value of any 'meat' sire must be based on 'in vivo' parameters which are highly related with those measured on the carcass. A good example of such a non destructive method is ultrasonic scanning.

MATERIAL AND METHODS

The study was carried out on 144 cattle of 4 different genetic types as reported in table 1. Every 4 weeks the live weight was monitored and the ultrasonic assay was made by a Scanogram Model 722 (Ithaco, USA) between the 12th and 13th thoracic vertebra and between the 4th and 5th lumbar vertebra. The animals were slaughtered when the scheduled live weights were reached. After 7 days of aging at $0-4^\circ$ C, the following

data were obtained: the side, hindquarter and forequarter weights
(separated between the 12th and 13th thoracic vertebra) and the weight of
the commercial cuts: a tracing of the eye muscle was taken on the thorax,
in the site corresponding to the ultrasonic assay (table 1).

TABLE 1 - Some characteristics of measured animals.

Genetic type (1)	Sex	N	Live weight, kg				eye muscle area, cm^2			
			initial		final		in vivo		cut face on carcass	
			$\overline{X}$	C.V.%	$\overline{X}$	C.V.%	$\overline{X}$	C.V.%	$\overline{X}$	C.V.%
CH x IF	M	18	357.9	7	568.3	4	102.3	11	105.5	14
IF	M	31	315.5	11	488.8	3	78.8	12	79.2	13
PF	M	35	176.8	10	427.7	5	79.8	10	80.3	10
RPB	M	40	343.5	7	509.5	3	93.5	8	94.0	9
CH x IF	F	20	240.5	19	391.0	4	76.3	10	77.5	9

(1) CH = Charolais; IF = Italian Friesian; PF = Poland Friesian; RPB = Red
    Pied Bavarian.

TABLE 2 - Thoracic eye muscle. Regression equations (*** = P<0.001).

Genetic type	Sex	Equation		R^2	F	
CH x IF	M	$Y_1 = -$	$4.4247383 + 0.18719498\ x$	0.75	451	***
IF	M	$Y_2 =$	$11.2904150 + 0.13602702\ x$	0.70	365	***
PF	M	Y_3	$18.1156450 + 0.13669073\ x$	0.79	981	***
RPB	M	Y_4	$0.0895522 + 0.17745042\ x$	0.72	569	***
CH x IF	F	Y_5	$18.5330570 + 0.14518010\ x$	0.63	208	***

RESULTS

For each genetic type the relationship between the variation of live
weight and that of eye muscle area estimated ultrasonically was studied.
Within the limits of our observation, the best function was found to be a
linear regression, probably because, the measurements coincided with the
ascendent and linear sections of the curve of growth. The use of the
ultrasonic technique showed different rates of maturity among the males of
the 4 genetic types examined. The PF subjects were the first to reach the
weight established as suitable for slaughtering; the IF were last. At

179

500 kg of live weight the IF animals had eye muscle areas 7cm^2 less than the PF, over 9*cm^2 less than the RPB and over 10*cm^2 less than the CH x IF.

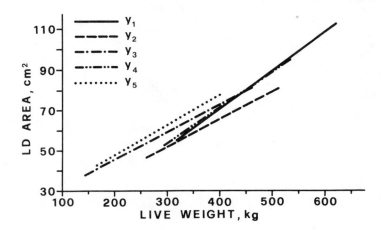

FIGURE 1 - Relationship between live weight and thoracic eye muscle (LD) area of considered genetic types.

TABLE 3 - Males. Live weight range in which the differences (D_x) in thoracic eye muscle area are significant (*=P<0.05; **=P<0.01).

Comparison			From		To	
			live weight	D_x	live weight	D_x
CH x IF	-	IF	340	1.7*	510	10.4**
CH x IF	-	PF	310	- 6.9**	410	- 1.8**
CH x IF	-	RPB	310	- 1.5*	320	- 1.4*
IF	-	PF	260	- 7.0**	470	- 7.1**
IF	-	RPB	310	- 1.6*	510	- 9.3**
PF	-	RPB	290	6.2**	410	1.3

REFERENCES

Matassino, D., Pilla, A.M., Cosentino, E. and Bordi, A. 1976. The use of an ultrasonic technique 'in vivo' for beef carcass evaluation. EEC Agric. Res. Seminar, Crit. Meth. Assess. Carcass Meat Charact. Beef Prod. Exper., Zeist (1975). EUR 5489, 71–80.

Bech Andersen, B. (Red.) 1982 – In vivo estimation of body composition in beef – Report on a CEC workshop, Copenhagen (1981). 524 Beretning Fra Statens Husdyrbrugs Forsøg. 195.

BODY COMPOSITION MEASUREMENTS OF RATS, SHEEP, PIGS AND HUMANS BY NEUTRON ACTIVATION ANALYSIS

T. Preston, B.W. East and I. Robertson

The Scottish Universities Research and Reactor Centre,
East Kilbride,
Glasgow G75 OQU,
U.K.

ABSTRACT

Data are presented comparing body composition of rats, sheep, pigs and humans by neutron activation analysis. Determinations include total body N, Na, P, Cl, K and Ca.

INTRODUCTION

In vivo body composition determination by neutron activation analysis (NAA) has proved to be a very useful diagnostic tool in the clinical sciences for over ten years, (Cohn, 1980). Although no single facility has been designed to measure all possible elements simultaneously, NAA methods have now been reported that in principle, enable measurement of the nine elements that comprise more than 99% of animal tissue to be made (Sharafi et al., 1983).

Results and Discussion

The NAA facility at East Kilbride and details of the NAA measurements on rats, sheep, pigs and humans are described in East, Preston and Robertson (1983).

Table 1 presents NAA data for the animal groups and humans. These are expressed as concentrations (g element/Kg tissue) to give a measure of carcass quality. The sheep data falls into two distinct groups, field grown and laboratory grown lambs. The results show good agreement within a population (e.g. field grown sheep nitrogen g/Kg tissue, 4% c.v., n = 8). Further data demonstrating that the lower carcass protein content can be related to greater fat content is given below.

	RATS n=12	SHEEP* n=8	SHEEP† n=15	PIGS n=3	HUMANS n=21
N	31·8	33·2	24·5	30·7	24·2
Ca	7·65	17·4	12·1	8·68	13·1
P	5·72	9·37	7·03	6·03	7·26
K	N.D.	3·18	2·42	2·37	1·78
Na	1·02	1·39	1·04	1·13	1·02
Cl	0·98	1·07	0·83	1·05	0·81

CARCASS QUALITY (g/Kg element)

*FIELD GROWN
†LABORATORY GROWN

TABLE 1

RATIO	RATS	SHEEP	PIGS	HUMANS
N:Ca	4·12	1·97	3·53	1·85
N:P	5·51	3·52	5·09	3·33
N:Na	30·8	23·8	27·0	23·8
N:Cl	32·0	30·3	29·3	29·8
N:K	N.D.	10·3	12·9	13·5

LEAN BODY QUALITY (elemental ratios)

TABLE 2

An assessment of lean body mass quality can be given by comparing tissue elemental ratios (Table 2). These data, from the animal and human populations used above, show little spread within the population (e.g. field reared sheep N:P and N:Na ratios, 7% C.V., n = 8). The two sheep populations show no significant differences in lean body mass quality, in contrast to their carcass quality. The relatively low bone mineral content of rat and pig tissue compared to that of sheep and humans is apparent. Little trend is seen in electrolyte content of these animal groups, however N:K ratio increases from 41Kg sheep to 85Kg humans. This possibly reflects the increasing non-muscle protein pool in larger animals, but developmental differences between the groups may also contribute. Compartmental analysis of N:K ratios in clinical studies has been used to resolve the muscle and non-muscle lean tissue (Burkinshaw, Hill and Morgan, 1978).

Accurate measurement of the major components of the lean body allows calculation of the body fat content, by difference. The rat population above were also analysed by destructive methods for comparison with NAA data. Total body water (TBW, by loss of weight after freeze drying) and body fat (by adiabatic bomb calorimetry or direct extraction) were also determined. Direct fat measurement was compared with indirect calculation using NAA data for protein and mineral estimation with TBW to give fat free mass. Fat estimates by these two methods are in good agreement (Table 3). NAA combined with TBW analyses have been used to study rat body composition development (Figure 1). These data include two animals of 450g from an obese rat strain which clearly alter the trend of body fat accumulation with size in the main population. Detailed analysis of these data show that although body fat variations can be predicted by changes in protein content, accurate measurement of TBW is important for accurate assessment of body fat by difference. Isotope dilution methodology can be used as a non-destructive method of TBW analysis but must be accurate to around 1% to be useful.

RAT WEIGHT, g	630	494	538	547	120	118	226	212
MEASURED FAT, g	47	27	31	33	87	68	175	154
CALCULATED FAT, g	41	21	22	30	101	96	182	158
RAT WEIGHT, g	316	376	423	397	445	550	549	447
MEASURED FAT, g	344	437	635	532	1167	1127	1123	1005
CALCULATED FAT, g	351	448	660	559	1145	1109	1096	993

MEAN WEIGHT = 275g MEAN MEASURED FAT = 438g
MEAN CALCULATED FAT = 437g MEAN RESIDUAL = 14g

TABLE 3 FAT CONTENT OF RATS

	PIG 1	PIG 2	PIG 3
WEIGHT	64.00	63.40	63.80
PROTEIN	10.62 (.37)	14.20 (.50)	11.80 (.41)
MINERAL	2.10 (.06)	2.57 (.08)	2.28 (.07)
WATER	38.72 (1.94)	44.74 (2.24)	41.74 (2.09)
FAT	12.56 (1.97)	1.89 (2.29)	7.98 (2.13)

PIG CARCASS COMPOSITION (kg), (S.D.)
TABLE 4

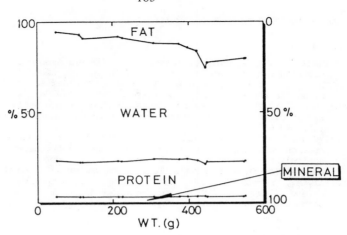

COMPOSITION OF THE DEVELOPING RAT
FIGURE 1

For larger animals, NAA can be used to measure total body O. Table 4 shows body composition calculations in 3 64Kg pigs based on NAA analysis of body O, N and Ca to give TBW, protein and mineral content using compartmental analysis of the known tissue elemental content. Pig 2 was known to be the most lean animal. It is intended to compare these data with results from destructive analysis.

Conclusions
1) NAA can provide precise measurements in In vivo body composition in a wide range of animal sizes.
2) Methods in routine use allow body protein, electrolyte and bone mineral determination.
3) Future work should concentrate on reducing the errors of body oxygen analysis, which may require counting arrangements within the irradiation facility. The aim is to provide TBW estimates in large animals routinely by NAA.

We wish to thank Dr. P.J. Reeds of the Rowett Research Institute,

184

Aberdeen,for measurements of rat body fat.

REFERENCES

Burkinshaw, L., Hill, G.L. and Morgan, P.B. (1978). Assessment of the
distribution of protein in the human by in vivo neutron activation
analysis. In: International Symposium on Nuclear Activation Techniques in the Life Sciences. Vienna: IAEA, 787-796 (SM-223/39).
Cohn, S.H. (1980). The present state of in vivo neutron activation analysis in clinical diagnosis and therapy. Atomic Energy Reviews, 18
(3), 599-655.
East, B.W., Preston, T. and Robertson, I. (1983). The potential of in vivo
neutron activation analysis for body composition measurements in the
agricultural sciences. In: CEC Workshop: in vivo measurement of body
composition in meat animals, Bristol, November 1983. - this volume.
Sharafi, A., Pearson, D., Oxby, C.B., Oldroyd, B., Krupowicz, D.W., Brooks,
K. and Ellis, R.E. (1983). Multi-element analysis of the human body
using neutron activation. Phys. Med. Biol., 28, (3), 203-214.

COMPARISON OF DIFFERENT TECHNIQUES
USED ROUTINELY FOR PREDICTING
COMMERCIAL BEEF CHARACTERISTICS
OF LIVING CATTLE

J. Raoult, and E. Rehben
Institut Technique de l'Elevage Bovin
149, rue de Bercy
75595 Paris Cedex 12, France

A) INTRODUCTION

Few results are available to compare the accuracy of different techniques used routinely either on farm or in station to evaluate beef
characteristics on living animals.

In general results do not concern comparisons but only isolated techniques. The purpose of this work is to provide elements to choose among
different techniques for beef recording programmes either for beef breeds
or for dual purpose breeds.

B) MATERIAL AND MEASUREMENTS

    B1- Studied techniques : - visual assessments

                                  - mensurations

                                  - ultrasonic measurements

    B2- The visual assessments consisted of the appreciation of 19
different anatomical sites and a commercial score. The ultrasonic measurements consisted of :

      - thickness of Longissimus dorsi obtained at the third lumbar
vertebra by a B-mode machine,

      - area of Longissimus dorsi and fat thickness obtained between
the first and the third lumbar vetebra by a multi-element
machine (Danscanner).

    B3- Measured animals : 58 young bulls of four different breeds
(Charolais, Charolais x Normand, Limousin, Holstein x Friesian).

    B4- Each measurement was made by two different operators. Most of
them were repeated by the same operator.

    B5- Beef characteristics : carcass measurements were made according
to a french commercial jointing of a half forequarter (all

muscles are deboned, trimmed, and cut ready for sale). They
consisted of :
- dressing percentage,
- bone in percentage of carcass weight,
- saleable lean meat ratio,
- fat in percentage of carcass weight minus bone weight.

C) STATISTICAL METHODS
First, all the measurements which did not discriminate the animals of
the same breed were eliminated.

Then among the measurements kept the ones performed by the operator
who had got the highest repeatability were used for predicting beef
characteristics.

The different beef characteristics were fitted by the following
model :
X = Bi + MA + FA + FT + VA + CS
X : beef characteristic
Bi : effect of breed "i"
MA : ultrasonic measurement of the muscle area
FA : ultrasonic measurement of the fat area
FT : ultrasonic measurement of the fat thickness
VA : average of five visual assessments
CS : assessed commercial score
This complete model was not used directly. We tried by elimination
of different measurements to determinate which ones had a significant
effect on the residual standard deviation of the prediction. The final
model showed which measurements were able to discriminate the beef chara-
teristics of animals of the same breed.

D) RESULTS
D1- Further results can be found in the complete report published by
    "Institut Technique de l'Elevage Bovin".
D2- 13 visual assessments out of 19, 7 mensurations out of 7, and
    muscle thickness performed by the B-mode machine were eliminated
    either because their repeatability was too low, or because they
    did not discriminate the animals of the same breed.
D3- An analysis of variance of the visual assessments kept showed a
    strong operator effect but not for ultrasonic measurements

performed by Danscanner.

D4- For predicting beef characteristics the elimination of the measurements according to the method described in C, showed that the only significant measurements were :
- ultrasonic muscle area and fat thickness for dressing percentage and saleable lean meat ratio,
- average of five visual assessments for bone ratio,
- fat thickness for fat percentage.

D5- The commercial score was not able to predict any of the four beef characteristics.

D6- TABLE 1

Predicted beef characteristics	dressing percentage	% fat	% meat
Standard residual deivation of a model fitted only by breed	1.28	2.39	2.01
Standard residual deviation of the models described in D4	1.11	2.25	1.88
Averages of predicted beef characteristics	59.25	10.45	68.11
Standard deviations of predicted beef characteristics	3.39	3.12	3.68

The differences (see table 1) between, on one hand the residual standard deviation of the models fitted only by breed and, on the other hand, the standard deivation of beef characteristics and the residual standard deviation of the models fitted by breed, and by the only significant measurements showed :
- for predicting beef characteristics of animals of the same breed the accuracy of different measurements were low, especially for fat percentage,
- the main variation of the beef characteristics depended on breeds.

SESSION VI

COST-BENEFIT ANALYSES

Chairman: D. Demeyer

COST-BENEFIT ANALYSES OF <u>IN VIVO</u> ESTIMATES

OF BODY COMPOSITION IN MEAT ANIMALS

A. J. Kempster

Meat and Livestock Commission, PO Box 44,
Queensway House, Bletchley, Milton Keynes, UK.

ABSTRACT

Criteria for determining the effectiveness of <u>in vivo</u> techniques in breeding schemes, the monitoring of commercial breeding stock and in marketing are discussed, and the approach to cost-benefit analyses outlined. Attention is drawn to the special requirements of these different applications and to the limited information available on the relative precision of techniques. The use of standard methods for testing techniques and presenting the statistical results is recommended.

INTRODUCTION

The purpose of this paper is to consider the cost-effectiveness of <u>in vivo</u> techniques for different applications in animal breeding, production and marketing. The subject is almost virgin ground because few techniques, other than simple body measurements and subjective assessments with minimal cost, have reached the point where general commercial application is feasible. The focus of attention remains in the laboratory with the search for techniques that work rather than with the commercial development of proven techniques. I shall concentrate, therefore, on <u>the approach</u> to cost-benefit analyses and the special requirements of potential applications.

At the Copenhagen seminar, King (1981) outlined the necessary features of <u>in vivo</u> techniques for use in breeding schemes. I shall try to avoid duplicating the points he made, aiming to complement his paper as far as possible.

COST EFFECTIVENESS AND THE DEVELOPMENT OF TECHNIQUES

This paper is concerned principally with the cost-effectiveness of techniques to individual users, but there are broader considerations which can affect commercial development. Manufacturers need to be reasonably sure that the development and marketing of a promising technique is cost-effective before investing their money. Returns will depend to a large extent on the size of potential markets so techniques suitable for use on all species of livestock and capable of both live body and carcase measurement will involve less financial risk; those which have still wider applications to other industries will be even safer. The marketing difficulties experienced by the manufacturers of ultrasonic scanning machines purpose-built for livestock measurement illustrates this point. Markets around the world are very limited and it is doubtful whether such machines will be able to compete in future, either in terms of cost or precision, with comparable medical machines built for larger and more demanding markets, and with a greater capability for exploiting the latest technological developments. The first indications of the strength of this competition has come from the results of the CEC-supported ultrasonic trial carried out in the UK and Denmark (Bech Andersen et al 1981). Two medical machines (Philips Diagnost R and the Ohio Nuclear Sonofluoroscope) were shown to be as precise as the Dans-canner and Scanogram (purpose-built animal machines) for predicting the lean content of live beef cattle, despite the fact that the operators were much less experienced in their use and the machines measured a smaller cross-section of the animal body. The medical machines were also competitively priced.

The other cost-benefit consideration is for the agencies that might become involved in the provision of live body estimation services. They will not be concerned directly with the benefits to individual users but with the benefits of finding as many users as possible to spread the over-head costs involved in purchasing and maintaining equipment.

The commercial development and uptake of in vivo techniques is much more likely, therefore, when they are suitable for a RANGE OF USES and the market is large. Research workers involved in basic developments should bear this point in mind.

CRITERIA FOR JUDGING THE SUITABILITY AND COST-EFFECTIVENESS OF TECHNIQUES FOR DIFFERENT APPLICATIONS

The following criteria are involved in determining the effectiveness of different techniques.

      (1)   Cost

      (2)   Practicability

      (3)   Precision

      (4)   Accuracy

COST would be taken as the overall cost of the technique, including depreciation and maintenance of equipment, operating costs and any costs involved in presenting the animals for measurement.   It is probably best expressed as a proportion of the cost involved in determining the actual carcase composition of the animal using the base-line method of evaluation (tissue separation, chemical analysis etc.,).   The relative merit of different base-line techniques has been discussed by Kempster, Cuthbertson and Harrington, 1982).

PRACTICABILITY may be considered in terms of the practical constraints associated with the use of a particular technique.   In some applications, for example, speed may be essential whereas in others portability or resistance to harsh environments may be required.   Such constraints would not necessarily be overcome by increased operational costs and might represent a major stumbling block to the use of a technique.   Indeed many promising techniques have not been used in commercial practice because of practicability.   King (1981) adds public acceptability to his list of criteria giving as examples the human health risk associated with the use of radioactive isotopes and the unacceptability of biopsy techniques on welfare grounds as examples.   But these too may be considered within the broad definition of practicability.   The third criterion is PRECISION. This is most effectively measured in terms of the residual standard deviation in the predicted carcase characteristic (base-line measurement) If carcase lean percentage (y) is being predicted from an ultrasonic measurement of backfat thickness, the residual s.d. is the square root of the variation in carcass lean percentage among animals with the same ultrasonic backfat thickness.   It is a better criterion to use than correlation coefficient because it takes account of the variation in y. A high correlation may simply reflect the fact that the technique was evaluated in a variable sample of animals.

However, the residual s.d. is concerned solely with consistency and self agreement; it is an optimistic criterion obtained when a regression line is fitted perfectly to a set of observations.   In practice, one does not often have the actual base-line measurements and it is necessary to assume that regression lines established in earlier studies hold in the new circumstances.   If the regression relationship does not hold the estimate of base-line composition will be biased to some extent.   The ACCURACY of a technique may be considered in terms the stability of the regression relationships to changes in the type of animals measured or the circumstances of measurement.

Reliance in many in vivo techniques on the measurement of subcutaneous fat thickness to predict carcase lean percentage is often a cause of bias because important differences can exist between animals in the way fat is partitioned between depots and in the lean to bone ratio. To avoid such bias, one ideally needs to have in vivo techniques which measure carcase lean content directly. (The relative accuracy of different predicting measurements and statistical methods of overcoming bias are discussed by Kempster et al (1982)).

THE APPROACH TO COST-BENEFIT ANALYSES

The criteria outlined above are not independent of one another: generally speaking the more detailed and costly techniques are more precise and less subject to bias. Consequently the first step in any cost-benefit exercise is to plot out precision and accuracy against cost for alternative techniques and determine how the new technique under examination compares with the general relationship. Similarly a user searching for the most cost-effective technique would examine such a relationship to find the technique offering the desired level of precision and accuracy for minimum cost.

However, this approach is difficult because there is limited information available on the relative precision of in vivo techniques. Although there have been numerous studies to examine different techniques most of the work has been carried out on a small scale using data collected as a secondary spin off from feeding and breeding trials. The samples of animals have rarely been ideal for examining techniques and, all too often, only a single technique was studied, making it difficult or impossible to compare its precision and accuracy with other techniques. More studies along the lines of Houseman (1972) are required to evaluate a series of techniques and determine their relative precision and complementarity. Additionally, research workers should agree to include a common technique in their trials as a reference method.

Figure 1 shows a typical precision-cost curve for beef carcase evaluation from Kempster, Cuthbertson and Jones (1976). If the stability of regression equations is plotted against cost, a similar pattern emerges. It is likely that in vivo curves will follow the same pattern as those for carcase evaluation with rapidly diminishing returns as cost increases. Clearly then, a primary objective for any new technique will be for it to be as far to the left and top of the curve as possible. Such techniques will be more cost-effective than the average.

An important implication of such a curve is that substantial precision can often be obtained at negligible cost from simple measurements such as body weight or subjective assessments. It is nonsense not to use these measurements where possible since the choice of technique depends on finding the best compromise between cost and precision: measurements of negligible cost should, therefore, be included automatically if they are likely to be useful predictors. By the same token, more expensive techniques should be evaluated in terms of the precision achieved over and above predictors of negligible cost. This point is, of course, not limited to body weight and subjective assessment. In circumstances where other simple growth performance characteristics are available, these should be used in the same way. For example in breeding schemes, live weight for age (or daily live-weight gain) will almost certainly be available as might food intake. The value of other predictors should then be examined with weight for age or food intake constant. This point is illustrated well by the results of Cuthbertson, Croston and Jones (1983) presented in a poster paper at this seminar. Several techniques were correlated with carcase lean percentage in a Suffolk ram performance test but did not significantly improve the precision of carcase lean prediction among rams of the same weight for age. Indeed the residual standard deviation among rams of the same weight for age was extremely low (about 1.5 percentage units carcase lean) and it is unlikely that any of the techniques used would provide further discrimination within this. Had the simple predictors been ignored in this trial, the cost-effectiveness of the live body measurements for use in ram performance testing would have been seriously overestimated. Much confusion exists, in fact, in the scientific literature because many workers have not followed the simple policy of automatically including predictors of negligible cost in their evaluation.

When determining the precision and bias of different techniques it is important to be aware that these can be improved in many circumstances by the judicious combination of measurements and the use of advanced statistical methods. In particular, there is flexibility for doing this when the mean carcase composition of groups of animals are being estimated (Coniffe and Moran, 1972; Evans and Kempster, 1979).

FIGURE 1   Possible relationship between precision of prediction
of carcase lean percentage and cost for a range of
in vivo predictors

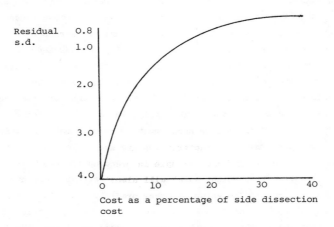

COST-EFFECTIVENESS OF TECHNIQUES IN DIFFERENT APPLICATIONS

There are four main areas in which in vivo techniques have a potential application as follows :

(1)   Performance testing in breeding schemes

(2)   Monitoring of the body composition of
commercial breeding stock on the farm

(3)   On-farm selection of stock for marketing
and slaughter

(4)   Valuation of commercial stock in the
marketing chain, in particular at auction
markets

The basic requirements of (2) and (3) are essentially the same but otherwise there are important differences in the importance attached to the criteria in different applications.   The relative importance of factors is outlined in Table 1.

TABLE 1   Relative importance of the different criteria for assessing the cost-effectiveness of techniques in different applications

	Cost	Practicability	Precision	Accuracy
Performance testing (1)✝	*	*	***	*
(2)✝	***	**	**	*
Monitoring of breeding stock	***	***	*	**
On-farm selection of stock for marketing	***	***	*	**
Valuation in the marketing chain	*	**	**	**

✝ (1)   Large-scale breeding operations
  (2)   Individual breeders

* to *** indicates increasing importance in determining the effectiveness of a particular technique.

Techniques for use in PERFORMANCE TESTING are considered under two separate headings in the table because there is a considerable difference between (1) national breeding programmes or those operated by large commercial breeding companies where costs can be set against genetic improvements disseminated to large populations of commercial stock and (2) the individual breeder whose scope for dissemination of improved genes and cost-recoupment is much less.

Cost and practicability will be more important for the individual breeder than for large-scale breeding operations. Precision will be much more important than accuracy because selection will be based on the relative performance of individuals. Experience also indicates that significant differences in regression slope occur rarely.

The assessment of cost-benefit ratios for breeding schemes is a difficult matter at the best of times because accurate estimates of genetic parameters are rarely available and may change as selection proceeds. It is also necessary to predict future market requirements and determine the economic weights to be placed on carcase characteristics, differences in which are often not reflected in producer returns. A further difficulty exists in the estimation of the rate of dissemination of improvement.

In view of these difficulties, it is more realistic to aim selection at general characteristics of long-term economic importance in particular the efficiency with which feed is converted into meat. When several of the characteristics that go to make up this objective (feed consumed, daily live-weight gain, killing-out percentage and carcase lean content) are assembled together in a selection index, the precision of individual carcase characteristics by in vivo methods is likely to be less critical. If the estimation of leanness is low this will be built into the index calculations and the selection weights obtained will place more emphasis on other characteristics that can be measured directly, so economic response is made in the right direction.

It is also relevant to consider alternatives to performance testing when determining the most cost-effective approach to selection especially when the in vivo techniques are towards the sophisticated/high cost end of the spectrum. In this context King (1981) refers to combined testing with sibs slaughtered for carcase assessment (a system commonly used in pig testing). He indicates that the techniques of multiple ovulation and ova transplants will make sib testing a more feasible option for cattle in future. Another possible alternative is proposed to store semen from young bulls and slaughter them for carcase evaluation. Cloning would provide a further elaboration of this method.

The cost-effectiveness of these techniques and also in vivo techniques in breeding schemes will depend critically on the dissemination of improvements. Sophisticated high cost techniques can more easily be justified in national schemes. This point may be illustrated by the calculations carried out by my colleague, David Steane (personal communication) as part of the work of the MLC Planning and Development team considering the most appropriate approach to beef improvement in Britain.

An index has been constructed to select for the efficiency of saleable meat production in a constant age performance test. Measured characteristics are live weights at birth, 200 and 400 days, a subjective assessment of muscling score, an assessment of calving difficulty, average feed intake and ultrasonically measured fat thickness. Table 2 shows the correlation of the index with overall economic merit, the relative progress achieved in the characteristics selected and the relative importance of the ultrasonic fat thickness measurements as the genetic correlation between ultrasonically measured fat thickness and saleable meat weight changes from

O to -0.35.   The full details of the index and calculations will be
published in a Planning and Development team report.

TABLE 2   Performance of the overall index as the genetic correlation
between ultrasonic fat thickness and saleable meat weight
changes (estimated values) ∤

	Genetic correlation		
	O	-0.20	-0.35
Correlation with economic merit	0.34	0.39	0.46
Relative progress in [#]			
weight of feed consumed	-0.08	-0.16	-0.16
saleable meat weight	+1.18	+1.21	+1.20
calving difficulty	-0.09	-0.06	-0.03
Percentage contribution of the ultrasonic fat thickness to the accuracy of the overall index	1	13	26

∤ D. E. Steane (personal communication)
\# Regression of economic merit for each trait on overall points score

It can be seen that an improvement in the genetic correlation from
O to -0.20 provides a 13% increase in accuracy.   Such changes would have
major significance on the cost of facilities to measure fat thickness.   At
-0.20 such a facility could be highly cost-effective when it is noted that
the response to selection in one year   might be worth £20 to £30 million
(when discounted over 20 years).   Assuming that a 10-fold return is
required for the investment, a cost of around £0.25 million/annum could
be justified for fat thickness measurement.   Argued in this way, there is
considerable scope for the development of sophisticated/high cost equipment.   But from the points raised at the very outset, it is important to
remember that the market for such a technique would be very limited and
there would be strong competition from new developments in methods of
testing.   In considering such techniques we should not overlook the need
for minimum cost in relation to precision.   As this ratio improves
the range of applications will increase.

One should also remember the needs of the smaller scale breeder for
practicable cheap and cost-effective techniques which would have a much
wider market if they were also suitable for applications (2) to (4) in
Table 1.

Techniques suitable for use in MONITORING BREEDING STOCK need to be cheap and practicable; precision is of less importance provided the extremes of body composition can be identified consistently.   Since one is concerned with the absolute body composition of individual animals, accuracy is relatively important.   ON-FARM SELECTION OF STOCK FOR MARKETING requires techniques with similar characteristics.   Again accuracy will be more important than precision because returns are likely to depend on the average performance of marketed stock: there is little point in being able to estimate the relative carcase characteristics of individual animals precisely if all of them fall outside the target area for marketing and return a lower price.

It is difficult to assess the cost-benefit of these applications in general terms because they depend critically on individual farm circumstances.   However, changes in the body composition of breeding stock can fluctuate dramatically during the reproductive cycle and an indication of when animals reach critical levels of fatness is likely to result in considerable cost advantages if remedial feeding can be given and the animals saved from culling.   In this context it is important to be aware of variations which may exist in the partition of fat between different depots (Wright, 1981).   The measurement of subcutaneous fat in the live animal may not provide a sufficiently accurate description of the total amount of fat available for metabolism in the body if there is substantial animal to animal variation in the ratio of subcutaneous fat to fat in other depots.   Again one ideally requires a direct assessment of total body fat rather than the measurement of an individual depot to avoid bias.

It is easier to identify the benefits from the use of techniques to select animals for market provided the producer is selling on a grade and deadweight basis.   Market requirements for weight and fatness are becoming tighter and producers are being penalised increasingly for stock which does not reach the basic market requirements.   It would be valuable, therefore, if the producer could be given a simple objective tool for determining market suitability.   This would enable him to find not only the most suitable time at which to slaughter but also the most appropriate market outlet.   He might also be able to improve his average returns by selecting his better stock for markets requiring and paying high premiums for this type of stock, poorer quality animals being sent to less

discriminating markets.   Cost-benefit analyses would be carried out by
using the target area concept as promoted by MLC (for example, Kempster,
1983) which sets out the various questions which should be asked when
considering the most appropriate ways of matching production to market
requirements.

The criteria for techniques suitable for the VALUATION OF ANIMALS
IN THE MARKETING CHAIN are rather different to those suited for on-farm
use.   In auction markets it might be possible to assess many animals in
a day and thereby spread the costs considerably so the overall cost of
the equipment might not be too critical.   Equal emphasis might be
placed on practicability, precision and accuracy.

The cost effectiveness of live assessment in auction markets will
depend on the extent to which such markets are important in the marketing
chain and the benefits that would accrue generally to the efficiency of
the industry if the payments to producers more closely reflected the
quality of stock sold.   These factors are very important in Britain where
55% of cattle and 65% of sheep are sold live with little obvious
relationship between quality and price.   An accurate method of determining carcase quality in auction markets would therefore have a considerable
impact on British livestock marketing.

Grading as a concept lends itself to economic analysis.   The
theoretical benefits in the context of meat trading have been explored,
for example, by Williams and Stout (1964) and the framework for detailed
cost-benefit studies of the proposed Australian classification systems
has been laid down by Griffith (1976).   However, factual information on
the detailed structure and costs of current meat marketing systems is
limited and so no one has yet been able to present a cost-benefit analysis
of a proposed scheme which is sufficiently convincing to influence the
degree of acceptance.

Harrington (1972) attempted an unsophisticated item-by-item approach
to beef and pig classification in Great Britain.   Each potential area of
impact was considered separately and the scale of the advantage (for
example) in accelerating improvement in carcase quality, in protection
against mispricing and in facilitating subsequent carcase and meat sales
estimated.   Under each heading, the potential benefits of the carcase
compositional information, if used, appeared to exceed substantially the
costs and it seemed reasonable to deduce a substantial cumulative net

benefit, even though some of the individual benefits to successive
participants in the distributive chain cancelled out.   It seems likely
that similar benefits would accrue if the classification were applied
in auction markets given that suitable in vivo techniques were
available.   Such developments might also stimulate the use of computer-
assisted remote bidding systems which are beginning to gain ground in
North America and Australia (reviewed, for example by Russell, Purcell
and Bell, 1983).

CONCLUSIONS

It has not been possible to review cost-benefit analysis in live
animal evaluation with any depth or sharpness because limited information
exists.   Not only is the subject embryonic in thought but the basic
information necessary to make specific cost-benefit decisions is limited.
It is recommended that standard methods are used to evaluate new
techniques in future.   These methods would involve the comparison with
a reference technique and the inclusion automatically of simple minimal-
cost predictors in regression equations.   Thought should also be given
to the possibility of evaluating techniques on standard samples of animals.

The review leads to the conclusion that the requirements of techniques
for different applications vary considerably and that there is a major gap
between the sophisticated/high cost techniques suitable for use in
national breeding schemes on the one hand and the more basic requirements
for ease of operation and for production and marketing on the other.   The
scientific community in their pursuit of accuracy and consistency should
not forget the operational needs for practicality and efficiency.   At
present the livestock industry relies essentially on subjective assessments of live animal evaluation.   Regardless of the extent of training
and supervision, it is difficult, if not impossible, to maintain high
levels of consistency and uniformity in such assessments.   The inherent
variability in such techniques must lead to inefficiency which might
easily be overcome by a simple cost-effective objective technique.

REFERENCES
Bech Andersen, B., Busk, H., Chadwick, J.P., Cuthbertson, A., Fursey,
    G.A.J., Jones, D.W., Lewin, P., Miles, C.A. and Owen, M.G. 1981.
    Ultrasonic techniques for describing carcase characteristics in live
    cattle. Commission of the European Communities, Luxembourg (EUR 7640).

Conniffe, D. and Moran, M.A. 1972.   Double sampling with regression in comparative studies of carcase composition.   Biometrics 28 : 1011 - 1023.

Cuthbertson, A., Croston, D. and Jones, D.W. 1983.   In vivo estimation of lamb carcass composition and lean tissue growth.   Paper presented at the CEC Workshop on 'In Vivo Measurement of Body Composition in Meat Animals' Bristol, November 1983. - this volume.

Evans, D.G. and Kempster, A.J. 1979.   A comparison of different predictors of the lean content of pig carcasses.   2.   Predictors for use in population studies and experiments.   Anim. Prod. 28 : 97 - 108.

Griffith, G.R. 1976.   The benefits of a national pig carcase measurement and information service.   Proceedings of the Carcase Classification Symposium, Adelaide, pp 1 to 10.

Harrington, G. 1972.   The potential advantages of carcase classification. Mimeograph.

Houseman, R.A. 1972.   Studies of methods of estimating body composition in the living pig.   Ph.D. Thesis, Edinburgh University.

Kempster, A.J. 1983.   Breeds required to meet market needs.   Paper presented at the Harper Adams Sheep Conference, January 1983 (mimeo).

Kempster, A.J., Cuthbertson, A. and Jones, D.W. 1976.   Prediction of the lean content of steer carcases of different breed types from the lean content of sample joints (and other measurements).   In 'Criteria and Methods for Assessment of Carcase and Meat Characteristics in Beef Production Experiments.   CEC, Luxembourg (EUR 5489) pp 209 - 219.

Kempster, A.J., Cuthbertson and Harrington, G. 1982.   Carcase Evaluation in Livestock, Breeding Production and Marketing.   Granada Publishing, St. Albans.

King, J.B.K. 1981.   Potential use of in vivo techniques for breeding purposes.   In 'In Vivo Estimation of Body Composition in Beef' (ed. B .Bech Andersen) 524 Beretning fra Statens Husdyrbrugs forsøg, pp. 86 - 83.

Russell, J.R., Purcell, W.D. and Bell, J.B. 1983.   Electronic marketing a summary of conceptual, theoretical and empirical considerations. Report of Department of Agricultural Economics, Virginia Tech. (MB 308).

Wright, I.A. 1981.   Studies on the body composition of beef cows. Ph.D. Thesis, University of Edinburgh.

DISCUSSION

Following Kempster's paper, Fuller suggested that the basis on which investment decisions had to be made must be a balance between national and commercial interests. He felt that investments in new technology of the kind discussed at this meeting were pertinent in the first instance to the national interest, for the scope of pilot trial investment was so large as to deter investment by potential users. King felt that the newer technologies should not be considered in isolation, but as members of a range of alternative options all of which may be subjected to, say, cost-benefit appraisal.

SESSION VII

FUTURE DEVELOPMENTS

Chairman: D. Demeyer

FUTURE DEVELOPMENTS IN THE <u>IN VIVO</u> MEASUREMENT OF BODY COMPOSITION IN PIGS

K.V. Ettinger, M.A. Foster and U.J. Miola

Department of Biomedical Physics and Bioengineering
University of Aberdeen
Foresterhill
Aberdeen AB9 2ZD
Scotland, U.K.

ABSTRACT

There are a number of techniques suitable for <u>in vivo</u> measurement of the body composition of pigs, and particularly the fat content of the animal. Nuclear Magnetic resonance measurements visualize the tissues according to their observable proton density and to the relaxation time T_1. The paper describes various pulse sequences which can be used to discriminate between fat and muscle tissues. Contrast i.e. the degree of discrimination attained using different pulse sequence modalities is shown on original photographs demonstrating transverse images of a pig, taken from the Aberdeen NMR imager. The technique of discrimination by means of the chemical shift of precession frequencies of protons involved in various types of chemical bond is also discussed.

Another technique of analysis of body composition, based on the use of neutron activation analysis, is capable of indicating the elemental composition of tissues, from which the content of fat, muscle, water etc. can be deduced. These techniques, originally developed for the purpose of human medicine, are particularly suitable for animal studies, owing to the relaxed requirements concerning the radiation dose administered to the animals. The paper describes briefly the principle of measurements of induced radioactivity following exposure to a neutron beam, as well as techniques based on the measurement of gamma rays accompanying neutron capture. The main source of errors appears to be the uncertainty of the spatial distribution of neutron flux, which is dependent on the size of the animal. This uncertainty can be reduced by an application of corrections derived from the calculated flux distributions which are known for simplified geometries. Finally, the paper discusses a new, proposed technique based on the use of an isotope scanner, either single photon or detecting coincidences (in the case of positron emitters). The animal is given a dose of labelled perhalo compounds, containing F-18 or Cl-38 or one of the bromine isotopes with a relatively short half life. These compounds, when included in the breathed air, dissolve in the adipose tissues and their presence can be subsequently detected by measuring the radioactivity of the animal. They can also be imaged to show local areas of concentration. The success of the proposed technique depends on the differential solubility of perhalo compounds in the adipose tissue and in the body fluids.

INTRODUCTION

A new technique for imaging human and animal tissues by means of nuclear magnetic resonance (NMR) produces images of outstanding quality of transverse sections (slices) through the body. To obtain the NMR sectional images of an animal it is necessary to place it inside an NMR Imager, of a type which has been designed and built in many laboratories, including our own laboratory in Aberdeen. The anatomic information provided by the NMR images is in this case less important than the nature of tissues revealed.

THE USE OF NUCLEAR MAGNETIC RESONANCE FOR TISSUE DISRIMINATION

It has already been shown that NMR can be used to discriminate fatty tissues from adjacent tissues of lower lipid content (Foster et al. 1984; for earlier qualitative considerations cf. Ettinger, 1982). NMR imaging techniques, with few exceptions, are designed to examine proton distribution and binding in the body.   They can only, however, observe those protons which are relatively mobile. The two major contributions to an NMR image are the hydrogen nuclei of water molecules and those of the $-CH_2$ groups of free lipids such as those in adipose tissue. If one examines a typical low lipid wet tissue such as muscle it is found to have a water content of about 75%, and an observable proton density of about 310* with a T_1 value of about 225 msec (measured in living leg muscle at 3.4 MHz). In comparison the water content of adipose tissue is very much lower – between 10 and 30%, but the density of NMR observable protons is higher than that in muscle at 350. The larger correlation time of the fat hydrogen, however, reduces the tissue T_1 value to about 150 msec. It is on the basis of these differences in proton density and T_1 relaxation time that fat is so clearly discriminated.

NMR imaging techniques can be used to produce a variety of different displays of the basic information on relaxation time and proton density. As well as displays of observable proton density, with little effect from relaxation and of calculated T_1 value, it is possible to obtain a large number of types of display of signals containing proton density information which is weighted to different extents by the relaxation process. In particular we have been interested in T_1-weighted images and these have been termed SATURATION RECOVERY, INVERSION RECOVERY and S1 – S2 images. To understand the origins of the images it is necessary to look at the pulse sequence used for spin warp imaging (Edelstein et al., 1980).

* The observable proton density number is the magnitude of corresponding signal generated by the NMR imager and not a direct physical quantity.

Pulse sequences

The sequence starts with a 90° shaped RF pulse delivered in the presence of a gradient (Fig. 1). This selects a specific slice where the Larmor frequency, defined by the field strength, matches the radio frequency and hence excitation of the spins can take place. In the second interval an orthogonal gradient is applied which is of programmable magnitude and direction. The effect of this is to define the position of spins in the anterior/posterior direction of the chosen slice. Also in this second time interval a third orthogonal gradient is applied across the slice at right angles to the second gradient. This alters the phase of the spins in this direction.

In the next time interval the second gradient is removed and the third gradient reversed.

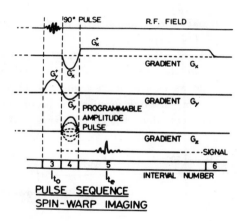

Fig. 1   Waveforms of the pulse sequence employed in the spin – warp imaging modality of NMR

Hence the effect of the second gradient remains, but the fans of spins created by the third gradient begin to close up until they come together again to generate a spin echo in the receiver coil. Because of the effects of the gradients this spin echo has a complex shape and 2 – D Fourier transformation of this separates out the different component frequencies. A combination of phase and frequency provides the information for the two dimensions of the image.

An image from the pulse response just described provides information only about the density of observable protons in the selected slice and the spin echo is the signal we term the S1 signal.

To obtain formation about relaxation characteristic it is necessary to invert the spins. This is done before every second 90° pulse. The spins are turned through 180° by adiabatic fast passage. The system is then given 200 msec to relax before the 90° pulse is applied. The extent of relaxation which occurs in these 200 msec has a considerable influence on the size of signal obtained from the 90° and gradient sequence. The spin echo obtained with adiabatic fast passage (AFP) is termed the S2 signal. From the S1 and S2 signals the four standard displays are obtained.

S1 alone yields the proton density image

S2 alone yields the inversion recovery image

S1 − S2 is a T_1-weighted difference image

The T_1 image is calculated from the signals by means of the following formula: $S1/S2 = 1 - 2\exp(\,-t/T_1\,)$

Another sequence which we use to produce an image with a different degree of T_1 weighting is a $90^O - \tau - 90^O$ response (see Fig. 2). This is also referred to as saturation recovery and is a splin warp pulse sequence, incorporating a selective gradient, a programmable gradient and the de-phasing and rephasing readout gradients. There is, however,

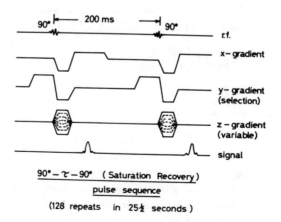

$90° - \tau - 90°$ (Saturation Recovery)

pulse sequence

(128 repeats in $25\frac{1}{2}$ seconds)

Fig. 2   Waveforms of the pulse sequence employed in the saturation recovery imaging modality of NMR

no inversion pulse and the interval between 90° pulses is very short; we use 200 msec at the moment. Because of the short interval there is insufficient time for most of the spins to relax back to their initial state before the next 90° pulse, hence there is partial saturation of the system, the degree of saturation depending on the T_1 relaxation time of the individual protons. Such a response is bound to show a considerable difference between fat with a short T_1 value and muscle which has a fairly long T_1 relaxation time.

Contrast due to different sequences

Contrast between fat and muscle can, to some extent, be predicted if we examine the response, in terms of signal size, produced by samples of the same proton density but of different T_1 (Foster et al., 1984). This can be demonstrated graphically (Fig. 3). The S1 (i.e. proton density) signal shows a fairly flat response for most T_1 values met in biological samples. Since this is to be expected because there is little T_1 effect in the S1 signal and, moreover, T_2 effect is also minimal because there is a fairly constant, short time interval (12 msec) between the 90° pulse and the generation of the spin echo. From the graph we would expect no discrimination between fat and muscle if they

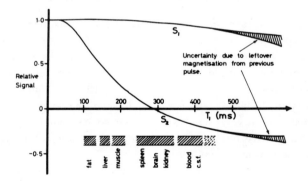

Fig. 3   Contrast between fat and muscle in S1 and S2 signals. T_1 values for other tissues are also shown

had the same proton density. There is, however, a small increase in PD in fat seen in S1 images, where the fat is rather brighter than muscle (see Fig. 4).

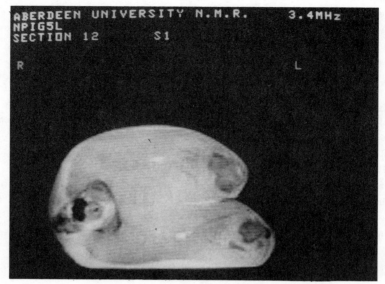

ABERDEEN UNIVERSITY N.M.R.   3.4MHz
NPIG5L
SECTION 12   S1

R   L

Fig. 4   NMR transverse section image employing S1 signal

The S2 image is much more affected by T_1 relaxation. The fixed interval of 200 msec between the AFP and the 90° pulse affects the size of signal obtained from each spin, to an extent which is dependent on its T_1 relaxation time. Where this is very short, as for fat, the spin will have relaxed back almost completely and so will contribute a large positive part to the echo, where the T_1 is long, however, the spin will have relaxed a relatively small amount and so its contribution to the echo will be positive or negative depending upon whether it has relaxed through the null point or not (Fig. 5).

The effect of this T_1-weighting on the S2 signal is to considerably reduce the signal size as T_1 increases. On this basis alone we would expect to get a good discrimination between fat and muscle in the S2 (inversion recovery) image. We must, however, also include the effect of the difference in proton density (PD) between the tissues. This would tend to elevate the fat signal relative to the muscle signal, which in this case causes an improvement in the contrast between the two tissues.

Separation of different relaxation times

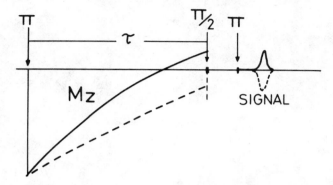

Fig. 5   Magnitude and sign of the contribution of spins to the
spin echo for long and short relaxation (T_1) times

Hence we would expect the inversion recovery image to distinguish very
well between fat and muscle – this is indeed the case (Fig. 6).

The combined signal, S1 – S2, shows a very different type of curve.
There is an increase (elongation) of T_1 relaxation time (Fig. 7 and see
Fig. 9). Purely on this basis fat and muscle would be reasonably well
discriminated but the effect of the difference in proton density is again
to elevate the fat signal relative to muscle. In this case, however, the
result is a reduction in contrast between the two tissues. A similar
effect is seen with T_1 which, naturally, also shows an increase in signal
size with increasing T_1, although discrimination here is better than with
the difference plot (Fig. 8).

If we turn to the saturation recovery, we find that this should show
fairly poor contrast because of the shape of the response curve. But the
effect of the proton density difference enhances the small contrast to
produce a clear discrimination between the two tissues (Fig. 10).

Fig. 11 shows the transverse section through a pig employing the
saturation recovery signal for imaging.

The overall picture from examination of different pulse sequences
can be summarised by taking an NMR section and selecting areas on the
image which are clearly fat or muscle and obtaining values for signal
size in these regions. The percentage difference in signal size between

214

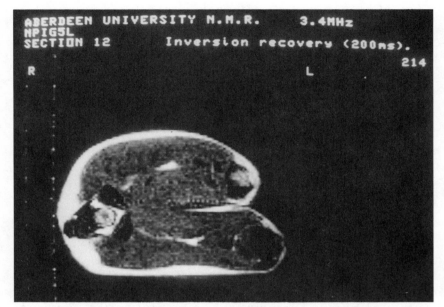

Fig. 6   Transverse section image employing inversion recovery
information

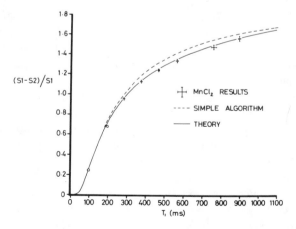

Fig. 7   Experimental and theoretical variation of signal ratio (S1- S2)
/S1 with the relaxation time T_1.   (Courtesy of Dr. T. Redpath)

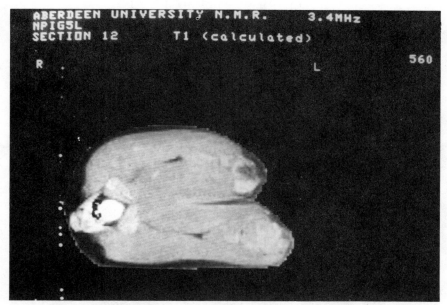

Fig. 8   Transverse section image employing T_1 information

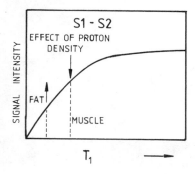

Fig. 9   Effect of differences in proton density on contrast in tissue discrimination, using S1 - S2 signal

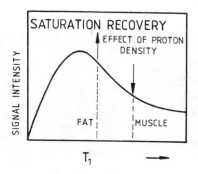

Fig. 10   Effect of differences in proton density on contrast in
tissue discrimination, using saturation recovery signal

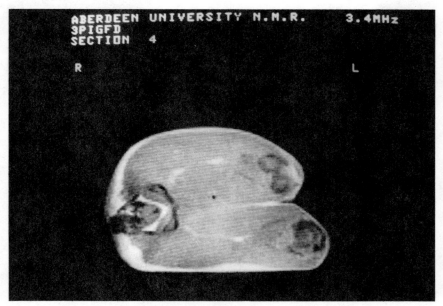

Fig. 11   Transverse section image employing saturation
recovery information

the tissues is a measure of contrast (Table 1).

TABLE 1   Sizes of signals from different pulse sequences*

Type of information	Fat	Muscle	Larger as % of smaller
Saturation recovery	304	216	140
Proton density (S1)	356	314	113
S1 - S2	192	264	138
T_1	148	228	154
Inversion recovery	164	48	342

*   The size (magnitude) of the signal is expressed in
    arbitrary units, specific for the Aberdeen NMR Imager

It can be seen that, as predicted, the proton density (S1) image
gives the lowest contrast, the saturation recovery and (S1 - S2) images
are moderate, and the T_1 image is a little better.   The inversion
recovery image however, gives by far the best contrast.   It appears,
therefore, that a T_1-weighted image can give much better fat/muscle
contrast than either PD or T_1 images alone.   It is, however, essential
to examine the response curve of the particular type of T_1-weighting
before choosing the image.   Other aspects of the imaging information can
also be varied to improve the contrast.   In particular these include the
time intervals between different parts of the pulse sequence (Wehrli et al,
1984).   The T_2 relaxation time could also be incorporated to improve
some aspects of tissue discrimination.

Chemical shift

Another area of interest is that of chemical shift imaging.   As well
as the difference between the relaxation times of protons there is a small
chemical shift difference between them.   This is only 4% for adipose
tissue and the muscle and for most of existing NMR imaging instruments
it is undetectable.   It may, however, be possible to make use of it at
very high fields.

The chemical shift arises from the effect of local magnetic fields
upon the proton.   The resonance frequency of the spinning nucleus is
precisely related to the strength of the magnetic field to which it is
exposed.   The main contribution to this field is the applied field of the
NMR instrument but there are also small components arising from
neighbouring nuclei and electrons which can add to or subtract from the
main field.   The alteration in resonance frequency due to the local

chemical environment is small, but is clearly defined by the molecular structure of the locality. Local electrons, acting as a moving cloud, can shield the proton from external fields (reducing Larmor frequency), whereas neighbouring nuclear spins can often increase the local field strength.

Very recent work has attempted to use this minute change in the local field strength to produce an independent picture of chemical shift (Edelstein et al., 1983). In essence what is being done is to produce an image based on a 3-dimensional Fourier transform technique. The spins are allowed to fan out and re-collect in essentially the same manner as described for spin warp imaging (which is a 2-dimensional Fourier transform method), and normally an extra gradient would supply the third dimension of the 3-D. For chemical shift imaging, however, the spins are allowed to fan out under the effect of their own local field strength. Hence those at one level of chemical shift, say water, will have a different phase to those at another, say the $-CH_2$ of fat. Hence they will contribute differently to the NMR signal. In effect, the technique uses 2-D of spatial information and 1-D of chemical shift information to form the image. Using this technique it has been possible to observe differences between normal liver and that undergoing fatty degeneration as a result of alcohol intake, and also to distinguish different levels of fat content in brain tissue. It should, therefore, be relatively simple to apply the same technique to examination of fat vs. muscle in an animal.

However, there are major problems in this technique. Because the chemical shift between H_2O and $-CH_2$ hydrogens is so small, the field necessary to produce an acceptable image is very high. Also it has to be extremely homogeneous. All the work reported so far has been performed on small animals since it is both simpler and cheaper to produce a homogeneous field of high strength over a smaller volume. Most imagers used for whole body studies of large animals and humans have lower fields and in general do not have the field homogeneity that is required. Since the variation in local field due to chemical shift is so small, any inhomogeneity in the main applied field will mask it.

Some efforts to produce higher field instruments of suitable specifications are being made. International General Electric Co., for example, are attempting to produce a machine to operate at 0.2 Tesla, which should also have a good field profile. Unfortunately any instruments of this type are likely to be very expensive, perhaps costing over £1 million, and so may be out of reach for animal studies. Other methods of examing the chemical shift at much lower field strength are being sought very urgently, but such methods are not envisaged for the near future.

ACTIVATION ANALYSIS IN VIVO FOR TISSUE DISCRIMINATION

The techniques of activation analysis in vivo were originally developed for the purposes of clinical and investigative medicine and their use for animal studies is only recently gaining recognition. The basic principle of activation analysis is that nuclei of one particular species emit prompt or delayed radiation as a result of the exposure to activating radiation field. This activating field can be produced by neutrons, gamma rays, X-rays or other nuclear active agents (protons, π - mesons, even perhaps heavy ions and electrons). Easy availability of isotopic and accelerator based neutron sources has helped to establish the techniques of activation analysis involving activation with the fast or slow neutron flux. Most work mentioned in this section has been done with neutron beams.

Principles of neutron activation analysis in vivo for light elements

A beam of neutrons entering the bulk of hydrogeneous material, such as human or animal body will undergo interactions which will change the intensity and composition of the beam. In the neutron energy range below 15 MeV, which is the region that mostly concerns us, the dominant form of energy loss by neutrons is its dissipation in collisions with the light nuclei, principally with protons of hydrogen and carbon nuclei.

This process of neutron energy loss results in formation of slow and even thermal neutron flux within the body at the expense of fast neutrons. If a pulse of fast neutrons enters the human body, it is completely thermalized within few hundred of microseconds. Both fast and slow neutrons take part in nuclear reactions with the nuclei of the body constituents and it is a task for those undertaking activation analysis to identify the nuclei which underwent these reactions by observation of energy and, sometimes, the half-lives of decay, of emerging radiations.

The easiest to observe and measure is hydrogen, owing to its large abundance in the body and fairly high energy of gamma radiation

accompanying capture of a thermal neutron by a proton (2.23 MeV).
No other reactions are available for the measurement of hydrogen content.
The determination of hydrogen by observation of gamma rays from
neutron capture is one of so called 'prompt' processes, without a
measurable decay time between the neutron capture and gamma ray
emission. This necessitates that the neutron irradiation facility and the
gamma ray detection system are integrated, due care being taken to
prevent neutron damage to the detectors or their activation. In practice
some compromise must be reached between the high detection efficiency
and the avoidance of above mentioned effects.

The techniques for measurement of nitrogen in vivo offer more
choice for the experimenter. In one available technique 14 MeV neutrons
are used to produce a short lived isotope of nitrogen following the
reaction $^{14}N(n,2n)^{13}N$. The ^{13}N has a 9.96 min half-life and decays by
positron emission which is followed by production of two anihilation
quanta, each of 0.511 MeV energy, which are easily detectable outside
the body. The threshold for this reaction is 10.6 MeV and the cross
section is rather small, only 6 mb. The technique requires a whole
body counter and suffers from the common difficulty encountered in fast
neutron reactions in vivo i.e. non-uniformity of fast neutron fast flux in
the body, owing to its attenuation. The changes in the intensity and
spectral composition of neutron flux within the soft tissues of animal
body are shown in Figs. 12 - 14. It is evident that the fast flux is
converted into a slow one fairly rapidly with the increasing depth in the
tissues. For fast neutron reactions employed for the purpose of analysis
this means that the number of neutrons available for producing these
reactions is diminished and a considerable calculational effort may be
needed to 'unscramble' the effects of attenuation of neutron flux from
the changes in the concentration of analysed elements.

Neutron distributions shown in Fig. 12 are typical for sources with
the average neutron energy in the range 3 - 5 MeV, which includes a
common Am-Be isotopic source. Distributions in Fig. 13 are typical for
neutrons produced by cyclotrons and it is evident that the penetration of
the fast neutron flux is deeper than for the isotopic sources. Finally,
the use of 14 MeV neutrons from d,T reactions, most commonly
encountered in neutron generators, gives still better depth penetration of
the fast flux.

The (n, 2n) reaction for determination of nitrogen suffers from another disadvantage: a correction is needed for ^{13}N formed as a result of $^{16}0(p,\alpha)^{13}N$ with the proton flux originating from recoils of hydrogen nuclei suffering collisions with fast neutrons.

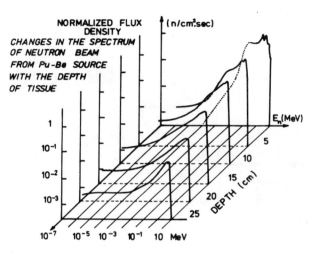

Fig. 12   The mean energy of neutrons from a Pu-Be source is 3.9 MeV.   Note the logarithmic scales for energy and flux denisty

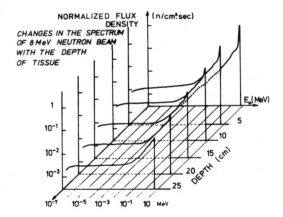

Fig. 13

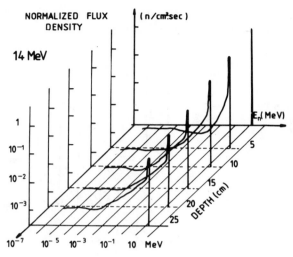

Fig. 14

The second, frequently used technique for the determination of nitrogen is based on the detection of gamma rays accompanying capture of thermalized neutrons i.e. $^{14}N(n,\gamma)^{15}N$. Among the photons emitted in this process there is a group of energy about 10.8 MeV, practically above any interfering energies which could be met in the experiments. These 10.8 MeV photons are thus detected and their intensity is a measure of the concentration of nitrogen. The practical systems employing this reaction use either an isotopic neutron source (e.g. Brookhaven installation) or a pulsed neutron beam (Ettinger et al., 1975). The temporal distribution of fast and slow neutron fluxes as well as location of the counting periods are shown in Fig. 15.

The proposed simple scanning installation for the detection of nitrogen in pigs using the capture neutron technique is shown in Fig. 17. It is based on the well proven design in Brookhaven National Laboratory, intended for humans. The neutron sources can be either isotopic or a cyclotron neutron target can be located underneath the moving couch. The animal is moved along the source aperture (in this particular design it takes form of a slit) and the capture gamma rays are counted by a collimated bank of NaI(T1) detectors. A judicious choice of the shielding materials and careful positioning of the detectors in relation to

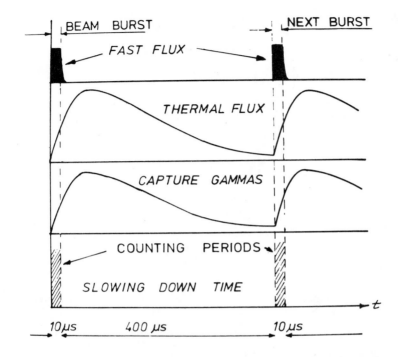

Fig. 15   Counting of gamma rays from capture, i.e. slow neutron
reactions takes place during the slowing down time;   the gammas
from fast reactions are counted during beam bursts

the irradiated area result in an acceptable amount of neutrons directly
interacting with the detectors, which is the source of increase in the
background, owing to the activation of the scintillators.   In this type of
installation it is customary to measure at the same time the intensity of
hydrogen capture spectral line, thus providing information on the
uniformity of the neutron flux along the scanned animal.   The flux in
question is the thermal flux, because (n,γ) reactions in the elements of
human (or animal) body are significant only with the thermalized
neutrons.

There exists also an interesting measurement technique which
obviates the need to build an expensive animal counter.   If a fast
neutron flux interacts with the hydrogeneous tissues of the body a large
number of recoil protons are produced, which give rise to secondary

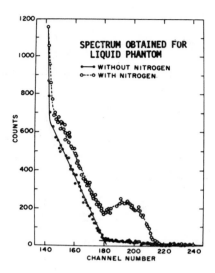

Fig. 16   Spectrum of gamma rays from radiative capture of
thermal neutrons in liquid phantoms. The composition of both
phantoms is identical apart from the presence or absence of
nitrogen. The system used a continuous neutron beam from a
Pu, Be source and large NaI(T1) scintillation detectors for
detection. A remarkable absence of interference in the high
energy region is evident. The broad spectral peak insludes
unresolved full energy peak and both single and double escape
peaks, differing by 0.51 and 1.02 MeV respectively from the
full energy value (Ellis et al., 1979)

nuclear reactions. Reaction with nitrogen nuclei $^{14}N(p,\alpha)^{11}C$, will
result in formation of 'hot' carbon atoms which will be immediately
oxidised to ^{11}CO and $^{11}CO_2$ and, then, a significant fraction of
radioactive carbon oxides will be carried by the blood to the lungs and
exhaled. If the exhaled gas is collected and both carbon monoxide and
carbon dioxide trapped (e.g. by haemoglobin solution and sodium
hydroxide solution respectively) their activity can be easily counted,
having in mind that the activity comes from a positron emitter which
produces pairs of gamma rays. These rays can be counted between two
sodium iodide crystals with a good efficiency in a coincidence mode.
The main limit to the use of this technique appears to come from the
uniformity of fast neutron flux which can be achieved in an animal. In
the human applications the exhaled gas technique requires an unacceptable

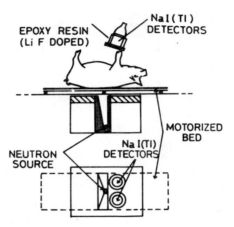

Fig. 17   Installation for the determination of body composition
in medium sized animals, based on human scanner in the
Brookhaven National Laboratory. This design can be used for
the measurement of N, H and if a pulsed beam of neutrons is
available, also for determination of O and C

radiation dose and thus was left undeveloped. It is worth investigating
the sources of errors and the accuracy which can be achieved in this
way.

The detection of oxygen in vivo is best achieved by means of fast
neutron reactions $^{16}O(n,p)^{16}N$ (7.1 sec) or $^{16}O(n,n')^{16}O$. The first of
these reactions yields a beta minus emitter, which produces a number of
gamma rays. The second reaction is known as inelastic scattering of
neutrons on oxygen nuclei. The excited nucleus produces a prompt
photon of energy 6.2 MeV, corresponding to the lowest excited state
(the same energy is involved in the detection of gamma rays from the
decay of ^{16}N). If the first reaction is used, the counting of gamma
rays can be done with the neutron beam switched off (multisecond
pulsing system). The use of gamma rays from the inelastic scattering
proceeds best if a fast (microsecond) pulsed system is used, as shown
in Fig. 15.

For the determination of carbon only one nuclear reaction has been
employed so far. It is the inelastic scattering process on ^{12}C,
$^{12}C(n,n')^{12}C$ which yields a prompt gamma ray of 4.41 MeV.

It is important to note, that the determination of the concentration

of the light elements in an animal can proceed in a single session.
Using a pulsed beam, from a neutron generator or from a cyclotron H
and N can be determined by counting the capture gamma rays, whilst the
presence of C and O can be evaluated from the intensity of gamma rays
from inelastic scattering of fast neutrons, before they become thermalized
and enter capture reactions. Some other elements, like Ca, Cl, Na and
K can be measured off-line, by transferring the animal to a whole body
counter following the irradiation.

Slow neutron flux penetration into the animal body

Fast neutron flux penetrating into the animal tissue generates at
certain depth the maximum of thermal flux. Position of this maximum
depends on the primary neutron energy and on the width of the beam.
Fig. 18 (courtesy of W.D. Morgan) shows the comparison of currently
available experimental data on the position of the thermal flux peak in
the soft tissues. For a broad beam one can expect the thermal peak
generated by primary 14 MeV neutrons to lie about 10 - 11 cm deep. It
is obvious that very little can be gained by further increase in the initial

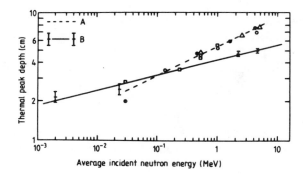

Fig. 18 (Courtesy of W.D. Morgan) Position of thermal peak as
a function of initial neutron energy, for narrow (B) and broad (A)
neutron beams

neutron energy. The usual technique for an improvement in the slow
neutron flux distribution is to apply bilateral irradiation, simultaneously
or sequentially. Bilateral irradiation coupled with the use of
pre-moderators i.e. layers of moderating material placed outside the
irradiated object, between the neutron source and skin, leads to a

significant improvement in the uniformity of slow flux with depth in the tissue. According to Cohn et al. (1973) the flux was uniform to within 5.14% throughout a 25 cm thick phantom when irradiated with 14 MeV neutrons. For lower initial neutron energy or for thicker phantom these uniformity obviously worsens (Boddy, 1973).

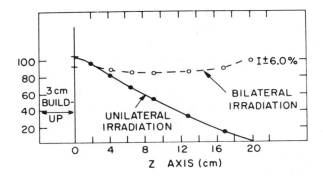

Fig. 19 Composite sensitivity of Brookhaven National Laboratory prototype of a scanner shown in Fig. 17, in the vertical direction. The object could be irradiated and counted bilaterally in two passages through the machine (Ellis et al., 1979)

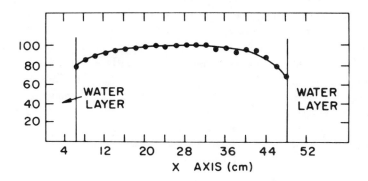

Fig. 20 Composite sensitivity of the same scanner in the direction in horizontal plane transversal to the direction of motion of the couch. (Ellis et al., 1979). The water layer acts as a premoderator. Vertical scale in arbitrary units.

Not only the distribution of the thermal neutron flux but the detection efficiency of gamma rays as well have a decisive influence on the uniformity of detection of elements within the body. The compsoite sensitivity of an installation for activation analysis _in vivo_ includes both the uniformity of neutron flux and the changes of detection efficiency. An example of a good engineering solution to the problem of uniformity of detection is given in Figs. 19 and 20 for the machine in the Brookhaven National Laboratory.

It is doubtful if the techniques developed for humans will be adequate for animals of larger thickness of the body. There are two possible approaches, which may yield the necessary correction factors for the non-uniformity of the thermal neutron flux. In the first of these techniques phantoms are fabricated of dimensions close to that of investigated animal and the known concentrations of investigated elements are placed within. This approach leads to a large collection of phantoms and may be expensive, at least in the initial stage of building up the stock. The other approach, of greater versatility is based on the existence of neutron transport codes developed originally for the needs of reactor physicists and engineers. These codes describe spatial and spectral distributions of neutrons introduced into an arbitrary medium with arbitrary initial neergy spectrum. The simplest of codes, e.g. ANISN is suitable only for systems with plane-parallel, cylindrical or spherical geometries. Codes similar to ANISN are known as one-dimensional codes, giving the changes in the flux density and spectrum as a function of one dimension e.g. along the radius of a cylinder or a sphere. A more sophisticated two-dimensional group of codes (e.g. DOT) can be used in more complex geometries. Finally, codes based on Monte-Carlo (e.g. MORSE, MONK) are, in principle, suitable for any geometry and are capable of taking into account the internal distribution of soft and calcified tissues, voids etc. The results of Monte-Carlo type calculations may be tabulated and there is indeed need for a set of comprehensive correction tables in order to accommodate flux non-uniformities in a typical range of animal sizes. If an access to a large computer is available, the computations can, in principle, be performed for any particular set of animal dimensions i.e. individually.

Dose problem in activation analysis _in vivo_ of animals

The authors are unaware of existence of regulatory dose limits for animals involved in studies using neutron irradiations for the purpose of

Fig. 21   The shape of a pig can be approximated by an ellipsoid
for calculations of flux distribution using two- or three-
dimensional computer codes.   These calculations can yield
corrections for the observed concentrations of elements

analysis of body composition.   This situation makes the task of the
designers of equipment much easier.   Obviously, techniques developed
and used on humans will be suitable, as far as the administered dose is
concerned, to animals.   Furthermore, certain techniques, including
recoil proton activation for nitrogen detection, unsuitable for dosimetric
reasons for man, is acceptable for animals.   The effect of neutron
energy on the imparted dose, shown in Fig. 22 is slight and if sources
of neutrons of higher energy than 14 MeV will become available in the
future for animal work, they should find use in the activation analysis,
enabling to obtain deeper penetration of the thermal flux, the other
factors remaining the same.   The distribution of neutron dose and dose
equivalent in an ellipsoidal phantom is shown in Fig. 23, for 14 MeV
neutrons.   It is evident that the dose through the phantom varies almost
by a factor of 3, for unilateral irradiation.

Calculation of the body composition

The elemental composition of body components is given in Table 2
(from ICRP 23 and ICRU 26).   It is evident that there are significant
differences in the concentration of elements in the tissues.   Furthermore, there is neither carbon nor nitrogen in the body water and there
is no nitrogen in fat.   The total body water can be measured by an
independent method, which does not rely on neutron activation e.g. by
deuterium oxide dilution, thus providing additional information on the
body composition.

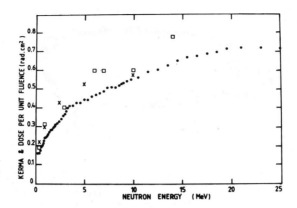

Fig. 22 Fluence – to – kerma conversion factors for neutrons in the energy range 0 – 25 MeV

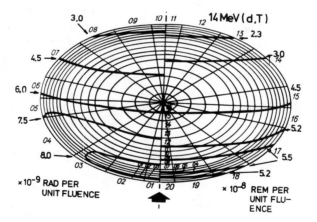

Fig. 23 Total dose and dose equivalent distribution in a phantom. The axes are 36 and 24 cm in length. The direction of the neutron beam is shown by an arrow

The last entry in Table 2 is given for illustration only; the average composition of animals will depend on the species and other factors.

TABLE 2   Elemental composition of body components

Component	% Carbon	% Hydrogen	% Nitrogen	% Oxygen
Water	0	11	0	89
Fat	77	12	0	11
Protein	52	7	16	23
Carbohydrate	42	6	0	52
Standard Man	18	10	3	65

The body composition may be expressed as a ratio of Fat/Lean Body Mass or in absolute values i.e. in kilogrammes of each component.   The particular nature of calculations depends whether total body water has been independently determined or is evaluated from the results of activation analysis and also on the availability of individual amounts of elements in absolute terms rather than as ratios.   The knowledge of the amount of potassium, measured e.g. by the whole body counter in which ^{40}K is counted, may provide additional information on the total body muscle, once suitable predictor equations are established for the investigated species of animals similarly to an analogous procedure known for man (Carlmark and Reizenstein, 1973).

USE OF FAT - SOLUBLE SHORT LIVED RADIOACTIVE GAS TRACERS
There exists a whole range of compounds with a particular affinity to adipose tissues, which includes a number of halogenated gases, some of which are used in anaesthesia.

Among such compounds are various freons (CCl_xF_{4-x}) and, in general perhalo compounds.   The commonly used anaesthetic halothane (2-Bromo-2-chlo-ro-1,1,1-trifluoroethane) can also be produced as a radioactive tracer.   The label can be either ^{11}C or ^{18}F or ^{77}Br or ^{38}Cl. The first three labels are short lived positron emitters, which yield pairs of anihilation photons of energy 0.511 MeV each.   It is proposed that the investigated animal is given some of these compounds to breathe, in concentration small enough not to have a noticeable anaesthetic effect. The amount of halogenated compound taken up by the adipose tissue can be found from the measurements in a whole body counter of conventional design or an equally conventional whole body scanner. · The distribution of the tracer can be deduced from the results of a scan.   The tomographic sections showing distribution of the tracer can be produced

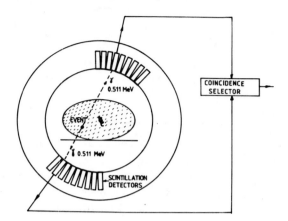

Fig. 24   Ring of radiation detectors surrounding the animal body can be used in coincidence mode for detection of positron emitting radionuclides.   This mode of detection makes possible to obtain tomographic sections, showing distribution of the tracer and thus localization of the tissue in which it became deposited

in a way analogous to the sections employed in Nuclear Medicine. Tomographic sections of particularly superior spatial resolution are obtainable from Positron Emission Tomographic Scanners (PET's), because the colinear nature of emission of anihilation photons permits a more accurate localization of the event than is the case in Single Photon Emission Tomography.   The method of radioactive fat tracers is proposed by us after the ease of manufacture of these compounds has been demonstrated (Brinkman and Visser, 1980;   Seevers and Friedman, 1983).   Obviously, a demonstration of the quantitative nature of the proposed method is still wanting, before it can be established as a technique for practical measurements of the amount and distribution of the body fat.

ACKNOWLEDGEMENTS

The authors are most obliged to Professor J.R. Mallard, Head of the Department of Biomedical Physics and Bioengineering, University of Aberdeen for his continuing encouragement and initiative.   We are also obliged to Prof. W. Wolf for permission to use Fig. 22 (Ettinger et al., 1984) from his forthcoming book.

REFERENCES

Boddy, K. 1973. Neutron Sources, Energy, Flux and Moderation in the
    Body. In "In Vivo Neutron Activation Analysis" (IAEA, Vienna)
    STI/PUB/322 pp. 49-64.
Brinkman, G.A. and Visser, J. 1980. High Yields of Labelled Perhalo-
    compounds Formed By the Reaction of ^{18}F and ^{38}Cl Recoil Atoms.
    Int. J. Appl. Radiat. Isot. 31. 415-419.
Carlmark, B. and Reizenstein P. 1973. Human Body Composition Studies
    pt. I. In "In Vivo Neutron Activation Analysis" (IAEA, Vienna)
    STI/PUB/322. pp. 113-125.
Cohn, S.H., Fairchild, R.G. and Shukla, K.K. 1973. Neutron Sources,
    Energy, Flux, Density and Moderation in Total Body Neutron
    Activation Analysis. "In Vivo Neutron Activation Analysis"
    (IAEA, Vienna) STI/PUB/322, pp. 37-47.
Edelstein, W.A., Hutchison, J.M.S., Johnson, G. and Redpath, T.W.
    1980. Spin Warp NMR Imaging And Applications To Human Whole-
    body Imaging. Phys. Med. Biol. 23, 751-756.
Edelstein, W.A., Mueller, O.M., Bottomley, P.A., Hart, H.R., Schenk,
    J.F., Smith, L.S., O'Donnell, M., Leue, W.M. and Redington, R.W.
    1983. NMR Images OF the Whole Human Trunk At 64 MHz. Proc.
    2nd Annual Meeting of Society of Magnetic Resonance in Medicine,
    San Francisco, August, 1983.
Ellis, K.J., Vartsky, D. and Cohn, S.H. 1979. A Mobile Prompt-
    gamma In Vivo Neutron Activation Facility. In "Nuclear Activation
    Techniques in the Life Sciences" (IAEA, Vienna) STI/PUB/492.
    pp. 733-742.
Ettinger, K.V., Biggin, H.C., Chen, N.S., Fremlin, J.H., Harvey, T.,
    Morgan, W.D., Thomas, B.T.. Vartsky, D. 1975. In Vivo Neutron
    Activation Analysis Using Capture Gamma Rays. Kerntechnik
    17. 89-93.
Ettinger, K.V. 1982. New Techniques For Measurement Of Body
    Composition. Proc. IAEA Symp. on Body Composition Measurement
    By In Vivo Neutron Activation Analysis, Brookhaven N.Y., 1982.
Ettinger, K.V. Miola, U.J. and Cohn, S.H. 1984. Instrumentation And
    Methods For Future Studies Of Elemental Body Composition by
    In Vivo Nuclear Activation Analysis. In "Non-Invasive Methods in
    Body Chemistry" (ed. by W. Wolf) Raven Press, N.Y. 1984 (in
    press).
Foster, M.A., Hutchison, J.M.S., Mallard, J.H. and Fuller, M. 1984.
    NMR Pulse Sequence And Discrimination Of High and Low Fat
    Tissues. Magn. Reson. Imaging. 2 (in press).
ICRP Publication 23. 1975. Report of the Task Group On Reference Man.
    Pergamon Press, Oxford.
ICRU Report 26. 1977. Neutron Dosimetry For Biology And Medicine.
    (Int. Commission on Radiation Units and Measurements,
    Washington D.C.).
Seevers, R.H. and Friedman, A.M. 1983. (^{77}Br)Halothane : A
    Radiobrominated Anesthetic. Int. J. Appl. Radiat. Isot. 34.
    1407-1408.
Wehrli F.W., Mac Fall, J.R., Glover, G.H., Wigsby, N., Haughton, V.
    and Johanson, J. 1984. The Dependence of Nuclear Magnetic
    Resonance (NMR) Image Contrast In Intrinsic And Pulse Sequence
    Timing Parameters. Magn. Reson. Imaging. 2. 3-16.

SESSION VIII

SUMMARY AND CONCLUSIONS

SUMMARY AND CONCLUSIONS

J. Robelin
Institut National de la Recherche Agronomique
Laboratorire de la Production de Viande
Centre de Recherches Zootechniques et Veterinaires
Theix, 63122 CEYRAT, France

This workshop on the measurement of body composition in living animals was devoted mainly to the description of new techniques such as X-ray computerized tomography (CT) or Nuclear Magnetic Resonance Spectroscopy (NMR). The principles of these techniques and examples of their use in man and farm animals have been extensively discussed. Shorter presentations of more "classical" methods (ultrasound, dilution, ^{40}K whole body counting, specific gravity) were also given. The technical aspects of these procedures were discussed in the light of the opportunities of their application in animal production and industry.

Methods for describing body composition can be classified into three groups:

In the first category, measurements are made on the whole body (for example, ^{40}K counting, specific gravity, water space) and an integrated value for the whole body is deduced.

In the second, measurements are made on a "sample", and a part to whole relationship is used to assess the composition of the body. The evaluation of subcutaneous fatty tissues by skinfold measurement, ultrasonics or adipose cell size is representative of this group of methods, and a statistical relationship between subcutaneous fat and whole body fat, or some other component, eg lean body, is used as the basis for calculation. The determination of the chemical composition of the body or part by CT or NMR analysis of a "slice" relies on a similar approach.

A third category of methods employs the measurement of metabolites in blood or the incorporation of labelled tracers in body tissues. These techniques are well adapted to the measurement of the dynamics of body composition.

The application of these methods is of great interest in many aspects of animal production, but the level of accuracy required by the methods differs widely according to the situation in which they are used. The measurement of body composition for balance trials in nutrition experiments requires a high degree of accuracy without bias. However the method of choice may be technically difficult, time consuming and costly and it may only be possible to study small numbers of animals. If body composition measurements are to be made in breeding experiments, a larger number of animals have to be measured within a short period of time. The method must be very quick, easy to carry out and relatively inexpensive.

Clearly only the evaluation of subcutaneous fat can enter these two last category of applications in which large numbers of measurements are needed. Ultrasonic scanning seems to give reasonably good results, but some problems of interpretation remain. The new technique of measuring ultrasound velocity could be an interesting tool. Similarly, the measurement of adipose cell size after biopsy may be useful in experimental conditions. Measurement of water space is well adapted to nutritional balance investigations and may be valuable for smaller animals. The more sophisticated methods, computerized tomography and NMR spectroscopy, have been used mainly in hospitals until now. Clearly we are at a very early stage of application in domestic animals and more research is needed in the interpretation of the data given by these techniques.

The presentation of all these methods has clarified their applicability but also their limits and some of their weaknesses. Further research is needed for all these methods but we may hope that cross comparisons of methods will be done in the near future in different countries. If this were done it would be valuable if at least one common technique was included in order to make the comparison of results easier. Finally, the lack of knowledge in the evaluation of the gut content and its variation, has been stressed. Some particular application of dilution techniques may improve our knowledge in this area.

PARTICIPANTS

BELGIUM

Dr J.J. Adam
Dept de Technologie
Chaire de Technologie
Agricole et Alimentaire
B-5800 GEMBLOUX

Mr J. Connell
CEC
Director General of Agriculture
Rue de la Loi 200
B-1040 BRUSSELS

Professor D. Demeyer
Studiecentrum Vleesproduktie
Proefhoesvestraat 10
89230 MELLE

DENMARK

Dr B.B. Andersen
Research Center Foulum
Postboks 39
8833 Ørum Sønderlying

Dr H. Busk
National Institute of Animal
  Science
Rolighedsvej 25
1958 Copenhagen V

Dr S.E. Sorensen
Danish Meat Research Institute
Maglegardsvej 2

Dr T.M. Sorensen
National Institute of Animal
  Science
Dept of Cattle Experiments
Rolighedsvej 25

IRELAND

Dr P. Allen
Meat Research Department
Agricultural Institute
Dunsinea Research Centre
Castleknock
Co Dublin

FRANCE

Dr F. Bocquier
INRA Theix Lab Prod Ovine
63122 CEYRAT

M. B. Desmoulin
INRA Saint-Gilles
35590 L'Hermitage

Dr E. Rehben
149 Rue de Bercy
75595 PARIS
CEDEX 12

Dr J. Robelin
Lab de la Production de Viande
CRZV de Theix
63110 BEAUMONT

GREECE

Dr A. Gogos
Director
Veterinary Public Health Directorate
Food Control Division
Ministry of Agriculture
Acharnon 2 str
Athens

FEDERAL REPUBLIC OF GERMANY

Professor Dr P Glodek
Institut für Tierzucht und
  Haustiergenetik
Albrecht Thaer Weg 1
D3400 GOTTINGEN

Dr E Groenevold
Institut für Tierzucht und
  Tierverhalten
FAI 305
Mariensee/Urber Wunstorf BRD

Professor Dr E. Kallweit
Institut für Tierzucht und
  Tierverhalten
FAI 305
Mariensee/Urber Wunstorf BRD

ITALY

Dott G. Bittante
Instituto di Zootecnica
Universita degli studi di Padova
Via Gradenigo
6-35131 Padova

Dott E. Cosentino
Instituto di Produzioni Animali
Facolta di Agraria
Dell'Universita di Portici
Napoli
Italy

NETHERLANDS

Dr J. Jansen
Dept Animal Science
Marijkeweg 49
6700 AH
Wageneningen

Dr E. Kanis
Dept Animal Science
Marijkeweg 49
PO Box 338
6700 AH
Wageneningen

Dr P. Walstra
Research Institute Animal Husbandry
  "Schoonoord"
PO Box 501
3700 AM ZEIST

NORWAY

Dr E. Sehested
Dept of Animal Genetics and Breeding
Agricultural University of Norway
BOKS 24
1432 AS NLH

Dr N. Standal
Dept of Animal Genetics and Breeding
Agricultural University of Norway
BOKS 24
1432 AS NLH

UNITED KINGDOM

Professor K. Boddy
Northern Region Medical Physics Dept
University of Newcastle
Newcastle

Mr A. Cuthbertson
Meat and Livestock Commission
Milton Keynes
Bletchley
Bucks MK2 2EF

Dr B.W. East
Scottish Universities Research
  and Reactor Centre
East Kilbride
Glasgow
Scotland

Dr K.V. Ettinger
Dept of Bio Medical Physics and
  Bio Engineering
University of Aberdeen
ABERDEEN
Scotland

Dr M.F. Fuller
Rowett Research Institute
Bucksburn
Aberdeen
Scotland

Dr J.P. Gibson
Animal Breeding Research
  Organisation
King's Buildings
West Mains Road
Edinburgh
EH9 3JQ
Scotland

Dr A.J. Kempster
Meat and Livestock Commission
MILTON KEYNES
Bletchley
Bucks MK2 2EF

Professor J.W.B. King
Animal Breeding Liaison Group
Edinburgh School of Agriculture
West Mains Road
Edinburgh
EH9 3JG
Scotland

Dr C. Knight
Hannah Research Institute
Ayre
KA6 5HL
Scotland

Dr David Lister
Animal Physiology Division
AFRC Meat Research Institute
Langford
Bristol   BS18 7DY

Dr C.A. Miles
Engineering and Development Division
AFRC Meat Research Institute
Langford
Bristol   BS18 7DY

Dr T. Preston
Scottish Universities Research
   and Reactor Centre
East Kilbride
Glasgow
Scotland

Dr R.C. Roberts
Ministry of Agriculture, Fisheries
   and Food
Chief Scientist's Office
Great Westminster House
Horseferry Road
London   SW1P 2AE

Mr Randal Rue
Oxford Research Systems Limited
Nuffield Way
ABINGDON
Oxon   OX14 1RY

Mr B.M. Scott
Regional Livestock Husbandry
   Advisory Officer
ADAS
Ministry of Agriculture, Fisheries
   and Food
Burghill Road
Westbury-on-Trym
Bristol   BS10 6NJ

Mr David Steane
Meat and Livestock Commission
PO Box 44
Queensway House
Bletchley
MILTON KEYNES   MK2 2EF

Mr M.H. Stranks
Chief Scientist's Office
Ministry of Agriculture, Fisheries
   and Food
Great Westminster House
Horseferry Road
London   SW1P 2AE

Dr P.N.T. Wells
Bristol and Weston Health Authority
Bristol General Hospital
Guinea Street
Bristol   BS1 6SY

Professor B.S. Worthington
Dept Diagnostic Radiology
Queens Medical Centre
Nottingham

MEAT RESEARCH INSTITUTE

Mr A.J. Brown

Dr B.W. Butler-Hogg

Mr A.V. Fisher

Dr A. Fortin
   (Visiting Worker, Agric. Canada)

Dr J.D. Wood